Also in the Variorum Collected Studies Series:

A.R. DISNEY
The Portuguese in India and Other Studies, 1500–1700

GLYNDWR WILLIAMS
Buccaneers, Explorers and Settlers
British Enterprise and Encounters in the Pacific, 1670–1800

M.N. PEARSON
The World of the Indian Ocean, 1500–1800
Studies in Economic, Social and Cultural History

BARRY M. GOUGH
Britain, Canada and the North Pacific: Maritime Enterprise and Dominion, 1778–1914

RODERICH PTAK
China, the Portuguese, and the Nanyang
Oceans and Routes, Regions and Trade (c. 1000–1600)

G.V. SCAMMELL
Seafaring, Sailors and Trade, 1450–1750
Studies in British and European Maritime and Imperial History

W.G.L. RANDLES
Geography, Cartography and Nautical Science in the Renaissance
The Impact of the Great Discoveries

C.R. BOXER
Dutch Merchants and Mariners in Asia, 1602–1795

RICHARD W. UNGER
Ships and Shipping in the North Sea and Atlantic, 1400–1800

URSULA LAMB
Cosmographers and Pilots of the Spanish Maritime Empire

S. ARASARATNAM
Maritime Trade, Society and European Influence in Southern Asia, 1600–1800

ASHIN DAS GUPTA
Merchants of Maritime India, 1500–1800

VARIORUM COLLECTED STUDIES SERIES

Essays in Naval History, from Medieval to Modern

N.A.M. Rodger

N.A.M. Rodger

Essays in Naval History, from Medieval to Modern

ASHGATE
VARIORUM

Published in the Variorum Collected Studies Series by

Ashgate Publishing Limited
Wey Court East
Union Road
Farnham, Surrey
GU9 7PT
England

Ashgate Publishing Company
Suite 420
101 Cherry Street
Burlington, VT 05401–4405
USA

Ashgate website: http://www.ashgate.com

ISBN 978–0–7546–5995–2

British Library Cataloguing in Publication Data
Rodger, N.A.M., 1949–
    Essays in naval history, from medieval to modern.
    – (Variorum collected studies series ; no. 930)
    1. Naval history. 2. Great Britain – History, Naval.
    I. Title II. Series
    359'.009–dc22

    ISBN 978–0–7546–5995–2

Library of Congress Cataloging-in-Publication Data
Rodger, N.A.M., 1949–
    Essays in naval history, from medieval to modern / N.A.M. Rodger.
    p. cm. – (Variorum collected studies series)
    Includes index.
    ISBN 978–0–7546–5995–2 (hardcover : alk. paper)
    1. Great Britain – History, Naval. 2. Great Britain. Royal Navy – History.
    I. Title.
    DA70.R559 2009
    359.00941–dc22

                                    2009008258

VARIORUM COLLECTED STUDIES SERIES CS930

Mixed Sources
Product group from well-managed
forests and other controlled sources
www.fsc.org Cert no. SGS-COC-2482
© 1996 Forest Stewardship Council

Printed and bound in Great Britain by
TJ International Ltd, Padstow, Cornwall

CONTENTS

This volume contains xii + 332 pages

PUBLISHER'S NOTE

The articles in this volume, as in all others in the Variorum Collected Studies Series, have not been given a new, continuous pagination. In order to avoid confusion, and to facilitate their use where these same studies have been referred to elsewhere, the original pagination has been maintained wherever possible.

Each article has been given a Roman number in order of appearance, as listed in the Contents. This number is repeated on each page and is quoted in the index entries.

PREFACE

These articles, written over about twenty years, and extending over more than ten centuries, illustrate a number of themes which seem to me to be central to naval history. Though the subjects and the styles vary a good deal, I hope they are linked by a common approach and some common ideas. Many, though not all of them, originated as detailed studies underpinning some part of the 'Naval History of Britain' on which I have been working for many years, and of which two (out of three) volumes have now appeared: *The Safeguard of the Sea, 660–1649* (1997), and *The Command of the Ocean, 1649–1815* (2004). I have always believed naval history to be not only, or even chiefly, a distinct area of special study, but rather a central theme running through the history of England, and of the whole British Isles. It, and in many cases it alone, has the power to tie together and to explain things which do not make sense in isolation. Hence many of these studies examine ways in which naval history has formed a key element in such subjects as intellectual, religious, administrative or medical history. At the same time naval history is undeniably a technical subject, which demands a willingness to understand warships – the most complex artefacts of every age – and the structure of large and complex organisations. Some of these articles start from a foundation of detailed and technical evidence about ships and weapons to build large conclusions, for example about late Anglo-Saxon government and military organisation, or about the nature of warfare at sea in the Renaissance era. Other, more broad-ranging, essays survey the nature and meaning of sea power as a theme in various periods and contexts. Some well-known historical concepts such as the 'Military Revolution' are revisited from a naval perspective. Though almost all of these essays are written from the British point of view, I do not consider that naval history can ever be written from a narrowly national standpoint. The sea links different nations, in peace or war, and there can be no true naval history which is not informed by international comparisons, and based on the sources from all the relevant countries and languages. Several of these essays explicitly survey naval developments over a range of countries, and I hope even the most narrowly focussed are at least implicitly aware of the wider world of war at sea.

Two of these articles have not been printed before in this form in English (IX and XIII), and one was originally issued in an on-line journal, with a more comprehensive collection of accompanying graphs than it has been possible to reproduce here (XV). These three have necessarily been newly typeset, but all the others are reproduced as they were originally printed, with no changes other than correcting misprints. I have resisted the temptation to bring them up to date, but in some cases I have added a note commenting on the piece in the light of more recent scholarship. A number of these were originally published in obscure journals or works of very limited circulation, and several were issued outside the English-speaking world. I know that would-be readers have found them hard to obtain, and I hope this collection will make them more accessible.

N.A.M. RODGER

All Souls College, Oxford
Easter 2009

ACKNOWLEDGEMENTS

Grateful acknowledgement is made to the following institutions and publishers for their kind permission to reproduce the articles included in this volume: *The English Historical Review*, Oxford University Press, Oxford (for articles I and II); *The Mariner's Mirror*, Society for Nautical Research, London (III); Boydell and Brewer Ltd, Woodbridge (IV); *Social Science Tribune*, University of Thessaly, Volos (V); Cambridge University Press, Cambridge (VI); Institut d'histoire, Université Michel de Montaigne Bordeaux 3, Bordeaux (VII); Institut für Geschichte der Medizin, University of Düsseldorf (VIII); the British Society for Eighteenth Century Studies, and Wiley-Blackwell Publishers, Oxford (X); Editions Honoré Champion, Paris (XI); Taylor and Francis Group, London (XII); the National Maritime Museum, Greenwich (XIV and XV); Four Courts Press, Dublin (XVI); and The Hudson Trust, Oxford University and the Royal Navy (XVII).

I

Cnut's Geld and the Size of Danish Ships*

IN A well-known passage, the *Anglo-Saxon Chronicle* (E text) relates
how Harthacnut in 1040 imposed a severe geld on the English to pay for
his fleet: 'hi gerædden þet man geald lxii scipon æt ælcere hamulan viii
marc.'[1] This sentence has attracted much study, because of the information it gives us, or appears to give us, about several matters of
importance for English history. The sums levied in geld, and the
numbers of ships which were thereby paid, are stated with what seems
to be pedantic accuracy.[2] We are told that £21,099 was paid to sixty-two
ships, and a further £11,048 to thirty-two ships, at the rate of eight marks
æt ælcere hamulan. From this various scholars, most recently M. K.
Lawson, have calculated the size of the Danish ships and the number of
men they carried; on his figures approximately eighty each, in addition
to the steersman in command.[3] Simon Keynes uses the same evidence to
arrive at a figure of sixty-five men;[4] and it can be applied as far back as
1013, when this geld was first imposed to pay for the fleet of Thorkell the
Tall, newly taken into the service of Æthelred II.[5] One aspect of these
calculations which has not attracted notice is that they rest on a chain of
unstated assumptions.[6] It is assumed that the word *hamele*, which with

* I am indebted to Dr Julia Crick, Dr Simon Keynes and Dr Gillian Hutchinson for their advice in
preparing this paper.

1. *Two of the Saxon Chronicles Parallel*, ed. Charles Plummer and John Earle (2 vols., Oxford,
1892–9) i, 161. The C text reads '*þ' wæs viii marc æt ha*''.
2. James Campbell, 'Some Agents and Agencies of the Late Anglo-Saxon State', in *Domesday
Studies*, ed. J. C. Holt (Woodbridge, 1987), pp. 201–18, at 202.
3. M. K. Lawson, 'The Collection of Danegeld and Heregeld in the Reigns of Aethelred II and
Cnut', *ante*, xcix (1984), 721–38; also his *Cnut: The Danes in England in the Early Eleventh Century*
(London, 1993), p. 183. It is not necessary for my purposes to support either side in the controversy
between Dr Lawson and Mr Gillingham on the plausibility of the *Chronicle*'s geld figures: see John
Gillingham, ' "The Most Precious Jewel in the English Crown": Levels of Danegeld and Heregeld in
the Early Eleventh Century', *ante*, civ (1989), 373–84; M. K. Lawson, ' "Those Stories Look True":
Levels of Taxation in the Reigns of Aethelred II and Cnut', ibid. civ (1989), 385–406; John Gillingham,
'Chronicles and Coins as Evidence for Levels of Tribute and Taxation in Late Tenth- and Early
Eleventh-Century England', ibid. cv (1990), 939–50; M. K. Lawson, 'Danegeld and Heregeld Once
More', ibid. cv (1990), 951–61.
4. Simon Keynes, *The Diplomas of King Æthelred 'the Unready', 978–1016: A Study in their Use as
Historical Evidence* (Cambridge, 1980), p. 225, n. 257.
5. Nicholas Hooper, 'Some Observations on the Navy in Late Anglo-Saxon England', in *Studies in
Medieval History Presented to R. Allen Brown*, ed. Christopher Harper-Bill et al. (Woodbridge, 1989),
pp. 203–13, at 205.
6. The assumptions seem to be common to all recent authorities writing in English: see for example
Lawson, 'Collection of Danegeld and Heregeld'; Hooper, 'Observations on the Navy'; Campbell,
'Some Agents and Agencies'; Keynes, *Diplomas of King Æthelred 'the Unready'*, p. 257.

one doubtful exception[1] is otherwise unknown in Old English,[2] means a 'rowlock',[3] that to every 'rowlock' belongs an oar, that every oar is pulled by one man, and that the oarsmen (with their steersman) make up the whole ship's company. Without, if possible, raising a Norse trireme controversy, the purpose of this note is to suggest that none of these assumptions is altogether safe, and that several of them are probably wrong.

Before addressing them directly, it will be useful briefly to traverse the current state of knowledge about Viking ships of the period.[4] The only standard work on the subject, Brøgger and Shetelig's *The Viking Ships*,[5] is now nearly fifty years old, and is essentially based on literary references, mainly from the sagas, on a limited range of iconography, and on the Gokstad and Oseberg ships.[6] These two remarkable survivals have exercised a fascination over generations of scholars, and are still very often cited as models for the ships of the Viking age. They are, however, of the same size and type, buried within a few years and a few miles of one another, and there is no reason to assume that they represent anything more than the mid-ninth-century *karfi* of the Vestfold.[7] Indeed, it is commonly argued that they are unusual even for their type and period in being in the nature of 'royal yachts', with many archaic

1. A gloss on Aldhelm's *De laude virginitatis*, rendering the Latin 'portisculo'. This is probably a mistake for 'hamor', which occurs in some MSS; it certainly does not seem to bear on the present problem. See *Anecdota Oxoniensia: Old English Glosses, Chiefly Unpublished*, ed. Arthur S. Napier (Oxford, 1900), p. 2; N. R. Ker, *Catalogue of Manuscripts Containing Anglo-Saxon* (Oxford, 1957), pp. 381–3. I owe these references to the kindness of Dr Keynes.

2. *An Anglo-Saxon Dictionary*, ed. Joseph Bosworth and T. Northcote Toller (Oxford, 1898), s.v. 'Hamele'. The supplements edited by Toller and Alistair Campbell (Oxford, 1921, 1955) add nothing on this word.

3. The translation offered by *The Anglo-Saxon Chronicle*, ed. Dorothy Whitelock *et al.* (London, 1961), p. 105. Bosworth and Toller render 'oar-loop', which they borrow from Vigfusson, who presumably invented it. Elsewhere Professor Whitelock also invokes 'rowlock' to translate 'hanon', a word of unknown meaning which may not even be a noun: see *English Historical Documents*. Vol. I: *c. 500–1042*, ed. Dorothy Whitelock (2nd edn., London, 1979), p. 581, and *The Crawford Collection of Early Charters and Documents now in the Bodleian Library*, ed. A. S. Napier and W. H. Stevenson (Oxford, 1895), pp. 23, 126–9.

4. The most useful recent surveys are: Roald Morcken, *Langskip, knarr og kogge: nye synspunkter på sagatidens skipsbygging i Norge og Nordeuropa* (Bergen, 1980); Ole Crumlin-Pedersen, 'Viking Shipbuilding and Seamanship', in *Proceedings of the Eighth Viking Congress*, ed. Hans Bekker-Nielsen *et al.* (Odense, 1981), pp. 271–86; id., *From Viking Ships to Hanseatic Cogs* (3rd Paul Johnstone Memorial Lecture, N[ational] M[aritime] M[useum], 1983); id., 'Ship Types and Sizes, AD 800–1400', in *Aspects of Maritime Scandinavia, AD 200–1200*, ed. Crumlin-Pedersen (Roskilde, 1991), pp. 69–82 (a reference I owe to Dr Hutchinson); Angela Evans, 'The Clinker-built Boats of the North Sea, 300–1000 AD', in *The North Sea. A Highway of Economic and Cultural Exchange: Character – History*, ed. Arne Bang-Andersen *et al.* (Stavanger, 1985), pp. 63–78; Arne-Emil Christensen, 'Viking Age Ships and Shipbuilding', *Norwegian Archaeological Review*, xv (1982), 19–28; Lucien Musset, 'Problèmes militaires du monde scandinave (VIIᵉ–XIIᵉ siècles)', *Ordinamenti militari in Occidente nell'alto medievo* (Spoleto, 1968), pp. 229–91. Detlev Ellmers, *Frühmittelalterliche Handelsschiffahrt in Mittel- und Nordeuropa* (Neumünster, 1972), is also valuable, and wider in scope than its title indicates.

5. A. W. Brøgger and Haakon Shetelig, *The Viking Ships, their Ancestry and Evolution*, trans. Katherine John (Oslo, 1953); originally published as *Vikingskipene: deres forgjengere og etterfølgere* (Oslo, 1950). The second English edition of 1971 has the same text as before.

6. Christensen, 'Viking Age Ships', 22.

7. Brøgger and Shetelig, *Viking Ships*, pp. 169–71.

and ostentatious features not typical of ordinary working craft.[1] Even if we had no other evidence, we could still have inferred from common sense and modern experience that the 'Viking' ship design must have assumed many different forms and sizes to meet local circumstances and particular requirements over the wide area and the very long period in which it was current. Since Brøgger and Shetelig was published, our knowledge has been greatly extended by a large number of archaeological discoveries, which allow us to see some of the diversity that existed within the 'Viking' shipbuilding tradition.[2] We now know, moreover, that there were at least three other major shipbuilding traditions existing in northern Europe during the Viking age.[3] Yet all this new evidence has only made it clearer how many types must once have existed of which we remain ignorant. In particular, our knowledge of Viking warships, of the type of which the fleets of Cnut were probably made up, remains painfully thin.[4] Moreover, there is a general problem that the literary and documentary evidence, which is mainly from the twelfth and thirteenth centuries, and refers particularly to Norway, is unreliable in itself, and not easy to match to the archaeological finds from other areas and earlier periods.

With these cautions, it is possible to venture some generalizations. Firstly, the Vikings seem from the earliest periods of which we have evidence to have understood the warship as a specialized type, the *langskip* or *herskip*, distinguished from others by her size and her long, narrow hull form, whence the common term *snekkja* or 'snake'. Ships of all sorts in the Viking tradition of double-ended, clinker-built vessels, were measured by *rými*, 'rooms', or *sessan*, thwarts. The 'room' is equivalent to the modern English shipwright's 'room and space', a section of the hull defined by two adjacent sets of frames and the beams spanning them. By convention, only the full-size rooms were counted, ignoring the smaller spaces created by the cant frames in the bows and stern. In undecked ships like the Nydam ship of about 300 AD and the Sutton Hoo ship of about 625, the rowers sat on thwarts spanning the frames, and the number of rooms was necessarily the same as the number of pairs of oars.[5] In such a case a *tvítugsessa* was equivalent to a

1. Alan Binns, 'The Ships of the Vikings: Were They "Viking Ships"?', in *Proceedings of the Eighth Viking Congress*, pp. 287–94, at 289–90. Crumlin-Pedersen, 'Viking Shipbuilding and Seamanship', p. 284.

2. Crumlin-Pedersen, *From Viking Ships to Hanseatic Cogs*; Christensen, 'Viking Age Ships'; Ellmers, *Frühmittelalterliche Handelsschiffahrt*, pp. 271–341; Arne Emil Christensen, 'Boat Finds from Bryggen', in *The Bryggen Papers*, main ser., vol. 1, ed. Asbjørn E. Herteig (Bergen, 1985), pp. 47–278. I owe the last reference to the kindness of Dr Hutchinson.

3. Crumlin-Pedersen, 'Viking Shipbuilding and Seamanship', pp. 274–6.

4. Ibid., p. 285.

5. Rupert Bruce-Mitford, *The Sutton Hoo Ship-Burial* (3 vols. in 4, British Museum, London, 1975–84). Harald Åkerlund, *Nydamskeppen: en studie i tidig Skandinavisk skeppsbyggnadskonst* (Gothenburg, 1963).

ship of twenty rooms, and our literary sources give the impression that this continued to be the case throughout the Viking age.[1]

It appears that ships of fewer than twenty rooms were not usually counted as longships, at least in the twelfth century.[2] This is not to say that smaller ships never went to war; *karfar*, in particular, seem to have been often used by Norwegian fleets when it was necessary to portage ships overland,[3] while the *knarr*, the typical merchantman of the Viking age, is also mentioned as taking part in battles.[4] On our present information, however, it is reasonable to assume that war fleets raised by Danish kings like Swein Forkbeard and Cnut would have been made up of longships, probably little if at all smaller than twenty rooms each, nor bigger than twenty-five. It has recently been argued that the ship-muster system known as the *leidang* (of which more below) relied on quite small ships,[5] but it is held that this fleet was not available (perhaps also not suitable) for overseas expeditions.[6] In the later Norwegian fleet organization, of which we are relatively well informed, almost all the ships were of twenty or twenty-five rooms.[7] Ships of thirty rooms and upwards, often called *drekkar*, 'dragons', are celebrated in the sagas as most unusual, indeed as famous and heroic. The earliest was possibly the ship of unstated size owned by Harald Fairhair in the tenth century. The first whose size we know was Olav Tryggvason's thirty-room *Tranin* ('Crane'), built at Nidaros in 995. By far the most famous in this period was his later ship the *Ormrinn Langi* ('Long Serpent') of thirty-four rooms, built over the winter of 999 to 1000,[8] the ship from which he plunged to his death at the disastrous battle of Svöld. We know for certain of only six ships as large as thirty rooms afloat in the eleventh century, the largest being Harald Hardrada's thirty-five-room ship built

1. Crumlin-Pedersen, 'Viking Shipbuilding and Seamanship', p. 279. Musset, 'Problèmes militaires', p. 255. Brøgger and Shetelig, *Viking Ships*, pp. 173–4.

2. Musset, 'Problèmes militaires', p. 255. Brøgger and Shetelig, *Viking Ships*, pp. 187–90.

3. Morcken, *Langskip, knarr og kogge*, pp. 29–35.

4. G. J. Marcus, 'The Evolution of the Knörr', *Mariner's Mirror*, xli (1955), 115–22, at 120. Plummer and Earle, *Saxon Chronicles* i, 109.

5. Ole Crumlin-Pedersen, 'Gensyn med Skuldelev 5. Et ledingsskib?', in *Festskrift til Olaf Olsen* (Copenhagen, 1988), pp. 137–56 (a copy of which was kindly lent me by Dr Hutchinson), discussing Rikke Malmros, 'Leding og Skjaldekvad', *Aarbøger for Nordisk Oldkyndighed og Historie*, 1985, pp. 89–139 (which latter reference I have not seen myself). Dr Crumlin-Pedersen's argument could be attacked as erecting a universal theory to explain the curious features of a single ship (Skuldelev 5); the connection between her and the *leidang* is entirely speculative.

6. Niels Lund, 'The Armies of Swein Forkbeard and Cnut: *leding* or *lið*?', *Anglo-Saxon England*, xv (1986), 105–18.

7. Brøgger and Shetelig, *Viking Ships*, pp. 187–90. Laurence M. Larson, *The Earliest Norwegian Laws, Being the Gulathing Law and the Frostathing Law* (New York, 1935), p. 200. *Kulturhistorisk Leksikon for Nordisk Middelalder* (22 vols., Copenhagen etc., 1956–78) [henceforth *KLNM*]), x, 435, s.v. 'Leidang'.

8. Or 998–9, if Svöld is to be dated to the autumn of 999: see Lawson, *Cnut*, p. 25.

in 1061–2.[1] Ten more were constucted during the twelfth and thirteenth centuries, culminating in the *Kristsúðin* of thirty-seven rooms, built at Bergen for King Håkon Håkonsson in 1262–3. This ship, unusual among the great ships, which seem mostly to have stayed in coastal waters, actually crossed the North Sea in support of King Håkon's Scottish campaign, and bore his body home from Orkney in 1264.[2]

We have evidence of the size of some of these *drekkar*. Snorri Sturlason claims to have measured the slip on which the *Ormrinn Langi* was built, showing her to be 145ft. long on the keel.[3] We know from excavation of some of the ship-houses in which Norwegian and other ships were kept in winter that ships at least one hundred feet long existed not later than the fifth century.[4] Later ship-houses have been excavated as long as 130 feet, with room for one or two ships each, and Håkon Håkonsson constructed a ship-house at Bergen to accommodate two ships abreast which is stated to have been 180ft. long and 120ft. broad.[5] This was before he built the *Kristsúðin*, which is given by a contemporary authority as 260ft. long (presumably overall).[6] By comparison the largest British wooden battleship ever built, HMS *Prince of Wales* of 1860, was just over 250ft. long on the keel.[7]

Before we return from the fleets of Queen Victoria to the fleets of King Cnut, it will also be useful to touch briefly on the *leidang* or ship-muster systems, known in their developed forms from all parts of the Scandinavian world in the twelfth and thirteenth centuries.[8] When and how these systems developed are subjects of controversy. According to the sagas, the Norwegian *leidang* was instituted by Håkon the Good in the mid-ninth century, but the first hard evidence of its organization there is not until two centuries later. In Denmark it is first mentioned in connection with the great fleet raised by Cnut II for the invasion of England in 1085. In both cases there are indications that it may have been English practice which inspired the Scandinavian mon-

---

1. Sir Frank Stenton, *Anglo-Saxon England* (3rd edn., Oxford, 1971), p. 413, refers to Cnut possessing a *drekkar* of 120 oars: the figure is incredible, and one naturally suspects a confusion between men and oars. Unfortunately he gives no authority, and nor do any of the historians who have copied the story from one another, according to R. C. Anderson, who attempted to trace it to its source: 'The Oars of Northern Long-Ships', *Mariner's Mirror*, xxix (1943), 190–5, at 192.

2. Brøgger and Shetelig, *Viking Ships*, pp. 192–207; at p. 192 they list all known Viking ships of thirty rooms or more.

3. Ibid., pp. 72, 106. Morcken, *Langskip, knarr og kogge*, pp. 36–7; here and elsewhere I follow Morcken on the length of the ell.

4. Ellmers, *Frühmittelalterliche Handelsschiffahrt*, pp. 147, 334. Morcken, *Langskip, knarr og kogge*, p. 28, dates the Kinsarvik ship-house to the second century.

5. Ibid., pp. 28, 42. *KLNM*, xii. 252–3, s.v. 'Naust'. Ellmers, *Frühmittelalterliche Handelsschiffahrt*, p. 147.

6. Morcken, *Langskip, knarr og kogge*, p. 40.

7. 252ft. on the gun deck: J. J. Colledge, *Ships of the Royal Navy* (2 vols., 2nd edn., London, 1987), i. 274.

8. *KLNM*, x. 433–46, s.v. 'Leidang'. Musset, 'Problèmes militaires', pp. 279–82. Else Roesdahl, *Viking Age Denmark* (London, 1982), p. 157.

archs.[1] Some scholars, however, derive the *leidang* from the earliest periods of Viking history, and it is certain that Danish and Norwegian kings were possessed of fleets, raised by some means, as far back as we meet them in history. Faint evidence has been drawn from rune-stones of a Danish fleet organization in the reigns of Swein Forkbeard and Cnut,[2] and it is argued that the Danish *leidang* may have existed at least as early as the eighth century. If Professor Lund is right, however, it was only available for defensive purposes, and Swein and Cnut would have had to make up their invasion fleets by gathering private raiding squadrons of their own and other Scandinavian leaders.[3] On this argument the Danish fleets would have been at least partly made up with people familiar with the *leidang*, even if they were not in this case using it. Since these kings undoubtedly had large fleets, apparently with some degree of organization and an established rate of pay, we may assume the influence of some *leidang*-like system; but once more we are driven to use twelfth- and thirteenth-century Norwegian evidence for want of the eleventh-century Danish information we really need.

Having briefly surveyed what we know of warship design and fleet organization in the eleventh century, we may return to Harthacnut's geld, levied at eight marks *æt ælcere hamulan*. *Hamele* is presumably the Danish *havna*, Norwegian *hamla*, which is still current in Norwegian, and whose basic meaning is not in doubt. It refers to the rope or withy grommet securing an oar to its single thole.[4] This was then the method of rowing small boats, and in Norway it still is.[5] There must once have been a time when it was also applicable to large ships: the Nydam and Sutton Hoo ships, as well as the Kvalsund ship of the seventh or eighth century, were rowed with single, hooked, tholes, which is an impossibility without some lashing to restrain the oar on the return stroke.[6] It is quite certain, however, that seagoing ships of the eleventh century were not rowed with tholes, still less with rowlocks, which are not known to have

1. C. Warren Hollister, *Anglo-Saxon Military Institutions on the Eve of the Norman Conquest* (Oxford, 1962), p. 113. James Campbell, 'The Significance of the Anglo-Norman State in Administrative History', in *Essays in Anglo-Saxon History* (London, 1986), pp. 171–188, at 186 (originally in *Histoire comparée de l'administration, IVe–XVIIe siècles*, ed. W. Paravicini and K. F. Werner [Munich, 1980], pp. 117–34). Musset, 'Problèmes militaires', p. 284.

2. Klavs Randsborg, *The Viking Age in Denmark: The Formation of a State* (London, 1980), pp. 37–43.

3. Lund, '*Leding* or *lið*?'.

4. *An Icelandic-English Dictionary*, ed. Richard Cleasby and Gudbrand Vigfusson (2nd edn., Oxford, 1957); Jan de Vries, *Altnordisches etymologisches Wörterbuch* (2nd edn., Leiden, 1977); Johan Fritzner, *Ordbog over det gamle norske sprog* (4th edn., Oslo, 1973), all s.v. 'Hamla'. Alexander Jóhannesson, *Isländisches etymologisches Wörterbuch* (Berne, 1956), p. 210.

5. Christensen, 'Viking Age Ships', 21, has a striking pair of photographs of the Gokstad *faering* and an *oselver* built in 1969, which demonstrates the remarkable conservatism of Norwegian boat-building.

6. See the plans in Åkerlund, *Nydamskeppen*, and Bruce-Mitford, *The Sutton Hoo Ship-Burial*, vol. i. For the Kvalsund ship, see Evans, 'Clinker-built Boats', pp. 68–9.

existed before the fourteenth century at the very earliest.[1] Ships with the freeboard necessary to carry sail in a seaway could not have been rowed with any kind of oar-lock on the gunwale unless the oarsmen stood up, or used impossibly long oars. All our evidence, iconographic, literary and archaeological, is unanimous that by the eleventh century all but the smallest ships had long been rowed through oar-ports cut at a convenient height in the hull.

It follows that *hamele* is not being used here in its literal sense. We know that in both Denmark and Norway it later bore a technical meaning in connection with the *leidang*. Applied to a ship in Norwegian usage, it was a unit of measurement of size, apparently equivalent to the oar or half-room.[2] By extension it referred to the man, or men, levied to man the half-room, and to the number of houses or households required to produce one such unit. In this sense the *hamla* was the product of dividing the whole ship's company by the number of oars, equivalent to the number of men pulling each oar, if every man were rowing at once. Danish scholars, on the other hand, seem to suggest that the *havna* was one man.[3] As the *Anglo-Saxon Chronicle*'s reference is evidently to the payment of men, it seems reasonable to propose that the word is used here as a technical term for a unit of men raised for naval service. The problem is to know what the unit was, for clearly the size of the Danish forces, and the rate of pay of each man, cannot be calculated without knowing whether *æt ælcere hamulan* refers to one man or several.

We could be sure that it meant a single man only if we could be sure that the half-roomful was one man – that is, that each man pulled an oar of his own, and there were no men who were not oarsmen. This is the assumption which is commonly made, but what evidence we have is clearly against it. The fragmentary wreck known as Skuldelev 2, a longship sunk as a blockship in Roskilde Fjord late in the eleventh century, was between twenty and twenty-five rooms and over one hundred feet long. Rowed single-banked (one man to an oar) she would have needed forty to fifty oarsmen, but she could easily have carried at least eighty men.[4] This ship, hitherto supposed to be Danish, has now been judged from study of her timber to have been built in the British

1. Seán McGrail, *Ancient Boats in NW Europe: The Archaeology of Water Transport to AD 1500* (London, 1987), pp. 212–14. The word 'rowlock' is not recorded in Bertil Sandahl's *Middle English Sea Terms* (3 vols. to date, Uppsala, 1951–82).

2. The fine for failing to build a new ship in place of one broken up was three marks a *hamla*: Christensen, 'Boat Finds from Bryggen', p. 245. Dr Christensen, writing in English, somewhat muddies the water by rendering 'hamla' as 'rowlock', but it is clear from his own illustrations (e.g. p. 226) that he does not mean it.

3. *KLNM*, vi. 96–101, s.v. 'Hamna'. Larson, *Earliest Norwegian Laws*, p. 423.

4. Olaf Olsen and Ole Crumlin-Pedersen, 'The Skuldelev Ships (II). A Report of the Final Underwater Excavation in 1959 and the Salvaging Operation in 1962', *Acta Archaeologica* [Copenhagen], xxxviii (1967), 73–174, at 118. Ole Crumlin-Pedersen, 'The Viking Ships of Roskilde', in *Aspects of the History of Wooden Shipbuilding* (NMM, Monographs and Reports, no. 1, 1970), pp. 7–23, at 9. Simon Keynes, 'The Historical Context of the Battle of Maldon', in *The Battle of Maldon, AD 991*, ed. Donald Scragg (Oxford, 1991), pp. 81–113, at 88, prints a sketch of this ship reconstructed which credits her with twenty-five rooms and sixty men, surely too small a crew.

Isles, possibly at Dublin.[1] Like some other longships excavated in Denmark, she had a particularly high length-to-beam ratio, that is to say with a narrow and relatively cramped hull.[2] The evidence of the Norwegian ship-houses, however, suggests beamier longships, and many references indicate that with them the half-roomful was two, three or more men, depending on the size of ship.[3] The Gokstad ship, admittedly an untypical example from an earlier century, but also smaller and therefore more cramped than most warships, had thirty-two oars but sixty-four shields.[4] Cnut's Norwegian contemporary Erling Skjalgsson had a twenty-two-room ship with a crew of two hundred, or four and a half to the half-room.[5] The *Ormrinn Langi* is said to have had two complete watches of four men to an oar, making 544 men in addition to the rest of the crew.[6] The *Maríasuðin* of thirty rooms, built for King Sverre in 1182–3, carried five men to the half-room, three hundred oarsmen plus twenty others.[7] This same monarch, wishing to limit the power of the Archbishop of Nidaros, forbade him to have a ship above twenty rooms, carrying ninety men – two and a quarter to the half-room.[8] Skuldelev 2, the nearest in time to Cnut's ships, is smaller and probably narrower than the Norwegian *drekkar*, but she could certainly have carried at least two men to an oar, and it is hard to see what military advantage would be gained by going on a warlike expedition with the ship half empty, and foregoing the opportunity to row double-banked if a burst of speed were required.

In practice, if prolonged rowing were called for, the limitations of human stamina would oblige the crew to row in watches,[9] but we can be sure they did not row when they could sail. This raises a further problem, for there is no reason to assume that each Danish ship was manned simply with an undifferentiated mass of soldier-oarsmen. If we know nothing else about the Vikings, we know that they were capable seamen: the fleets which crossed and recrossed the North Sea, and voyaged around the coasts of the whole of Western Europe, were not handled by peasants taken from the plough's tail. We might perhaps believe that Norwegian ships, manned from districts where to this day all communication is by water, could rely on every man knowing how to trim a sail, but there is no reason to assume as much of Denmark (or of England). Yet there must undoubtedly have been good seamen aboard. Unless we are to imagine whole fleets of thousands of men recruited entirely from regular seafarers, we must assume some division of skills

1. Crumlin-Pedersen, 'Ship Types and Sizes', n.1.

2. *KLNM*, xv. 484, s.v. 'Skibstyper'.

3. Morcken, *Langskip, knarr og kogge*, pp. 28, 37, 59. *KLNM*, x. 435, s.v. 'Leidang'. Brøgger and Shetelig, *Viking Ships*, pp. 72, 203.

4. Ibid., p. 126.

5. Ibid., p. 207.

6. Morcken, *Langskip, knarr og kogge*, pp. 36–7.

7. Brøgger and Shetelig, *Viking Ships*, p. 203.

8. Ibid., p. 210.

9. McGrail, *Ancient Boats*, p. 216.

aboard. Perhaps the mass of muster-men were taught to pull an oar (not as easy as it looks, especially in a seaway) by a small professional crew belonging to each ship. If they were regarded as separate from the oarsmen-soldiers, were they included in the *hamele*? The answer to that question, could we know it, would further affect our calculations.

Moreover, we do not know that references to the number of oars a ship carried are necessarily to the number she rowed. Those who have studied oared warships from administrative documents will be familiar with the difficulty of distinguishing the number of oars a ship rowed from her total outfit. Oars break easily, and no one puts to sea intending to use them without taking spares. The English ship with sixty-four oars which Bishop Ælfwold of Crediton bequeathed some time in Æthelred II's reign, did not necessarily, or even probably, row thirty-two a side, which would have put her among the giants of the Viking age.[1] Nor is there any reason to assume that a Danish fleet, however well organized, consisted of ships all of the same size.[2]

Yet a further complication has to be introduced. For men to row sitting in files one abaft the other, they need to sit at least three feet apart, but we have hints that some eleventh-century ships may have used an unconventional oaring arrangement. Skuldelev 5, a small ship of about twelve rooms with frames at a conventional interval, had some reused strakes of planking in her, including part of the strake in which her oar-ports were cut. This had served the same function in an earlier ship with ports only 32in. apart, which must have been too close together for the crew to row in the conventional fashion with any comfort.[3] Possibly she was rowed by oarsmen sitting staggered, with oars of different lengths, an arrangement which has been proposed for thirteenth-century English galleys built in the Viking tradition.[4] Moreover, in Skuldelev 2 both frames and oar-ports were only 28in. apart, so that the number of half-rooms and oars was the same, but the conventional rowing arrangement was impossible.[5]

These discoveries tend to complicate our calculations by making it difficult to reckon the number of oars from the length of the ship, or vice versa. In Skuldelev 2 there is one oar to the half-room, but the number of both is one-fifth greater than in the conventional arrangement for a ship of the same size. If, however, she was built in Dublin, we cannot assume that she had much in common with Cnut's ships. What we can deduce is

---

1. Napier and Stevenson, *Crawford Charters*, pp. 23, 126–9; the English is 'ænne scegð lxiiii ære'.

2. *English Historical Documents*, ed. Whitelock, p. 334, quotes Thord Kolbeinsson's *Eiríksdrápa* on the ships of various sizes in the 1016 fleet.

3. Olsen and Crumlin-Pedersen, 'The Skuldelev Ships (II)', 140–1, 167.

4. Ole Crumlin-Pedersen, 'The Vikings and the Hanseatic Merchants, 900–1450', in *A History of Seafaring Based on Underwater Archaeology*, ed. George F. Bass (London, 1972), pp. 181–204, at 188. R. C. Anderson, *Oared Fighting Ships from Classical Times to the Coming of Steam* (London, 1962), pp. 44–5. J. T. Tinniswood, 'English Galleys, 1272–1377', *Mariner's Mirror*, xxxv (1949), 276–315, at 296.

5. Olsen and Crumlin-Pedersen, 'The Skuldelev Ships (II)', 167. Crumlin-Pedersen, 'Viking Ships of Roskilde', p. 9.

that the builder of this ship was anxious to have as many oars as possible, which must mean that speed under oars was valuable to him, and we can be sure that he would have wished to fit in as many men as he could to pull them. The possibility of unorthodox oaring arrangements makes our calculations even more uncertain, but it suggests that they should yield the highest figures for the size of the crew consistent with the size of ship. We also need to consider the problem of the mark, which may be understood as a unit of weight, or a money of account worth 10s. 8d., 13s. 4d., or 16s. Of these alternatives, both the mark weight and the mark of the value of 10s. 8d. (which is Dr Lawson's choice) yield a crew of about eighty men for each ship, but a mark of 13s. 4d., as used by Dr Keynes for his calculation,[1] suggests only about sixty-five men, and one of 16s. implies only fifty.[2]

Taking stock of all these complications, we may now ask where this leaves the calculations of Dr Keynes, Dr Lawson and others. It may be that they are not hopelessly perplexed. Once we dispose of the 'row-locks' and accept that the *hamele* is not in this context a part of a ship at all, we cut out many of our difficulties. All the mentions of oars, and corresponding calculations of the size of the ships, are modern inferences not called for by the text. All we are given is a rate of taxation, and by implication pay, of eight marks to a unit of men which may be one man or several, and a number of ships to which those men belonged. We cannot say for certain what is the size of the *hamele*, but the balance of probability seems to be in favour of one, for (assuming a mark of 10s. 8d.) any much larger figure would call for improbably large ships. A *hamele* of one man on Dr Lawson's calculations gives a ship's company, or at least the oarsman-soldier part of it, of about eighty men, which would fit a longship of twenty rooms or somewhat more, either with the conventional oaring arrangements, or with the tight spacing of Skulde-lev 2.[3] Eighty men could not possibly man the ships of eighty oars, or forty rooms, which he proposes. If such monsters had ever existed, they would have required crews many times that size to move them under oars, and it is rather unlikely that Cnut possessed scores if not hundreds of ships, larger than any known ever to have been built of wood in any period of history. If the *hamele* were eight or ten men, such ships could at least have been manned, but the army then becomes exceedingly large, and its rate of pay diminishes almost to vanishing point.

It is surely simplest and most satisfactory to take the *hamele* as one man and the ships as twenty rooms or thereabouts on average, and to abandon the unnecessary idea of one man to an oar which creates so much difficulty. This is certainly the interpretation of 'Florence' of Worcester, who renders this passage, 'octo marcas unicuique suae classis

1. Keynes, *Diplomas of King Æthelred 'the Unready'*, p. 225, n. 257.
2. Lawson, '"Those Stories Look True"', 386. Id., *Cnut*, p. 177. Campbell, 'Some Agents and Agencies', p. 203, n. 11.
3. Lawson, 'The Collection of Danegeld and Heregeld', 737–8.

remigi et xii unicuique gubernatori praecepit dependi'.[1] All this accepts the mark of 10s. 8d., for a ship's company as small as sixty-five looks less plausible on the archaeological evidence, and one as small as fifty looks most unlikely. If, however, the mark were proved to be 16s., it might suggest that the *hamele* was actually two men, which would give a crew of one hundred men, and a high, but not impossibly high, rate of pay of 8s. a year for each. If there were seamen not included in the total paid *æt ælcere hamulan*, the calculations become more complex, but we could accommodate them in several ways, such as by supposing slightly larger ships, or by valuing the mark at 13s. 4d. and reducing the crews to sixty-five or so.[2] It is very much to be hoped that in due course the numismatists will be able to settle the value of the mark with more confidence, which would remove one of our major uncertainties.

In our present state of knowledge, it looks as though a great many complications might be boiled down to leave us roughly where we were to begin with on this specific question. Many other calculations, however, have been made on the assumption that one man equals one oar, and will have to be revised if we accept that warships were often manned on twice or thrice this scale.[3] Clearly this conclusion affects the debate about the size of Danish armies expressed in numbers of ships.[4] Whatever view one takes of the accuracy of our sources, it will be very difficult to push the number of men per ship as low as fifty, let alone thirty, and a figure as high as a hundred would not be out of the question. If the rate of pay on eleventh-century Danish warships, however the crew had actually been recruited, was expressed by a technical term of the *leidang*, it should imply that the system (or at least some system for manning a fleet) was already old enough to have established its own terminology – especially as the term in question is derived from a feature of warship design which was already at least two hundred years out of date. There are also implications for English naval history. It will no longer do to make connections between Alfred's ships of sixty oars and the sixty-man ship-sokes of the tenth century and later.[5] If Alfred's ships were really of thirty rooms and more – nearly

---

1. *Chronicon ex Chronicis*, ed Benjamin Thorpe (2 vols., London, 1848–9), i. 194.

2. Lawson, 'The Collection of Danegeld and Heregeld', 722, n. 3.

3. Examples are Stenton, *Anglo-Saxon England*, p. 413; Eric John, *Land Tenure in Early England: A Discussion of some Problems* (Leicester, 1960), pp. 121–5; *Alfred the Great: Asser's Life of King Alfred and Other Contemporary Sources*, ed. and trans. Simon Keynes and Michael Lapidge (Harmondsworth, 1983), p. 289; Hollister, *Anglo-Saxon Military Institutions*, p. 106; Hooper, 'Observations on the Navy', pp. 212–13. An honourable exception is Richard P. Abels, *Lordship and Military Obligation in Anglo-Saxon England* (Berkeley, 1988), p. 109.

4. P. H. Sawyer, *Kings and Vikings: Scandinavia and Europe, AD 700–1100* (London, 1982), p. 93. James Campbell, Eric John and Patrick Wormald, *The Anglo-Saxons* (Oxford, 1982), p. 147. N. P. Brooks, 'England in the Ninth Century: The Crucible of Defeat', *Transactions of the Royal Historical Society*, 5th ser., xxix (1979), 1–20. Lawson, '"Those Stories Look True"', 396–7.

5. Campbell, *Anglo-Saxons*, p. 150. Hooper, 'Observations on the Navy', pp. 210–13. H. R. Loyn, *The Governance of Anglo-Saxon England, 500–1087* (London, 1984), p. 168.

I

twice as long as the Danish ships, as we are quite plausibly informed[1] – they would have needed crews of several hundred to row or fight them to effect. A unit of sixty men, on the other hand, would be adequate to man a ship of only fifteen rooms or so – if the sixty men raised from villages in inland shires really manned their ship without professional assistance, in other words if they were really the whole ship's company and not just the military part of it.[2] These are puzzling questions, but not beyond all conjecture; and we shall do well in considering them to make no unfounded assumptions about the relationship between size of ship, size of crew, and number of oars.

Additional Note [2009]

This paper was published just too soon to take advantage of Niels Lund's essential study *Lið, leding og Landeværn: Hær og samfund i Danmark i ældre middelalder* (Roskilde, 1996), which greatly extends our understanding of the leding and analagous organisations in the Northern world. In addition our knowledge of English and Scandinavian nautical vocabulary in the Viking age has been transformed by two books: Judith Jesch, *Ships and men in the late Viking Age: the vocabulary of runic inscriptions and skaldic verse* (Woodbridge, 2001); and Katrin Thier, *Altenglische Terminologie für Schiffe und Schiffsteile: Archäologie und Sprachgeschichte 500–1100* (Oxford, 2002). Nautical archaeology, and practical experience of sailing reconstructed Viking ships, continues to expand our understanding of many aspects of seafaring. A replica of the big warship Skuldelev 2, believed to have been built near Dublin, has been constructed by the Viking Ship Museum and named *Havhingsten fra Glendalough* ('Sea Stallion from Glendalough'). In the summer of 2007 she sailed to Dublin around the North of Scotland, returning up the English Channel. Not much has been published yet about this voyage, but remarkable film of the ship under way under oars and sail can be seen on the Museum's website, www.vikingeskibsmuseet.dk/. A most important new discovery of nine early medieval shipwrecks was made on the shores of Roskilde Fjord in 1996–97 during the construction of a new building for the Viking Ship Museum. These wrecks include that of an eleventh-century longship which is the largest Viking warship ever excavated. At the time of writing, however, no proper reports of these discoveries have been published, only preliminary notices, of which one is in English: Morten Gøthche, 'The Roskilde Ships', in *Connected by the Sea: Proceedings of the Tenth International Symposium on Boat and Ship Archaeology, Denmark, 2003* eds Lucy Blue, Fred Hocker & Anton Englert (Oxford, 2006), pp. 252–8. With these and other recent publications it would be possible now to fill out the argument of this article, but I am not aware that its conclusions have been fundamentally challenged, or that the big questions it poses have been answered.

---

    1. Whitelock, *Anglo-Saxon Chronicle*, p. 57. A ship of thirty rooms might well be nearly double the overall length of one of about twenty.

    2. David Hill, *An Atlas of Anglo-Saxon England* (Oxford, 1981), maps 165 and 166, shows that even the bishops of London and Sherborne, whose estates bordered the coast, recruited most of the men for their ships from inland villages where seafarers are unlikely to have lived.

II

The Naval Service of the Cinque Ports[*]

IT was for long an accepted truth of medieval history that the Cinque Ports, 'these powerful and privileged towns',[1] furnished the essential core, if not actually the whole, of the naval strength available to the kings of England. Some scholars are still prepared to describe the Cinque Ports in such terms without further qualification,[2] but the tendency among those recent writers who are aware of the existence of naval warfare in English medieval history (which not everyone is), has been to claim, or more often allow by implication, that the Cinque Ports, though admittedly of declining or negligible naval value in the period under study, had provided essential service in some undefined, earlier, era.[3] The question of when this period was has been rather evaded, but it still seems to be generally accepted that the charters of the Cinque Ports reflected their naval importance: 'a monopoly of naval power and an effective control of the Channel', in the words of K. M. E. Murray;[4] a 'virtual control' of the Straits of Dover in the later fourteenth century, according to Professor Allmand (one of the few prepared to hazard a date).[5] The problem is that the more closely the subject is studied, the more difficult it becomes to identify a time when this 'monopoly' or 'virtual control' actually existed. There is no doubt that the Ports'

[*] I am indebted for helpful suggestions to Dr Julia Crick, Professor John Gillingham, Professor Janet Nelson and Professor Michael Prestwich.

1. F. W. Brooks, *The English Naval Forces, 1199–1272* (London, 1932), p. 80.

2. Timothy J. Runyan, 'The Organization of Royal Fleets in Medieval England', in *Ships, Seafaring and Society: Essays in Maritime History*, ed. T. J. Runyan (Detroit, 1987), pp. 37–52, at pp. 38 and 41; Stephen Morillo, *Warfare under the Anglo-Norman Kings, 1066–1135* (Woodbridge, 1994), p. 60 (referring to that period specifically).

3. A. L. Poole, *From Domesday Book to Magna Carta 1087–1216* (Oxford, 1951), pp. 433–4; May McKisack, *The Fourteenth Century 1307–1399* (Oxford, 1959), p. 243; C. F. Richmond, 'The War at Sea', in *The Hundred Years War*, ed. Kenneth Fowler (London, 1971), pp. 96–121, at p. 104; Michael Prestwich, *War, Politics and Finance under Edward I* (London, 1972), pp. 137–150; Jonathan Sumption, *The Hundred Years War*, Vol. I: *Trial by Battle* (London, 1990), pp. 175–6; J. W. Sherborne, 'The Hundred Years War. The English Navy: Shipping and Manpower 1369–1389', *Past and Present*, xxxvii (1967), 163–175, at 167; David Loades, *The Tudor Navy: An Administrative, Political and Military History* (Aldershot, 1992) p. 12. As far as I know, Sir Maurice Powicke, *The Thirteenth Century 1216–1307* (Oxford, 1953), p. 523, is alone in suggesting that the Ports' privileges were earned by shipbuilding for the Crown.

4. *The Constitutional History of the Cinque Ports* (Manchester, 1935), p. 210.

5. Christopher Allmand, *The Hundred Years War: England and France at War, c.1300–c.1450* (Cambridge, 1988), p. 85.

eleventh- and twelfth-century charters conferred valuable privileges, and there is no need to return to their complex constitutional history, so thoroughly studied by Miss Murray. No historian, however, has ever specified exactly when and how the Cinque Ports were 'a great maritime power'.[1] If their privileges were really granted in expectation of naval service to be performed, or in acknowledgement of service already performed, it should be possible to identify what, and when, this service was, or was supposed to be. If they were not connected with naval service, it would be good to know why they were granted.

It may be helpful as a preliminary to sketch the forms of English naval warfare in the four centuries or so following the Conquest. This is a big subject, to be treated properly elsewhere,[2] but for present purposes we may briefly identify three types of naval activity. Specialized warships, in northern waters as in the Mediterranean, were oared (but also rigged) vessels, of shallow draught and relatively high speed, mainly employed in coastal, or inland, amphibious warfare, especially in the ubiquitous raids which corresponded to the campaigns of destruction so prominent in warfare on land. They were the means by which large bodies of men could be transported with speed and surprise to any point within reach of navigable water, but they were expensive to build and maintain, and their operating range was very short.[3] Several English kings assembled, or tried to assemble squadrons of these galleys, barges or balingers, but none succeeded in maintaining such a force for long. Oared vessels could also be found in small numbers in the English merchant fleet, but for English kings Bayonne was usually the best source of galleys, and of the professional skills needed to handle them.[4] For most of this period, and especially in the fourteenth century, it was France and France's allies (Castile, Genoa and Portugal) which deployed galley squadrons in English waters, and met little effective opposition.

In addition to oared vessels, sailing ships belonging to the Crown or, more often, taken from the merchant fleet, were employed for specifically warlike purposes, notably convoy escort. They were distinguished from other merchantmen by carrying a double crew (*duplex eskippamentum*), the addition often being made up of troops, and by having

---

1. Sumption, *Trial by Battle*, p. 176.
2. N. A. M. Rodger, *A Naval History of Britain*. Vol. I: *The Safeguard of the Sea* (forthcoming).
3. John H. Pryor, *Geography, Technology and War: Studies in the Maritime History of the Mediterranean, 649–1571* (Cambridge, 1988), pp. 71–85; *The Age of the Galley: Mediterranean Oared Vessels since Pre-Classical Times*, ed. John Morrison (London, 1995), pp. 115, 130, 132, 194, 208, 210, 218–23; P. E. Russell, *The English Intervention in Spain and Portugal in the Time of Edward III and Richard II* (Oxford, 1955), pp. 232–235; Francisco-Felipe Olesa Muñido, *La galera en la navegación y el combate* (2 vols., Madrid, 1971), i. 207–211. Pryor gives a theoretical maximum radius of operations in Mediterranean conditions of about 500 miles, but in practice it is rare to find galleys operating more than 100 to 150 miles from their base.
4. Jacques Bernard, *Navires et gens de mer à Bordeaux (vers 1400 – vers 1500)* (3 vols., Paris, 1968), i. 242–5.

temporary castles fitted.[1] By the fourteenth century these ships were often referred to as 'warships' (*naves guerrinas, naves de guerra, nefs defensables*, etc), which seems to have indicated larger ships fitted with permanent castles.[2] Like galleys, these ships were essentially instruments of inshore warfare. Though it was feasible to patrol along the coast, cruising in the open sea was either impossible or pointless; deliberate interception of the enemy, though sometimes attempted, was rarely achieved; and all fighting was hand to hand, usually in sheltered waters. The vast majority of ships on war service for the English Crown, however, were unmodified merchantmen with their usual crews, taken up to transport troops or supplies overseas. They were expected to proceed from one friendly port to another, under escort if necessary. Their men would be accustomed to facing the risks of piracy which were endemic in that age, but they were not normally expected to meet regular forces in action. Many hundreds of such ships were levied to lift the larger overseas expeditions of the thirteenth, fourteenth and fifteenth centuries.

With these distinctions in mind, we may return to the Cinque Ports. The form of their obligation presents the first puzzle, for it is difficult to think of any period and circumstance in which the service of fifty-seven ships, each with a master and twenty-one men, for a fortnight,[3] was or could have been of real military value. It can safely be asserted that there never was any period in English medieval history when a useful naval operation could be accomplished in a fortnight. This service, like the paid service of other ports, was always counted from the date of sailing from the port of assembly, after a process of mustering which usually took many months, but the movement of squadrons or fleets of sailing vessels was at least as slow after assembly as before. Only a galley force, already full operational and based within striking range of the enemy, could hope to complete an operation in fifteen days. It is sometimes suggested that the Cinque Ports' function was to provide such a force,[4] but the evidence does not seem to support the idea. The documents seldom mention more than a few galleys, barges or balingers among their squadrons; in one of about 1295, for example, there were three galleys out of about seventy-five vessels.[5] More often than not when galleys are mentioned they were evidently operating under sail, as the

---

1. E.g.: *Rotuli Scotiae* (2 vols., London, 1814–19, i. 192; C[alendar of] C[lose] R[olls], 1369–74, p. 177.

2. E.g. *CCR, 1333–37*, pp. 22, 414, 431; P[ublic] R[ecord] O[ffice] E.372/180 rot.44 m.2; cf. C.71/15 m.29.

3. A fortnight *more latino*, i.e. fifteen days.

4. Sherborne, 'English Navy', p. 168; Richard W. Unger, *The Ship in the Medieval Economy, 600–1600* (London, 1980), p. 172.

5. PRO, E.101/684/54/4; total approximate as the entry for Winchelsea is illegible. I have not counted ten ferry-boats (*passagers*) from Dover.

crews were too small to have manned the oars.[1] In 1300, for example, the barge *Holy Ghost* of Sandwich carrying despatches to Ireland had a crew of thirty-five, while in the same year John le Skirmesour of Winchelsea was escorting victuallers from Ireland to the Solway Firth in a barge with a crew of only twenty-six.[2] In a list of seven barges and balingers belonging to the Ports in 1379–80, none has a crew of more than 30 for ships big enough to carry 45–70 troops, which must be too few to man all their oars.[3] There is nothing surprising in this, for medieval English oared vessels usually sailed, and even in wartime only embarked a full crew of oarsmen when it was really necessary.[4] If the Cinque Ports had really been providing a squadron of galleys for war service, however, full crews would have been called for, and they would have been a great many more than twenty-one men, for oared warships were generally manned on a scale approaching one man to the ton,[5] and their military value derived largely from the number of men they carried. Nor would Henry III have been likely to have based a squadron of royal galleys at Rye and Winchelsea in the 1230s, if the Cinque Ports had had galleys available for his service.[6]

By contrast the ships of the Cinque Ports often served on ordinary transport service. The twenty-one men specified in their charters represented the typical crew of a ship of sixty tons or so in peacetime trade, and this was about the smallest which was normally taken up for transport duty, except in grave emergency.[7] In the thirteenth or fourteenth century three or four tons a man was a common ratio for ships trading to Gascony.[8] In 1324 orders were issued for a fleet assembling to carry Edward II to Gascony to be manned on a scale ranging from twenty-one men for sixty tons up to sixty men for a ship of 240 tons.[9] 124 ships gathered to transport an expedition in 1326 had a mean of a master and 29½ men each.[10] The Ports usually contributed a proportion

1. E.g. PRO, E.372/195, rot.44; E.352/120, rot.49; E.101/3/26; Nicholas Harris Nicolas, *A History of the Royal Navy from the Earliest Times to the Wars of the French Revolution* (2 vols., London, 1847), i. 294–295; *CCR, 1323–27*, pp. 608–12.

2. *Liber Quotidianus Contrarotulatoris Garderobae Anno Regni Regis Edwardi Primi Vicesimo Octavo*, ed. J. Topham *et al.* (London, 1787), pp. 273–4.

3. Bertil Sandahl, 'Names in English Naval Documents, 1280–1380', in *Medieval Ships and the Birth of Technological Societies*. Vol. I: *Northern Europe*, ed. Christiane Villain-Gandossi, Salvino Busuttil and Paul Adam (Malta, 1989), pp. 175–92, at p. 178, citing PRO, E.101/39/2.

4. Unger, *Ship in the Medieval Economy*, pp. 172, 204; J. T. Tinniswood, 'English Galleys, 1272–1377', *Mariner's Mirror*, xxxv (1949), 276–315, at 279; Dorothy Burwash, *English Merchant Shipping 1460–1540* (Toronto, 1947), pp. 103–8; J. W. Sherborne, 'English Barges and Ballingers of the Late Fourteenth Century', *Mariner's Mirror* lxiii (1977), 109–114; Ian Friel, 'Archaeological Sources and the Medieval Ship: Some Aspects of the Evidence', *International Journal of Nautical Archaeology*, xii (1983), 41–62, at 55; *Liber Quotidianus*, ed. Topham, pp. 272–9.

5. Friel, 'Archaeological Sources', p. 55.

6. Brooks, *English Naval Forces*, pp. 150–1.

7. C[lose] R[olls], 1237–42, pp. 401, 429, 431–2 *CR, 1253–54*, p. 124.

8. Nicolas, *Royal Navy*, i. 285.

9. PRO, C. 66/160 m.13; translated in *British Naval Documents, 1204–1960*, ed. John B. Hattendorf *et al.* (Navy Records Soc., vol. cxxxi., 1993), No. 27.

10. *CCR, 1323–27*, pp. 608–12.

of such fleets, but there was nothing especially 'naval' about this duty, and nothing they were doing which was not being done by dozens of other ports of similar size.

For service as 'warships' twenty-one men was too few. This would have been the double complement of a ship of only thirty tons, much too small to be valuable in action in an age when all sea fighting was hand to hand, and the freeboard of the bigger ship allowed her to dominate the battle. The Cinque Ports' ships were small, but not that small. The forty which served in the Welsh war of 1282 bore on average just under thirty-two men, including troops added to double their complements.[1] In 1299 a Cinque Ports squadron of thirty ships had just under thirty-four men each.[2] A force of twenty-three of their ships in 1326 had a mean of forty-five men each, double-manned.[3] Either from their own resources, or with the addition of royal troops, they could fit out 'warships' with a double complement, but the crews required were typical of those of similar ships taken up from any small or middle-sized port of the period,[4] and bore no obvious relation to the Ports' due service. Undoubtedly their help in this and in transport duty was worth having, but it is hard to see that it was worth so much more than the contribution of other ports as to justify special privileges.

If, therefore, the Cinque Ports really earned their status by actual or prospective naval service, we still have to identify a valuable service which they were capable of discharging, which was not being performed at the same time by every other English port, and which bore some relation to the obligation specified in their charters. The obvious answer is to derive these obligations from different circumstances in some earlier period. F. W. Brooks, still the only scholar to have examined the subject in detail, dated the Ports' corporate existence from the late twelfth century, and thought that the thirteenth was their heyday, before their harbours silted up. He attached weight to the group of charters issued in 1205, which he presented as intended to adapt an existing organization to the new strategic situation resulting from the loss of Normandy.[5] He implied that the original service of the ports had been to run a ferry service to Normandy. There is obvious attraction in the theory that the Cinque Ports' obligations were originally designed to link the two halves of the Anglo-Norman empire. Such a service was undoubtedly necessary, and it is one duty which could easily be fulfilled by a large number of small ships each available for a fortnight. The theory also has the effect, convenient for the historian, of pushing the

1. PRO, E.101/3/26, mm.1–2.

2. Nicolas, *Royal Navy*, i. 294–5.

3. PRO, E.352/120, rot.49; the presence of a constable for each ship indicates that they were double-manned, though not with soldiers in this case.

4. E.g. Nicolas, *Royal Navy*, i. 335.

5. F. W. Brooks, 'The Cinque Ports', *Mariner's Mirror*, xv (1929), 142–91; idem, 'The King's Ships and Galleys, mainly under John and Henry III', *Mariner's Mirror*, xv (1929), 15–48, at 19.

ports' origins back into a period from which relatively little written evidence survives. Unfortunately there are several reasons why it cannot be true.

In the first place, it seems virtually certain that the earliest privileges granted to ports which later came to be part of the Cinque Ports federation, predate the Conquest. The right to annual ship-service from several ports in Kent and Sussex, including those which later became the head-ports of the Cinque Ports (Sandwich, Dover, Hythe, Romney and Hastings), was apparently acquired by Edward the Confessor in or before 1051. Dover and Sandwich each provided twenty ships for a fortnight, with crews of twenty-one men, and Fordwich, Romney and possibly Hythe and Hastings, probably served on a similar basis.[1] It is difficult to prove administrative continuity from the eleventh century to the thirteenth; but if the original Cinque Ports already owed a number of ships for a fortnight, each with twenty-one men, as they did later, it can hardly be a coincidence.[2]

We shall return to the circumstances of their origin. For the moment it is sufficient to observe that whatever King Edward wanted from the Ports in 1051, it was presumably not a ferry service to Normandy. Nor, had he wanted such a thing, could he have found it there. Lying at the extreme leeward end of the Channel, up which the prevailing south-westerlies blow for most of the year, the Cinque Ports were very ill placed to be a base of operations anywhere to the westward, especially with the relative inefficiency of medieval hulls and sailing rigs in working to windward.[3] From the westernmost of the Cinque Ports, Hastings, to Dieppe, the easternmost port of Normandy, is a feasible passage of eighty miles or so, but the other ports would have been very hard put to participate.[4] In the twelfth century, when the documents allow us to see the royal ferry service in operation, the Cinque Ports were scarcely involved. Between 1154 and 1189, according to the chroniclers, Henry II crossed the Channel certainly twenty-six, and probably twenty-eight times. Four of these crossings were on the Dover-Wissant route, when the King had occasion to visit Flanders, and one (in January 1188) was from Dieppe to Winchelsea. All the others were between Southampton, Portchester or Portsmouth; and Barfleur, Cherbourg, or another of the

---

1. Nicholas Hooper, 'Some Observations on the Navy in late Anglo-Saxon England', in *Studies in Medieval History Presented to R. Allen Brown*, ed. Christopher Harper-Bill, Christopher J. Holdsworth and Janet L. Nelson (Woodbridge, 1989) pp. 203–13, at pp. 206–7; C. W. Hollister, *Anglo-Saxon Military Institutions on the Eve of the Norman Conquest* (Oxford, 1962), pp. 116–22.

2. Murray, *Constitutional History*, p. 21.

3. It is not easy to understand the argument of A. Z. Freeman ('Wooden Walls: The English Navy in the Reign of Edward I', in *Changing Interpretations and New Sources in Naval History*, ed. R. W. Love [New York, 1980], pp. 58–67, at p. 61) that 'with prevailing winds out of the northwest and ships at their best running, the Ports could dominate the Channel.'

4. John Le Patourel, *The Norman Empire* (Oxford, 1976), p. 167, suggests that William I and II favoured the Cinque Ports for crossings, but Henry I transferred the ferry service to Portsmouth and Hampshire. This seems most unlikely on geographical grounds, but even if it were true, it could not explain the origins of the ports' privileges if they predated either William.

Cotentin ports.[1] The pipe rolls tell the same story. The ferry service was based at Southampton, with some sailings from Portsmouth, Portchester or Bosham, and its Norman terminus was at Barfleur.[2] From the first mention of her in 1160,[3] the King's own ship lay at Southampton, and other ships to supplement her were usually found there. Neither the King nor his court ever sailed from any of the Cinque Ports to Normandy. The Cinque Ports themselves are mentioned, under that name, but with one possible exception in 1160,[4] they were not employed on the ferry service.

It could of course be argued that they do not figure in the pipe rolls because they were not being paid, and it is difficult to prove that they were not performing unpaid service of some sort, but they certainly were being paid for passages from Dover to the Continent,[5] among other things, and there is very little to suggest that there was unpaid activity going on at the same time. Money was paid to fit out unspecified Kentish ships to go with Henry II's Irish expedition in 1171 without mention of wages,[6] which might indicate that the ports were serving unpaid – but there was no reason why the King should have paid for their equipment if they were performing their due service, and it seems unlikely that they could have completed the expedition in a fortnight. The great bulk of the ships for the Irish expedition came from elsewhere,[7] and for obvious reasons it was based on west coast ports, which makes it difficult to credit Miss Murray's suggestion that the Cinque Ports' charters of 1155–56 were connected with Henry II's plans to sail to Ireland.[8] The Ports were certainly a source of ships – Richard I bought thirty-three of them for his crusade in 1189,[9] and he chartered others later[10] – but as far as the records go they seem always to have been paid for. The Ports' ships were certainly serving for pay in wartime not later than the 1180s.[11] The same was true of transport service. In the twelfth century and later Dover continued to be a ferry port for the Continent, but whenever the king or his servants travelled that way, they seem to

1. John Le Patourel, 'Le gouvernment de Henri II Plantagenêt et la mer de la Manche', in *Recueil d'Etudes offert au Doyen M. de Bouärd* (*Annales de Normandie*, extra issue, Caen, 1982) ii. 323–33, at 324–6.

2. There are numerous references in the pipe rolls of Henry II's and Richard I's reigns (as printed by the Pipe Roll Society) under 'Hampshire' and 'Southampton'. See also *Rotuli Normanniae in Turri Londinensi asservati Johanne et Henrico Quinto Angliae Regibus*, ed. Thomas Duffus Hardy (London, 1835), pp. 27, 28, 58, 63.

3. *Pipe Roll 7 Henry II*, p. 56.

4. *Pipe Roll 7 Henry II*, p. 56; £34 to Cinque Ports ships 'qui perrexerunt cum thesauro'.

5. *Pipe Roll 29 Henry II*, p. 160; *Pipe Roll 31 Henry II*, p. 224.

6. *Pipe Roll 17 Henry II*, p. 139.

7. *Pipe Rolls 17, 18, 19 Henry II, passim.*

8. Murray, *Constitutional History*, p. 13.

9. *Pipe Roll 2 Richard I*, p. 8.

10. *Pipe Roll 5 Richard I*, p. 170: £45 0s. 3d. 'in liberatione navium rentatarum per V portus'.

11. *Pipe Roll 30 Henry II*, p. 146.

have paid their passages like everyone else, and even paid for repairs to the ferry boats.[1]

The arguments of geography also tell against Brooks's suggestion that the Ports took on a new importance with the loss of Normandy.[2] Clearly they were now more open to attack than they had been, like everywhere on the English coast, but there is no obvious reason why they should have been chosen as centres of a naval effort against France. As before, they lay on the leeward edge of the likely area of operations. Any English king planning the reconquest of Normandy would have chosen a port further down Channel. King John in fact built up his fleet at Portsmouth, where he constructed something like the first English dockyard; Henry V, with a similar strategic objective, chose Southampton. Neither the Cinque Ports nor their service were especially relevant to John's plans, and his naval administrator William of Wrotham, 'Keeper of the King's Ports and Galleys', appears to have treated the Cinque Ports as providing naval service on the same basis as other ports.[3] In the thirteenth century the Ports sometimes performed their due service, but a fortnight's service, even counted from the date of sailing from the port of assembly, contributed nothing but a short delay before the ships had to be taken into pay. It was presumably useful, as a means of mobilization as well as of saving some money, but we know that in some cases the Cinque Ports' ships, whether or not they had been summoned to perform their due service, were taken into the king's pay immediately.[4] As early as 1217 the Ports were summoned to appear with their ships 'tam nuper lucrato quam alio'.[5] In any case the Ports could make a major contribution only to small campaigns. In the first Welsh War they provided eighteen ships; in the second, forty, and two galleys.[6] In both cases the naval requirement was low, as the armies marched overland and there were no enemies at sea. When a major expedition was called for, the Cinque Ports contributed in proportion to their economic strength, but again their formal service bore no relation to the actual requirement. They provided 73 out of 305 ships for the 1297 Flanders expedition, of which 46 served free for a fortnight 'por ce qe eles font lour service qe du vous est des ports'.[7] When Edward I next summoned their service he asked for all the men (1,254) in half the ships; they

1. C[alendar of] L[iberate] R[olls], 1226–40, 39, 49; CLR, 1245–51, p. 21; CR, 1254–56, p. 8; CR, 1259–61, pp. 250–251; Book of Prests for the King's Wardrobe for 1294–5, Presented to John Goronwy Edwards, ed. E. B. Fryde (Oxford, 1962), pp. 109, 111.

2. Brooks, English Naval Forces, p. 87; idem, 'The Cinque Ports', p. 151.

3. Pipe Roll 14 John, pp. xvii–xix.

4. CR, 1251–53, pp. 471, 508–9. C[alendar of] P[atent] R[olls], 1247–58, p. 230; CLR, 1226–40, pp. 39, 49; CLR, 1245–51, p. 21; CLR, 1261–72, no. 2297 E and G.

5. P[atent] R[olls], 1216–25, p. 89.

6. Prestwich, War, Politics and Finance, p. 137; John E. Morris, The Welsh Wars of Edward I (Oxford, 1901), pp. 106–8, 173.

7. Michael Prestwich, Documents Illustrating the Crisis of 1297–98 in England (Camden Fourth Ser., vol. xxiv, 1980), nos. 49, 105 (quoted); idem, War, Politics and Finance, p. 142.

actually sent 1,106 men in 30 ships.[1] In all these cases their due service, like the service of the feudal host, seems to have survived as an acceptable method of mobilization rather than a practical organization for war.

The thirteenth century was certainly the Cinque Ports' naval heyday, and the charters of 1278 and 1290 are the only ones which make any explicit mention of gratitude for naval services performed,[2] but even so it was only in the smaller campaigns that they provided a major component of the English effort at sea, and for the most part their service was paid like that of other ports without special privileges. In one respect, however, they did make a distinctive contribution; as a source of expert advice and advisers, sometimes almost as a primitive naval staff.[3] In 1225 they were asked to advise the king's council how to resist the threatened French invasion.[4] Ten years later Henry III again summoned representatives of the Ports 'ad loquendum nobiscum de negociis nostris'.[5] In 1301 they provided a suggested mobilization scheme, with the numbers of ships which might be raised in each port 'saunz graunt grevaunts'.[6] Sometimes they contributed experts like Thomas Alard of Winchelsea, who accompanied the royal clerk William of Thorncroft arresting ships along the south coast and the Bristol Channel in 1295.[7] The Ports were also used as a convenient source of expert (but invariably paid) manpower for the king's own ships.[8] In 1252 they were asked to send pilots for the king's voyage to Gascony, 'qui melius et securius sciant et possint nos ad partes illas conducere, et de quibus magis confidere possimus'.[9]

In the early fourteenth century the Ports were summoned to perform their naval service on a number of occasions, but it does not appear that they ever performed it in full,[10] and it is difficult to believe that it was either expected or desired that they should serve in a way which was so ill-adapted to the demands of war. Advice and expertise were now being sought from seaports at large rather than the Cinque Ports in particular,[11] and their naval service continued to decline in value, both relatively and absolutely. Several of the Ports were no longer able to provide any ships at all.[12] Whether or not a notional summons was issued for their full service, what was actually wanted was always fewer, larger ships

1. Prestwich, War, Politics and Finance, p. 143.

2. Murray, Constitutional History, pp. 237–239; Calendar of Charter Rolls, 1257–1300, p. 344.

3. J. R. Alban, 'National Defence in England, 1337–89' (Liverpool Ph.D. thesis, 1976), p. 270.

4. D. A. Carpenter, The Minority of Henry III (London, 1990), p. 379; PR, 1216–25, p. 503.

5. CR, 1234–37, p. 161.

6. PRO, SC.1/16/No. 37.

7. Book of Prests, ed. Fryde, p. 96.

8. PR, 1225–32, pp. 34, 36, 276; CPR, 1232–47, pp. 27–8; CLR, 1261–72, no. 2191; CR, 1242–47, p. 245; CR, 1251–53, pp. 508–9.

9. CR, 1251–53, p. 245.

10. CCR, 1302–7, p. 433; CCR, 1318–23, p. 708; CPR, 1301–7, p. 431.

11. CCR, 1323–27, p. 566; CCR, 1341–43, p. 519; CCR, 1369–74 pp. 109–110; Foedera, [Conventiones, Literae & Acta Publica], ed. Thomas Rymer (Record Commission edn., 3 vols. in 6, London, 1816–30), III, i. 4.

12. CPR, 1313–17, pp. 292, 294; CCR, 1341–43, p. 263; Calendar of Fine Rolls, 1337–47, p. 238.

with bigger crews.[1] In 1301, for example, the barons advised Edward I that they could provide twelve good large ships, and twelve were duly summoned.[2] It is not certain that they performed any free service by this date. There are more accounts of payments to them in terms which imply,[3] and some which directly state,[4] that they were in the king's pay from the date of setting sail. They were called on for their full service in 1314, and failed to provide it.[5] They were only summoned to perform their due service twice in Edward III's reign, in 1327 and 1332, and the second summons was cancelled. Otherwise they served for wages like any other port,[6] except in 1339 when they forewent their wages in return for being paid half their costs.[7] Their ships were arrested for service like those of other ports,[8] and they complained like any other port when they did not get paid. When Robert of Burgersh came to Winchelsea to arrest ships some time late in Edward I's reign he was met by 'une grande criee de gentz de la vile qui diseyent que il ne poeynt le service le roy aprester pur grant duresce que on leur fist'; they spoke of the king's unpaid debts, and of tallies which 'briserent saunz fere a eux bref ou allowance ou autre chose qui valer leur peuft ... il sunt mout angussez'.[9] Somehow it seems not to have occurred to them that they should have been happy to serve unpaid in return for their chartered privileges.

By the mid-fourteenth century only Sandwich of the original head ports was still able to make even a modest contribution to English fleets, and all the Ports and members together provided less than 5 per cent of requisitioned shipping.[10] Even in the great fleet raised in 1347 to blockade Calais and support the English army, an operation of the first importance mounted within sight of Dover, their ships formed only 14 per cent of the total.[11] They were again summoned to deliver their full

1. Albert E. Prince, 'The Army and Navy', in *The English Government at Work, 1327–1336*. Vol. I: *Central and Prerogative Administration*, ed. James F. Willard and W. A. Morris (Cambridge, Mass 1940), pp. 332–93, at p. 385; C. F. Richmond, 'The War at Sea', in *The Hundred Years War*, ed. Kenneth Fowler (London, 1971), pp. 96–121, at p. 104; Sherborne, 'English Navy', pp. 167–8.

2. PRO, SC.1/16/No. 37; *CCR, 1296–1302*, pp. 482–3, 486–7; *CPR, 1297–1301*, pp. 583–4.

3. PRO, E.352/120, rot.49; *Issue Roll of Thomas de Brantingham*, ed. Frederick Devon (London, 1835), pp. 180, 198, 243–4, 262–6, etc.

4. PRO, E.372/195, rot.44.

5. *Foedera*, II.246; *CPR, 1313–17*, pp. 292, 294.

6. Adrian T. Hall, 'The Employment of Naval Forces in the Reign of Edward III' (Leeds M.A. Thesis, 1955), pp. 42–3; Ranald Nicholson, *Edward III and the Scots: The Formative Years of a Military Career, 1327–1335* (London, 1965), p. 209; *CCR, 1327–30*, p. 118; *CCR, 1330–33*, p. 581.

7. *Rotuli Parliamentorum* (6 vols., London, 1767–83) ii. 108.

8. Hall, 'The Employment of Naval Forces', p. 47; *CPR, 1385–89*, p. 213.

9. PRO, SC.1/47/No. 172 (R. de Borgerssche to J. de Drokensford, 1300 × 1307).

10. Timothy J. Runyan, 'Naval Logistics in the Late Middle Ages: The Example of the Hundred Years' War', in *Feeding Mars: Logistics in Western Warfare from the Middle Ages to the Present*, ed. John A. Lynn (Boulder, Colorado, 1993), pp. 79–100, at p. 86.

11. The original wardrobe account of Walter of Wetwang which contained the list of this fleet cannot now be found in the PRO, and the list is known from three equally unsatisfactory transcripts: a late sixteenth-century version (now B[ritish] L[ibrary] Cott.MS Titus F.3 fos. 265–6), printed by Richard Hakluyt, *The Principal Navigations Voyages Traffiques & Discoveries of the English Nation* (2nd edn. of 1599–1600, as printed in 12 vols., Glasgow, 1903–05) i. 297–299; another copy of the same MS made in 1604 by the herald Rafe Brooke (now BL Harl.MS 782, fos. 62–67), printed in *A Collection*

service at various times between 1394 and 1421, but in most of these cases a major mobilization was called for at the same time, to which all ports were expected to contribute,[1] and it seems that 'full service' was always understood to mean some such figure as the ten ships with 600 men for twenty days which was agreed in 1387.[2] By 1417 the only real difference between them and any other port was that they continued to receive their summons from the hand of the Lord Warden rather than an admiral or royal official,[3] and by the 1430s, even that had ceased.[4] Their naval service was occasionally called for again,[5] and with great reluctance they put some ships to sea in 1588,[6] but no one but themselves any longer pretended that they had any important naval role to play. Already in the 1390s privileges were going to other ports like Dartmouth 'which above other places in the realm has long been and still is strong in shipping, and therewith has wrought great havoc on the king's enemies in time of war'.[7]

Besides their expertise, certain qualities distinguished the Portsmen at sea, notably violence and indiscipline. The word 'piracy' has to be applied with caution in the medieval context, when the sea was widely perceived as a lawless realm beyond the frontiers of all nations, where neither law nor truce nor treaty ran. Since no medieval jurist thought to deny the right of a merchantman to take prizes in wartime, every man was his own privateer, and none but the most scrupulous were unduly careful to distinguish neutral from enemy, or indeed peace from war.[8] The Portsmen were not among the most scrupulous. Matthew Paris's phrase *classis pyratica* is no more than a reference to their professional abilities,[9] but it could perfectly well be read in the modern sense. Throughout the Middle Ages, English piracy repeatedly caused diplomatic embarrassment to English kings, sometimes with serious consequences. In the thirteenth and fourteenth centuries, the Cinque Ports were prominent among the offenders. As early as 1225 Henry III had to

---

of Ordinances and Regulations for the Government of the Royal Household (Soc. of Antiquaries, London, 1790), pp. 6–8; and a version allegedly taken from a 'MS of the Dean and Chapter of Canterbury' (not now identifiable in the Cathedral Archives), printed by John Charnock, *History of Marine Architecture* (3 vols., London, 1801), i. xxxviii–xliii.

1. *CPR, 1391–96*, p. 518; *CCR, 1392–96*, pp. 307–8, 468–9; *CCR, 1409–13*, pp. 166, 273–4, 391; *CCR, 1419–22*, pp. 141–2; *Foedera*, ed. T. Rymer (20 vols., London, 1704–35), viii. 700.

2. *CCR, 1385–89*, pp. 208–9. In 1400 it was 20 ships with 800 men: *CCR, 1399–1402*, p. 170.

3. *CCR, 1413–19*, p. 336.

4. *CPR, 1429–36*, pp. 71, 130, 133, 153, 202, 474.

5. *CCR, 1468–76*, no. 1427.

6. Ada Haeseler Lewis, *A Study of Elizabethan Ship Money, 1588–1603* (Philadelphia, 1928), pp. 10–11.

7. *CPR, 1388–92*, p. 338.

8. D. A. Gardiner, 'The History of Belligerent Rights on the High Seas in the Fourteenth Century', *Law Quarterly Review*, xlviii (1932), 521–546; Marie-Claire Chavarot, 'La pratique des lettres de marque d'après les arrêts du Parlement (XIIIᵉ – debut XVᵉ siècle)', *Bibliothèque de l'École des Chartes*, cxlix (1981), 51–89.

9. Brooks, 'The Cinque Ports', 184. Cf. William le Breton's description of the Poitevins, *quibus ars piratica ... notus est*, quoted by F. W. Brooks, 'The Battle of Damme – 1213', *Mariner's Mirror*, xvi (1930), 263–71, at 266.

pay compensation to a Norman victim.[1] In 1314 a Gascon merchant shipped wine to England in the ship owned by John Perbroun, a future admiral then in the king's service. They were robbed by the Cinque Ports fleet commanded by a recent admiral, Gervase Alard.[2]

Indiscriminate piracy naturally tended to make enemies, and itself fed upon the Portsmen's notorious rivalries with Yarmouth and other ports. When Prince Edward chose a Yarmouth ship to carry him to Gascony in 1252, the jealous Winchelsea men attacked her and killed many of the crew.[3] Before the Welsh campaign in 1277, the King with difficulty imposed a truce between the Portsmen and Bayonne.[4] In 1297 Edward I's Flemish expedition was wrecked by a major battle between the Cinque Ports and Yarmouth contingents of his fleet, with the loss of at least seventeen ships and 165 men.[5] In 1321 the men of Winchelsea attacked Southampton, burning seventeen ships.[6] The Cinque Ports were not the only offenders – there was a battle between Lyme and Dartmouth in 1264,[7] and Yarmouth had enemies among other ports[8] – but they were undoubtedly the worst.

It is clear from all this that the Cinque Ports, individually and collectively, contributed to English strength at sea little if anything more than other ports of similar size. There was a seaport whose long and loyal service, whose ships, money and skills, provided an indispensable core of English naval strength in the thirteenth and fourteenth centuries – but that port was Bayonne. It has been described as being 'in a sense the sixth Cinque Port'; it might be better to say that it was in that sense the only one.[9] The most that can be claimed of the other five is that in the thirteenth century they made a significant contribution to the land campaigns in Poitou[10] and Wales. At this period they were also valued as a convenient source of expert advice and manpower, and feared as a very inconvenient source of piracy and indiscriminate violence. None of the services they performed bore any close relation to the naval obligations prescribed in their charters, and as the Hundred Years War at sea became increasingly intense (and for the English, increasingly disastrous) during the fourteenth century, those obligations seem to have been almost forgotten. Even if the service due had matched the service

1. Nicolas, *Royal Navy*, i. 233.

2. Ibid., 359.

3. Michael Prestwich, *Edward I* (London, 1988), p. 10.

4. Nicolas, *Royal Navy*, i. 265. This feud went back at least to 1226: *PR, 1225–32*, p. 53.

5. *Crisis of 1297–98*, ed. Prestwich, no. 134; idem, *Edward I*, p. 392; idem, *War, Politics and Finance*, p. 143; E.163/2/8.

6. Colin Platt, *Medieval Southampton: The Port and Trading Community, AD 1000–1600* (London, 1973), p. 107.

7. *Documents relating to Law and Custom of the Sea*, ed. R. G. Marsden (Navy Records Soc., vols xlix–l, 1915–16), i. 7.

8. *CPR, 1334–38*, pp. 576–577.

9. Malcolm Vale, *The Angevin Legacy and the Hundred Years War, 1250–1340* (Oxford, 1990), pp. 149–150, 194, 204–206, quoted at p. 149.

10. Michael Weir, 'English Naval Activities, 1242–1243', *Mariner's Mirror*, lviii (1972), 85–92.

then required, it could not explain the origins of an obligation which predated the Conquest. Neither economic collapse nor the silting of their harbours can account for the ports' declining naval value,[1] for they had never had any unique naval value at any stage in their history. Only once in eight centuries of corporate existence did the Ports' ships alone perform a notable naval feat: the raid on Boulogne in January 1340 which destroyed eighteen French galleys and indirectly contributed to the victory of Sluys later that year.[2] Coming when their shipping was in decline and their charters already ancient, it cannot explain their unique situation. No sea service which the Cinque Ports were obliged to perform, could have performed, or actually did perform, is sufficient to explain the privileged status granted and confirmed to them by successive sovereigns from Edward the Confessor to Charles II.

We are left with a mystery, which perhaps cannot be properly resolved without further research. It may be suggested, however, that the Ports' real significance never had much to do with naval service, and particularly not against France. Geography, diplomacy and politics provide a more plausible context in which to locate their charters. Even if their ships were not of unique value, their harbours were ideally situated for operations in the Straits of Dover. In Anglo-Saxon times Sandwich was often used as the anchorage of the English fleet.[3] Twice English squadrons (neither of them known with any confidence to have been provided by the Ports themselves) sailed from them to achieve that most difficult of all medieval naval feats, the interception of an enemy fleet under way: from Sandwich in 1217, and from Winchelsea in 1350.[4] Their roadsteads were often chosen as the assembly points for fleets intended for Flanders, and sometimes for east coast shipping bound for Gascony. Indeed, if the great anchorage of the Downs can be regarded as belonging to the Ports, their strategic significance lasted to the very end of the age of sail. From the diplomatic point of view, they were equally critical. Entirely in the wrong place to dominate the Channel or mount a naval offensive against France, the ports faced directly across the Narrow Seas to Flanders, the part of the Continent which attracted the intense interest of English kings as far back as we have records of diplomacy. In Flanders successive exiles and pretenders took refuge, from Flanders successive invasion attempts were mounted. For any

1. Murray, *Constitutional History*, pp. 208–210; James A. Williamson, *The English Channel: A History* (London, 1959), pp. 104–112.

2. Sumption, *Trial by Battle*, pp. 264–6, 320–1; Charles de la Roncière, *Histoire de la Marine Française* (6 vols., Paris, 1899–1932) i. 432–6 (dating the raid to August 1339).

3. Hollister, *Anglo-Saxon Military Institutions*, p. 125; Nicholas Hooper, 'The Anglo-Saxons at War', in *Weapons and Warfare in Anglo-Saxon England*, ed. Sonia Chadwick Hawkes (Oxford, 1989), pp. 191–202, at pp. 192–3; David Hill, *An Atlas of Anglo-Saxon England* (Oxford, 1981), p. 14.

4. The narratives of the Battle of Dover mention some of the Portsmen as advising Hubert de Burgh, but their ships apparently made off before the action: Matthew Paris, *Chronica Majora*, ed. H. R. Luard (7 vols., Rolls Ser., 1872–83) iii. 29; Nicolas, *Royal Navy* i. 176–181, 427–30; Brooks, *English Naval Forces*, pp. 217–19; *Histoire des ducs de Normandie et des rois d'Angleterre*, ed. Francisque Michel (Paris, 1840), pp. 201–2.

government wanting to observe developments across the water, and to control movement thence and thither, the co-operation and loyalty of the Cinque Ports were essential.

It is in this context that they first appear in history, during the succession crisis of 1051–52, while Earl Godwin was in exile in Flanders, waiting his opportunity.[1] Many aspects of this episode remain unclear, but it is certain that ships and seapower played central parts in the struggle. We know that in 1051 King Edward paid off the last of his Danish mercenary force, the lithsmen,[2] and it has been assumed that his grants to the Cinque Ports were intended to create one naval force to replace another,[3] but it is neither necessary nor safe to make such a deduction. The form of the future Cinque Ports' service was extremely ill-adapted to replace this or any other standing force, and we do not know for sure that it was first established (rather than first mentioned) at this time. In any case there is another context in which it may better be located. In the words of the *Anglo-Saxon Chronicle*: 'King Edward had forty small boats manned which lay at Sandwich in order that they might keep watch for Earl Godwin who was at Bruges'.[4] It is plausible to suppose that these 'forty small boats' represented the service of the original head ports, and for this job – patrol and scouting, with a succession of small vessels unobtrusively watching the Flanders shore – their due service was perfectly suitable. It is conceivable that this was one of the few occasions in their long history on which the future Cinque Ports ever performed the service specified in their charters, though we know that they were similarly employed in 1174,[5] and in 1217 Matthew Paris mentions their ships among others, 'qui semitas maris sollerter speculantes Francorum explorarent et præpedirent adventum'.[6]

But there were other reasons for Edward the Confessor to favour the Ports besides the service they had to offer. The political significance of the Kentish coast needed no pointing. Edward had to gain – if necessary, buy – the loyalty of the Ports. In this case he failed, for when Godwin

1. *The Anglo-Saxon Chronicle*, ed. Dorothy Whitelock (London, 1961), pp. 122–3; F. M. Stenton, *Anglo-Saxon England* (3rd edn., Oxford, 1971), pp. 566–9.

2. Nicholas Hooper, 'Military Developments in the reign of Cnut', in *The Reign of Cnut: King of England, Denmark and Norway*, ed. Alexander R. Rumble (Leicester, 1994), pp. 89–100; M. K. Lawson, *Cnut: The Danes in England in the Early Eleventh Century* (London, 1993), pp. 177–8, 190; idem, 'The Collection of Danegeld and Heregeld in the Reigns of Aethelred II and Cnut', *ante*, xcix (1984) 721–38, at pp. 737–8; N. A. M. Rodger, 'Cnut's Geld and the Size of Danish Ships', *ante*, xc (1995), pp. 392–403.

3. Frank Barlow, *The Feudal Kingdom of England, 1042–1216* (London, 1961), p. 60; H. R. Loyn, *The Governance of Anglo-Saxon England, 500–1087* (London, 1984), pp. 121, 168–9.

4. *Anglo-Saxon Chronicle*, ed. Whitelock, p. 123; *Two of the Saxon Chronicles Parallel*, ed. Charles Plummer & John Earle (2 vols., Oxford, 1892–99) i. 179. 'þa læt Eadward cyng scypian xl snacca þa lagon æt Sandwic'. 'Small boats' must be correct if they only had 21 men each, but *snacca* (O. N. *snekkjar*) were often large warships; for the word and its cognates see Rudolf Simek, *Die Schiffsnamen, Schiffsbezeichnungen und Schiffskenningar im Altnordischen* (Vienna, 1982), pp. 174–5.

5. Le Patourel, 'Henri II Plantagenêt et la mer de la Manche', p. 331.

6. *Chronica Majora*, iii. 26.

landed next year the Ports were among the first to rally to his cause;[1] but their untrustworthiness only emphasized their political importance. After the Conquest the doubtful loyalty of the Cinque Ports continued to be the focus of well-founded anxiety on the part of successive sovereigns. The charters issued by Henry II, probably in 1155,[2] perhaps bespeak the natural concerns of a new king on an unstable throne. If so, he was right to worry, for eighteen years later, at the time of the Young King's rebellion in 1173, ships had to be gathered from ports along the coast from Yorkshire to Hampshire, 'qui missi fuerunt Sandwich' contra naves v Portuum'.[3] Much the same happened at the time of the baronial rebellion against King John, when the Ports went over to the rebels and helped to ensure free communication with the Continent.[4] Again in January 1259 they were commanded to watch by day and night to prevent any magnates leaving the country,[5] but they were soon firmly in the baronial camp, which rewarded them in 1260 with a new charter.[6] In 1264 they formed the core of a fleet gathered at Sandwich to prevent foreign assistance reaching Henry III.[7] After the King's victory at the battle of Evesham, the Ports indulged in an orgy of piracy which was suppressed with great difficulty, and during which they were proclaimed to be public enemies of the king and every nation round about. Only the feeblest attempt was made to punish them afterwards, and that provoked them into burning Portsmouth.[8] In 1293 a major battle on the coast of Brittany between the Cinque Ports, Bayonne and the Normans, followed by an attack on La Rochelle, led to the confiscation of English Gascony.[9] Piracy was only the proximate cause of the war with France, but it was an unqualified disaster for Edward I in the midst of his Scottish operations. When he reproved the Cinque Ports, they replied with undisguised threats.[10] Nothing was achieved by attempts to put pressure on them by investigating their obligations,[11] nor by hints that their failure to safeguard the sovereignty of the 'English Sea' (*Mier*

1. Hooper, 'Observations on the Navy', pp. 206–7.

2. Murray, *Constitutional History*, pp. 232–4.

3. *Pipe Roll 19 Henry II*, pp. 2, 13, 31, 43 (quoted), 117, 132–4.

4. Brooks, *English Naval Forces*, pp. 207–219.

5. *CPR, 1258–66*, p. 8.

6. Murray, *Constitutional History*, pp. 37–8, 236–7.

7. *CR, 1261–64*, pp. 356, 384; *CR 1264–68*, p. 80; *CPR, 1258–66*, pp. 345, 349, 351; Murray, *Constitutional History*, pp. 38–9.

8. *CPR, 1258–66*, pp. 547, 551, 652–3, 655; *English Historical Documents*. Vol III: *1189–1327*, ed. Harry Rothwell (London, 1975) p. 181; Brooks, *English Naval Forces*, pp. 223–225; Murray, *Constitutional History*, pp. 39–40.

9. Prestwich, *Edward I*, pp. 377–379; Malcolm Vale, 'Edward I and the French: Rivalry and Chivalry', in *Thirteenth Century England II: Proceedings of the Newcastle upon Tyne Conference, 1987*, ed. P. R. Coss and S. D. Lloyd (Woodbridge, 1988), pp. 165–76; Nicolas, *Royal Navy*, 267–270; La Roncière, *Marine Française* i. 324–30.

10. PRO, C.47/29/3/No. 7, printed (very inaccurately) by A. Champollion-Figéac, *Lettres des rois, reines et autres personnages des cours de France et de l'Angleterre ... 1162–1515* (2 vols., Paris, 1839–47), i. 396–397; also in part (misdated) by Marsden, *Law and Custom of the Sea*, i. 50–56.

11. Morris, *Welsh Wars*, p. 106; Murray, *Constitutional History*, pp. 241–2.

Dengl') was undermining English diplomacy.[1] In the fifteenth century the Ports continued to be a major security risk. In the crisis of 1460 they favoured the Earl of Warwick, and undoubtedly countenanced the raid of June in which he captured the royal fleet and its commanders in Sandwich. Using that port as his base, Warwick went on to the campaign which installed Edward IV on the throne.[2] It was the same story in May 1471, when even after the disasters of Barnet and Tewkesbury the Bastard of Fauconberg was able to raise the Ports for an attack on London.[3] In all these transactions the Ports do not appear as providers of valuable naval services, but as dangerous troublemakers willing to sell their geographical advantages to the highest bidder.

This seems to be a more plausible context than naval warfare in which to locate the Cinque Ports' privileges. These grants long predate the Ports' brief period of naval usefulness in the thirteenth century; and they were confirmed and even added to long after the Ports' ships had ceased to have any significant naval value. The service specified in the charters was never closely related to any wartime requirement. But geography had placed their harbours in a key position to control movement across the Narrow Seas to Flanders and Calais, and the Portsmen well knew how to exploit the opportunity. Perhaps they spoke more truth than they realised when they claimed in the seventeenth century that 'they are the gates that open or shutt to the perill or safety of this kingdome'.[4]

Additional Note [2009]

Very little has been published on the maritime history of the Cinque Ports since 1996, other than my own larger study *The Safeguard of the Sea. A Naval History of Britain, Vol.1, 660-1649* (London, 1997). We now have, however, some valuable studies of mediaeval naval warfare in general; in particular Susan Rose, *The Medieval Sea* (London, 2007), and a chapter in Michael Prestwich's *Armies and Warfare in the Middle Ages: The English Experience* (New Haven and London, 1996).

1. *Calendar of Documents Relating to Scotland*, vol. v (supplementary), ed. G. G. Simpson and J. D. Galbraith (1986), no. 567. This must be connected with the Montreuil negotiations (for the recovery of Gascony) in 1306, at which the English commissioners claimed that the kings of England 'du temps qil ny ad memoire du contraire, averoient este en paisible possession de la sovereigne seigneuries de la meer Dengeleterre et des isles esteans en ycele': Pierre Chaplais, *English Medieval Diplomatic Practice* (2 vols. in 3, London, 1975–82), i. 206.

2. C. F. Richmond, 'Royal Administration and the Keeping of the Seas, 1422–1485' (Oxford D.Phil. thesis, 1962), pp. 281–5; M. E. Meehan, 'English Piracy, 1450–1500' (Bristol M.Litt.Thesis, 1971), pp. 72–6; Cora L. Scofield, *The Life and Reign of Edward IV* (2 vols., London, 1923), i. 51.

3. Charles Ross, *Edward IV* (London, 1974), pp. 173–4.

4. Murray, *Constitutional History*, p. 218.

III

THE DEVELOPMENT OF BROADSIDE GUNNERY, 1450-1650

On 1 April (N.S.) 1588 King Philip II of Spain wrote to the Duke of Medina Sidonia, newly appointed Captain-General of the Ocean Sea and commander-in-chief of the Armada assembled at Lisbon. It is a long letter of advice and instruction, which includes a well-known reference to English gunnery tactics:

> That you might be forewarned, you will receive a detailed report of the way in which the enemy arranges his artillery so as to be able to aim his broadsides low in the hull and so sink his opponent's ships.[1]

That, at least, is what the king is made to say in English in the most recent translation,[2] but though the original Spanish has been in print for over a century,[3] it seems not to have been noticed that in one small but crucial respect the king has been mistranslated. There is no reference in the original to 'broadsides'; the word is *cañonazos*, 'gunfire'. The translator has assumed, as the majority of modern writers have assumed and continue to assume,[4] that heavy gunfire from sailing warships was essentially from broadside-mounted guns, and that for literary purposes the two words may be treated as synonyms. This is part of a general view of gunnery, tactics, and warship design in the sixteenth century, according to which a naval revolution took place which replaced an obsolete type, the galley, with an obviously superior design, the sailing ship, armed with heavy guns on the broadside. Thus Sir Julian Corbett, one of the earliest and still weightiest exponents of this view, speaks of Drake entering Cadiz Bay in 1587, 'ready to pit bowline and broadside against oars and chasers'.[5] It was moreover for Corbett, and still is for many writers, an integral part of the argument that the superior modern design was an English invention.[6]

Accompanying this view of sixteenth-century developments come a number of other common assumptions which bear scrutiny. The effects of a classical education still lie so heavily on the world of scholarship that it is often taken for granted that sixteenth-century galleys were fitted with rams,[7] though it is beyond question that they had in fact lost them by a date not later than the tenth century.[8] More damaging confusion surrounds discussion of the line ahead and the line of battle, which are frequently regarded as equivalent terms, by which means the line of battle has been discovered as far back as the fifteenth century,[9] and could no doubt be uncovered in yet earlier periods. The line of battle is of course a form of line ahead, but a very specific form, in which an entire fleet forms a single, straight line, in a predetermined order. Sailing in line ahead does not in the least imply adopting a line of battle, as the term came to be understood by the late seventeenth century.

Corbett himself initiated this confusion in his anxiety to show how far ahead Drake was of his time, and added to it by mistranslating the Spanish term *en ala* (as used to describe the English fleet in 1588) as 'line ahead'.[10] *En ala* (literally 'in wing') is in fact a technical term of galley tactics meaning a line of bearing or bow-and-quarter line, referring to a galley fleet in fighting formation, line abreast with the wings either advanced or refused, so as to form a sort of crescent with the horns pointing either towards the enemy (*lúnula* in Spanish) or away from him (*arco* or *falcata*).[11] It is quite distinct from the Spanish *en hila* or *en fila*, line ahead, but unfortunately Corbett's authority has carried some eminent modern historians with him.[12] Further perplexity has recently been added by the new term 'line astern', which seems to mean line ahead with the senior officer leading.[13] To escape from these confusions we must be careful not only to attend to the meanings of words, but to make no anachronistic assumptions about what things 'naturally' belong together. In particular it is essential to separate the three elements of the full-rigged ship, the heavy gun at sea, and the broadside armament, for they did not arrive together in the sixteenth century, and were not securely combined until well into the seventeenth.

The story of how the heavy gun came to go to sea must begin in the mid-fifteenth century. By that time light guns were an established part of the armament of large ships, and very heavy guns of the 'bombard' type were used for the attack and defence of fortresses ashore. About the 1460s or 1470s small bombards began to be mounted on the decks of ships, in the waist firing on the broadside either over the bulwarks, or through small ports cut in the bulwarks.[14] These were not very large guns, and they did not essentially modify the traditional fighting tactics of the sailing warship of the day, as described in contemporary manuals.[15] The first essential for the captain taking a ship into action was to get the weather gage, which was a clear sign of hostility in a stranger, and a gross breach of respect in a friend. Having got the wind of the enemy, one bore up and ran down to board. As the ships closed, all available missile weapons laid down their fire on the enemy's decks, including the bombards at the last possible moment, as the ships came alongside. For contemporaries, their contribution was essentially to stun the enemy with concussion and blind him with smoke more than to kill men, but it was recognised that in certain circumstances it might be imprudent to attempt boarding, in which case one might keep to windward of the enemy, near enough to fire at him with bows and guns. These guns did not significantly modify either the tactics or the construction of sailing warships, which remained largely unaltered well into the 1530s.[16]

The technical problems of carrying battering guns to sea were solved first not by sailing ships in northern waters, but by galleys in the Mediterranean. The Venetians in the 1470s, soon followed by the other Mediterranean navies, began to mount a single heavy gun on a fixed mounting right forward. Initially these guns were long wrought-iron breech-loaders of the type known as 'basilisks', but by the opening years of the sixteenth century they were being replaced by cast bronze muzzle-loaders firing anything from 30 to 60-pound ball (or stone shot of equivalent calibre). In the 1520s galleys began to adopt sliding carriages, recoiling along or beneath the central gangway (*coursia, crujía* etc. in the various Mediterranean languages, whence the gun was called the *coursier* or *pieza de crujía*), and at the same time the single heavy gun was flanked by two, and eventually four, lighter pieces.[17]

The adoption of the heavy gun, which of course meant carrying heavy weight right forward in a vessel of fine lines and light construction, involved developments in the construction and employment of the galley which in the long run pushed it towards obsolesence. The immediate effect, however, was to overturn the traditional relationship between galleys and sailing ships. Though naval battles of any sort were rare in the Middle Ages, it was everywhere understood that if galleys met ships in action, the high freeboard and thick sides of the ship gave her an overwhelming advantage over the exposed crew of the galley. The heavy gun reversed the equation, and swiftly displaced the carrack from Mediterranean war fleets.[18] It is not clear how quickly the English appreciated the naval revolution which had taken place, but they certainly knew all about it after the disastrous afternoon of 22 April 1513, when a squadron of French Mediterranean galleys forced their way through the English fleet off Brest, sinking one ship outright, and badly damaging another. Three days later Sir Edward Howard, Lord Admiral of England, was killed attempting a counter-attack, and within a week the entire fleet had retreated in disorder to Plymouth. It is hard to convey to a modern reader the terror induced by these 'basilisks', in men for whom guns had hitherto been a noisier kind of crossbow: 'Never man saw men in greter fere then all the masters and maryners be off the galies, insomoche that in a maner they had as leve go into Purgatory as to the Trade'.[19]

It must have become clear then if it had not been before that the navies of the northern world faced a very grave, and apparently insoluble problem: how to match the heavy gun-armed galley. One answer of course was to build oared vessels themselves, which Henry VIII and most of his contemporaries did, but the galley's serious limitations of range and seaworthiness (growing as a result of adopting heavy guns) meant that this alone could not be a satisfactory response. The challenge was to arm a sailing ship to match the galley. It was not an abstract question of how best to arm a ship in theory, but a very concrete matter of how to imitate the only known method of mounting heavy guns at sea, on a fixed mounting in the eyes of the ship. Even if any other solution had presented itself, it was not easy to see how heavy guns could be used offensively against other vessels unless they could fire forward, for it was hardly plausible to imagine the ship sailing into action sideways or astern. Yet the construction of sailing ships in general, and in particular of the carracks with their lofty 'forestages' which had dominated northern naval warfare for a century, seemed to make it difficult or impossible to mount heavy guns firing forward. Moreover contemporaries placed great stress on the need to mount a heavy gun low in order to hit the enemy on or about the waterline.

From another point of view the dilemma was not unlike that which faced naval architects in the 1830s. A new propulsion system was available (the ship rig in one case, the paddle steamer in the other) which was so much more powerful and effective than its predecessor that it was inconceivable that it should not be used for war, but it seemed to be incompatible with a serious armament. This was the problem which faced English naval men at the start of the sixteenth century, and which they did not begin to solve until more than seventy years after the galley had first taken heavy guns to sea. What they were trying to do was not to develop the broadside armament, but to supersede it; to design a sailing ship with a powerful ahead-firing armament which could beat the galley at her own game.

How heavy guns were first mounted in sailing ships is very obscure, but it seems to be fairly clear that about 1500, ships of war began to mount a pair of large, long guns (usually 'basilisks') right aft on the lowest deck, in the flat which soon became known as the gunroom, firing through ports cut in the stern on either side of the sternpost. This was made possible by the adoption at this period, and possibly for this purpose, of the transom stern, in whose flat planking it was relatively simple to fit a watertight port.[20] Thus Philip of Cleves recommends that a flagship should have:

> auz deux costes du gouvernail, à chacun un [scil. canon de fonte, ou de fer], affustez comme ils doibvent estre en tel cas. Et doibvent avoir les portes qui se lievent à cordes, quand on veult, pour tirer desdicts bastons, quand le temps le peult porter.[21]

Which ships, and indeed which nations first began this movement, it is at present difficult to say. The invention of the gunport is traditionally ascribed to a Breton in 1501, which is not implausible, and a Danish ship wrecked at about this time carried her heaviest guns fore and aft, but the first big ship which we know to have mounted two basilisks at stern ports was the Scottish *Michael*, completed in 1512.[22] She was almost certainly the inspiration for the English *Henry Grâce à Dieu*, whose two stern-chasers were forged iron breech-loaders respectively 20ft 6ins and 22ft long without their breech chambers.[23] Another English ship of this period with a similar armament was the *Mary Gonson*.[24]

Almost as soon as heavy guns appeared in the gunroom, others began to be mounted in ports on the broadside. Philip of Cleves proposes for his flagship 'entre les deux tillasses à chacun costé quatre canons de fonte, ou de fer, iectant feu ou pierres'.[25] It appears from early illustrations that the first broadside ports were in the quarters (that is, in the gunroom), and that from there they spread forward, and perhaps also aft from the forecastle, until by the 1540s if not before big ships like the *Mary Rose* had a complete line of gunports.[26] It is significant, however, that the broadside guns seem to have been shorter and lighter than the stern-chasers, and that when a ship's armament is listed according to its disposition (which is not often) it is usually the stern-chasers which are mentioned first, as though they were regarded as the main armament.[27] Moreover pictures and drawings of sailing warships between about 1500 and 1560, but not earlier or later, usually view them from the stern or quarter, as though showing off their principal military strength.[28]

By the 1540s, therefore, the larger sailing warships mounted a substantial (though heterogenous and rapidly changing) armament of heavy guns. Their stern-chasers protected them from galley attack at their most vulnerable point.[29] Unfortunately they were still no nearer beating the galleys at their own game, for they had little or no armament firing forward, or mounted low. The *Michael* is said to have had one bow chaser, but we have no information as to how or where it was mounted.[30] Philip of Cleves recommends mounting two long guns on the first level of the aftercastle, firing forward on arcs just clearing the forecastle on either side:

> ...sur le premier estage du chasteau derriere, lá ou lon tire le cabestain, debvez avoir deux grosses coulouvrines, à chacun coste du mast une, lesqueles tirent en devant: car pour leur grande longueur, ne scauroient tourner pour tirer de costé.[31]

The *Mary Rose* did exactly this, but it was still not a satisfactory solution. Not only did she have a blind arc right ahead, but guns mounted high up were ill placed to hit a small, low and fast-moving target like a galley. What contemporaries wanted were guns mounted low as well as firing forward, to meet the galleys on equal terms.

Since they did not have them, they were obliged to make the best they could of a very awkward tactical situation. Only galleys could match galleys, so every fleet had to have them, which presented the acute difficulty of co-ordinating galleys and ships. Ships could only fight galleys by turning, or half turning their broadsides toward them, which was difficult to do in any kind of formation. In the campaign of 1545 when the French and English fleet clashed at Spithead, and later off Shoreham, both sides tried to draw up the ships in successive ranks or lines, with the oared ships forming one or two wings.[32] In the Cowdray engraving which provides our best evidence for the Spithead action, the *Henry Grâce à Dieu* is advancing towards the French galleys firing a gun from her foremost broadside port, apparently canted round as far forward as possible. The *Mary Rose* foundered while going about to try to bring her other broadside to bear. In the Shoreham action only the oared vessels were engaged, and Lord Lisle reported that:

> The *Mistress*, the *Ann Gallant* and the *Greyhound* with all your Highness's shallops and rowing pieces did their parts well, but especially the *Mistress* and the *Ann Gallant* did so handle the galleys, as well with their sides as with their prows, that your great-ships in a manner had little to do.[33]

Meanwhile, however, the shipwrights of England and other countries, had continued their efforts to build a sailing ship which should incorporate the essential strength of the galley. Most historians of naval warfare in this period have remarked on the spread of new types of warship with names having an element in common: 'galleass', 'galliot', 'galleon' and the like. Terminology has to be used with great caution in a period of rapid change when names were used in fluid and imprecise ways, but we may infer that these vessels were thought to derive from, or resemble in some way the galley, and we know that both the galliot and the galleon in their earliest forms were small oared vessels.[34] It is a mistake, however, to assume that oars were the only important feature of a galley likely to be reflected in a name. As far as oars went, all small sailing vessels used them on occasion, including types like the English pinnace or the Portuguese caravel which did not derive from galleys; while on the other hand undoubted galley types such as the brigantine, fregata and fusta had unrelated names. What was really distinctive about these early galleasses and galleons was not the use of oars, but the form of the hull, and in particular the design of the bows.[35]

The term 'galleass' was only used in England for a fairly short period from the 1520s to the 1550s, and particularly of four very interesting ships, the *Bull*, *Hart*, *Antelope* and *Tiger*, described in 1546 soon after their completion as 'fast wingers', and probably meant to counter the galley 'wings' of the French fleet. They are shown in the Anthony Roll in their original form, which is strikingly unlike other sailing warships, for they are low in the water and virtually flush-decked. They have a bank of oars, with a single deck over the rowers. These ships were notable for their 'exceeding nimbleness in sailing and swiftness of course', and having been rebuilt (the *Antelope* and *Hart* in 1558, the other two in 1570) and having lost their oars, they went on to long and successful careers in the Elizabethan Navy.[36]

They were probably the immediate origin in English service of a type which developed more or less simultaneously around the middle of the century in England, Portugal, France, Denmark, and probably elsewhere: the galleon. The looseness with which this name was used in the sixteenth century is exceeded only by the promiscuity with which modern authors apply it to almost anything afloat, but it does seem to have had a fairly precise meaning, similar in most languages,[37] in the years between about

1540 and 1570, though the English tended to use it more of foreign warships than of their own. The essence of the galleon was, crudely, that she combined the forepart of a galley with the afterpart of a ship. The hull was considerably longer in relation to beam than was customary in sailing ships, and the bow design (the 'Gallyon noose very letyll' of one English ship in the 1540s)[38] was adapted from the galley. Two heavy chase guns were mounted under the low forecastle (corresponding to the *arrumbada* or fighting platform which in Spanish galleys covered the guns), firing either side of the galley spur or beakhead, on or through which the bowsprit was stepped. In the bigger ships two more heavy chase guns on the gun deck below fired from ports either side of the stem. Thus after more than half a century of effort, northern shipwrights finally arrived at a satisfactory solution to their problem: a fast and handy sailing ship with a powerful ahead-firing armament, combining the power of sail with the military qualities of the galley.[39] They achieved this, not by adopting broadside-mounted guns – which had been in use for over a century – but by abandoning them, or rather, relegating them to the secondary armament.

It was clearly this advance which inspired and permitted the English building-programme of the 1570s which is often associated with the name of Sir John Hawkins, and it was ships built or rebuilt in this style which formed the principal strength of the English fleet in 1588. The prototype is variously identified as the *Foresight* of 1570, the *Revenge* of 1577 or others,[40] but they must have been developed from the experiments of the 1540s, very probably influenced by foreign experience. Their characteristic feature was the low forecastle with its powerful bow chasers, of which the queen's principal master shipwright, Matthew Baker, has left us several impressive sketches.[41]

At this point it is worth digressing for a moment to look at a different solution to a related problem in naval architecture which was produced in the Mediterranean at about the same time. The gun-armed galley was formidable in attack, but herself vulnerable to attack on the beam, and still more astern. That meant that a galley fleet in the usual fighting order of line abreast was at great risk if its formation was disrupted. This encouraged naval men to think of a type which could develop heavy fire astern as well as ahead, and which could be pushed ahead of the galley line to break up the enemy's formation. The result was the Venetian galleass (quite distinct from the English ships of the same name), which was developed from the older mercantile 'great galley'. These galleasses had a full rig and a continuous deck over the rowers mounting a light broadside armament. It is customary among English-speaking historians to regard them as an inferior attempt to imitate the broadside-armed sailing warship. In fact the galleass, like the galleon, was designed to mount the bulk of her armament firing forward and aft. The primary function of the oars was not so much to propel the galleass, which was so sluggish that in the absence of wind she often had to be towed into action, but to wind the ship to bring her powerful end-on fire to bear as required. At the battle of Lepanto in 1571 the galleasses were a triumphant success in their designed role of breaking up the enemy battle line.[42]

The English, the Portuguese, and others taking galleons to sea at about the same date did not have the same fighting experience with their new ships, but this did not mean that they were at a loss as to how to use them. They had designed the type to meet a well-known tactical requirement, and well-known tactics were naturally what they adopted. One gained the weather gage of the enemy (always the indispensable preliminary), and bore up to 'give him the prow', meaning to fire the bow chasers, as one ran down to board. Broadside guns, as before, might be fired at the moment of running alongside, but were not an essential requirement. As before, the line abreast was the only established fleet formation. As before, boarding was the only known means of bringing the action to a decision, though if the weaker (but faster) party desired to avoid decisive action, it was possible to haul off to windward after an exchange of fire. These tactics were common to all seafaring nations, and did not differ essentially from those used by carracks a century before. The only novelty was the possibility of 'giving the prow' as one attacked, with the implication that heavy guns, mounted low and firing low, might damage or even sink the enemy.[43]

With a handy warship, however, mounting an effective armament of stern chasers and broadside guns as well as bow chasers, it was soon clear that one could improve on the indecisive form of action by firing the entire armament in succession. Having got into the wind of the enemy, one bore up, 'gave him the prow', hauled onto a parallel course to windward to fire the lee broadside guns, luffed up to bring the stern chasers to bear, then paid off onto the other tack to fire the other broadside. One then withdrew to a safe distance to reload before returning to 'give the charge' again. As a variation some preferred to wear rather than tack. Though often practised by the English, this was an international tactic, used by Spanish or Portuguese ships when opportunity offered.[44] As early as 1540 the English ship *Barbara* was intercepted off the coast of Brazil by a Portuguese who 'shote off his hole syde of ordynaunce at us. And then he caste aboute on thother syde of us also, and shotte all his hole syde at us agayne to thentente to have soncke us'.[45] The tactic may have been even older, for Alonso de Chaves has an ambiguous passage, apparently speaking of shifting guns from one side to the other, which may refer to tacking to bring the other side to bear.[46]

Against a stationary target ashore, ships did not need to use their broadsides at all. Instead they developed the heaviest fire at the least risk by remaining 'end-on' to the target. There is a well-known sketch of Sir William Winter's squadron bombarding the Papal landing force entrenched at Smerwick in 1580, probably drawn by Sir William's son, also William, who commanded the *Achates* in this operation. The big ships have anchored offshore while the smaller ones remain under sail, coming in to deliver repeated 'charges' at the fort, but all of them are using either their bow or stern chasers. None of them has chosen to open her broadside.[47]

Most of the fighting experience gained by English seamen with their new galleons in the 1570s and 1580s was in privateering. It is axiomatic that the object of privateers in attacking another ship was to capture her; the last thing they wanted was to stand off at a distance and knock their prey to pieces, so that it makes no sense to suggest that the English in 1588 had learnt 'stand-off' tactics from their experience as privateers.[48] What they learnt was the advantage of speed and surprise, with a minimal use of artillery for psychological as much as practical effect. When Drake attacked the *Nuestra Señora de la Concepción* off the Peruvian coast in 1579, he fired two shots and boarded at once under cover of musketry and arrows.[49] Attacking the carrack *Madre de Deus* in 1592, the Earl of Cumberland's *Assurance* 'coming up unto her, laid her aboard, discharging even withal four or five cast pieces and a volley of small shot, and ranging up along the starboard quarter of the carrack, shot forward into the *Foresight*'s stern...'. When a third English ship came alongside, they finally carried the great carrack, after prolonged fighting hand to hand, but relatively little heavy gunnery.[50] Attacking a really formidable opponent like the carrack *Cinco Chagas* it might be necessary to 'charge' several times to soften up the target before boarding, but that was always the end of the action: 'The shot which we wee made at her in great Ordinance before we layde her aboord might be at seven bouts which we had, and sixe or 7 shot at a bout...'.[51] Likewise Richard Grenville in the *Tiger* attacked the *Santa María de San Vicente* in the Caribbean in 1585: 'she bore down on them, firing her guns with the intention of disabling them, and so cut up their rigging that they were disabled' – and surrendered at once.[52] Even when it was manifestly wiser to stand off and fight at a distance, the tactic did not come naturally to English privateers. When Cavendish attacked the *Santa Ana* off the Pacific Coast of Mexico in 1588, he made three successive attempts to board, each preceded by a few shots and repelled with loss, before it occurred to him that his heavy guns might be used with more advantage from a distance against an enemy whose main armament was two muskets.[53] Standing off and engaging in a gunnery duel held few attractions for those who had tried it:

> our enimie playenge upon us with theyr ordinance made our gunnors fall to it ere we were at musket shott & no nerer could I bringe them though I had no hope to take any of them but by boordinge, heere wee popt away powder and shot away to no purpose for most of our gunnors would hardly have striken Paules steeple had it stoode there...'[54]

'How much the neerer, so much the better' was Sir Richard Hawkins' maxim; certainly less than point-blank range, and Sir William Monson echoed him: 'he that shooteth far off at sea had as good not shoot at all'.[55]

But the orthodox, ordinary and decisive tactic of naval battle was to board the enemy after the exchange of a few opening rounds, and even after the experience of 1588 it was still possible for an orthodox and unimaginitive captain like Sir Richard Grenville to do precisely this even in the most unpromising circumstances. Older accounts of the last fight of the *Revenge* pictured her surrounded by the Spanish fleet, holding them at bay with her great guns. We now know that she fired them only briefly before closing with her nearest opponents and fighting hand to hand for fifteen hours. When she surrendered, the Spaniards gained not only what was possibly the finest set of heavy guns afloat, but most of their ammunition; she had fired very little except small arms.[56]

There were those who thought that Lord Howard of Effingham should fight that way in 1588, but it is clear that he and his senior officers (with the possible exception of Sir Martin Frobisher) had no intention of doing so; 'in which course all wise men think he did discreetly and like a true man of war'.[57] The best available fleet tactics of the day were still those derived from galley warfare, attacking in line abreast.[58] These were the tactics which had won the Marquis of Santa Cruz a decisive victory in 1582 over a Franco-Portuguese fleet of sailing ships, and Philip II had no doubt that they would work again against the English.[59] As an alternative there was the 'wedge' formation, also a galley tactic, which Lord Lisle had contemplated in 1545, which the Danish admiral Herluf Trolle had used with success in 1564, and which was still being advocated by conservative writers well into the seventeenth century.[60] The problem, for the English, was that all these implied a decision reached in the conventional style, by boarding. They intended to apply the traditional tactic of the indecisive action, firing at the enemy from the windward without closing. The Spaniards describe the English fleet as first sighted, close-hauled and working up to gain the weather gage, as being *en ala*,[61] but it seems to be clear that they initially attacked as individual ships, in no particular order except that there was a natural tendency for ships 'giving the prow' to come down abeam of one another or in line of bearing to avoid fouling one another's range.[62] After Lord Howard reorganised his fleet into four squadrons, there was a tendency to attack in squadrons, or at least in small groups, formed in line ahead. Each ship in turn bore down on her target, fired all her guns in succession in the usual fashion, and hauled off to windward to give place to her next astern. 'He came bragging up at the first, indeed, and gave them his prow and his broadside; and then kept his luff', as Frobisher put it, accusing Drake of cowardice in not closing with the enemy.[63] In this way the English could keep the enemy under more or less continuous bombardment by a succession of ships, each of which came into action perhaps once an hour. The formation was 'follow-my-leader' in a circle or figure of eight; line ahead, undoubtedly, but very far removed from the line of battle as it later developed.[64]

This squadronal attack in line ahead was the standard battle tactic of English ships in the later years of the war against Spain, and it remained so well into the seventeenth century:

> The whole fleet shall follow the admiral, vice-admiral, or other leading ship within musket-shot of the enemy; giving so much liberty to the leading ship as after her broadside delivered she may stay and trim her sails. Then is the second ship to tack as the first ship and give the other side, keeping the enemy under a perpetual shot. This you must do upon the windermost ship or ships of an enemy, which you shall either batter in pieces, or force him or them to bear up and so entangle them, and drive them foul of one another to their utter confusion.[65]

The tactic was the same for an individual privateer as for a squadron:

> Give him a chase peece with your broad side, and run a good berth ahead of him... Edge in with him againe, begin with your bow peeces, proceed with your broad side, & let her fall off with the wind, to give her also your full chase, your weather broad side, and bring her round that the stern may also discharge, and your tackes close aboord againe![66]

> In the first place, your chase guns are to be given; and coming up somewhat nearer, your whole broadside in order, as your pieces will be brought to bear. This done, you are to run a good berth ahead or beyond your enemy's ship, if it may be, and then to edge up into the wind... that so either your consort (if you have one) may have the opportunity to come up with the enemy and do as you have done; or that the enemy's ship herself may shoot ahead of you, and help you to a better opportunity to charge upon her a second time.[67]

It exploited the handiness as well as the heavy armament of English ships to deliver an unequalled weight of fire, for which reason the new three-deckers of the early Stuart Navy like the *Prince Royal* were deplored by many: 'A ship of six hundred tons will carry as good ordnance as a ship of twelve hundred tons; and though the latter have double her number, the lesser will turn her broadsides twice, before the greater can wind once, and so no advantage in that overplus of ordnance'.[68] It was clearly the experience of 1588 which inspired these thoughts:

> As for the use and employment of their great guns, the good sailers shall even in this particular be able to over-press the other; for being nimble and yare of steerage, and having sea-room, by a sudden clapping into the wind and bringing of themselves on the backstays after they have bestowed one of their broadsides, they may speedily give the other; whereas the hundred bad sailers, being closed and shuffled up together, and being heavy and unwieldy withal, they can never use save one, the same beaten side.[69]

In the action off the Isle of Pines in 1595, the only other battle fought between English and Spanish squadrons of sailing warships in the course of the war, the English faithfully followed these tactics:

> As soone as they discried us, they kept close upon a tacke, thinking to get the winde of us: but we weathered them. And when our Admirall with all the rest of our fleet were right in the winds eye of them, sir Thomas Baskervil putting out the Queenes armes, and all the rest of our fleete their braverie, bare roome with them...[70]

Essentially the same tactic was ordered by Lord Wimbledon, commanding the 1625 Cadiz expedition, except that as a soldier, dismayed by the casual approach of the seamen, he attempted to instill some order and discipline into their attacks. He envisaged his fleet of 27 ships divided into three divisions each of three files of three, to 'discharge and fall off three and three as they are filed in this list', retiring to the rear to reload much like musketeers firing by volley.[71]

Contemporaries were so impressed by the volume of fire that English ships could deliver by these tactics that they fell into hyperbole which has persuaded many modern scholars that they were achieving a high rate of fire per gun. Ubaldino describes the *Revenge* in 1588 as 'letting fly every way from both her broadsides, so that she seemed to repeat her fire as rapidly as any harquebusier'.[72] Figures have been offered which would have aroused admiration in the Navy of Nelson's time,[73] and it has been powerfully argued that these high rates of fire were made possible by the English having adopted the truck gun carriage, while the Spaniards continued to use two-wheeled carriages with trains, adapted from the ordinary field carriages of land service. From this it is deduced that the English were able to load inboard and run their guns out to fire, while the Spaniards were condemned to load outboard, which in the circumstances of the Armada fight was effectively impossible except at night.[74]

Powerful evidence has been produced to support this argument. In the first place it is clear that the English did use truck carriages, indeed had been using them for at least forty years, while the Spaniards did use large two-wheeled carriages with trains.[75] Informed contemporaries were equally clear that the English did develop a much greater volume of fire than the Spaniards: three times greater was the estimate of eye-witnesses in 1588.[76] Captain Alonso de Vanegas, an artillery officer aboard Medina Sidonia's flagship, calculated that in a morning's action the English had fired 2,000 rounds against 750; his own ship (with 48 heavy guns) had fired 120 rounds in about one hour.[77] He does not, however, distinguish the calibre of shot, which is important, because we know from documentary evidence concerning Spanish ships which survived the 1588 voyage, and from underwater excavation of some which did not, that they had shot off all or a great part of their small-calibre ammunition, but little or none of that provided for their heavy guns.[78] It is therefore clear that when Medina-Sidonia reported to Philip II that his ships could not renew the fight for want of ammunition,[79] he was not referring to the heavy guns, and it must follow that some other consideration prevented the Spaniards using them effectively in action.

There are, however, some substantial difficulties in the way of the argument that the rate of fire was governed by the design of the gun-carriages. A practical experiment has suggested that Spanish-style carriages could be run in and out, albeit not as fast as the English.[80] Though both Spanish and English contemporaries remarked on the disadvantage of the large Spanish carriages, they do not mention this disadvantage.[81]

Above all, we have serious reason to question whether, or in what circumstances, the English were accustomed to run their truck carriages in and out.

There are in fact three possible ways by which naval heavy guns may have been reloaded. The most obvious is the method familiar from later centuries, by which the gun was loaded inboard, run out, fired, and allowed to run in on the recoil. It is often assumed that this must have been how the guns were handled, and it has been explicitly argued from evidence of the breechings and tackles supplied to English warships by the Ordnance Board.[82] It seems to be implied by a letter of 1588 from Sir William Winter, mentioning 'a hurt that I had received in my hip, by the reversing of one of our demi-cannons in the fight'.[83] Alternatively, it is proposed that the guns were secured outboard and fired 'non-recoil' before being cast loose and hauled inboard to reload.[84] Lastly it has been argued that the guns were secured outboard for the duration of the action and reloaded by men sitting astride the gun or standing on the wales.[85]

Any of these three methods would have been feasible. Carronades were often fired 'non-recoil' during the Napoleonic War, applying greater strains than could have been generated by Elizabethan naval guns, to weaker parts of the ship's structure.[86] The gunner William Bourne refers to chocking the carriages when the guns had been run out; Mainwaring positively states that breechings, 'we do not use in fight'; and Smith's definition of them is 'the ropes by which you lash your Ordnance fast to the Ship's side in foul weather', all of which imply 'non-recoil' firing.[87] Outboard loading was certainly practised (on the windward, disengaged side), and we have both contemporary illustrations of it and descriptions of what it was like to do it.[88] The evidence seems to refer chiefly to other countries, to merchantmen rather than warships, and to the seventeenth rather than the sixteenth century, but it would be rash to say that the English never loaded outboard.

It is at present difficult to say with certainty which of these theories is correct. There is a particular problem that much of the English evidence comes from retired officers like Sir William Monson, Sir Richard Hawkins, Sir Walter Ralegh, and Sir Henry Mainwaring, looking back to the Spanish War but writing some time afterwards (which makes it difficult to know if their remarks reflect current or past practice), together with others like the colonial governor Nathaniel Butler[89] and the soldier Captain John Smith, who wrote about the same time but had less sea experience. The earliest unequivocal English reference to guns run in after firing is Monson's suggestion, written in the 1630s, that one should cut the port-ropes of a ship boarded 'that at her coming off again, when she shall begin a new fight, her pieces may serve for no purpose because her ports will be clogged and not able to put forth a piece of ordnance...'.[90] His objections to three-deckers included the difficulty of hauling in their lowest tier of guns if the sea got up: 'and when they are out, and forced to haul them in again, it is with great labour, travail and trouble to the gunners when they should be fighting' – which might suggest that gunners were not expected to haul guns inboard, at least without help.[91] At least a generation earlier Bourne complained in similar terms that 'it is very troublesome to haul them [the guns] in and lade them, especially if the ship doth heel with sail bearing'.[92] Monson's contemporary Butler objected to fitting the cookroom where it would obstruct 'a free reverse to those great guns that lie in the forecastle', and unequivocally advised that 'the lids and covers of your ports are carefully and suddenly to be let down, as often as any of your great guns do make their reverse within board upon their firing and discharge...'.[93] This seems to make it clear that by then recoil firing was known, and it may have been adopted in 1625, when Wimbledon's second orders call for an increase in gun's crews which implies some development in gunnery practice.[94] Since Butler refers to chase guns, as Winter possibly did in 1588, it may be that recoil firing was initially confined to these guns which had room to recoil, and only later extended to the broadside. We might also infer that the adoption of the more powerful and reliable corn powder, apparently in the early 1580s in the Queen's ships, pushed in the direction of recoil firing.[95] At present it is difficult to say with any certainty.

Some things, however, can be said with confidence. The first is that guns were regarded as fixed, each on an individual bearing, to be aimed by the ship. For this reason the gunner was expected to con the ship as she went into action, bringing each gun to bear in turn as she swung.[96] Though the chase guns may possibly have been fired together, the broadside guns certainly were not, for they did not all point in the same direction. On the contrary, those in the fore part of the ship, sometimes the whole broadside, were 'bowed' or 'traversed' round to fire as nearly forward as possible, while those further aft might be 'quartered' to fire aft.[97] For Englishmen this was the great advantage of their compact gun carriages, that they allowed the gun to be canted round as far as possible, while the Spanish carriages 'cannot be traversed from side to side but must be shot off directly forward as they lie'.[98] Gun ports were to be cut as wide as possible, 'that the ordnance may have leave to traverse as much bowing and quartering as may be'.[99] This style of fighting strongly implies that the guns were secured before going into action, and that each gun was fired only once in each 'charge'. Moreover guns which had been 'traversed' in this way would have run in diagonally if they were allowed to run in at all', with obvious risk of hitting other guns, or of capsizing the gun as the strain came unequally on the tackles.

Secondly, we know roughly the number of men quartered at the guns in English ships. Up to the 1570s, the figure seems to have been around one man a gun at most. In the course of half a century, the proportion of soldiers to seamen had fallen sharply, but the number of gunners remained much the same.[100] According to one contemporary rule, gunners should form one-seventh of a wartime ship's company calculated at three men for 5 tons: 28 gunners for a 500-ton ship, which would have carried at least that many guns of demi-culverin calibre and above.[101] In the light of the experience of 1588, one commentator argued for a large increase, sufficient 'to traverse, run out and haul in the guns', but his idea was not adopted,[102] and by the early seventeenth century the figure had risen only to two or three men per gun.[103] By the 1630s expert opinion was prepared to contemplate as many as four men to handle a demi-cannon (weighing 2½ tons),[104] but contemporary critics still complained that English ships were undermanned to fight their guns properly.[105] Of course it was possible to borrow men from on deck to add to the guns' crews ('some to assist the gunners in the traversing of the ordnance'),[106] but the English tactic of attacking from the windward, necessarily with the advantage of speed ('the only thing we could presume upon in our war against the Spaniards')[107] and therefore under full sail, then tacking to haul out of action, called for a large part of the ship's company to handle the sails. A ship obliged to go into action unprepared might find herself unable to supply the manpower to run out and traverse more than a few guns:

In the beginning of the fight I had all my gunnes in, and all my sailes out (for otherwise I could not have reached them), so that I suffered much for want of men before I could fitt the sails and bring the gonnes to their due bearing, otherwise they should have had many more shottes out of my shippe.[108]

If sixteenth-century guns were handled in the same way as eighteenth, it was with fewer than a quarter of the number of men later considered necessary; and if the guns were run in as well as out by hand, they were doing twice as much work. In the absence of train tackles (not supplied to English ships until much later) the likely methods of securing a gun inboard to reload (presumably chocks or handspikes) imply a large gun's crew.[109] The conclusion seems to be inescapable that however the guns were being reloaded, there were not enough men available to load all of them at once. We have to imagine teams of men moving from gun to gun. Reloading the whole armament, by whatever method, must have taken a long time, and there was no advantage in lingering within range of the enemy while one did so.

We also know how much ammunition was supplied to English ships, and in some cases how much they expended in a given time. The figures given by the Anthony Roll in 1545, the official Ordnance Board allowances of 1572, a survey of 1576, and the records of the 1585 West Indies and 1596 Cadiz expeditions are all fairly consistent in allowing 20 to 25 rounds a gun (plus three to five crossbar shot) for guns of about 6 pdr upwards.[110] English privateers appear to have been armed on a similar scale, though the 1595 West Indies squadron carried rather greater quantities of ammunition.[111] In view of these figures it is not surprising that English ships ran short of ammunition during the 1588 campaign; the surprise is that after a week of fighting on and off they still had powder and shot to fight at Gravelines. Their expenditure during the preceding week cannot on average have much exceeded five rounds per gun per day.

One thing seems to be clear: however the English reloaded their guns, they did not do it in action. Whether the 'charge' was made by single ships or whole squadrons, it was invariably the case that having fired off their guns, the attackers withdrew to reload at leisure. Attempting to slow down the *Madre de Deus*, the *Dainty* 'gave her a broadside of ordnance and falling astern came (having laden his ordnance) again and again to deliver his peals to hinder her way till the rest of the fleet could come...'.[112] It is not clear in this case how long it took to reload, but in some cases we are given clues. At Gravelines in 1588, Sir William Winter claimed that his ship the *Vanguard* fired 500 rounds of demi-cannon, culverin and demi-culverin shot in nine hours; with a total of 32 guns of these calibres, her rate of fire per gun was 1¾ rounds an hour.[113] Winter clearly regarded this as an extraordinary figure, and it probably was. As late as 1652 the *Sapphire*, in action against two Royalist privateers:

bore down upon Colaert stem for stem, and in two ships' lengths clapt upon a wind, and fired all his lower tier with round shot and bar shot, and his upper tier with round shot and partridge (or bags of old iron) and all his muskets at Colaert. Then down mainsail and stood away, keeping firing at one another while in shot. In less than two glasses all their great guns and muskets being loaded... then about ship and served Spragge as his brother was served before.[114]

Two glasses is of course an hour, and an hour seems a fair approximation of the time usually taken to make a charge, withdraw and reload for the next. The Dutch traveller Jan Huyghen van Linschoten, who experienced an action against English ships as a passenger in a Portuguese vessel, describes how 'when wee shot off a peece, wee had at the least an houres worke to lade it againe...',[115] a passage which has been cited to demonstrate the incompetence of enemy gunners,[116] but it seems to be tone rather than substance which distinguishes his report from this stirring account, of English East Indiamen in action against the Portuguese in 1625:

> Without any wordes or parly of ether wee tanguled and mixed our fleetes one with another... ashooting pellmell one aganst the other. Our ordinance went off licke musketes; the dromes beate, and our trumpeters sounding, and the flying shoot tearing eath other sayles and rigging macking such a wherling noyse in the ayere, and our men couragiusly chering ourselves with a hubbub, shouting, whisling, and stiring in there severall places, had not the least thought of feare, but laded and discharged there ordnances at the ennymie. The fight continued hott and fearse one bouth sides... [we fired] broadsides as fast as wee could laied them and worck them and trim our sayles, having a good gale of wend... giving broadside after broadside, and ware not answered above one in tenn.[117]

Having read this it comes as something of a shock to the modern reader to discover that the English too were firing at best only one and a half rounds an hour from each gun.[118] In that same year the Indiaman *Lion* was taken off Gombroon, boarded from small boats while the crew were trying to reload.[119] In 1636 the English pinnace *Nicodemus* (a former Dunkirk privateer), defending a convoy in the Straits of Dover, fired 34 or 35 rounds from six guns in two hours, but these were very small pieces.[120]

Taking stock of all this evidence, we may say with some confidence that English shipwrights and naval men in the late Elizabethan age did not think of themselves as having designed the prototypes of the future ship of the line, but as having at length achieved a sailing warship which could beat the galley at her own game. Their main armament was their bow chasers, and with these they invariably attacked first: 'a man-of-war pretends to fight most with his prow'.[121] Drake's *Golden Hind* in 1574 mounted four bow chasers and seven guns a side.[122] The *Elizabeth Bonaventure*, his flagship in the West Indies in 1585, is said to have carried no less than six culverins in the bow and four in the stern.[123] In 1590 the Spaniards were advised by an English exile that to match the English they would have to build ships with six bow and six stern chasers, though the *Warspite* of 1595 is given with only four of each.[124] All of these ships fitted the recommendations of Mainwaring: 'Her chase and bow must be well contrived to shoot as many pieces right forward, and bowing, as may be (for those pieces come to be most used in fight)'.[125] Butler likewise proposed 'Bows and chases be so contrived that out of them as many guns as possibly may be, may shoot right forwards, and bowing (as the sea word is)'.[126] For many late Elizabethan naval men, their greatest triumphs were not the defensive fights against the Armada in 1588, but their unambiguous victories over the Spanish galleys at Cadiz in 1587 and 1596, and at Cezimbra in 1602: 'a precedent which has been seldom seen or heard of, for ships to be the destroyers of galleys.'[127] Even then the brief success of Federico Spinola's galley squadron in the Narrow Seas in 1601-02 inspired hasty galley-building programmes in both England and the Netherlands.[128]

For this generation what distinguished warships from merchantmen was that the men-of-war fought offensively with their bows, 'the place where the chief offensive force of the ship should lie', but merchant ships defensively with their sterns.[129] An example was the action between the Levant Company's *Mary Sampson* and a squadron of galleys of the Knights of Malta in 1628. After some time completely becalmed and obliged to fight only with his broadside:

> Captaine William Rainsborow (who behaved himselfe with brave courage and temper) finding a breath of wind to give the ship motion; considering that he was a great marke on the broad-side, and the galleys very narrow, keeping their prowes sharpe toward him, and that he could beare little upon them, trimmed his sailes before the winde, and brought them to a sterne fight... the *Sampson* could then beare upon them two whole culverin in her stern-chase, and two transome-culverins in the gunne-room and two sakers in the great Cabbin.[130]

It remains to consider a number of incidents and texts which have frequently been cited to prove that broadside armament and the line of battle originated in the sixteenth century. The first is Vasco da Gama's battle off Calicut in 1502, when the Portuguese caravels under Vicente Sodré are reported to have gained the weather gage and gone into action in line ahead, keeping aloof from their opponents. The Portuguese were under orders not to risk their precious manpower by boarding, but to fire on the enemy from a distance. This has been hailed as a precocious example of modern gunnery tactics,[131] but there was nothing done here which would have struck any admiral of the fifteenth century as unusual (it is exactly what Philip of Cleves recommends for such a situation),[132] except perhaps that the Portuguese guns succeeded in sinking some of the flimsy Indian craft.[133] It must also be said that only one Portuguese historian of this voyage mentions the battle at all, that the narrative is vague and impressionistic, and that the crucial reference to sailing in line is not present in all the manuscripts.[134]

Another action in which ships can be shown to have fought in line ahead, and which has been cited as an early instance of the 'line of battle', is that fought by William Towerson and a French ship, caught interloping on the Guinea Coast in 1557, against a small Portuguese squadron which is described as 'driving off the interlopers with repeated broadsides'.[135] We have only a confused account of what was evidently a confused affair, but certainly both sides strove for the weather gage, apparently in some sort of line ahead, and at one point Towerson was directly to windward of the Portuguese. At this stage neither his ship nor the larger Portuguese vessels could fire effectively; his own, 'because our ship was so weake in the side, that she laid all her ordinance in the Sea'; the enemy because they were to leeward, though they 'caried such ordinance that if they had had the weather of us, they would have troubled 3 of the best ships that we had... they shot not at us, because we had the weather of them...'.[136] Possibly we are to understand that the Portuguese had their heaviest guns mounted in chase and so could not fire from the leeward position. No broadsides were fired either at or by Towerson's ship: the only occasion that they are mentioned is when the Portugese later attacked the disabled French ship to leeward; 'every one went roome with him, and gave him the broad side, and after they cast about againe...'.[137] All the elements concerned – the striving for the weather gage, the bearing up to attack an enemy to leeward – were standard practice, with a long history behind and ahead of them.

Just the same may be said of George Fenner's fight in the *Castle of Comfort* in 1567 against a Portuguese squadron off Terceira.[138] On the first day 'the great shippe shot at us all her broad side, and her foure greatest pieces that lay in her sterne, and therewith hurt some of our men... the ship and the Caravell gave us the first day three fights'. Next day the Portuguese attempted boarding, but Fenner 'gave them such a heate with both our sides, that they were both glad to fall asterne of us'. On this day there seem to have been three more 'fights' or charges, and Fenner's reference to 'crossebarres, chaineshotte and haileshot' makes it clear he was firing at the enemy's rigging and decks to repel boarders. Finally, on the third day there were four further fights before the Portuguese abandoned the struggle, having 'made in our ship some leakes with their shot.' The whole was a typical action in the traditional style, with boarding attempted and repelled, using small arms and great guns chiefly against men and rigging. The only novelty in this, as in Towerson's narrative, was the early use of 'broad side' to refer to guns, and this may reflect the usage of the 1590s when Hakluyt collected and edited the accounts, rather than of the period when the actions actually occurred.[139]

More of a puzzle is a letter written in 1574 by an anonymous Spanish agent in England, to Don Luis de Requeséns y Zúñiga, Governor of the Spanish Netherlands:

> If the fleets come to hostilities it would be well to give orders when they [scil. the Spaniards] approach them [scil. the English], that the ordnance flush with the water should be at once discharged broadside on, and so damage their hulls and confuse them with the smoke. This is their own way of fighting, and I have many times seen them do it to the French 30 years ago.[140]

From this Sir Julian Corbett deduced that the English were using broadside firing as early as the 1540s.[141] The English version, however, is a bold reconstruction of a difficult original of which about one-fifth has been lost by fire, and the remainder is written in an indifferent hand and rather odd Castilian, apparently by a Portuguese speaker.[142] It certainly refers to firing at the enemy's side, but there is nothing which can be safely translated 'broadside', nor is it clear what exactly the writer saw done thirty years before. Here again the evidence provides little support for anachronistic suppositions about broadside firing and the line of battle.

Yet there is no doubt that eventually both of these did become general practice, and we have still to explain how and when the transition from Elizabethan tactics was made. By the end of the sixteenth century English warships had long carried far more heavy guns than they could possibly mount in chase, and the remainder were of necessity mounted on the broadside. Occasions would and did occur when these guns could be used to advantage instead of the chasers, and in the reports of the last years of the war Englishmen show themselves increasingly aware of their broadside guns.[143] The word itself, referring to gunfire rather than a part of the ship, first becomes common in English in the 1590s. By the seventeenth century, contemporaries seem to have been confused; sometimes they repeated the orthodox view that, 'her Bow and chase so Gally-like contrived, should beare as many Ordnances as with conveniency she could, for that alwaies commeth most to fight... neither should her Gunroome be unprovided...'.[144] In this spirit they objected to the new two- and three-deckers because they were too clumsy to tack in action, and insufficiently lofty to resist boarding: 'The only strength of the James at this present is in her broadside'.[145] At other times they wrote as though the broadside were obviously the main armament.[146] In actions of this period we find the same confusion: sometimes the bow chasers were used as the primary armament, sometimes the broadside, sometimes a mixture of both.[147] Fighting instructions and other commentaries of this period often looked no further than bringing the two fleets into contact;[148] and there were still many like Sir William Monson who explicitly denied the possibility of squadrons of ships being handled in formation, regarded the heavy guns as valuable chiefly to clear the enemy's decks, and found it hard to envisage any form of decisive action other than boarding.[149]

Meanwhile the trend of English naval architecture was towards big, heavy ships, unable to tack quickly to turn the other broadside, and mounting a decreasing proportion of their guns in chase. At the same time the Dunkirkers were building their frigates, the fastest ships afloat, which carried few and small guns, mostly amidships, with none of the penalty in seakeeping associated with a heavy armament fore and aft.[150] These represented the warship types of the future; neither could be fought 'end-on' with any advantage, and neither was well defended against boarding. Even so, Elizabethan tactics were still very much in evidence in the period of the First Dutch War. In 1650 the *President*, bombarding Burntisland, missed stays attempting to go about to fire the other broadside,[151] while as late as 1652 Sir George Ayscue attacked a Dutch squadron off Plymouth by twice 'charging' them from the windward.[152] But by this time the logic of warship design as it had developed was pushing rapidly towards new tactics.[153] Within twenty years the line of battle had become an established ideal (however hard to attain), while guns' crews had been increased to a level which allowed one broadside to be fought continuously (all that was necessary when fighting in line) – though it has been calculated that even with 'continuous' firing, the English rate of fire still did not exceed one round an hour on average, and as late as 1691 the Ordnance Board was resisting an increase in 'the antient and settled allowance of this Office which has bin no more than 40 Rounds in all times past and was found sufficient for a four days fight in the Dutch Warr'.[154]

So in the end the English, and with them no doubt the other northern nations, discovered that in setting out to match the galley, they had arrived at an entirely unexpected destination, with a new type of warship and a new style of fighting. In material terms, they were ready for the line of battle by the 1580s if not before, in that they already had ships which mounted a majority of their guns (though not usually their heaviest guns) on the broadside – but this does not mean that they had yet understood the tactical implication, clear though it may be in hindsight. They formed their ideas as all men do, by reference to a known past and an imagined future, neither of which involved the line of battle or the line-of-battle ship. For Corbett and his generation of historians, history was a practical instrument of current naval policy; it was important to understand the Elizabethans in terms of their contribution to the modern Royal Navy, and natural to see Drake and his contemporaries as forerunners of Nelson. Our purposes are different, and we need no longer maintain the anachronistic vision which the nineteenth-century historians inadvertently conjured up.

Acknowledgements

I am indebted for helpful comments to Professor Geoffrey Parker, Dr Gillian Hutchinson and Mr Richard Barker.

References

1 G.P.B. Naish, ed., 'Documents Illustrating the History of the Spanish Armada' in *The Naval Miscellany IV*, ed. Christopher Lloyd (Navy Records Society [NRS] Vol. 92, 1952), 1-84, quoted at p.16.

2 The earlier version by M.A.S. Hume in the *Calendar of State Papers Spanish* IV, 247, is more accurate.

3 Cesáreo Fernández Duro, ed., *La Armada Invencible* (Madrid, 1884-85, 2 vols), No. 94;

also in Gabriel Maura Gamazo, Duque de Maura, *El Designio de Felipe II y el episodio de la Armada Invencible* (Madrid, 1957), 250. It repeats the terms of a letter of 14 September 1587 to the Marquis of Santa Cruz which is printed by Enrique Herrera Oria, *Felipe II y el Marqués de Santa Cruz en la Empresa de Inglaterra* (Madrid, 1946), 72; and now in *La Batalla del Mar Océano: Corpus Documental de las hostilidades entre España e Inglaterra (1568-1604)*, ed. Jorge Calvar Gross *et al* (Madrid, 1988ff, 3 vols to date) III, 1067-8.

4. For example Michael Lewis, *The Spanish Armada* (London, 1960), 125; Garrett Mattingley, *The Defeat of the Spanish Armada* (London, 1959), 98; Geoffrey Parker, *The Military Revolution: Military Innovation and the Rise of the West, 1500-1800* (Cambridge, 1988), 94; *Armada 1588-1988: An International Exhibition to Commemorate the Spanish Armada*, ed. M.J. Rodríguez-Salgado *et al* (London, 1988), 34. A particularly egregious mistranslation is in E.M. Tenison, *Elizabethan England* (Leamington Spa, 1933-60, 12 vols in 14) IV, 214, rendering *grandes cargas de arcabuçaços y cañonaços* as 'heavy volleys of harquebus shots and broadsides of artillery'.

5 Julian S. Corbett, *Drake and the Tudor Navy* (London, 2nd edn, 1899, 2 vols), II, 75.

6 In an article looking at the English case from English sources, I can only glance at other countries, but there are good reasons to believe that at least in some developments, the English followed the Portuguese, Scots, and Danes.

7 See for example Corbett, *Drake* I, 51; Lewis, *Armada*, 69; Mattingley, *Armada*, 98; Peter Padfield, *Guns at Sea* (London, 1973), 44.

8 John H. Pryor, *Geography, Technology and War: Studies in the Maritime History of the Mediterranean 649-1571* (Cambridge, 1988), 59-66. Noël Fourquin, 'Galères du Moyen-Age', in *Quand voguaient les galères* (Paris, Musée de la Marine, 1990), 67-87. John E. Dotson, 'Merchant and Naval Influences on Galley Design at Venice and Genoa in the Fourteenth Century', in *New Aspects of Naval History*, ed. Craig L. Symonds (Annapolis, Md, 1981), 20-32. *The Age of the Galley: Mediterranean Oared Vessels since pre-classical Times*, ed. John Morrison (London, 1995), 101-16. P.E. Russell, *The English intervention in Spain & Portugal in the time of Edward III & Richard II* (Oxford, 1953), 229-31. Christiane Villain-Gandossi, *Le Navire Médiéval à Travers les Miniatures* (Paris, 1985), 28. Federico Foerster Laures, 'The warships of the Kings of Aragón and their fighting tactics during the 13th and 14th centuries AD', *International Journal of Nautical Archaeology* XVI (1987), 19-29. Lawrence V. Mott, 'Ships of the 13th-century Catalan Navy', *Ibid.*, XIX (1990), 101-12.

9 Notably by William Maltby, 'Politics, Professionalism, and the Evolution of Sailing-Ship Tactics, 1650-1714', in *Tools of War: Instruments, Ideas and Institutions of Warfare, 1445-1871*, ed. John A. Lynn (Urbana, Illinois, 1990), 53-73. Cf. Parker, *Military Revolution*, 96.

10 Corbett, *Drake* II, 206-7; but see his *The Successors of Drake* (London, 1900), 57-8, where he is much clearer, and his *Fighting Instructions 1530-1816* (NRS Vol. 29, 1905), 9, where he translates *en ala* correctly.

11 Francisco-Felipe Olesa Muñido, *La galera en la navigaciòn y el combate* (Madrid, 1971, 2 vols), II, 107-19. Ricardo Cerezo Martínez, 'La táctica naval en el siglo XVI', *Revista de Historia Naval* I (1983), No. 2, 29-61; *idem.*, *Las Armadas de Felipe II* (Madrid, 1988), 141-4.

12 Colin Martin & Geoffrey Parker, *The Spanish Armada* (London, 1988), 166.

13 The term seems to have been coined (or borrowed from Air Force terminology?) by J.F. Guilmartin, *Gunpowder and Galleys: Changing Technology and Mediterranean Warfare at Sea in the Sixteenth Century* (Cambridge, 1974), 91. Martin & Parker, *Spanish Armada*,166, use it to translate *en ala*.

14 L.G. Carr Laughton, 'Early Tudor Ship-Guns', ed. Michael Lewis, *M.M.*, XLVI (1960), 242-85, at p.245. Villain-Gandossi, *Le Navire Médiéval*, Pl. 76. Eric Rieth, 'La question de la construction navale à franc-bord au Ponant', *Neptunia* 160 (1985), 8-21, at p.17. Frank Howard, *Sailing Ships of War 1400-1860* (London, 1979), 12 & 26-7. Carlo M. Cipolla, *Guns and Sails in the Early Phase of European Expansion 1400-1700* (London, 1965), 80-1. R.A. Konstam, 'Naval Artillery to 1550: Its Design, Evolution and Employment' (St.Andrews M.Litt. thesis, 1987), 12-16.

15 Of which the most important is Philip of Ravenstein, Duke of Cleves, *Instruction de toutes manieres de guerroyer, tant par terre que par mer, & des choses y servantes* (Paris, 1558) (but actually written *c.* 1505); the best modern edition of this work is Johanna K. Oudendijk, *Een Bourgondisch Ridder over ten Oorlog ter Zee: Philips van Kleef als Leermeester van Karel V* (Amsterdam, 1941). See also the Burgundian

orders of 1474 printed by R.E.J. Weber, *De Seinboken voor Nederlandse Oorlogsvloten en Konvoien tot 1690* (Amsterdam, 1982), 23-7; J.C. de Jonge, *Geschiedenis van het Nederlandsche Zeewesen* (Haarlem, 2nd edn, 1858-62, 5 vols) I, 736-46; Antoine de Conflans, 'Le livre des "faiz de la Marine et navigages"', ed. Michel Mollat du Jourdin & Florence Chillaud-Toutée, *107e Congrès nationale des Sociétés savantes, Collection d'histoire maritime* (Brest, 1982), 9-44; extracts from the *Espejo de Navegantes* of Alonso de Chaves, printed by Cesáreo Fernández Duro, *Armada Española desde la unión de los Reinos de Castilla y de Aragón* (Madrid, 1895-1903, 9 vols) I, 379-91, and translated by Corbett, *Fighting Instructions*, 6-13; Jehan Bytharne, 'Book of War by Sea and Land, Anno 1543', in *The Naval Miscellany I*, ed. J.K. Laughton (NRS Vol. 20, 1902), 1-21; and the English orders wrongly attributed to Thomas Audley, printed by Corbett, *Fighting Instructions*, 14-17, and discussed by C.S.L. Davies, 'Naval Discipline in the Early Sixteenth Century', *M.M.*, XLVIII (1962), 223-4.

16 F.C. van Oosten & Ph.M. Bosscher, 'Het Taktisch Gebruik van het Zeilschip', *Marineblad* LXXXI (1971), 863-89. Kelly R. DeVries, 'A 1445 reference to shipboard artillery', *Technology and Culture* XXXI (1990), 818-29. Gillian Hutchinson, *Medieval Ships and Shipping* (Leicester, 1994), 156-8. Ian Friel, 'Winds of Change? Ships and the Hundred Years War', in *Arms, Armies and Fortifications in the Hundred Years War*, ed. Anne Curry & Michael Hughes (Woodbridge, 1994), 183-93, at p.186. Howard, *Ships of War*, 38-9. *Naval Accounts and Inventories of the Reign of Henry VII, 1485-8 and 1495-7*, ed. M. Oppenheim (NRS Vol. 8, 1896), 194-5, 204-5, 261, 264 & 274.

17 The best general treatments of galleys are Olesa Muñido, *La galera*, and Guilmartin, *Gunpowder and Galleys*. See also *idem.*, 'The Early Provision of Artillery Armament on Mediterranean War Galleys', *M.M.*, LIX (1973), 257-80; Pierre Boyer, 'Artillerie et tactique navale en Méditeranée au XVIe siècle', *Revue Historique des Armées* No.174 (1989), 110-21; Fernández Duro, *Armada Española* I, 323-4; Padfield, *Guns at Sea*, 19; and Michel Mollat du Jourdin, '"Etre roi sur la mer": Naissance d'une ambition', in *Histoire Militaire de la France I, Des origines à 1715*, ed. Philippe Contamine (Paris, 1992), 279-301, at pp.294-5.

18 Jan Glete, *Navies and Nations: Warships, Navies and State Building in Europe and America, 1500-1860* (Stockholm, 1993, 2 vols) I, 140.

19. *Letters and Papers relating to the War with France, 1512-1513*, ed. Alfred Spont (NRS Vol. 10, 1897), 121-33 & 159. Charles de la Roncière, *Histoire de la marine française* (Paris, 1899-1932, 6 vols) III, 104-6. The 'Trade' is the Raz du Four, the northern entrance into Brest Roads.

20 R. Morton Nance, 'The Ship of the Renaissance', *M.M.*, XLI (1955), 180-92 & 281-98, at p.291. Laughton, 'Early Tudor Ship Guns', 251-4. Konstam, 'Naval Artillery', 144. Howard, *Sailing Ships of War*, 45.

21 *Toutes manieres de guerroyer*, 128.

22 Mollat du Jourdin, '"Etre roi sur la mer"', 291. Laughton, 'Early Tudor Ship Guns', 250-1. Frank Howard, 'Early Ship Guns', *M.M.*, LXXII (1986), 439-53 & LXXIII (1987), 49-55, at p.440. Norman MacDougall, '"The greatest scheip that ewer saillit in Ingland or France": James IV's *Great Michael*', in *Scotland and War AD 79-1918*, ed. MacDougall (Edinburgh, 1991), 36-60.

23 Laughton, 'Early Tudor Ship Guns', 259, 264-6 & 275-8.

24 R.C. Anderson, 'The *Mary Gonson*', *M.M.*, XLVI (1960), 199-204.

25 *Toutes manieres de guerroyer*, 128.

26 Laughton, 'Early Tudor Ship Guns', 250-6. Howard, *Sailing Ships of War*, 46 & 75. For discussion of the armament of the *Mary Rose* I am much indebted to Dr Alex Hildred and her colleagues at the Mary Rose Trust.

27 *British Naval Documents 1204-1960*, ed. John B. Hattendorf *et al* (NRS Vol. 131, 1993), 120-1. G.V. Scammell, 'War at Sea under the Early Tudors: some Newcastle upon Tyne Evidence', *Archaeologia Aeliana* 4th S.XXXVIII (1960), 73-97 & XXXIX (1961), 179-205, at p.187.

28 The best-known examples are the ships of the Anthony Roll, the rather fanciful 'Embarkation of Henry VIII for the Field of the Cloth of Gold' at Hampton Court, the Portuguese carrack *Santa Caterina do Monte Sinai* of about 1520 at the National Maritime Museum, and all but one of the ships sketched by Thomas Pettyt off Calais about 1540 (British Library: Cott.MSS Aug.I.i.23). See also the hulk by Breughel reproduced by Nance, 'Ship of the Renaissance', Fig.22b.

29 Howard, *Sailing Ships of War*, 45.

30 MacDougall, 'James IV's *Great Michael*'.

31 *Toutes manieres de guerroyer*, 128-9.

32 Corbett, *Fighting Instructions*, 20-4. La Roncière, *Marine française* III, 419-24.

33 Corbett, *Drake* I, 57-8.

34 Peter Kirsch, *The Galleon: The Great Ships of the Armada Era* (London, 1990; translated from *Die Galleonen*, Coblenz, 1988), 3-6. Carla Rahn Phillips, *Six Galleons for the King of Spain: Imperial Defense in the Seventeenth Century* (Baltimore, 1986), 40-6; eadem, 'The Caravel and the Galleon', in *Cogs, Caravels and Galleons*, ed. Richard W. Unger (London, 1994), 91-114, at pp.98-9. Jacques Bernard, *Navires et Gens de Mer à Bordeaux (vers 1400-vers 1550)* (Paris, 1968, 3 vols) I, 255-6. *Papers relating to the Navy during the Spanish War, 1585-1587* ed. Julian S. Corbett (NRS Vol.11, 1898), 337-40. Parker, *Military Revolution*, 92.

35 A.H. Taylor, 'Carrack into Galleon', *M.M.*, XXXVI (1950), 144-51. Francisco-Felipe Olesa Muñido, 'La Marina oceanica de los Austrias', in *El buque en la Armada Española*, ed. Enrique Manera Regueyra (Madrid, 1981), 109-46, at pp.122-3.

36 Tom Glasgow, 'H.M.S. Tiger', *North Carolina Historical Review* XLIII (1966), 115-21. David Loades, *The Tudor Navy: An Administrative, Political and Military History* (Aldershot, 1992), 95 & 195. Howard, *Sailing Ships of War*, 81-3. Kirsch, *Galleon*, 11-12.

37 The significant exception is Dutch, in which *galjoen* refers not to the ship, but to her characteristic feature, the beakhead.

38 Scammell, 'War at Sea', 180.

39 Rodríguez-Salgado, *Armada 1588-1988*, 162-3. Bjorn Landström, *The Royal Warship Vasa*, trans. Jeremy Franks (Stockholm, 1988), 9-10. Phillips, *Six Galleons*, 44; & 'The Caravel and the Galleon', 98-106 & 114. Nance, 'Ship of the Renaissance', 294. José Luis Casada Soto, *Los barcos españoles des siglo XVI y la Gran Armada de 1588* (Madrid, 1988), 193. Niels M. Probst, 'The Introduction of Flushed-Planked Skin in Northern Europe – and the Elsinore Wreck', in *Crossroads in Ancient Shipbuilding: Proceedings of the Sixth International Symposium on Boat and Ship Archaeology, Roskilde 1991*, ed. Christer Westerdahl (Oxbow Monograph 40, Oxford, 1994), 143-52. Corbett, *Successors of Drake*, 417 n.3 & 421. C. Martin, 'The Ships of the Spanish Armada', in *God's Obvious Design: Papers for the Spanish Armada Symposium, Sligo, 1988*, ed. P. Gallagher & D.W. Cruikshank (London, 1990), 44-68, at pp.45-8.

40 David B. Quinn & A.N. Ryan, *England's Sea Empire, 1550-1642* (London, 1983), 65. James A. Williamson, *Hawkins of Plymouth* (London, 2nd edn, 1969), 250. Ronald L. Pollitt,

'The Elizabethan Navy Board: A Study in Administrative Evolution' (Northwestern Ph.D. thesis, 1968), 225.

41 Corbett, *Drake* II, 179. Baker's sketches are in the 'Fragments of Ancient Shipwrightry', Pepys MS 2820 in the Pepysian Library, Magdalene College, Cambridge.

42 Martin, 'Ships of the Spanish Armada', 52-6. Olesa Muñido, *La galera* I, 268-81. Parker, *Military Revolution*, 87. *The Naval Tracts of Sir William Monson*, ed. M. Oppenheim (NRS Vols 22-3, 43, 45 & 47, 1902-14) IV, 101.

43 There are many narratives of actions fought in this style in Richard Hakluyt, *The Principal Navigations Voyages Traffiques & Discoveries of the English Nation* (2nd edn of 1599-1600, as printed Glasgow, 1903-05, 12 vols), e.g. VII, 103 (the *Amity* of London, 1592); X, 179 (the *Content*, 1591).

44 Olesa Muñido, 'La marina oceanica de los Austrias', 117. Felipe Fernández-Armesto, *The Spanish Armada: The Experience of War in 1588* (Oxford, 1988), 135-41.

45 'Voyage of the Barbara to Brazil, Anno 1540', ed. R.G. Marsden, in *The Naval Miscellany II*, ed. J.K. Laughton (NRS Vol. 40, 1912), 3-66, at p.31.

46 Fernández Duro, *Armada Española* I, 388; but John Smith, *A Sea Grammar*, ed. Kermit Goell (London, 1970), 79 unambiguously recommends shifting guns to empty ports on the engaged side.

47 Tom Glasgow, jr & W. Salisbury, 'Elizabethan Ships pictured on the Smerwick Map, 1580', *M.M.*, LII (1966), 157-65. The authors speculate as to why the artist should have omitted the broadsides which they take for granted must have been fired.

48 David Loades, 'From the King's Ships to the Royal Navy 1500-1642' in *The Oxford Illustrated History of the Royal Navy*, ed. J.R. Hill (Oxford, 1995), 24-55, proposes this at p.43.

49 Calvar Gross, *La Batalla del Mar Océano* I, 147. *New Light on Drake: A Collection of Documents relating to his Voyage of Circumnavigation 1577-1580*, ed. Zelia Nuttall (Hakluyt Soc. 2nd.S.34, 1914), 157-8 & 164-75.

50 'The Taking of the Madre de Dios, anno 1592' ed. C.L. Kingsford, in Laughton, *Naval Miscellany II*, 85-121, at pp.107-8.

51 Hakluyt, *Principal Navigations* VII, 123.

52 *Further English Voyages to Spanish America 1583-1594*, ed. Irene A. Wright (Hakluyt Soc. 2nd S.99, 1951), 13.

53 Calvar Gross, *La Batalla del Mar Océano* III, 1684 & 1775.

54 *The Last Voyage of Drake & Hawkins*, ed. Kenneth R. Andrews (Hakluyt Soc. 2nd.S. 142, 1972), 104-5. The superfluous 'away' does not occur in the same passage as printed in Thomas Maynarde, *Sir Francis Drake his Voyage, 1595*, ed. W.D. Cooley (Hakluyt Soc. Vol. 4, 1849), 23.

55 *The Observations of Sir Richard Hawkins*, ed. James A. Williamson (London, 1933), 130. Monson, *Naval Tracts* IV, 43.

56 Peter Earle, *The Last Fight of the Revenge* (London, 1992), 122-4.

57 The opinion of Sir Arthur Gorgas: Tom Glasgow, jr, 'Gorgas' SeaFight', *M.M.*, LIX (1973), 179-85, at p.182.

58 Corbett, *Fighting Instructions*, 20-3.

59 Magdalena de Pazzis Pi Corrales, *Felipe II y la Lucha por el Dominio del Mar* (Madrid, 1989), 225-9. Cerezo Martínez, 'La tactica naval', 55-7. La Roncière, *Marine Français* IV, 183-92.

60 Corbett, *Drake* I, 55. Fernández Duro, *Armada Española* I, 388. Cerezo Martínez, *Las Armadas de Felipe II*, 142-3. R.C. Anderson, *Naval Wars in the Baltic during the Sailing Ship Epoch, 1522-1850* (London, 1910), 6. *Boteler's Dialogues*, ed. W.G. Perrin (NRS Vol. 65, 1929), 315.

61 Corbett, *Drake* II, 207.

62 The form of attack is clearly shown in the Adams charts drawn for Lord Howard.

63 *State Papers relating to the Defeat of the Spanish Armada, anno 1588*, ed. J.K. Laughton (NRS Vols 1 & 2, 1894) II, 102.

64 Brian Lavery, 'The Revolution in Naval Tactics (1588-1653)', in *Les Marines de Guerre Européennes, XVII-XVIIIe siècles*, ed. Martine Acerra, José Merino & Jean Meyer (Paris, 1985), 167-74; a neglected and valuable article which sums up much of the argument of this paper. Brian Tunstall, *Naval Warfare in the Age of Sail: The Evolution of Fighting Tactics 1650-1815*, ed. Nicholas Tracy (London, 1990), 11. L.G. Carr Laughton, 'Gunnery, Frigates and the Line of Battle', *M.M.*, XIV (1928), 339-63. Taylor, 'Carrack into Galleon', 149. Glasgow, 'Gorgas' SeaFight', 180-1.

65 Corbett, *Fighting Instructions*, 42, quoting Raleigh's 1617 orders; cf. *The Works of Sir Walter Ralegh...*, ed. Thos. Birch (London, 1751, 2 vols) I, cii.

66 Smith, *Sea Grammar*, 77-8.

67 Perrin, *Boteler's Dialogues*, 296.

68 Ralegh, *Works* II, 94.

69. Perrin, *Boteler's Dialogues*, 253.

70 Hakluyt, *Principal Navigations* X, 242. Andrews, *Last Voyage of Drake & Hawkins*, 123-4 & 236-48 prints this with other narratives of this action. To 'bear room' is to bear up.

71 *The Voyage to Cadiz in 1625, being a Journal written by John Glanville*, ed. Alexander B. Grosart (Camden Soc. N.S.Vol. 32, 1883), 16-17. Corbett, *Fighting Instructions*, 63-72. Tunstall, *Naval Warfare*, 12-13.

72 Corbett, *Drake* II, 260.

73 Jean Meyer, 'La marine française de 1545 a 1715', in Contamine, *Histoire Militaire de la France I*, 485-525, suggesting at p.491 that by the 1630s the English could fire one round every 2 minutes.

74 The argument is set out in Parker, *Military Revolution*, 93-5, and elaborated in Martin & Parker, *Spanish Armada*, 199-211. It is also given by Colin Martin and David Lyon in Rodríguez-Salgado, *Armada 1588-1988*, 173-6.

75 Adrian B. Caruana, *The History of English Sea Ordnance 1523-1875: Volume 1, The Age of Evolution, 1523-1715* (Rotherfield, Sussex, 1994), 172-80. John F. Guilmartin, jr, 'Guns and Gunnery', in Unger, *Cogs, Caravels and Galleons*, 139-50, at p.146. C.J.M. Martin, 'A 16th century siege train: the battery ordnance of the 1588 Spanish Armada', *International Journal of Nautical Archaeology* XVII (1988), 57-73; idem., *Full Fathom Five: Wrecks of the Spanish Armada* (New York, 1975), 215-18. Spanish carriages are illustrated by Phillips, *Six Galleons*, 98, and Rodríguez-Salgado, *Armada 1588-1988*, 179.

76 Historical Manuscripts Commission, *Salisbury Manuscripts* III, 345.

77 Fernández Duro, *La Armada Invencible* II No. 185.

78 Martin & Parker, *Spanish Armada*, 199-204. Geoffrey Parker, 'The *Dreadnought* Revolution of Tudor England' (in this issue), assembles much more evidence on this point; I am indebted to Professor Parker for allowing me to consult this paper before publication.

79 Fernández Duro, *La Armada Invencible* II, 226; cf. *La Armada Invencible: Documentes Procedentes del Archivo General de Simancas*, ed. Enrique Herrera Oria (Valladolid, 1929), 245-6.

80 Simon Adams, 'The Gran Armada: 1988 and After', *History* LXXVI (1991), 238-49, at p.242.

81 Monson, *Naval Tracts* V, 147. *The Life and Works of Sir Henry Mainwaring*, ed. G.E. Manwaring & W.G. Perrin (NRS Vols 54 & 56,

1920-22) II, 119. Juan Martínez de Recalde to Philip II, 13 Dec. 1586, in Calvar Gross, *La Batalla del Mar Océano*, II, 462.

82 Caruana, *Sea Ordnance*, 25-6.

83 Laughton, *Spanish Armada* II, 11.

84 Martin & Parker, *Spanish Armada*, 208.

85 Laughton, 'Gunnery, Frigates and the Line of Battle', 339-41. R.A. Konstam, '16th century naval tactics and gunnery', *International Journal of Nautical Archaeology* XVII (1988), 17-23. Kirsch, *Galleon*, 59. Padfield, *Guns at Sea*, 62 & 69.

86 Brian Lavery, *The Arming and Fitting of English Ships of War, 1600-1815* (London, 1978), 132.

87 William Bourne, *The Arte of Shooting in Great Ordnance* (London, 1587), 52 & 57. Mainwaring, *Works* II, 110. Smith, *Sea Grammar*, 85 (but note that Smith borrows much from Mainwaring).

88 It is shown in Van Wieringen's painting of the action off Gibraltar in 1602 (in the Scheepvaart Museum, Amsterdam), and in a Van de Velde sketch of about 1664 (National Maritime Museum No. 106). There is a personal account in *The Life of the Icelander Jón Ólafsson...*, ed. Bertha S. Phillpotts (Hakluyt Soc. 2nd S.Vols 53 & 68, 1923-31) II, 48-9.

89 Perrin, *Boteler's Dialogues*: the editor preferred the spelling under which the book was first printed to that invariably used by the author himself.

90 *Naval Tracts* V, 148.

91 *Naval Tracts* IV, 95; cf. IV, 61, proposing that idlers be trained 'to the labour in hauling, and doing other helps to the gunner about his ordnance'.

92 Brian Lavery, *The Colonial Merchantman Susan Constant* (London, 1988), 38, quoting Bourne's *Inventions or Devices*, which he dates to 1578. *English Maritime Books printed before 1801*, ed. Thomas R. Adams & David W. Waters (Providence R.I. & Greenwich, 1995), 21, lists a 1st edn of *c*.1577, of which no copy is traced, and a 2nd of 1590.

93 Perrin, *Boteler's Dialogues*, 90 & 303.

94 Padfield, *Guns at Sea*, 67. Taylor, 'Galleon into Ship of the Line', 268.

95 Caruana, *Sea Ordnance*, 184-7.

96 Monson, *Naval Tracts* IV, 33. Mainwaring, *Works* II, 184. Bourne, *Great Ordnance*, 53-4.

97 Perrin, *Boteler's Dialogues*, 259. Hawkins, *Observations*, 130. The 'bowing' of

guns is clearly visible in contemporary illustrations.

98 Monson, *Naval Tracts* V, 147. Bourne, *Great Ordnance*, 57. But Hawkins, *Observations*, 134, mentions a Spanish gunner killed traversing his piece in action.

99 Mainwaring, *Works* II, 200.

100 Loades, *Tudor Navy*, 97. M. Oppenheim, *A History of the Administration of the Royal Navy from 1509 to 1660...* (London, 1896), 56. Konstam, 'Naval tactics and gunnery', 18. Hattendorf, *British Naval Documents*, 103-6. Corbett, *Spanish War*, 270-2. Charles Derrick, *Memoirs of the Rise and Progress of the Royal Navy* (London, 1806), 14-15, 19, 25 & 303-6.

101 Corbett, *Spanish War*, 265.

102 Corbett, *Drake* II, 288-9. Complements in 1588 are in Laughton, *Spanish Armada* II, 324-5.

103 Monson, *Naval Tracts* IV, 91. Mainwaring, *Works* I, 54-5. John Brand, 'The Names of his Majesties Shipps...', *Archaeologia* XV (1806), 53-8.

104 *Trinity House of Deptford Transactions, 1609-35*, ed. G.G. Harris (London Record Soc. Vol. 19, 1983), 115-16.

105 Monson, *Naval Tracts* II, 243 & IV, 224.

106 Perrin, *Boteler's Dialogues*, 293.

107 Monson, *Naval Tracts* II, 180.

108 *Journal of a Voyage into the Mediterranean by Sir Kenelm Digby, A.D. 1628*, ed. John Bruce (Camden Soc. Vol. 96, 1868), 12.

109 Caruana, *Sea Ordnance*, 25.

110 S.B. Bull, 'The Furie of the Ordnance: England's Guns and Gunners by Land 1600-1650' (Wales Ph.D. thesis, 1988), 107-8. N.A.M. Rodger, 'Elizabethan Naval Gunnery', *M.M.*, LXI (1975), 353-4. Caruana, *English Sea Ordnance*, 199. Michael Lewis, 'Armada Guns. A Comparative Study of English and Spanish Armaments', *Ibid.* XXVIII (1942), 41-73, 104-47, 231-45 & 259-90; XXIX (1943), 3-39, 100-21, 163-78 & 203-31; at XXIX,112-14. W.G. Perrin, 'Early Naval Ordnance', *Ibid.* VI (1920), 51-3. Laughton, *Spanish Armada* I, 339. Corbett, *Spanish War*, 27-33.

111 *English Privateering Voyages to the West Indies 1588-1595*, ed. K.R. Andrews (Hakluyt Soc. 2nd.S. CXI, 1959), 74-7 & 231. Harris, *Trinity House Transactions*, 85. Andrews, *Last Voyage of Drake and Hawkins*, 72-3.

112 Samuel Purchas, *Hakluytus Posthumus, or Purchas his Pilgrimes* (Glasgow, 1905-07, 20 vols) XVI,16. The common metaphor of a 'peal'

(implying that the guns were fired in succession) is worth noting.

113 Laughton, *Spanish Armada* II, 11. The *Vanguard*'s designed armament in 1586 (Corbett, *Spanish War*, 312) and her actual armament in 1596 (Caruana, *English Sea Ordnance*, 35) differ, but the total is the same.

114 *Letters and Papers relating to the First Dutch War*, ed. S.R. Gardiner & C.T. Atkinson (NRS Vols. 13, 17, 30, 37, 41 & 66, 1899-1930) I, 21-2.

115 Hakluyt, *Principal Navigations* VII, 63.

116 Martin & Parker, *Spanish Armada*, 207.

117 *The English Factories in India 1624-1629*, ed. William Foster (Oxford, 1909), 51-2.

118 Foster, *English Factories*, 81.

119 G.V. Scammell, *The Engish Chartered Trading Companies and the Sea* (National Maritime Museum, n.d. [1983]), 26.

120 *High Court of Admiralty Examinations 1637-1638*, ed. Dorothy O.Shilton & Richard Holworthy (London, 1932), 272 & 279.

121 Mainwaring, *Works* II, 131.

122. Lewis, 'Armada Guns', XXVIII,273.

123 Wright, *Further English Voyages*, 44.

124 David Goodman, *Power and Penury: Government, Technology and Science in Philip II's Spain* (Cambridge, 1988), 108. Oppenheim, *Administration of the Royal Navy*, 156.

125 Mainwaring, *Works* II, 184.

126 Perrin, *Boteler's Dialogues*, 259.

127 Monson, *Naval Tracts* II, 163; cf. Corbett, *Successors of Drake*, 369-77, & Sir Richard Leveson's account in Historical Manuscripts Commission, *Salisbury Manuscripts* XII, 183-4. The Lord Admiral had specifically warned Leveson not to risk the Queen's ships within reach of the Spanish galleys: *Salisbury Manuscripts* XII, 162. Merchantmen which fought off galleys were also much celebrated: *Naval Songs and Ballads*, ed. C.H. Firth (Navy Records Society Vol. 33, 1908), xx.

128 Randal Gray, 'Spinola's Galleys in the Narrow Seas, 1599-1603', *M.M.*, LXIV (1978), 71-83. L.Th. Lehmann, *Galleys in the Netherlands* (Amsterdam, 1984), 12-14 & 50-86; *idem.*, 'Dutch Galleys', *ibid.* LXV (1979), 63.

129 Mainwaring, *Works* II, 131-2.

130 Michael Strachan, 'Sampson's Fight with Maltese Galleys, 1628', *M.M.*, LV (1969), 281-9, at p.286.

131 Parker, *Military Revolution*, 94. Peter Padfield, *Tide of Empires: Decisive Naval Campaigns in the Rise of the West* (London, 1979-82, 2 vols) I, 42-53; see also his *Guns at Sea*, 25-7.

Maltby, 'Evolution of Sailing-Ship Tactics', 53, explicitly claims this as an example of the line of battle.

132 *Toutes manieres de guerroyer*, 139.

133 *The Three Voyages of Vasco da Gama... from the Lendas da India of Gaspar Correa*, ed. H.E.J. Stanley (Hakluyt Soc. Vol. 42, 1869), 366-70.

134 I am indebted to Mr Richard Barker for this point.

135 Parker, *Military Revolution*, 94, citing Guilmartin, *Gunpowder and Galleys*, 89-93. The same interpretation is offered by Quinn & Ryan, *England's Sea Empire*, 61-2; & Taylor, 'Carrack into Galleon', 148. Cf. J.D. Alsop, 'The Career of William Towerson, Guinea Trader', *International Journal of Maritime History* IV (1992), 45-82.

136 Hakluyt, *Principal Navigations* VI, 221-3.

137 Hakluyt, *Principal Navigations* VI, 222.

138 Cited as an example of an early gunnery action by Quinn & Ryan, *England's Sea Empire*, 63; & Taylor, 'Carrack into Galleon', 148.

139 Hakluyt, *Principal Navigations* VI, 281-3.

140 *Calendar of State Papers Spanish* II, 480, rendering British Library: Cott.MSS Galba C.5 f.32.

141 Corbett, *Drake* I, 137.

142. I am indebted to my brother Mr A.D.A. Rodger and my sister-in-law Sra. Leticia Martínez Aguilar for advice on the language of this document. Fernández-Armesto, *Spanish Armada*, 140 identifies the spy as a Portuguese named Fogaza.

143 Monson, *Naval Tracts* II, 158 & V, 186. Cf. the sources quoted at notes 65-9 above.

144 Smith, *Sea Grammar*, 72.

145 Monson, *Naval Tracts* IV, 94; cf. Lavery, 'Revolution in Naval Tactics', 169.

146 Perrin, *Boteler's Dialogues*, 291. John Hollond, *Two Discourses of the Navy, 1638 and 1659*, ed. J. R. Tanner (NRS Vol. 7, 1896), 376-7.

147 C.R. Boxer, 'The Action between Pater and Oquendo, 12 September 1631', *M.M.*, XLV (1959), 179-99, at pp.190-1. Purchas, *Purchas his Pilgrimes* V, 245. Christopher Lloyd, *English Corsairs on the Barbary Coast* (London, 1981), 38. Calvin F. Senning, 'Piracy, Politics and Plunder under James I: The Voyage of the *Pearl* and its Aftermath, 1611-1615', *Huntington Library Quarterly* XLVI (1983), 187-222, at p.192.

148 Eg. Buckingham's of 1626, cited by Norman Clayton, 'Naval Administration, 1603-

1628' (Leeds Ph.D. thesis, 1935), 434; Lindsay's of 1635 in Monson, *Naval Tracts* IV, 8-9 & Tunstall, *Naval Warfare*, 13-16; Northumberland's of 1636 in *ibid.*, 16.

149 Monson, *Naval Tracts* IV, 91-8.

150 Lavery, 'Revolution in Naval Tactics', 170. Andrew Thrush, 'In Pursuit of the Frigate, 1603-40', *Historical Research* LXIV (1991), 29-45. Laughton, 'Gunnery, Frigates and the Line of Battle', 361. Johan E. Elias, *De Vlootbouw in Nederland in de eerste Helft der 17e Eeuw, 1596-1655* (Amsterdam, 1933), 40-58.

151 M.L. Baumber, 'The Navy during the Civil Wars and the Commonwealth, 1642-1651' (Manchester M.A. thesis, 1967), 320-1.

152 Gardiner & Atkinson, *First Dutch War* II, 105-6.

153 Tunstall, *Naval Warfare,* 16-37. Laughton, 'Gunnery, Frigates and the Line of Battle', 344. Taylor, 'Galleon into Ship of the Line', 271-4. Padfield, *Guns at Sea,* 71-4. Weber, *De Seinboken,* 108; *idem.*, 'The Introduction of the Single Line ahead as a Battle Formation by the Dutch 1665-1666', *M.M.*, LXXIII (1987), 5-19. Julian S.Corbett, *England in the Mediterranean: A Study of the Rise and Influence of British Power within the Straits, 1603-1713* (London, 2nd edn 1917, 2 vols) II, 569-80.

154 Tunstall, *Naval Warfare,* 25. Rodger, 'Elizabethan Naval Gunnery', 354.

IV

THE NEW ATLANTIC:
NAVAL WARFARE IN THE SIXTEENTH CENTURY

It has long been customary to regard naval warfare as the business of navies, and it usually still is. This creates an obvious problem, for navies, as the word is generally understood today, are instruments of the state; permanent fleets of warships, manned by professional officers and men, supported by an elaborate infrastructure and maintained from the revenues of central government. These are the normal instruments of naval warfare in the modern world, and it is easy to assume that they are the natural if not the only ones. Yet even a superficial knowledge of European history will show that navies in this sense were unusual if not unknown before the Renaissance. Byzantium and Venice have some claims to have possessed navies in something like the modern form, at some periods, but medieval naval warfare was generally conducted without navies. Historians have been reluctant to confront the fact. In the British case, Sir William Laid Clowes in the 1890s began his history of the Royal Navy in the third century BC, though he believed that the Navy, as an institution, had been founded in the sixteenth century AD.[1] Even a modern publisher might hesitate at so wide a discrepancy between title and contents, yet a century after Laird Clowes, the *Oxford Illustrated History of the Royal Navy*[2] adopts the same approach on a slightly more modest scale, beginning eight hundred years before the foundation of the Royal Navy. The basic confusion arises from a refusal to acknowledge that navies, in our modern sense of the word, are a modern creation, a product of the early modern and modern state. Naval warfare existed long before navies, but it took other institutional forms.

We may distinguish at least six different forms of naval organisation that existed in Europe alone at various times before the seventeenth century: (1) Requisitioning, (2) Ship Musters, (3) Chartered Squadrons, (4) Local Navies, (5) Feudal Navies, and (6) Private Forces.

1. Requisitioning. The simplest of all forms of naval organisation, this called for the prince to use his authority to call up unmodified (and usually unpaid) merchant ships for war service. Once assembled, fleets of this sort were used

---

[1] *The Royal Navy: A History from the Earliest Times to the Present*, 7 vols. (London, 1897–1903).
[2] Ed. J. R. Hill (Oxford, 1995).

IV

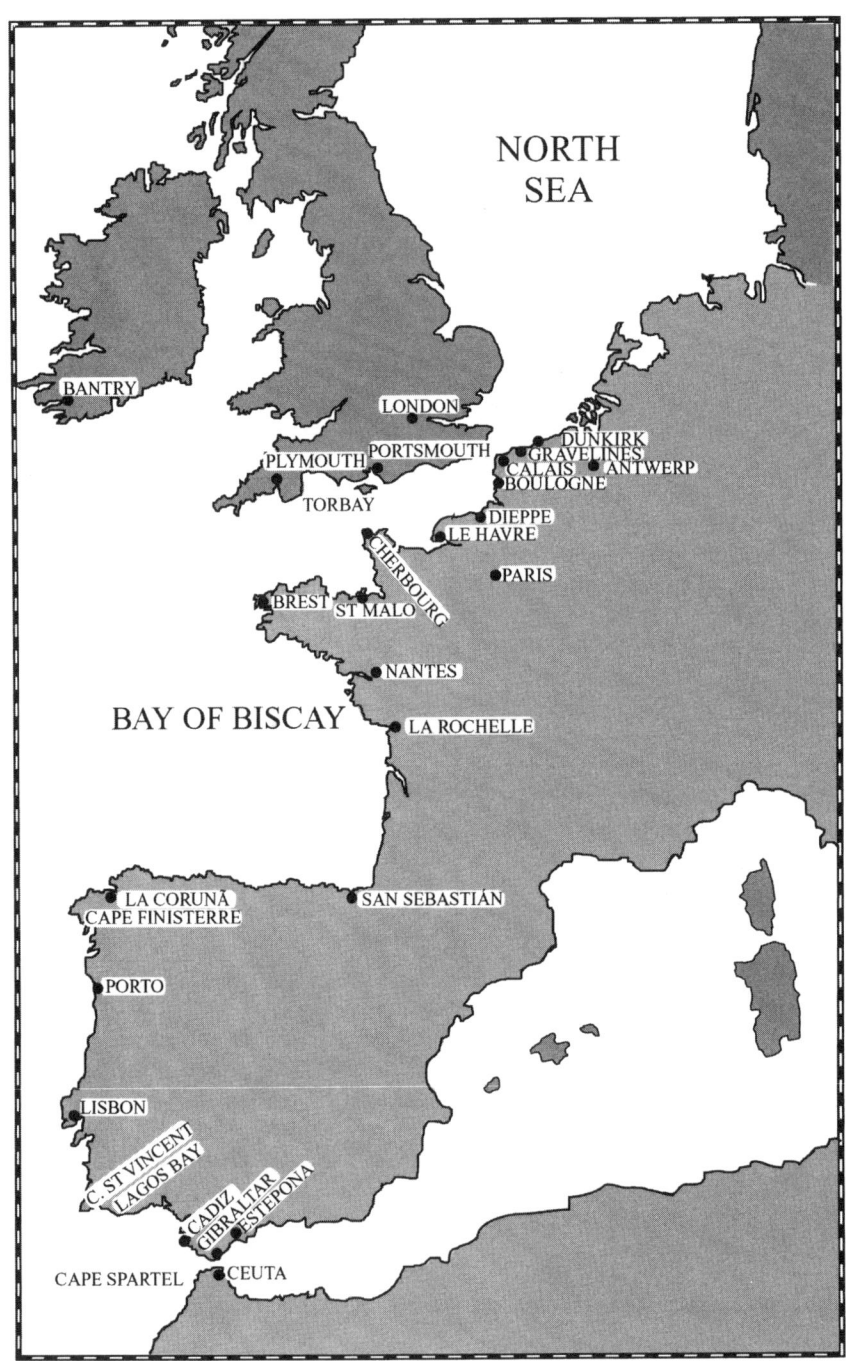

Map 1. The European Atlantic Coast

mainly to transport troops overseas, but the ships might also be fitted as 'warships', with 'castles' or fighting platforms, or simply by adding a number of soldiers to the usual crew. The system was incapable of providing any specialised warships, and it was extremely slow and cumbersome to operate, but it cost the prince very little and laid all the burden of naval war on his ship-owning subjects. This was the method by which medieval English kings assembled the large fleets that they needed to carry English armies overseas to France, Flanders, Scotland, Ireland and Wales.[3]

2. Ship Musters. In some countries, notably in Scandinavia but also in England before the Norman Conquest and in parts of the Celtic world, law or custom laid an obligation on coastal districts to build and man one or more warships each, available for national service in specified circumstances and for a fixed period. It is unclear to what extent, and when, the Scandinavian *leidang* existed as an operational force rather than a legal fiction, but the English equivalent certainly functioned in the tenth and eleventh centuries. Such a system was capable of providing a large national fleet of warships at no direct cost to the Crown, and with no known central organisation.[4]

3. Chartered Squadrons. Warships might be owned by private entrepreneurs who chartered their squadrons to the Crown, in some cases contracting to build as well as operate them. By this method the Crown subcontracted the organisational, and many of the operational requirements of naval warfare, retaining only the financial obligation to pay for them. Mediterranean galley fleets were often made up partly or wholly of such private squadrons, and Spain applied the same method to obtain the bulk of its naval forces in the Atlantic in the sixteenth century. The Genoese and Ragusans were noted specialists in this business, while Basque contractors built and owned much of the Spanish Atlantic fleet.[5]

4. Local Navies. Another approach to sea power was to create squadrons on the basis of local rather than national government. Provinces or individual seaports might organise their own forces, paid from their own revenues, to protect their

---

[3] N. A. M. Rodger, *The Safeguard of the Sea: A Naval History of Britain, Volume I: 660–1649* (London, 1997), 117–30, deals with the organisation of these English fleets.

[4] Rodger, *Safeguard of the Sea*, 23–7; Hans Kuhn, *Das altnordische Seekriegswesen*, ed. Sigrid Engeler and Dietrich Hofmann (Heidelberg, 1991), 54–87; Lucien Musset, 'Problèmes militaires du monde scandinave (VIIe–XIIe siècles)', in *Ordinamenti militari in Occidente nell'alto medievo* (Spoleto, 1968), 229–91, at 279–84; Niels Lund, 'The Armies of Swein Forkbeard and Cnut: *leding* or *lið*?', *Anglo-Saxon England*, 15 (1986), 105–18; Hugh Marwick, 'Naval Defence in Norse Scotland', *Scottish Historical Review*, 28 (1949), 1–11; John Bannerman, *Studies in the History of Dalriada* (Edinburgh, 1974), 140–1.

[5] Kenneth R. Andrews, *The Spanish Caribbean: Trade and Plunder 1530–1630* (New Haven, 1978), 90–4; Huguette and Pierre Chaunu, *Séville et l'Atlantique (1504–1650)*, 8 vols in 11 (Paris, 1955–9), VIII, i, 255–7; Francisco-Felipe Olesa Muñido, *La organización naval de los estados Mediterráneos y en especial de España durante los siglos XVI y XVII*, 2 vols (Madrid, 1968), I, 463–88; I. A. A. Thompson, *War and Government in Habsburg Spain 1560–1620* (London, 1976), 164–204 and 267–73; J. F. Guilmartin, *Gunpowder and Galleys: Changing Technology and Mediterranean Warfare at Sea in the Sixteenth Century* (Cambridge, 1974), 26–34.

own interests. Depending on the power of the centre, these might also be combined on occasion to form a national fleet. Renaissance Spain again is an outstanding example of this approach: it had at least eight navies operational at one time or another. The galleys of Castile were paid for from Castilian revenues, and the galleys of Aragon from Aragonese revenues; the ships of the *Guarda de Indias* were provided by the *Casa de Contratación* of Seville and paid for by the *avería* charged to the merchantmen which sailed under their convoy; the *Armada de Flandes* in the North Sea, the *Armada de Barlovento* in the Caribbean and the *Armada del Mar del Sur* in the Pacific were paid for by the local authorities. Only the Portuguese royal galleons (acquired by conquest in 1580) and the *Armada del Mar Océano* could be regarded as elements of a national fleet, albeit the latter was largely provided by contractors.[6] The Dutch adopted the same approach with greater success. Five provincial admiralties (nominally federal institutions but in practice dominated by local interests) each maintained a fleet and a naval establishment from their own taxation. Two great joint-stock companies, the East and West India Companies, each financed substantial naval forces from their shareholders' capital. Six individual seaports provided municipal navies (the '*directieschepen*') to protect their own shipping. All of these forces could coalesce in wartime to make up a national fleet, but not until 1653 did the Dutch Republic possess any ships that had been directly paid for out of central-government revenues and were unequivocally the property of the Republic, and not until 1795 did it have a single national naval organisation.[7]

5. Feudal Navies. It was possible for the military obligations of feudal or quasi-feudal systems to be discharged by naval service. In such a system landholders built and manned warships, which they were obliged to put to sea at their lord's command under specified conditions. Feudal naval service of this nature existed in Norman Sicily, and in the West Highlands and Western Isles of Scotland it provided the fleets that preserved into the seventeenth century the naval architecture and fighting traditions of the Viking Age.[8]

6. Private Forces. In the majority of countries private ship-owners built or used ships for warlike purposes on their own account. This might be done in wartime, and the ships might be combined with forces raised by other methods, but it was very often done in peacetime. To understand this to modern eyes anomalous or improper situation we need to discuss the objectives of medieval and Renaissance naval warfare.

Just as the forms of naval warfare have been confused, so also have been the

---

6   Ricardo Cerezo Martínez, *Las Armadas de Felipe II* (Madrid, 1988); José Luis Casada Soto, *Los barcos españoles del siglo XVI y la Gran Armada de 1588* (Madrid, 1988), 25–34.

7   J. R. Bruijn, *Varend Verleden: De Nederlandse Oorlogsvloot in de 17de en 18de eeuw* (Amsterdam, 1998).

8   D. P. Waley, ' "Combined Operations" in Sicily, A.D. 1060–78', *Papers of the British School at Rome*, 22 (1954), 118–25; Alexander Grant, 'Scotland's "Celtic Fringe" in the Late Middle Ages: The Macdonald Lords of the Isles and the Kingdom of Scotland', in *The British Isles 1100–1500: Comparisons, Contrasts and Connections*, ed. R. R. Davies (Edinburgh, 1988), 118–41.

functions. A modern navy is an instrument of the state, and in peace or war, it is employed about the purposes of the state. Modern navies therefore are political animals, and their objects are naturally and properly understood in political terms, as they have been by theorists from Mahan to our own times. Medieval and Renaissance sea power, however, was often private rather than public, and served commercial rather than political ends. Even the public, political objectives of naval warfare were not usually those about which naval theorists since Mahan have built their analyses. The concept of 'command of the sea' had been known in the classical world (the Greek is θαλασσωκρατος) and, consequently, it was known to educated medieval writers, but it was not often of practical relevance to the naval warfare of their time. Some medieval examples can be found of maritime warfare as it has been understood in the modern era: the wars of the Venetians and Genoese, fought for the control of the trade routes on which the belligerents depended for their prosperity, can be plausibly seen in quasi-Mahanian terms as a struggle for command of the sea.[9] To some extent the Baltic naval wars of the mid-sixteenth century could be fitted into the same mould.[10] This is unusual, however, anywhere in European naval warfare before the seventeenth century.

Most medieval naval warfare fell into one of two broad categories, which we may call public and private, or military and commercial. Public, military naval warfare was auxiliary to the operations of armies on land. The function of the ships was to transport the troops to the theatre of war, or to support their operations. This was the most important duty of galleys and other oared warships, which were essentially short-range instruments of amphibious warfare. Even when they did fight one another, they did so in a military fashion, commanded by soldiers, using military tactics. The prestige of the galley, which rose in the seventeenth century to be the supreme symbol of royal power even as it declined into insignificance as a practical warship, derived from its intimate association with armies, and consequently with princes.[11] Sailing ships did not have this connection or this status, but they too were frequently employed in this sort of warfare, both in the Mediterranean and in northern waters. This public, military, sea warfare, being an aspect of the warfare of armies and princes, was normally conducted at times of public, declared war between kingdoms.

Private or commercial naval warfare, on the other hand, was a normal aspect of the use of the sea at all times. The objective of the private ship-owner was business, but few if any medieval ship-owners could expect to make money without being willing to fight for it. Modern historians often present an implicitly dualist contrast between the peaceful trader and the aggressive pirate, but in

9   John E. Dotson, 'Naval Strategy in the First Genoese–Venetian War, 1257–1270', *American Neptune*, 46 (1986), 84–90.

10   Jan Glete, *Warfare at Sea, 1500–1650: Maritime Conflicts and the Transformation of Europe* (London, 2000), 133–44.

11   Marc Vigié, 'Galères et "Sea-power" en France au XVIIe siècle', *Revue historique des armées*, 182 (1991), 45–56.

medieval reality the two were usually the same. In northern waters the sea was often seen as a debatable land lying beyond the frontiers of settled society, where no sovereign could impose his peace, and no court had jurisdiction. Though at various periods English and French kings claimed some jurisdiction over the sea or those who used it, the claim was difficult or impossible to make good.[12] Robbery under arms was a normal aspect of sea-borne trade. All merchant ships went armed, and were prepared to gain a good cargo by paying for it or not, as opportunity might offer. There were no non-combatants at sea. Even in periods of profound peace, ships of rival nations, or simply rival ports, frequently attacked one another. For English ships, it appears to have been almost a reflex action to attack all foreigners; in the case of the Cinque Ports, to attack other English ships as well.[13] The English were the most notorious pirates of northern Europe, but all ships, of all nations, had to be prepared to fight on occasion.

Insofar as any legal cover was necessary for this private naval warfare, it could be found in the doctrine of reprisals. In such attacks the crews of the victims were usually murdered, but if the shipmaster or ship-owner survived, it was open to him to seek legal redress in the courts of the nation or seaport from which his attackers came. Such a suit was usually a civil action for the recovery of losses, not a criminal prosecution for assault or murder. In English law piracy was not even recognised as a crime until 1536, and English courts intervened, if at all, only to moderate a settlement between disputants whom they regarded as being essentially on the same footing. It was rare in any country for courts to treat suits between foreigners and locals with impartiality. The aggrieved ship-owner who had failed to gain legal redress, however, like the merchant or traveller who had been robbed by bandits ashore, could appeal to his own sovereign to grant him a letter of reprisal under marcher law, a *lettre de merk* in French, which authorised him to seize goods up to the value of his losses from the fellow-countrymen or fellow-citizens of those who had robbed him. Reprisals under marcher law were by definition available only in time of peace; they assumed, however unrealistically, that the attack had been improper and that foreign courts were open to a suit for redress. Reprisals might be a diplomatic weapon in a time of tension between princes, but there was no reason in theory or practice why they could not coexist with peace and good international relations. Kings were not necessarily much interested in the private misfortunes of their trading subjects. Then as now, legal disputes between persons of different nationality did not oblige their governments to go to war on their behalf. Reprisals allowed a legal dispute to issue in private war, but this private war remained private, not public.[14]

[12] Rodger, *Safeguard of the Sea*, 78–9.
[13] N. A. M. Rodger, 'The Naval Service of the Cinque Ports', *English Historical Review*, 111 (1996), 636–51, at 646–7.
[14] D. A. Gardiner, 'The History of Belligerent Rights on the High Seas in the Fourteenth Century', *Law Quarterly Review*, 48 (1932), 521–46. René de Mas Latrie, 'Du droit de

In the Mediterranean world there existed from the sixteenth to the nineteenth centuries a different system of private naval war, the *corsa* of the North African Regencies. Often misrepresented by English-speaking historians as 'Barbary piracy', their naval warfare was by no means piratical either in its legal status or its structure. The three Regencies of Tunis, Tripoli and Algiers engaged in open, public war against some Christian powers, and observed treaties of peace with others, generally with a more scrupulous regard for their obligations than the Christian powers showed in return. It was necessary for them to maintain permanent war against at least some of the trading nations of the Mediterranean for political rather than economic reasons. The Turkish Janissary garrisons of these quasi-independent states, nominally subject to the Ottoman Empire, were the leading factor in their internal politics, accustomed to make and unmake (meaning murder) the local rulers with uncomfortable frequency. The *corsa* provided a harmless and profitable outlet for their energies, which kept them out of mischief at home. Thus the naval warfare of the Barbary States, though declared public war, was largely or entirely conducted by private interests. It was a permanent necessity generated by the internal political structure of the Regencies, not a temporary response to external threats or opportunities. Moreover it differed from other private naval warfare in that the principal profit came not from ships or goods but people. Slaving, in turn, required and depended on extensive trade between enemies, for only poor and friendless slaves were retained in the labour force. The best profits were made by selling slaves for ransom, or trading them for Muslims enslaved by the Christian counter-*corsa* practised by the Knights of Malta, the Knights of St Stephen and other Christian navies. This traffic was made possible by slave markets on both sides of the Mediterranean, linked by extensive commercial and diplomatic contacts. The *corsa* differed from the naval traditions of the northern Europeans, but it had a similar effect in generating a system of warfare that blended symbiotically with trade. Though native to the Mediterranean, it was extended to the eastern Atlantic and even the Channel in the late sixteenth century, mainly by the Algerines.[15]

The *corsa* of the Regencies should in turn be distinguished from the activities

---

marque ou droit de représailles au Moyen Âge', *Bibliothèque de l'École des chartes*, 27 (1866), 529–77, and 29 (1868), 294–347 and 612–35; Marie-Claire Chavarot, 'La Pratique des lettres de marque d'après les arrêts du Parlement (XIIIe–debut XVe siècle)', *Bibliothèque de l'École des chartes*, 149 (1981), 51–89; Pierre Chaplais, 'Règlement des conflits internationaux franco-anglais au XIVe siècle (1293–1377)', *Le Moyen Age*, 57 (1951), 259–302; Florence E. Dyer, 'Reprisals in the Sixteenth Century', *Mariner's Mirror*, 21 (1935), 187–97; *Documents Relating to Law and Custom of the Sea*. Navy Records Society 49 and 50, ed. R. G. Marsden (1915–16), I, 119–24.

[15] Sir Godfrey Fisher, *Barbary Legend: War, Trade and Piracy in North Africa 1415–1830* (Oxford, 1957); Peter Earle, *Corsairs of Malta and Barbary* (London, 1970); J. de Courcy Ireland, 'The Corsairs of North Africa', *Mariner's Mirror*, 62 (1976), 271–83; *El comerç alternatiu: corsarisme i contraban (ss. XV–XVIII)*, ed. Gonçal López Nadal (Palma de Mallorca, 1990).

of Salee and other Moroccan Atlantic ports. They were not subject to the Sultan, nor affected by the same internal political pressure, but for long periods under weak or non-existent political control by the Moroccan emperor, and heirs to a private war against Spain and Portugal in particular. The style and legal status of this warfare fell midway between the *corsa* of the Mediterranean and the traditional private war of northern waters, while the cruising range of the Saletines reached far into both seas.[16]

Private, commercial war was fought by individuals for financial profit, not by states for political objectives. Medieval and Renaissance princes might find themselves in either category. Often they made war for identifiably political objectives, usually the conquest of territory, and their accompanying naval operations, if any, fell into the public, military category. But in political theory a Renaissance prince was simply an exceptionally great nobleman who was expected to support his state from his own revenues. Like his subjects, he badly needed to make money, and like them, he might engage in private, commercial war. Even at times of open war between princes, private operations might take place alongside public ones. The Anglo-Spanish War of 1585–1603, which was never formally declared on either side, was waged from the point of view of English law as a campaign of reprisals, in which Queen Elizabeth participated as an aggrieved party like her subjects. Though her primary objective (survival) was unequivocally political, she had an urgent need to make money to finance the war.

The legal regime of reprisals has been easily and frequently confused with the quite different system of privateering, as developed in English law in the mid-seventeenth century.[17] A privateer was a privately owned warship licensed in time of open war to attack the shipping of the public enemy.[18] As the name implies, a privateer was the private exception to what had become the public rule: it was inherent in the concept of privateering that ships not owned by the state might not legitimately engage in warfare, even in wartime, without licence. Warfare had become an exclusive activity of state; a formal, public undertaking entered into by a prince for a limited period, and concluded with proper ceremony. Privateering belonged to an entirely different legal and strategic system that evolved during the seventeenth century. There could be no privateering in the Elizabethan age or earlier, because there was no private exception; private, commercial warfare was the normal form of warfare in the open sea. Unfortu-

---

16 Roger Coindreau, *Les Corsaires de Salé* (Paris, 1948).

17 But English law was slow in this respect. The Flemish or Dutch *kaperbrief*, for example, provided for privateering roughly in the modern sense from the late fifteenth century: Louis Sicking, *Zeemacht en Onmacht: Maritieme politiek in de Nederlanden 1488–1558* (Amsterdam, 1998), 214–21; C. G. Roelofsen, 'Grotius and the International Politics of the Seventeenth Century', in *Hugo Grotius and International Relations*, ed. H. Bull, B. Kingsbury and A. Roberts (Oxford, 1990), 95–131; L. H. J. Sicking, 'Recht aan zee. De afhandeling van prijszaken na het bestand van Bomy en de Vrede van Nice met Frankrijk (1537–1538)', *Stichting tot uitgaaf der bronnen van het Oud-Vaterlandse Recht: verslagen en mededelingen*, n.s. 10 (1999), 163–80. I am indebted to Dr Sicking for a copy of this article.

18 David J. Starkey, *British Privateering Enterprise in the Eighteenth Century* (Exeter, 1990), 19–34.

nately the English jurists who devised the concept of privateering used the old term to name their new licences: they called them 'letters of marque'. It cannot be too strongly emphasised that the '*lettre de merk*' and the 'letter of marque' were entirely different things. However often we may speak or write of 'Elizabethan privateers', the term is strictly anachronistic; there were no privateers in the sixteenth century.

In this and other aspects, however, this was a period of transition, in which the naval traditions of the Middle Ages developed and combined to create new forms of warfare at sea. It was a period of rapid technical change, in which ideas and terminology were in a state of flux. Contemporaries reached into the past in search of words and ideas with which to make sense of their situation, with limited success. Later historians attempted, and sometimes still attempt, to force the sixteenth century into the framework so familiar from the eighteenth.

Moreover the problem was not simply one of rapid change over time, reflected in anachronistic words and concepts. Geography was changing as well as technology. As Spain and Portugal expanded from the Mediterranean to the 'Mediterranean Atlantic' and thence to the transatlantic world, they carried the language and ideas of the Mediterranean into a different geographical and political situation. There in due course they came into collision with French, English and Dutch seamen who themselves were venturing into a new geographical space, a new legal and political context, armed with attitudes and concepts derived from the naval warfare of late medieval northern Europe. At the same time the *corsa* of the North African Regencies, and the raids of Salee, extended from the Mediterranean to cover most of the Atlantic world, and in the early seventeenth century blended with the quite different private warfare of the English to create a unique, and for a while uniquely effective, hybrid form of naval warfare. Thus words and ideas borrowed from the past were mixed with words and ideas borrowed from other cultures, all subjected to extensive mistranslation by contemporaries, and extensive misconstruction by later historians.

In the sixteenth century, the Atlantic, the Mediterranean and northern Europe collided. The northerners brought the private, commercial style of war, combined with the new three-masted ship rig to give an instrument of much greater range and power than had been available to private owners before. The Mediterranean powers, above all Spain, brought the public, military tradition of naval warfare. They also attempted to apply the legal regime of the Mediterranean to the Atlantic. Where seafaring was seasonal and coastal, the passage of ships could be controlled and taxed in much the same way as the passage of merchants was controlled and taxed ashore. Coastal fortresses such as Monaco, Villafranca, Gibraltar, Piombino, Amalfi, Messina, Durazzo, Cerigo, Monemvasia, Rhodes and hundreds of others divided the sea into jurisdictions like the land.[19] Whereas the northern seas were effectively lawless, the southern seas were subject to local and national government.

---

[19] Fernand Braudel, *The Mediterranean and the Mediterranean World in the Age of Philip II*, 2 vols, trans. Siân Reynolds (London, 1972), I, 103–8.

This legal tradition was completely disconnected from the geographical and technical realities of the Atlantic. For a time Spaniards and Portuguese were the only deep-sea navigators in the world and their new empires were protected by distance, but by the 1540s French and Scottish ships were already crossing the Atlantic, followed a generation later by the English, and later the Dutch. There was no possible physical barrier that could prevent foreigners penetrating into the waters from which they were excluded by Spanish and Portuguese law. Spain did not simply reserve her colonial trade to her own shipping, as other colonial powers were to do; she pretended to forbid all foreign presence, even under pain of death. Moreover Spain's object was not to preserve a flourishing commerce in her own hands, as the Dutch and English were to do. The Spanish colonial system was not directed to promoting or preserving any sort of trade; it was designed solely to protect the flow of bullion. It served the private interests of the monarch, not the public interest of his people. Trade was permitted to use the convoys to reach the ports which they served, but almost nothing was done for the rest of the Spanish empire. Many Spanish colonial ports had in practice no legal means of exporting or importing anything. As the official convoy system declined, even the major ports ceased to have any legal trade. In 1707, the newly appointed Viceroy of Peru reported that it was more than ten years since his government (the whole of Spanish South America) had had any official trading contact with Spain.[20] This was an anti-colonial policy. The object was to preserve the Empire intact from the taint of foreign contact at any price. The Spanish government was even prepared to destroy and depopulate a colony (the northern part of Hispaniola in 1604) rather than see its people profit in any way from foreign contact.[21] The policy can perhaps best be understood in terms of the drive for *limpieza de sangre*, 'purity of blood', which marked Spain's internal policies in this era. The effect of the law was to criminalise all foreign activity or presence. Until 1670 Spain explicitly denied that any of her treaties with foreign powers had force west of the Azores or south of the Tropic of Capricorn. As a consequence there was literally 'no peace beyond the line', and no restraint on the activities of foreigners whom Spain had made outlaws.[22] By attempting to apply an inappropriate and unenforceable legal system to its over-seas empire, the Spanish Crown contributed powerfully to justify and perpetuate a style of mingled war and trade in which violence, or the threat of violence, was always present. Thus, the medieval northern form of private, commercial warfare was artificially preserved long after it had disappeared from European waters. The raiders of the sixteenth century, and the buccaneers of the seven-teenth, were not simply the offspring of Spanish colonial policy, but that policy acted to promote and prolong their activities, and to prevent them settling into

---

[20] Henry Kamen, *The War of Succession in Spain 1700–15* (London, 1969), 145.

[21] Andrews, *The Spanish Caribbean*, 208–10; K. R. Andrews, *Elizabethan Privateering: English Privateering during the Spanish War, 1585–1603* (Cambridge, 1964), 183–4.

[22] A. P. Thornton, *West-India Policy under the Restoration* (Oxford, 1956), 76–7, 87, 97–101 and 122–3.

peaceful channels.[23] In particular it gave the English, later British and Dutch, governments powerful and plausibly legitimate reasons for supporting violence, which they would otherwise have cooperated to suppress. This issue brought Britain and Spain to war as late as 1739, more than a century after the English government had turned against all other forms of piracy.

While Spain carried the public, military tradition of naval warfare from the medieval Mediterranean to the sixteenth-century Atlantic, the Barbary 'pirates' spread their tradition of private, commercial war. Both the Regencies and the Moroccan ports were affected in the late sixteenth century by northern European influence. Christian renegades who had 'turned Turk' helped the Muslim fleets to adopt sailing ships in place of galleys, greatly increasing their cruising range and putting both coasts of the North Atlantic at risk of slave raids virtually from the Equator to the Arctic. Next, some northern pirates, chiefly English, started to operate out of Muslim ports, with the agreement of the local authorities. This movement reached its apogee after the Anglo-Spanish peace of 1603, and the accession of James VI and I the same year, which turned adrift many ships and men, especially in the West Country, who had been employed in raiding the Spanish Empire, and gradually made English ports less comfortable bases for private war. For about fifteen years Moroccan ports, especially Mamora and Sallee, became the winter bases of English raiders who in summer worked from West Country or Irish ports, and who combined the attack on Spanish ports and shipping to which they had long been accustomed with the slave-raiding they learnt from the *corsa*.[24] The most famous of these pirates was the lexicographer Sir Henry Manwaring. A maker of dictionaries, but by no means a harmless drudge, Sir Henry was in his day the most feared man in the North Atlantic.[25]

Thus the naval warfare of northern Europe and the Atlantic in the sixteenth century was shaped by the collision and mingling of public and private naval warfare in both their northern and southern versions. This alone would have been sufficient to generate a great deal of novelty and confusion, but there were several other new factors affecting, and changing, the nature of naval war. First among these was the fracture of the Christian world, and the civil wars that followed in several European states. Religion, which had always been a factor in the naval warfare of the Mediterranean, now influenced war at sea in northern waters as well. In particular there was in practice, though not in theological principle, a powerful connection between Calvinism and private naval war. The French Atlantic and Channel ports, especially Dieppe and La Rochelle, were

---

23 Andrews, *The Spanish Caribbean*, 74–80 and 208–22; R. H. Boulind, 'The Strength and Weakness of Spanish Control of the Caribbean, 1520–1650: The Case for the *Armada de Barlovento*' (Ph.D. dissertation, University of Cambridge, 1965), 61–5 and 405–10.
24 C. M. Senior, *A Nation of Pirates: English Piracy in Its Heyday* (Newton Abbot, 1976); D. D. Hebb, *Piracy and the English Government, 1616–1642* (Aldershot, 1994); Christopher Lloyd, *English Corsairs on the Barbary Coast* (London, 1981).
25 *The Life and Works of Sir Henry Mainwaring.* Navy Records Society 54 and 56, ed. G. E. Manwaring and W. G. Perrin (1920–2).

both Huguenot strongholds and the centres of a school of navigators, pilots and cartographers who were the first Christians outside Iberia to learn the skills necessary for oceanic naval warfare. Joined at an early stage by Scottish ships and navigators, these men expressed their religious sympathies and professional skills by mounting the first raids on the Spanish Empire. When the Wars of Religion broke out in France, the Protestant cause was heavily supported by the profits of private war conducted under the cover of letters of reprisal issued by Huguenot leaders like Condé and Coligny (as Admiral of France). By the 1560s the English, especially the West Countrymen, were keen participants in this war, sailing under French letters of reprisal, and learning the professional skills of their new allies.[26] A generation later the Dutch in turn attached themselves to the Calvinist International, sailing out of English ports under letters of reprisal issued by the Prince of Orange, and learning from the English the techniques of navigation which they themselves had but lately acquired. The break-up of kingdoms and empires multiplied the number of leaders willing, indeed desperate, to finance their war-effort and assure their survival by issuing letters of reprisal. The legal mechanism itself was easily flexible enough to accommodate itself to civil war and rebellion, while religious hatred endowed it with renewed moral legitimacy. The experiment of 'general reprisals' under proclamation, which permitted any ship to make any prizes of a named enemy without any restriction or supervision, was tried by the English three times, in 1544, 1557 and 1563,[27] but it proved unsatisfactory: indiscriminate, uncontrollable, and barely distinguishable from a public declaration of war, it carried heavy diplomatic and commercial penalties. The ambiguity, flexibility and profitability of private war much better suited the situation of the English, Huguenots and Dutch.

Overlaying all these changes in the motives and contexts of naval warfare were developments in ships and weapons. The forms of naval warfare, both in northern waters and in the Mediterranean, had remained more or less stable for several centuries, and were not essentially changed by the introduction of 'man-killing' guns in the fourteenth century. So long as all fighting was hand to hand, the size of sailing ships gave them an overwhelming advantage over galleys, with their exposed crews and low freeboard. As a result the two types did not often face one another in action, but fulfilled distinct roles in different forms of naval warfare. The galley was the instrument of coastal operations, raids and landings. Wherever shallow draught was essential and short range no obstacle, galleys were the natural choice. For long passages in the open sea, for carrying men and goods in quantity, and for fighting other ships, sailing ships, and above all the great carracks developed in the fifteenth century, were essential. When a ship fought at sea, the first necessity was to gain the weather gage,

---

[26] Martine Acerra and Guy Martinière, eds, *Coligny, les protestants et la mer* (Paris, 1997); N. A. M. Rodger, 'The Myth of Seapower in English Politics, 1568–1815' (forthcoming); Brian Dietz, 'The Huguenot and English Corsairs during the Third Civil War in France, 1568 to 1570', *Proceedings of the Huguenot Society*, 19 (1952–58), 278–94.

[27] Marsden, *Law and Custom of the Sea*, I, 155–8, 162–5 and 174.

from which position she bore up to attack. All available missile weapons, including guns, were fired as the two ships closed, and as they grappled together the issue was settled by hand-to-hand fighting.[28]

I have argued elsewhere that the adoption of the heavy gun by galleys about the beginning of the sixteenth century caused a crisis in naval warfare. By allowing galleys to engage and even sink ships outside small-arms range, it rendered them obsolete, without providing any effective alternative. The challenge for ship designers was now to devise an effective counter to the galley. The problem was much more acute in northern waters, for the limited range and sea-keeping capacity of the galley were much more serious disadvantages in these open seas. Moreover the adoption of the heavy gun pushed galleys to adopt the *a scaloccio* oaring system, which further reduced their speed and range, while increasing the demand for oarsmen which the northern powers (with no tradition of the *corsa* and no slave markets) found it impossible to meet.[29] Those who had very lately developed the three-masted ship rig, who had experience of the novel combination of power and manoeuvrability which it provided, were not prepared to abandon it in favour of oars. Their requirement was to combine two apparently incompatible novelties: the ahead-firing heavy gun which gave the galley its uncontestable military superiority, and the new ship rig whose speed and power made ocean passages possible. They were not looking for just any method of mounting heavy guns in a sailing ship, but one in particular. By the early years of the sixteenth century if not before, ships already carried stern-firing heavy guns in their gunrooms, and were beginning to mount some lighter pieces below decks on the broadside. But there was no method of attacking the enemy while sailing astern or sideways. Moreover contemporaries wanted to sink ships, as galleys could, by firing at the waterline, and at the very short fighting ranges of the period this required the gun itself to be mounted low.[30]

I believe that the solution to this problem was the development, apparently between the 1530s and 1550s, of the galleon. The essence of the galleon seems to have been the bow and lines of a galley, grafted onto the stern and hull structure of a ship, giving the characteristic crescent shape of the true galleon. This preserved and indeed improved the speed and endurance of the ship rig, while mounting a heavy armament of ahead-firing guns. The galleon could beat the galley at her own game, without sacrificing the capacity to make long sea passages at high speed. How and where the galleon first emerged is as yet obscure. It may have been in England, Scotland, Portugal, Denmark, Venice, Genoa or elsewhere. What is reasonably clear is that the new type was rapidly

---

[28] N. A. M. Rodger, 'The Development of Broadside Gunnery, 1450–1650', *Mariner's Mirror*, 82 (1996), 301–24, at 302.

[29] Francisco-Felipe Olesa Muñido, *La galera en la navegación y el combate*, 2 vols (Madrid, 1971). Mauro Bondioli, René Burlet and André Zysberg, 'Oar Mechanics and Oar Power in Medieval and Later Galleys', in *The Age of the Galley: Mediterranean Oared Vessels since Pre-Classical Times*, ed. John Morrison (London, 1995), 172–205.

[30] Rodger, 'Broadside Gunnery', 303.

246

adopted by the Huguenots and the English, and formed a key element in their style of private, commercial warfare. These fast warships with their heavy armament, fine lines but limited stowage were designed to overwhelm the defences of individual merchantmen, convoys, and coastal forts, while avoiding close action with powerful forces. They suited those who penetrated the Spanish Empire to conduct raids or illegal trade, not those who sustained distant colonies and oceanic commerce themselves. They were better adapted to disrupting command of the sea than to gaining or keeping it. Though they were in structural terms the first true sailing warships and the ancestors of the eighteenth-century ship of the line, in function they were the last and most effective exponents of medieval private, commercial war.[31]

For these and other reasons the type, though successful, was also transitional. Though Huguenot sea power disappeared, the English and Dutch prospered by naval war against Spain. Soon they themselves were possessors, with rich home and colonial trades to conduct and protect, with waters of their own from which they aspired to exclude foreign traders. First the Dutch and then the English ceased to sponsor and began to suppress the private warfare of their subjects. In England the old style of warfare was briefly revived during the Civil Wars, partly because the Protestant radicals who created the English Republic warmly embraced the ideology of their Elizabethan predecessors. By the 1660s, however, the sixteenth-century style of naval warfare, the tactics and ship designs associated with it, were extinct everywhere except in the Caribbean. Only the word 'galleon' survived to be used with ever-decreasing precision down to our own day.

This has been the fate the naval warfare of the period as a whole; that is, to be dressed in clothes of the wrong period. Treating peace and war as mutually exclusive and coterminous categories, historians have described naval warfare in 'peacetime' as piracy, and private men-of-war in 'wartime' as 'privateers'. In reality war and peace were blended in various ways which have no modern parallels, and for which modern languages provide an inadequate vocabulary. There was, for example, and to an extent there still is a meaningless controversy as to whether Sir Francis Drake was or was not a 'pirate'.[32] This arose from the discomfort of Victorian popular writers like Charles Kingsley and Sir Henry Newbolt at the suggestion that their model of manly Christian heroism might have been a common criminal. It was an entirely bogus controversy, setting a figure who never existed against anachronistic legal and moral criteria, and it rested on mistranslation, the assumption that Drake's Spanish contemporaries had accused him of being a pirate, whereas they usually used the word *corsario*, not *pirata*. *Corsario* itself, of course, is a borrowing from another context, but it

---

[31] Ibid., 305–6; and Rodger, 'Guns and Sails in the First Phase of English Colonization, 1500–1650', in *The Oxford History of the British Empire, Volume I: The Origins of Empire*, ed. Nicholas Canny (Oxford, 1998), 79–98, at 82–8 and 96–87.

[32] It has been revived by Drake's latest biographer: Harry Kelsey, *Sir Francis Drake: The Queen's Pirate* (New Haven, 1998).

is an intelligent adaptation of a word that does convey much of the style of warfare Drake undertook. Unfortunately the English word 'corsair' is now so encrusted with spurious Byronic romanticism that it is probably irrecoverable for any serious purpose. Moreover English historians have long been accustomed to echo the error of the Frenchmen who first applied the phrase *guerre de course* to the very different legal and strategic situation of seventeenth and eighteenth-century privateering – and thus made it harder to describe the *corsa* itself with any clarity.

Thus the limitations of language continue to baffle our attempts to understand the sixteenth century at sea, and it continues to be treated as a sort of historical junk-room from which historians may borrow all sorts of scraps to construct ambitious intellectual edifices. It has long been customary to see the period through eighteenth-century spectacles. Indeed it is often analysed in terms of categories which themselves are anachronistic constructs developed in the late nineteenth century in order to understand the eighteenth. In recent years attempts have been made to discover the line of battle in the sixteenth century and even earlier, generally by reading any use of the word 'line' (not even 'line ahead') to mean 'line of battle', in one case with the help of terminology apparently borrowed from fighter-aircraft tactics.[33] This ruthless perversion of language and confusion of ideas makes it impossible to speak or write clearly about a period of rapid change to which many of our natural modern assumptions are inapplicable. No prince or state then possessed or claimed any monopoly on the use of force, which remained a normal means of settling all sorts of private as well as public disputes. The distinction between sailing warships and merchantmen was only beginning to emerge, because, under sail at least, war and trade were still usually combined. None of these circumstances can easily be accommodated to our preconceptions or our terminology. We shall never understand this period until we cease to stage it in modern dress.

Additional Note [2009]

Although there has been a good deal of writing in recent years on naval warfare in the Renaissance era, much of it is still undermined by a failure to think clearly about the contemporary meanings of words and ideas, and a fatal tendency to impose anachronistic modern concepts. This article, which goes beyond what I wrote in *The Safeguard of the Sea* in 1997, is an attempt to provide a theory, or at least a typology, of war at sea in this period.

---

[33] William Maltby, 'Politics, Professionalism, and the Evolution of Sailing-Ship Tactics, 1650–1714', in John A. Lynn, ed., *Tools of War: Instruments, Ideas and Institutions of Warfare, 1445–1871* (Urbana, Illinois, 1990), 53–73; Rodger, 'Broadside Gunnery', 301–2.

V

The military revolution at sea[1]

Historians and political scientists have long been interested in the rise of the modern state, and have very frequently connected it with what Michael Roberts called the 'Military Revolution'. At its crudest, the idea he popularised is that at a date usually located in or around the sixteenth century, armies became very much larger and more costly, subjecting the states which sought to raise them to severe strains. Many early modern states failed to meet this challenge, were conquered, absorbed or marginalised. A few succeeded in generating the permanent tax-raising powers needed to sustain modern armies, and so become the great military powers of modern Europe. These powers – France, Prussia, Sweden, sometimes Russia, Austria and even Spain are usually cited – are often described as having followed a particular route to modernity, sweeping away the archaic medieval representative institutions which had hampered the power of princes, and becoming autocratic, centralised and bureaucratic powers in which the power of the state had the full play necessary to meet the military and governmental challenges of the modern world.

There seems to be a number of difficulties inherent in this approach. By focusing attention on the rise of the great powers, it implicitly assumes that only power and success are of interest to history. Political scientists in particular, seeking to identify the two (or, in the more sophisticated versions, three) variables which explain the rise of the great powers, have largely ignored the experience of states and nations which did not succeed, or succeeded in different ways.[2] Moreover the concept of the 'military revolution' explains the fate of nations by reference to the form and functions of government. It assumes that the state shaped society, rather than society the state. Finally, historians have with few exceptions considered only armies, not navies.[3] This is beginning to change, but it is still possible to read eminent historians comparing Britain and Prussia as military powers who are apparently quite unaware that the British navy had any historical importance, or indeed had ever existed.[4]

Broadening the perspective to consider small and transient states as well as great powers, naval as well as military influences on them, and society as much as government, draws our attention to states which seem to have been formed in very different ways. Genoa, for example, no longer survives as an independent state, let alone as a mother of states, and yet medieval Genoese seapower gave rise to several naval republics. Some of them were not very far from here, on Aegean islands;[5] and one of them, Monaco, still survives as a mute witness to the Genoese seapower of the thirteenth and fourteenth centuries.[6]

Considering states which never became great powers teaches us, among other things, that modernity and bureaucracy in central government are not necessarily sufficient for success. In 1588, for example, one of the best-known of European states radically reformed its system of government, sweeping away the untidy mixture of offices and institutions inherited from the Middle Ages, and replacing them with a coherent and logical system of fifteen boards or departments which divided the business of government on functional lines, each department headed by a minister responsible to his sovereign for its affairs. It was then a unique approach to government, and it has since become universal, which makes it curious that so influential a development has been so little studied. The state in question is of course the Papal State, and it is Sixtus V's great constitution *Immensa aeterni Dei* which ushers in the modern era of government.[7] If the organisation of the state was what was required to make a great power, the Pope's divisions should have dominated Europe. Reality, as we know, was different. The Papal State, admirably equipped for greatness at the level of central government, nevertheless lacked many of the essential requirements of a modern state.[8]

Just as the Papal State was being refounded, another European state was struggling into existence, and organizing its nascent naval forces, with very few of the blessings of good government provided by Sixtus V. The Dutch Republic in over two centuries of existence never managed to agree on a permanent constitution to replace the temporary political arrangements with which it had begun. Its navy, or rather navies, consisted of a large number of more or less independent organizations.[9] Five provincial admiralties (notionally federal institutions, but in practice dominated by local interests) each maintained from their own revenues a fleet, an establishment of officers, and one or more naval yards. The two great joint stock companies, the East and West India Companies, each possessed substantial numbers of men-of-war. A number of individual seaports provided municipal navies (the 'directieschepen') to protect their own shipping. Private syndicates, especially in Zealand, commissioned squadrons of privateers to prey on enemy shipping. None of these were directly controlled by the central government – indeed it is not obvious that the 'Generaliteit' of the Dutch Republic can be called a central government in the ordinary acceptance of the phrase, when it had no ministers, or ministries, and hardly any permanent national institutions. Sovereign authority resided in the States-General, when it was in session, but the assembly itself consisted of delegates (not representatives) who could not act without a mandate from their principals, the provincial estates, which in turn were obliged to consult their electors before reaching a decision. No political scientist could possibly accept such a government as a plausible candidate for the military revolution, or even the modern world. Yet it was this system which created one of the foremost of the new armies of the sixteenth century, and by 1639 had made the United Provinces the leading European naval power. Not until 1654 did it acquire its first national fleet, paid for out of national revenues and unequivocally the property of the Republic – though even then the fleet formed but a part of the available naval forces, and its actual building and operation was perforce entrusted to the provincial admiralties, since the state possessed no other naval administration. Such a republic, where government was an abstract noun, where authority was endlessly divided and disputed, seems to historians today and seemed to many observers then to be completely unfitted for survival in a competitive world. Yet here again, theory and practice were very different.

By the mid-seventeenth century, there was another great power in Europe, one which deployed a first-class army and navy in spite of lacking most of the obvious requirements of a great power. Sweden was a poor and marginal country with a small population and no significant shipping interest. So far from being dominated by a powerful monarch, Sweden experienced a twelve-year regency from 1632 to 1644, followed by the reign of a woman, Queen Christina. Certainly her father Gustaf Adolf had been a great military leader and tactical innovator, but it was not absolutist power which enabled him to mobilize Sweden's resources. On the contrary, the rise of the Vasa dynasty to national and international power depended on creating a representative institution, the Riksdag, which incorporated the aristocracy and gave them a strong interest in the state. This was not so much an imposition of royal power as a dispersal of it. The state also developed efficient systems of local taxation and military mobilisation which were built from below rather than imposed from above, and which rested on a large measure of co-operation and consensus. In the 1640s and 50s, at the same time as aristocratic and popular revolts were tearing apart France, Spain and England, the Swedish political system was smoothly coping with a royal minority, the rule and subsequent abdication of a queen, and the accession of a new dynasty. At the same time it made possible a high level of effective taxation, by which a poor country with a small population supported the army and navy of a first-class power.[10]

It has not entirely escaped historians' notice that the Dutch, the Swedes and finally the British rose to the status of great powers; the Dutch without much that could be described as a central government, the British without much that could be called an army, and none of them with large populations or despotic forms of government. Attempts have therefore been made to explain, or at least to explain away, these apparent exceptions from the rule that the demands of the military revolution created centralised, autocratic or bureaucratic military powers. The sea itself has always been a favourite explanation, allegedly making England 'invasion-proof', and allowing it the luxury of retarded development until at length it became wealthy enough to support both a navy and a first-class army – the latter implicitly constituting the admission ticket to the great powers' club.[11] Unfortunately there are several difficulties with this theory. In reality the sea was never in the least impassable; certainly not by the standards of early modern roads. Until, and indeed for some time after, the English developed effective naval forces, the country was repeatedly invaded by sea. English governments have been overthrown by seaborne invasions at least nine times since the Norman Conquest: in 1139, 1153,[12] 1326, 1399, 1460, 1470, 1471, 1485 and 1688; to which should be added the 1332 invasion of Scotland, and at least seven other successful landings of major forces in England (in 1069, 1101, 1215, 1405, 1462, 1469 and 1487) which went on to campaign but did not overthrow the regime. These figures take no account of lesser raids and landings, or of seaborne assistance against England sent to Wales, Scotland or to English rebels; they ignore all expeditions which did not succeed in putting troops ashore, and they do not include landings of any kind in Ireland.[13] Countries like Spain which were protected by high mountains might genuinely claim to be insulated by geography from the military revolution, but England could not, and still less Sweden or the Netherlands. Nor is it in the least persuasive to argue that the English navy did not exist, or did not cost very much, or did not experience any significant technical developments, until the country was already a wealthy great power.[14] On the contrary, it is abundantly clear that a real 'naval revolution', both technical and administrative, took place in England in the mid-sixteenth century, which posed an enormous challenge for the essentially medieval structure of English government.[15] Though Queen Elizabeth's income was no higher in real terms than that of her medieval predecessors, in wartime she regularly spent one-third of it on her Navy,[16] and this high expenditure was no passing fancy but a sustained long-term national policy. It was established well before England had a large merchant fleet, or any significant oceanic trade, or any distant colonies. Certainly naval expenditure placed immense strains on the English political system, and contributed substantially to its collapse in the 1640s. In that sense England was indeed one of the casualties of the military revolution.[17] In the event, however, the country, and its constitution, and its navy, survived the crisis and emerged from it greatly strengthened, but even less autocratic than before. The Dutch had meanwhile become the world's leading naval power, surmounting in the process immense technical, administrative and financial obstacles, entirely without a national navy and almost without a national government. What England, the Netherlands and Sweden had in common was a structure of government which required an unusually large degree of consent and co-operation by the governed, and permitted a much higher level of effective 'resource extraction', through the medium of taxation, loans and private participation in the national war effort.

We must be absolutely clear that maintaining even a small permanent navy was (and indeed still is) extremely complex, costly and demanding. The industrial, technical and managerial resources required to build and operate warships vastly exceeded in kind and quality anything needed by an early modern army. In the 1560s the manufacture of hand guns was still a cottage industry and the casting of heavy guns (invariably in bronze) a luxury business for the gratification of princes. Yet in England the Ordnance Board had already spent thirty years and considerable sums of money in developing a large private iron gun founding industry. In an age when the largest private enterprises employed fewer than a score of people, the English dockyards were already employing six or seven hundred, in a wide range of skilled trades, with a substantial managerial and administrative structure. Even the largest sixteenth-century armies did not call for anything like the skills, the capital investment and the long-term commitment of a small navy.[18] It is no coincidence that Sweden, in most respects a peasant economy on the margins of international trade, had by the mid-seventeenth century developed one of the most advanced iron, and in particular gunfounding, industries in Europe (though this was greatly the work of Dutch investment, and exported its guns to arm Dutch ships). It was navies, not armies, which first confronted the demands of the industrial age.

The needs of an early-modern army were essentially those of mobilizing manpower on a large scale. The first requirement was a large number of unemployed peasants to make soldiers, and a smaller number of unemployed noblemen to make officers. The actual raising, training and, often, the equipping of the troops was left to the regimental officers. The feeding and paying them was as far as possible laid on the populations of conquered or occupied territories, to such an extent that in the (admittedly extreme) case of Swedish armies during the Thirty Years' War, it was even possible to wage major campaigns at a notional profit.[19] The huge fortresses of the artillery age required mass manpower and a good deal of masonry and timber revetment, but in engineering terms they were hardly larger or more sophisticated than the hill-forts of the Iron Age.[20] Raising the great armies of the early-modern age certainly imposed costs and strains on government, but they did not present a new challenge to society. They called for noblemen to do, and peasants to bear, what noblemen had always done and peasants had always borne. In social terms, a large seventeenth or eighteenth-century army was not very different from a small thirteenth or fourteenth-century one. These armies belonged naturally to societies which had not changed, and did not intend to change the conservative social order, societies in which the three estates kept to their God-given conditions, societies built around throne and altar.[21] 'The military hierarchy reproduced the fundamental social hierarchy, with all its privileges and inequalities.'[22] If this was a military revolution, its effects on society were the opposite of revolutionary. Government may have been changed, at least in some countries, by the development of modern bureaucracy, but society was ossified rather than revolutionised. The military revolution may have equipped absolutist monarchies to face the relatively simple challenge of mobilizing mass manpower, but it is not at all clear that it did anything to prepare them for the industrial world.

The great survivor, of course, was the great failure: Britain, the country which failed to rise to the challenge of the military revolution.[23] The question for the historian is how and why Britain survived, and there does not seem to be any agreed answer. It has been argued that British government or British bureaucracy were uniquely efficient,[24] and strikingly inefficient;[25] that the country was surprisingly militarized, and unusually free of military influence. It has been described as unique in combining the 'urban, capital-intensive' path to modernity with a strong central government.[26] For some scholars, England was different because it had a strong Navy, and a strong Navy was what made England different.[27] For others England was different because it had a strong Parliament, and a strong Parliament was what made England different.[28] Neither observation seems to have quite the explanatory force we need, and in any case weighty scholarly opinion argues that the English Parliament in the seventeenth century was just as weak as the English Crown, and weaker than its Continental analogues.[29]

It is not original to suggest that navies and constitutional government go together as naturally as armies and absolutism. Aristotle was quite clear on the point,[30] and other political scientists have followed him.[31] It is a matter of observation that army officers have traditionally been noblemen or gentlemen, while navies have tended to be run by middle-class professionals on whom the aristocratic concept of honour sat somewhat awkwardly.[32] What has not, to my knowledge, been seriously examined is why this should be so. Is it coincidence, or is it in the nature of a navy to favour constitutional rather than autocratic government? If there is a connection, which is cause and which effect? How far can this line of enquiry explain the British case? My answer starts from the argument of Jan Glete that successful navies require the support of a coalition of 'interest groups', united in supporting a strong navy, and capable of translating that support into long-term political commitment.[33] This argument has force regardless of the type of government in question, and one of its obvious merits is that it tends to draw attention away from the form of central government towards the nature of society, or at least of the political classes of society. Glete is quite clear that in the early modern period at least, efficient navies could be organised by provincial government or private individuals, though in the long run only states could meet the huge cost of major fleets.[34] Indeed this argument could be taken much further back, for in the early Middle Ages England, the Scandinavian countries and some parts of the Celtic world organised very large fleets by the *leidang* or ship-muster system, which depended on societies possessing advanced technical capabilities in shipbuilding and shiphandling, and a well-developed sense of mutual obligation and common purpose, but hardly on central government at all.[35]

Glete's argument helps to explain one of the obvious paradoxes of navies and state-formation. The examples of Spain in the late sixteenth century, England in the mid-seventeenth, France in the late seventeenth, Germany in the late nineteenth, and Russia in more than one period, all show that autocratic, militarised states are perfectly capable of building large and efficient navies, often with astonishing speed. What they do not seem to be capable of is sustaining their creations. Spanish seapower enjoyed a brief period of strength in the 1590s followed by a steep decline. The English Republic (and the English army which dominated it) took barely ten years to create the most formidable navy in Europe, and then to collapse. Louis XIV's fleet rose to be the largest in the world in less than thirty years, and had largely disappeared within another thirty. The fleet that Tirpitz built on borrowed money ran out of credit in the budget crisis of 1912. All these cases can be well explained by the argument that the temporary influence of a dominant favourite or the capricious will of the All-Highest were no substitute for the solid support of entrenched interest groups.[36]

It may be, however, that the argument needs to be taken further, for there is clear indication that absolutist governments were not merely bad at assembling a broad political constituency to support seapower; they seem actually to have had structural difficulties in sustaining a navy and using it rationally, regardless of the degree of government support.[37] In the case of Spain the stresses of war, and particularly war at sea, corroded the fabric of the absolutist state. More and more of the functions of government, including the function of building and operating fleets, were ceded to private contractors and private interests because the state was incapable either of organising or paying for them. At the same time the burdens imposed by the state largely contributed to ruining the country, impoverishing agriculture, destroying industry and reducing the largest merchant fleet and shipbuilding industry in the world to a miserable condition from which they have scarcely since recovered.[38] Perhaps the case of Spain is exceptional, but in the long run Oliver Cromwell had little more success than Olivares. Born of the insecurity and vulnerability of a minority regime, floated on extraordinary revenues which could not be sustained,[39] the English fleets of the 1650s lacked any the conditions for long-term survival. In the event the Republic collapsed before its navy could, leaving the restored monarchy to continue the search for a long-term foundation of seapower. Charles I with his Ship-Money fleets, Charles II with the Third Dutch War, both tried to use their navies as a lever for establishing something like absolutist government, and both found the instrument working to overturn their own ambitions. Even France under Louis XIV, which enjoyed unequalled revenues and apparently complete political stability, seems to have needed more than political commitment to endow its impressive fleet with lasting vigour. The latest study bluntly concludes that the navy's status as the personal creation of Colbert fatally weakened it from the start, making it an instrument of court politics rather than national policy. What was worse, its effectiveness was compromised precisely by its bureaucratic character as an accountant's navy, dedicated to efficiency rather than effectiveness: a sign of modernity to gladden the heart of Max Weber, no doubt, but an obstacle to victory, which so often depends on the deliberate sacrifice of efficiency.[40] Certainly the eighteenth-century French navy, even in the periods in which it enjoyed political backing and adequate finance, always lacked many of the essential elements of seapower, both human and material.[41] Always it remained a creature of the state, every element of it dependent on the support of the state. If foundries ran out of orders for anchors or guns, they closed, for they had no private customers. If the dockyards could not build enough ships of the line, there were no private yards to turn to. A century's effort to purge the officer corps of bourgeois, Protestants and other social undesirables turned it into the perfect expression of the absolutist regime, but a very imperfect instrument for winning wars.[42]

In all of these cases, moreover, the power of the absolutist or military state to impose taxation to pay for its naval ambitions was a key to success in the short term, and disaster in the long term. Absolute monarchies could destroy themselves, either by laying intolerable burdens on their economies, as in the case of Spain; or by incurring intolerable debts, as in the case of seventeenth-century England and eighteenth-century France.[43] Then as now, it seemed very much quicker and more efficient for an enlightened ruler to impose his will than for a pluralist government to assemble a coalition in support of a policy. Only a broad coalition, however, could ensure that the burden of war was distributed in the most equitable and least damaging fashion. Only a system capable of arousing and expressing popular support could make possible the high levels of effective taxation necessary to support industrial warfare.[44]

In Britain the Navy was always shaped by the nature of society as much as the will of the state. The English navy from its Tudor origins depended on a close alliance between the Crown and private interests. The naval war united nobility, gentry, merchants and seamen in 'the directest expression of the nation-in-arms'.[45] The Navy Royal was part of this coalition, and not exclusively under the control of the Crown. This has been described as a consequence of the weakness of the state, which in a way it was; and as a kind of decay or corruption, 'a disintegration of power, resulting from the conjunction of an antiquated system of government and the acquisitive drive of vigorous private interests';[46] which is true only from a quasi-Marxist perspective which sees the state as the only true expression of society and the only legitimate instrument of military force. Even when the English (later British) state became more efficient and wealthier, in the late seventeenth and early eighteenth centuries, the Navy and the state continued to rely heavily on private interests to perform functions which in France or Spain were the monopoly of the state. Private industry cast guns and manufactured powder, provided all sorts of stores and equipment and built many of the ships. Senior officers were almost entirely responsible for selecting and training their own officers and men; not until well into the nineteenth century did the Admiralty gain control of the entry of officers into the Navy.[47] It is true that there were important elements of naval administration which were more centralised in Britain than in France, notably victualling and central finance, but the French *trésoriers-généraux* and *munitionnaires* were not private contractors operating in a free market so much as privileged monopolists exploiting a private relationship with the centres of power.[48] They represented key points of weakness in French naval administration, where the British Navy's extensive networks of private suppliers and contractors gave it resilience and formed so many roots anchoring the Navy in the soil of civil society. Above all, 'Dutch finance' in both its Amsterdam and London versions, invoked private skills and public markets to spread the financial burden and risk of war across the whole breadth of the propertied classes at home and abroad. The funded debt represented the political nation's solid commitment to the wars which were a real expression of national will, not the private ambitions of kings or ministers. Two important recent studies have now shown in detail how Britain rose as a 'fiscal-military' state, combining a remarkably high and sustained level of taxation with an open and representative system of government. Though the essential technical advances in taxation and borrowing were made by the English republic in the 1650s, they were continued by the restored Parliament of the Restoration, and developed in the late seventeenth and early eighteenth centuries.[49]

Comparing Britain, Sweden and the Netherlands with the other great powers of the seventeenth and eighteenth centuries suggests that open and pluralist societies were not only better at assembling political support for navies, but better at the organization of seapower. To integrate the wide range of human, industrial, technical, commercial and managerial resources required to build, maintain and fight a seagoing fleet was simply beyond the unaided competence of any state in the early modern period, and perhaps it still is. Nations in which public policy was based on a broad consensus of interests, in which numerous private businesses serviced and influenced government, in which land and trade overlapped, were much better equipped to sustain a navy.[50] Effective seapower was the product of society as well as the state – if not instead of the state, in the case of the Dutch Republic. Only flexible and integrated societies could surmount the very considerable difficulties involved. Money was certainly necessary, but money alone did not

V

suffice. The events of 1588 amply demonstrate that even ten times the financial resources of England were no substitute for the efficient administration and extensive networks of support from private industry and trade which Spain lacked.[51]

This is a statement about the nature of society as much as about the form of government. Absolutist government had difficulty sustaining effective seapower because it had difficulty mobilizing the broad coalition of interests needed to support so complex an enterprise. Indeed it did not wish to mobilize many elements in society, either because they were actively undesirable (Moriscos in Spain, Huguenots in France, Jews in many countries), or because the absolutist system did not allow them freedom of action, or because it did not wish to involve them in the business of the state. Merchants, industrialists, tradesmen, skilled craftsmen; all had a place in absolute monarchies, but it tended to be a subordinate or marginal place. Indeed it is striking how often in absolutist societies the place of trade and industry was literally marginal; geographically remote from inland capitals, on the frontiers or seacoasts of the state.

All this suggests a link between the nature of societies, the nature of governments, and the nature of their military activities. Middle-class participation in public life, professional skills, commerce, industry and private finance directly favoured and were favoured by navies. Seapower was most successful in countries with flexible and open social and political systems.[52] They were the same which favoured trade and industry, and for the same reason, for a navy was the supreme industrial activity. The armed forces of early modern states were the blueprint of their modern societies: a complex, integrated, industrial world for the naval powers; a rigid, archaic world of great landed estates for the military powers.[53] It has been argued that a Europe of warring states eventually came to dominate a world much of which was occupied by vast territorial empires, precisely because the ceaseless competition of European warfare bred forces and weapons which were much more capable than the products of closed, monopolistic societies – in short, that the free market was more efficient than the plan.[54] If this was true on an international level, it should have been equally true within nations. If free competition is more economically efficient than government direction, then those forms of military activity which best harmonise with free markets are likely to be more successful in themselves, and best promote (or least hamper) the growth of flexible and competitive economies. In a world which was steadily moving away from land and population as the sole sources of wealth and towards commerce and industry, naval powers and open societies were much better placed to adapt than military powers and autocratic monarchies. It as not simply that sea-power gave access to overseas wealth, important though that was, for absolutist states could and did elect to become seapowers. They, however, were conspicuously less successful than other states, not richer than they and in some cases much poorer, but better equipped to mobilize their whole resources, either for war or for peace. The critical difference was the nature of society, and government as an expression of society, rather than constitutional forms taken in isolation. Open societies were best at naval warfare for the same reason that they were later best at meeting other challenges of the modern world, because a navy was an image of the modern world in miniature. 'Warfare on the British model was a triumph for an enterprising and acquisitive society, not an authoritarian one.'[55] Britain did not simply survive centuries of warfare relatively unscathed because of geographical and historical accident,[56] to profit from the industrial revolution because there were no competitors left undevastated by war. Naval warfare was Britain's apprenticeship for commercial and industrial supremacy.

Notes

1. In its original form this paper was first given at the Canadian Nautical Research Society's International Conference on Maritime History, Calgary, 1998. I am indebted to Professor Jan Glete for suggestions and references which have greatly improved it.

2. See for example: Richard Bean, 'War and the Birth of the Nation State', *Journal of Economic History* XXXIII (1973) pp. 203-221; Samuel E. Finer, 'State and Nation-Building in Europe: The Role of the Military', in *The Formation of National States in Western Europe* ed. Charles Tilly (Princeton, 1975) pp. 84-163; Ronald W. Batchelder & Herman Freudenberger, 'On the Rational Origins of the Modern Centralized State', *Explorations in Economic History* XX (1983) pp.1-13; Charles Tilly, 'War Making and State Making as Organized Crime', in *Bringing the State Back In* ed. Peter B. Evans, Dietrich Rueschmeyer & Theda Skocpol (Cambridge, 1985) pp. 169-191. The most recent contributions are: *Power Elites and State Building* ed. Wolfgang Reinhard (Oxford, 1996); Thomas Ertman, *Birth of the Leviathan: Building States and Regimes in Medieval and Early Modern Europe* (Cambridge, 1997); and *idem,* 'The Sinews of Power and European State-Building Theory', in *An Imperial State at War: Britain from 1689 to 1815* ed. Laurence Stone (London, 1994), pp. 33-51.

V

3. This applies to most of the very numerous books on the subject. Honourable exceptions are: Geoffrey Parker, *The Military Revolution: Military Innovation and the Rise of the West, 1500-1800* (Cambridge 1988); and Jeremy Black, *A Military Revolution ? Military Change and European Society 1550-1800* (London, 1991). Jaime Vicens Vives, 'Estructura administrativa estatal en los siglos XVI y XVII', *Rapports IV, XIe Congrès International des Sciences Historiques,* (Stockholm, 1960) pp. 1-24 (also in *Obra Dispersa* ed. M. Batllori & E. Giralt (Barcelona, 1967, 2 vols) II, 359-377; and translated by Frances M. Lopez-Morillas as 'The Administrative Structure of the State in the Sixteenth and Seventeenth Centuries', in *Government in Reformation Europe, 1520-1560* ed. Henry J. Cohn (London, 1971) pp. 58-87), was perhaps the first to mention the naval contribution to state formation. Jan Glete, *Navies and Nations: Warships, Navies and State Building in Europe and America, 1500-1860* (Stockholm, 1993, 2 vols) is an outstanding study which eschews the 'military revolution' as such; Professor Glete has now followed it with *War and the State in Early Modern Europe: Spain, the Dutch Republic and Sweden as fiscal-military states, 1500-1660* (London, 2002). Brian M. Downing, *The Military Revolution and Political Change: Origins of Democracy and Autocracy in Early Modern Europe* (Princeton, 1992), pp. 72-73, 165 & 224, is a rare political scientist who is uneasily aware that the existence of navies somewhat undermines his argument. *War and Competition between States* ed. Philippe Contamine (Oxford, 2000) has a chapter by Jaap R. Bruijn, 'States and their Navies from the Late Sixteenth to the End of the Eighteenth Centuries', pp. 69-98.

4. *Rethinking Leviathan: The Eighteenth-Century State in Britain and Germany* ed. John Brewer & Eckhart Hellmuth (Oxford, 1999).

5. William Miller, 'The Gattilusi of Lesbos, 1355-1462', *Byzantische Zeitschrift XXII* (1913), pp. 406-447. Michel Balard, *La Romanie Génoise* (Genoa, 1978, 2 vols); *idem,* 'Les Génois en mer Egée', *Mediterranean Historical Review* IV (1989), pp. 158-174.

6. Gustave Saige, *Monaco, ses origines et son histoire* (Monaco, 1897), pp. 42-56. Léon-Honoré Labande, *Histoire de la Principauté de Monaco* (Monaco, 1934), pp. 27-44. Michel Balard, 'Course et piraterie à Genes à la fin du Moyen Age', in *El comerç alternatiu: corsarisme i contraban (SS.XV-XVIII)* ed. Gonçal López Nadal (Palma de Mallorca, 1990) pp. 29-40, at p. 33.

7. Pio Pecchiai, *Roma nel Cinquecento* (Bologna, 1949), pp. 173-177. Paolo Prodi, *The Papal Prince. One Body and Two Souls: The Papal Monarchy in Early Modern Europe* trans. Susan Haskins (Cambridge, 1987), p. 87. Niccolò Del Re, *La Curia Romana* (Rome, 2nd edn 1952), pp.19-20 & 175-176. Jean Delumeau, 'Le progrès de la centralisation dans l'État pontifical au XVIe siècle', *Revue Historique* 226 (1961) 399-410, at p. 403. The text is printed in *Bullarium Romanum Novissimum* ed. L. Cherubini et al. (Rome, 3rd edn 1638, 4 vols) II, 464-468. Curiously enough these authorities do not agree on the actual date of the bull. Most modern authorities (e.g. Prodi,

p.87; Del Re, p.87) plump for 22 Jan 1588; Alberto Guglielmotti, *Storia della Marina Pontificia* (Rome, 1886-93, 10 vols) VII, 22, prefers the same day in 1587, Pecchiai (pp.176 & 207) offers both, while the actual text in Cherubini's (indifferent) edition is dated 1 Feb 1587.

8. Cf Delumeau, 'l'État pontifical', p. 410: 'Ce qui a manqué à l'État pontifical de la Contre-Réforme, ce ne sont pas tant les structures administratives que la santé sur le plan économique et social.'

9. What follows is a substantial simplification. Good introductions to Dutch naval administration are J.R. Bruijn, *Varend Verleden: De Nederlandse Oorlogsvloot in de 17e en 18e eeuw* (Amsterdam, 1998), and the appropriate sections of the *Maritieme Geschiedenis der Nederlanden* ed. G. Asaert et al. (Bussum, 1976-78, 4 vols). Glete, *War and the State,* pp. 140-173, considers Dutch government and war more generally.

10. Jan Glete, 'La construccion de un Impero con recursos limitados: Suecia y el desarrollo de las organizaciones militares', in *España y Suecia en la época del Barroco (1600-1660)* ed. E. Martinez Ruiz & M. de Pazzis Pi Corrales (Madrid, 1998), pp. 307-339. Glete, 'Absolutism or Dynamic Leadership? The rise of large armed forces and the problem of political interest aggregation from a mid-17th-century perspective', in *Politics and Culture in the Age of Christina* ed. Marie-Louise Roden (Stockholm, 1997), pp. 23-28. I am indebted to Professor Glete for copies of these papers, now conveniently summarised in his *War and the State,* pp. 174-212.

11. Perry Anderson, *Lineages of the Absolutist State* (London, 1974), p. 123. John Brewer, *The Sinews of Power: War, Money and the English State, 1688-1783* (London, 1989), pp. 12-13. *The Medieval Military Revolution: State, Society and Military Change in Medieval and Early Modern Europe* ed. Andrew Ayton & J.L. Price (London, 1995), p. 6. Downing, *Military Revolution,* pp. 179-183.

12. Perhaps 'seriously undermined' would describe these two occasions better than 'overthrown'.

13. N.A.M. Rodger, *The Safeguard of the Sea. A Naval History of Britain,* Vol. I, 660-1649 (London, 1997), p. 429.

14. Michael Mann, *The Sources of Social Power. I: A History of Power from the Beginning to A.D. 1760* (Cambridge, 1986), p. 457. Cf the comments of Ertman, *Birth of the Leviathan,* pp. 14-19.

15. Ronald Pollitt, 'Bureaucracy and the Armada: the Administrator's Battle', *Mariner's Mirror* LX (1974) pp. 119-132.

16. P.K. O'Brien & P.A. Hunt, 'The Rise of a Fiscal State in Britain, 1485-1815', *Historical Research* LXVI (1993) pp. 129-176. Geoffrey Parker, 'The *Dreadnought* Revolution of the Sixteenth Century', *Mariner's Mirror* LXXXII (1996) pp. 269-300.

17. Kenneth R. Andrews, *Ships, Money and Politics: Seafaring and Naval Enterprise in the Reign of Charles I* (Cambridge, 1991), p. 3. Conrad Russell, *Parliaments and English politics, 1621-1629* (Oxford, 1979) pp. 64,

V

418 & 431. Simon Adams, 'Spain or the Netherlands? The Dilemmas of Early Stuart Foreign Policy', in *Before the English Civil War: Essays on Early Stuart Politics and Government* ed. Howard Tomlinson (London, 1983) pp. 79-101, at p. 80.

18. Rodger, *Safeguard of the Sea*, pp. 228-237.

19. Downing, *Military Revolution*, pp. 193-202. Parker, *Military Revolution*, pp. 66-67. But Professor Glete is clear that the Swedish state (as distinct from generals and military entrepreneurs) never made a true profit.

20. I have failed to find directly comparable figures for the quantities of earthwork and masonry required, but there are some suggestive calculations in *The Experimental Earthwork on Overton Down, Wiltshire, 1960* ed. P.A. Jewell (British Association for the Advancement of Science, London, 1963), pp. 51-58, and John Coles, *Archaeology by Experiment* (London, 1973), pp. 73-74.

21. This is true regardless of whether you believe the military revolution was the cause of absolutism, or (like Black, *Military Revolution*) the consequence.

22. Christopher Storrs & H.M. Scott, 'The Military Revolution and the European Nobility, c. 1600-1800', *War in History* III (1996) pp. 1-41, at p. 34.

23. Jean Meyer, *Le poids de l'état* (Paris, 1983), pp. 128-129.

24. Brewer, *Sinews of Power, passim.*

25. Wallace T. MacCaffrey, Elizabeth I, *War and Politics 1588-1603* (Princeton, 1992), pp. 23-41. Lawrence Stone, introduction to *An Imperial State at War: Britain from 1689 to 1815* (London, 1994), pp. 14-17.

26. Charles Tilly, Coercion, *Capital and European States, AD 990-1990* (Oxford, 1990), pp. 56-61.

27. Aristide R. Zolberg, 'Strategic Interactions and the Formation of Modern States: France and England', in *The State in Global Perspective ed. Ali Kazancigil* (Paris & Aldershot, 1986) pp. 72-106, at pp. 94-95.

28. This seems to sum up the argument of Ertman, *Birth of the Leviathan.*

29. C.S.R. Russell, 'Monarchies, Wars and Estates in England, France and Spain, c. 1580-c. 1640', *Legislative Studies Quarterly* VII (1982) pp. 205-220.

30. *Politics* VI. 6 §2.

31. Mann, *Sources of Social Power*, I, 478-481. Anderson, *Lineages of the Absolutist State*, p. 134.

32. N.A.M. Rodger, 'Honour and Duty at Sea, 1660-1815', *Historical Research* LXXV (2002) pp. 425-447.

33. Glete, *Navies and Nations* II, 477-489.

34. Glete, *Navies and Nations* I, 159-161.

35. Hans Kuhn, *Das Altnordische Seekriegswesen* ed. Sigrid Engeler & Dietrich Hofmann (Heidelberg, 1991), pp.54-87. Nicholas Hooper, 'Some Observations on the Navy in Late Anglo-Saxon England', in *Studies in Me-*

dieval History presented to R. Allen Brown ed Christopher Harper-Bill et al. (Woodbridge, 1989), pp. 203-213. *Kulturhistorisk Leksikon for Nordisk Middelalder* (Copenhagen &c, 1956-78, 22 vols) X, 433-446, s.v. Leidang. Lucien Musset, 'Problemes militaires du monde scandinave (VIIe-XIIe siecles)', in *Ordinamenti Militari in Occidente nell'alto Medievo* (Spoleto, 1968) pp. 229-291, at pp. 279-284. Else Roesdahl, *Viking Age Denmark* (London, 1982), p. 157. Klavs Randsborg, *The Viking Age in Denmark: The Formation of a State* (London, 1980), pp. 32-43. Niels Lund, 'The Armies of Swein Forkbeard and Cnut: *leding or lið?*', *Anglo-Saxon England* XV (1986) pp. 105-118. John Bannerman, *Studies in the History of Dalriada* (Edinburgh, 1974), pp. 140-141. Hugh Marwick, 'Naval Defence in Norse Scotland', *Scottish Historical Review* XXVIII (1949) pp. 1-11.

36. Martine Acerra & Andre Zysberg, *L'essor des marines de guerres européennes (vers 1680 - vers 1790)* (Paris, 1997), p. 53. Michel Vergé-Franceschi, *La marine française au XVIIIe siècle: Guerres, Administration, Exploration* (Paris, 1996), pp. 49, 110 & 124-126. Daniel Dessert, *La Royale: Vaisseaux et marins du Roi-Soleil* (Paris, 1996), pp. 74-76, 101-110, 170-174, 238-261 & 284-286.

37. Glete, *Navies and Nations* I, 222.

38. I.A.A. Thompson, *War and Government in Habsburg Spain 1560-1620* (London, 1976), pp. 211-283. Somewhat more optimistic views are offered by R.A. Stradling, *The Armada of Flanders: Spanish Maritime Policy and European War, 1568-1668* (Cambridge, 1992), and David Goodman, *Spanish Naval Power, 1589-1665: Reconstruction and Defeat* (Cambridge, 1997).

39. J.S. Wheeler, 'Navy Finance, 1649-1660', *Historical Journal* XXXIX (1996) pp. 457-466.

40. Dessert, *La Royale*; cf. his 'La marine royale, une filiale Colbert', in *Patronages et clientelismes 1550-1750 (France, Angleterre, Espagne, Italie)* ed. Charles Giry Deloison & Roger Mettam (Lille & London, n.d.) pp. 69-83. Martin van Creveld, *Technology and War from 2000 B.C. to the Present* (New York, 2nd edn 1991), pp. 317-319.

41. Vergé-Franceschi, *La marine française.* Acerra & Zysberg, *L'essor des marines de guerres.* N.A.M. Rodger, 'The Continental Commitment in the Eighteenth Century', in *War, Strategy and International Politics: Essays in Honour of Sir Michael Howard,* ed. Lawrence Freedman, Paul Hayes & Robert O'Neill (Oxford, 1992) pp. 39-55, at pp. 47-50.

42. On French sea officers see the works of Michel Vergé-Franceschi, in this case especially *Marine et Éducation sous l'Ancien Régime* (Paris, 1991).

43. Glete, *Navies and Nations* I, 207-208.

44. The dualist contrast presented by Tilly in 'War Making and State Making as Organized Crime' (p.170), between the 'coercive and self-seeking entrepreneurs' who made wars and states, and the heroic (by implication, pacifist) ordinary people who resisted them and in some cases succeeded in preserving representative institutions, seems to me to bear no relation to rea-

V

lity, and is admitted by its author to be supported by 'no evidence worthy of the name'. His *Coercion, Capital and European States,* however, takes a more plausible line.

45. Kenneth R. Andrews, *Elizabethan Privateering: English Privateering during the Spanish War 1585-1603* (Cambridge, 1964), pp. 233-235. cf Paul M. Kennedy, *The Rise and Fall of British Naval Mastery* (2nd edn 1983), pp. 22-24.

46. Andrews, *Elizabethan Privateering,* p. 238.

47. N.A.M. Rodger, 'Officers, Gentlemen and their Education, 1793-1860', in *Les Empires en Guerre et Paix, 1793-1860* ed. Edward Freeman (Vincennes, Service Historique de la Marine, 1990) pp. 139-151.

48. James Pritchard, *Louis XV's Navy, 1748-1762: A Study of Organization and Administration* (Kingston, Ontario & Montreal, 1987) pp. 186-205. Henri Legohérel, *Les Trésoriers généraux de la Marine (1517-1788)* (Paris, 1965). Dessert, *La Royale,* pp. 54-77. Acerra & Zysberg, *L'essor des marines de guerres,* pp. 248-250.

49. James Scott Wheeler, *The Making of a World Power: War and the Military Revolution in Seventeenth-Century England* (Stroud, 1999). Patrick O'Brien, 'Fiscal Exceptionalism: Great Britain and its European Rivals. From Civil War to Triumph at Trafalgar and Waterloo', in *The Political Economy of British Historical Experience, 1688-1914* ed. Donald Winch & P.K. O'Brien (Oxford, 2002). Cf Philip Harling & Peter Mandler, 'From «Fiscal-Military» State to Laissez-Faire State, 1760-1850', *Journal of British Studies* XXXII (1993), pp. 44-70.

50. Anderson, *Lineages of the Absolutist State,* p. 135. P.J. Cain & A.G. Hopkins, *British Imperialism: Innovation and Expansion 1688-1914* (London, 1993), pp. 64-89.

51. Rodger, *Safeguard of the Sea,* pp. 257-260, 327-329 & 340-341.

52. This is the central argument of Peter Padfield, *Maritime Supremacy and the Opening of the Western Mind: Naval Campaigns that shaped the Modern World, 1588-1782* (London, 1999).

53. Glete, *Navies and Nations* I, 13. André Corvisier, 'Armées, état et administration dans les temps modernes', *Francia* IX (1980) pp. 509-519, at p. 509. Vicens Vives, 'Estructura administrativa estatal', p. 361.

54. William H. McNeill, *The Pursuit of Power: Technology, Armed Force and Society since A.D.1000* (Oxford, 1983) pp. 113-116. Paul Kennedy, *The Rise and Fall of the Great Powers: Economic Change and Military Conflict from 1500 to 2000* (London, 1988), pp. 21-29. Jeremy Black, *War and the World: Military Power and the Fate of Continents, 1450-2000* (London, 1998), p. 4.

55. Paul Langford, *A Polite and Commercial People: England, 1727-1783* (Oxford, 1989) p. 697.

56. Roughly the argument of Otto Hintze, for whom see Anderson, *Lineages of the Absolutist State,* pp. 134-135; and Ertman, '*The Sinews of Power* and European State-Building Theory', pp. 34-35.

Additional Note [2009]

This short piece was my first published approach to a subject which seems to me to be of great importance. Printed in a provincial Greek journal, it did not attract much notice in the English-speaking world. I referred to some of these ideas in *The Command of the Ocean: A Naval History of Britain, 1649–1815* (London, 2004), and they formed one of the themes of a conference on 'Navies and State Formation' held in 2004, whose proceedings have not yet been published. Though the connections between navies and state formation have been very generally neglected, one very important book does deal with them (from a rather different perspective to my own): Jan Glete, *Navies and Nations: Warships, Navies and State Building in Europe and America, 1500–1860* (Stockholm, 1993, 2 vols).

VI

QUEEN ELIZABETH AND THE MYTH OF
SEA-POWER IN ENGLISH HISTORY

This is a study of things that never happened, or never in the way they were understood and remembered. It is a history of ideas, but not an intellectual history, for it deals with the thoughts of men who were not accustomed to thinking in any profound and analytical fashion. It is a study of the memory of the Elizabethan age as it was shaped into an English national myth[1] about sea-power, the distorting lens through which generations of public men perceived and understood real naval activity. In this subject historians have sometimes been too apt to believe that political debate had to do with reality, that the issues discussed in parliament and print were real issues. This is curious, for it is a matter of common experience that even in our own day, when information circulates more freely than it ever did in the past, public policy is often formed and discussed in terms dictated more by politicians' preconceptions than by a dispassionate regard for facts. We ought to expect the same thing in a greater degree in the past, and so indeed we find it. For centuries sea-power and naval affairs mattered a great deal in English political life, but the shipping which men discussed in parliament was not exactly the same as the shipping which actually put to sea.

The English naval myth was built on the events of Queen Elizabeth's reign, but its precise origin does not seem ever to have been located. This may possibly be because it is to be found somewhere where British naval

---

[1] I use the word 'English' deliberately, even for the period after the union of the crowns, because the tradition I want to outline is essentially English. Scotland has, or had, its own ideas about the sea, but they were not the same.

historians have not traditionally looked for patriotic inspiration; namely France, and specifically in English cooperation with the Huguenots of La Rochelle and the Norman ports during the wars of religion. Until the 1560s English seamen were skilled in the coastal pilotage of northern European waters, but lacked any knowledge of deep-sea navigation. In the West Country especially, they had centuries of expertise in piracy, and the three English experiments with 'reprisals by general proclamation' in 1544, 1557 and 1563 did a good deal to revive the pirate culture in England, but it remained a matter of local rather than national importance, and it was only beginning to acquire any religious overtones. All this was changed by English support for the French Huguenots, and in particular by covert government assistance in the years 1568 to 1572. This support came via a group of West Country seamen led by Sir Arthur Champernowne, the vice-admiral of Devon, and his old business associates the Hawkins brothers of Plymouth, veterans of many joint ventures with Huguenot interests. Together they organised a joint Anglo-Huguenot fleet, sailing under letters of reprisal issued by the Huguenot leaders Henry of Navarre (as admiral of Guyenne, 1563–89) and Gaspard de Coligny (as admiral of France, 1552–72) out of Plymouth and La Rochelle as opportunity offered, against the shipping of all nations, but especially of Spain. By March 1569 there were as many as forty Huguenot cruisers in the Channel. At the same time Queen Elizabeth's own ships and seamen were supplying the French rebels. When Sir William Winter escorted the annual wine convoy to Bordeaux in December 1568, he sent ammunition into La Rochelle in passing, while next year John Hawkins with another squadron relieved the city, returning with cargoes of wine, prize goods and church bells.[2] The bells are an apt symbol of the wars of religion by land and sea; the fruit of the destruction of French country churches, carried to England to the profit of English ship-owners to be melted down and recast into guns with which to continue the war of religion.

The tie that bound the Huguenots to their English associates was religion, for Calvinism and piracy were intimately connected. The connection was not of course a theological one; the reformers did not encourage armed robbery in principle. In practice, however, in France, the Netherlands, Scotland and elsewhere, even the most scrupulous of

[2] Charles de La Roncière, *Histoire de la marine française* (6 vols., Paris, 1899–1932), IV, 102–18; B. Dietz, 'The Huguenot and English Corsairs during the Third Civil War in France, 1568 to 1570', *Proceedings of the Huguenot Society*, 19 (1952–8), 278–94 [hereafter *Proc. Hug. Soc.*]; James A. Williamson, *Hawkins of Plymouth*, 2nd edn (1969), 165–70; Patrick Villiers, *Les corsaires du Littoral: Dunkerque, Calais, Boulogne, de Philippe II à Louis XIV (1568–1713)* (Villeneuve d'Ascq, 2000), 26–7; D. J. B. Trim, 'The "Secret War" of Elizabeth I: England and the Huguenots during the Early Wars of Religion, 1562–77', *Proc. Hug. Soc.*, 27 (1999), 189–99 (I am indebted to Dr Trim for copies of this and his other paper cited below).

Protestant dissidents found themselves fighting to preserve their liberty of conscience, and obliged to find the sinews of war by whatever means the Lord might put into their hands. One of the best means was reprisals at sea,[3] and their best allies were the English. Thus the English, and at the same time the Dutch, rebels joined the Huguenots and their long-standing Scottish associates in what we may call the Calvinist International. Religion now sanctioned a private war against the shipping of the Catholic powers, which, providentially, formed much the largest and richest part of the sea-borne trade of Europe.[4] Most English seamen were now conscientiously convinced 'that we cold not do God better service than to spoyl the Spaniard both of lyfe and goodes, but indeed under color of religion al ther shot is at mens mony'.[5]

Though the immediate crisis passed in 1572, the links that the West Countrymen had established remained active. With French advice and encouragement, the English began to move out into the Atlantic and even, in small numbers, across to the West Indies.[6] Huguenot navigators like Guillaume Le Testu now took English seamen by the hand and

---

[3] For the legal doctrine of reprisals see: D. A. Gardiner, 'The History of Belligerent Rights on the High Seas in the Fourteenth Century', *Law Quarterly Review*, 48 (1932), 521–46; René de Mas Latrie, 'Du droit de marque ou droit de représailles au moyen âge', *Bibliothèque de l'Ecole des Chartes*, 27 (1866), 529–77, 29 (1868), 294–347, 612–35; Marie-Claire Chavarot, 'La pratique des lettres de marque d'après les arrêts du parlement (XIIIe-debut XVe siècle)', *Bibliothèque de l'Ecole des Chartes*, 149 (1981), 51–89; Pierre Chaplais, 'Règlement des conflits internationaux franco-anglais au XIVe siècle (1293–1377)', *Le Moyen Age*, 57 (1951), 259–302; Florence E. Dyer, 'Reprisals in the Sixteenth Century', *Mariner's Mirror*, 21 (1935), 187–97 [hereafter *MM*]; *Documents relating to Law and Custom of the Sea*, ed. R. G. Marsden (Navy Records Society vols. 49–50, 1915–16), I, 119–24 [hereafter NRS].

[4] Mickaël Augeron, 'Coligny et les Espagnols à travers la course (c. 1560–1572): une politique maritime au service de la cause protestante', in *Coligny, les protestants et la mer*, ed. Martine Acerra and Guy Martinière (Paris, 1997), 155–76; Ralph Davis, *The Rise of the Atlantic Economies* (1973), 77–80; David Loades, *England's Maritime Empire: Seapower, Commerce and Policy, 1490–1690* (2000), 85–114; Timothy George, 'War and Peace in the Puritan Tradition', *Church History*, 52 (1984), 492–503; D. J. B. Trim, 'Protestant refugees in Elizabethan England and confessional conflict in France and the Netherlands, c. 1562–c. 1610', in *From Strangers to Citizens: The Integration of Immigrant Communities in Britain, Ireland and Colonial America, 1550–1750*, ed. Randolph Vigne and Charles Littleton (Brighton, 2001), 68–79; Alan James, 'Between "Huguenot" and "Royal": Naval Affairs during the Wars of Religion', in *The Adventure of Religious Pluralism in Early Modern France*, ed. Keith Cameron, Mark Greengrass and Penny Roberts (Oxford and New York, 2000), pp. 101–12.

[5] *An Elizabethan in 1582: The Diary of Richard Madox, Fellow of All Souls*, ed. Elizabeth S. Donno (Hakluyt Society, second series, CXLVI, 1976), 144. Few English sea chaplains were as sceptical as Madox, who made himself very unpopular by preaching that armed robbery was not invariably warranted by Scripture.

[6] Kenneth Andrews, *Trade, Plunder and Settlement: Maritime Enterprise and the Genesis of the British Empire, 1480–1630* (Cambridge, 1984), 128–38; *Documents concerning English Voyages to the Spanish Main 1569–1580*, ed. I. A. Wright (Hakluyt Society, second series, LXXI, 1932), xxx–xxxv; G. V. Scammell, 'The English in the Atlantic Islands c.1450–1650', *MM*, 72 (1986), 295–317, at 302–3.

showed them how to raid the Spanish empire. The young Francis Drake and his contemporaries who began to range the Caribbean in search of 'some little comfortable dew from heaven'[7] were strongly motivated by religion as well as money. More eminent figures like Sir Richard Grenville, who owned men-of-war but did not go to sea himself until much later, belonged to the same current of opinion. His powerful galleon the *Castle of Comfort* was often encountered in the 1570s, and never in honest trade. She sailed with French letters of reprisal against the enemies of reformed religion, while at home in Cornwall, Grenville enthusiastically persecuted his Catholic neighbours and their priests, whom most of the Cornish gentlemen would have been quite happy to ignore. He was responsible for the execution of Cuthbert Mayne, the first of the seminary priests, at Lostwithiel in 1577.[8]

Religious war at sea, 'to God's glory and our comfort',[9] was linked with religious persecution at home. At first it was only in the West Country, but Pius V's bull *Regnans in excelsis* of 1570, which excommunicated Queen Elizabeth, made Protestantism patriotic and Catholicism matter of treason, while the outbreak of the Spanish War in 1585 allowed the West Country seamen to teach the nation the skills they had learnt from the Huguenots. Without this connection, founded on a common religion and a common sense of a mortal threat from resurgent Catholicism, it is far from certain that English piracy would have spread beyond the coasts of the Channel and the Bay of Biscay. Though the period of active cooperation in open war lasted less than four years, it gave a powerful impetus to the future development of English sea-power, and English ideas about sea-power. The intimate connection between Protestantism, patriotism and plunder that the English learnt at La Rochelle was to become a distinctive and formative part of the English national myth. In France, ironically, it was the ideology of the losers, destined to be rubbed out and overwritten by the very different ethos of royal absolutism.[10]

The Spanish War of 1585 to 1603 fixed the essential elements of the English idea of sea-power in the national consciousness. This was a war fought only partly by the queen's ships. Their strategic role was largely defensive, their operations for the most part confined to nearby waters. Only once, in 1588, did the Royal Navy take the lead in a campaign

---

[7] *The Expedition of Sir John Norris and Sir Francis Drake to Spain and Portugal, 1589*, ed. R. B. Wernham (NRS, CXXVII, 1988), 179, quoting Drake to Sir Francis Walsingham, 2 June 1589.

[8] A. L. Rowse, *Sir Richard Grenville of the Revenge: An Elizabethan Hero* (1937), 117–21, 132–44.

[9] *English Privateering Voyages to the West Indies 1588–1595*, ed. K. R. Andrews (Hakluyt Society, second series, CXI, 1959), 339 n. 4, quoting the account book of the London privateer owner Thomas Middleton for the voyage of the *Vineyard* in 1603.

[10] Jean Meyer, 'La course: romantisme, exutoire sociale, réalité économique', *Annales de Bretagne*, 78 (1971), 307–44, at 311. The recent collection, *Coligny, les Protestants et la mer*, ed. Acerra and Martinière, marks a stirring of French interest in this long-neglected subject.

that caught the national imagination. The offensive part of the naval war was largely in private hands, the work of a coalition of seamen (notably but no longer solely from the West Country), gentlemen and London capitalists making war on the common enemy for profit. The intellectual and political leadership of this coalition came from the radical Protestant group at court. The queen was unable and unwilling to take their wilder projects seriously; it was not in her interest to overthrow Spanish power, and it was not remotely within her capabilities, but many of them truly believed, in Sir Walter Raleigh's words, that 'if the late Queen would have believed her men of war as she did her scribes, we had in her time beaten that great empire in pieces and made their kings kings of figs and oranges as in old times'.[11]

By the end of the war the essential elements of the English naval myth were securely in place. The war had been fought for England's freedom, against the mortal threat of Catholic tyranny. It had been a naval triumph, and would have been more so but for the queen's hesitancy and parsimony. It had been fought at little public expense, and yielded enormous private profit. It had endowed English history with an ample stock of Protestant heroes. Above all, that part of the naval war which had seized the national imagination had been fought by private interests rather than by the crown, so that the prestige did not go to strengthen an image of royal power, but one of national liberty. It made English sea-power the ideal expression of the nation in arms. Reality, of course, did not altogether correspond with the myth, but it is too dismissive to follow a recent historian's judgement: 'the idea that the privateers were Protestant crusaders is nonsense. Like the lord admiral and his chief judge, they were primarily cheerful thieves.'[12] In fact the idea is not complete nonsense; there was some truth in it, and in each of the elements of the new naval myth, for cheerful theft and Protestant crusading were entirely compatible.[13]

At the core of the English political idea of sea-power as it was now established lay a trinity of associations: religion, freedom and money. True, natural and national English sea-power was securely attached to these three, and the three belonged together as inseparable parts of a single system. First, English sea-power was essentially Protestant, exercised for the defence of true religion and the destruction of Catholicism. English

[11] R. B. Wernham, 'Elizabethan War Aims and Strategy', in *Elizabethan Government and Society: Essays Presented to Sir John Neale*, ed. S. T. Bindoff, J. Hurstfield and C. H. Williams (1961), 340–68, quoted at 340.

[12] Bruce Lenman, *England's Colonial Wars 1550–1688: Conflicts, Empire and National Identity* (Harlow, 2001), 85.

[13] Kenneth R. Andrews, *Elizabethan Privateering: English Privateering during the Spanish War 1585–1603* (Cambridge, 1964), 6, 9, 16, 232–5; Andrews, *Trade, Plunder and Settlement*, 17–36, 248; Loades, *England's Maritime Empire*, 111–25; Geoffrey Scammell, *The World Encompassed: The First European Maritime Empires, c. 800–1650* (1981), 498.

sea-power fought for religious freedom, therefore; meaning the religious freedom of the people who mattered, English Protestants, and it was naturally associated with that most English of religious freedoms, the freedom to persecute Catholics. It was equally integral to its character to be on the side of political freedom, not simply by defending the country against foreign invasion, but by associating with those domestic policies which defended the liberties of Englishmen, and in particular the liberties of parliament. Finally, true English sea-power was profitable; it was the means by which the English nation in general, English seamen and merchants in particular, made their fortunes. Initially these fortunes came mainly from plunder; later foreign trade came to play the dominant part, but the underlying idea remained the same.

Throughout the seventeenth and eighteenth centuries the national use of the sea was commonly understood as a unity, in which merchant shipping and trade formed a common system with the Royal Navy and private men-of-war. In the words of a 1615 pamphlet,

> As concerning ships, it is that which every one knoweth and can say, they are our weapons, they are our ornaments, they are our strength, they are our pleasures, they are our defence, they are our profit; the subject by them is made rich, the Kingdom through them strong, the Prince in them mighty.[14]

Various terms were used to refer to this 'maritime-imperial system';[15] I have chosen to use the word 'sea-power', but I do not mean to limit it to the Royal Navy as an organisation. Public debate very often centred on the Navy, if only because it cost so much money and public money was the proper business of the House of Commons, but the subject as a whole is broader.

The modern observer naturally thinks of sea-power in the context of foreign policy, economics and war. For public men in seventeenth- and eighteenth-century England, however, its leading associations were more domestic than foreign. The political liberty which belonged to true English sea-power was English liberty, at home in England, a permanent and prominent element of English political life, not just the occasional military requirement for defence against foreign invasion. Likewise the religious liberty native to English sea-power was chiefly invoked in the domestic context; it was both a privilege and an obligation flowing from the status of the English as God's new elect, his chosen instruments to

[14] Norman Clayton, 'Naval Administration, 1603–1628' (Ph.D. thesis, University of Leeds, 1935), 281, quoting Robert Kayll, *The Trade's Increase* (1615). Cf. Brian Dietz, 'The Royal Bounty and English Merchant Shipping in the Sixteenth and Seventeenth Centuries', *MM*, 77 (1991), 5–20, at 5.

[15] The phrase used by Daniel A. Baugh in 'Maritime Strength and Atlantic Commerce: The Uses of "A Grand Marine Empire"', in *An Imperial State at War: Britain from 1689 to 1815*, ed. Lawrence Stone (1994), 185–223.

defeat the hellish designs of the Antichrist. It certainly involved defence against Catholic powers overseas, but even more it called for the proper enforcement of the penal laws against Catholics at home, for Rome was the centre of a single, worldwide conspiracy whose agents were at work everywhere, and had to be fought everywhere.[16] Foreign policy and war were remote and difficult subjects belonging to the prerogative of the crown. Domestic policy was within the competence and the understanding of members of parliament, and it was mainly in their sphere of home affairs that their ideas of sea-power were deployed.

Naval policies which conformed to the true and proper character of English sea-power could be confident of public support. War which promised to put money in the pockets of Englishmen (if not always of their government), war which strengthened the authority of parliament rather than the crown, above all war against Catholic rather than Protestant enemies, was warmly received by the political nation. But naval policies which appeared to serve the interests of the crown rather than the private citizen; policies tainted with arbitrary government, or its natural associate, religious toleration; above all policies of alliance with Catholic powers, were liable to be rejected as a false, unnatural and unpatriotic perversion of true English sea-power.

For the early Stuarts, the English naval myth was a minefield lying in the path of every attempt to use English sea-power. English parliamentarians of the day were not trying to assume the crown's prerogative powers to handle foreign policy and war. Their business was to represent their localities, and to avoid taking responsibility for these complex and expensive national burdens. Fortunately, there was no need for them to do so, since the secret of making war at sea without taxes was already discovered. In so far as taxes might be needed, they should be granted as a reward for virtue, that is to say after an aggressively Protestant foreign policy had proved its inevitable success. There was no point of contact here with the reality of James I's situation. To guard English independence from resurgent Habsburg power, to achieve his main foreign-policy objective of restoring his nephew to the Palatinate, called for alliance with France, which could only be bought by some relaxation of the penal laws against Catholics. For the House of Commons, this was popery and tyranny, the negation of a true English naval policy. What was worse, it was promoted by the duke of Buckingham, a kinsman of Catholics, a commander of armies and consequently an enemy of true freedom. So the naval expeditions of the 1620s were wrecked, and

---

[16] David Cressy, *Bonfires and Bells: National Memory and the Protestant Calendar in Elizabethan and Stuart England* (1989), 110–23; Carol Z. Wiener, 'The Beleaguered Isle: A Study of Elizabethan and Jacobean Anti-Catholicism', *Past and Present*, 51 (1971), 27–62 [hereafter *P&P*]; John Miller, *Popery and Politics in England 1660–1688* (Cambridge, 1973), 67–90.

Charles I inherited a situation in which his naval ambitions and those of his subjects were incompatible. For them the first essential of naval policy was to enforce the penal laws against Catholics; to invoke the blessing of God, and to bring in the rich prizes that were the inevitable fruit of a good and godly use of sea-power. 'We may enjoy peace and prosperity', as Isaac Pennington proclaimed; 'I mean peace with all the world, but war with Spain.' Sir John Eliot agreed: 'War only will secure and repair us' – meaning war with Spain, to be paid for by recusant fines.[17] Meanwhile the earl of Warwick and his associates of the Providence Island Company showed what a truly English naval policy should be, mounting a private naval war in the Caribbean against Spain, and in other seas against all comers. Warwick's piratical activities split the Virginia Company and nearly destroyed the East India Company, but in the eyes of public opinion they were a standing example, and reproach, to Charles I. It was no accident that it was John Hampden who was put up to oppose the legality of Ship Money, for as a director of the Providence Island Company he was a representative of true, patriotic English naval warfare.[18] Charles I's great fleet was a symbol of all his opponents regarded as wrong in his policy. It was maintained by extra-parliamentary taxation levied by prerogative power. It was associated with Laudian policies at home, and *de facto* Catholic alliance abroad. Without going to war it deterred foreign powers and supported the authority of the crown; instead of fighting to protect English trade and bring home lucrative prizes, as it should have done. When the civil war broke out and parliament gained control of the fleet, Warwick, the man who had shown Charles I how it ought to be done, was parliament's inevitable choice as its naval commander-in-chief.[19]

Under the Commonwealth and Protectorate the realities of power exposed some of the contradictions inherent in the English tradition of

[17] G. M. D. Howat, *Stuart and Cromwellian Foreign Policy* (1974), 52; S. R. Gardiner, *History of England from the Accession of James I to the Outbreak of the Civil War, 1603–1642* (10 vols., 1883–4), V, 191.

[18] Conrad Russell, *Parliaments and English Politics 1621–1629* (Oxford, 1979), 8, 71–83, 284–5, 290; Thomas Cogswell, 'Foreign Policy and Parliament: The Case of La Rochelle', *English Historical Review*, 99 (1984), 241–67 [hereafter *EHR*]; Roger Lockyer, *Buckingham: The Life and Political Career of George Villiers, First Duke of Buckingham, 1592–1628* (1981), 190, 244, 266, 467–74; S. L. Adams, 'Foreign Policy and the Parliaments of 1621 and 1624', in *Factions and Parliament: Essays on Early Stuart History*, ed. Kevin Sharpe (Oxford, 1978), 139–71; Simon Adams, 'Spain or the Netherlands? The Dilemmas of Early Stuart Foreign Policy', in *Before the English Civil War: Essays on Early Stuart Politics and Government*, ed. Howard Tomlinson (1983), 79–101; W. Frank Craven, 'The Earl of Warwick, a Speculator in Piracy', *Hispanic American Historical Review*, 10 (1930), 457–79; 'The Earl of Warwick's Voyage of 1627', ed. Nelson P. Bard, in *The Naval Miscellany V*, ed. N. A. M. Rodger (NRS, CXXV, 1984), 15–93; Nelson P. Bard, 'The Ship Money Case and William Fiennes, Viscount Saye and Sele', *Bulletin of the Institute of Historical Research*, 50 (1977), 177–84.

[19] Miller, *Popery and Politics*, 81–4; N. A. M. Rodger, *The Safeguard of the Sea: A Naval History of Britain*, I: *660–1649* (1997), 379–86, 393–4.

sea-power. For the first time since the tenth century, a fleet was built powerful enough to raise England to the first rank of European powers – a fleet paid for by arbitrary taxation illegally imposed by a military dictatorship which had ruthlessly slaughtered every one of the sacred cows of English liberty for which the civil war had supposedly been fought. This fleet launched into a war of aggression against fellow-Protestants, the Dutch, justified by the tortuous argument that a Presbyterian was next kin to a Jesuit, and that as insufficiently pious Protestants they constituted the first obstacle to the march on Rome. The Spanish War which followed brought disillusionment from another quarter. It was beyond question that such a war must be blessed by God, who had so often blessed the Good Old Cause, all the more so since 'the Spaniards cannot oppose much, being a lazy, sinfull people, feeding like beasts upon their lusts, and upon the fat of the land, and never trained up to warres'.[20] Instead, the war brought heavy expense, heavy loss to trade and no profit whatever. Cromwell's confidence never recovered from the humiliating Hispaniola disaster, the worst defeat the New Model Army ever suffered. In the end the war served not for 'the ruining and the utter fall of Romish Babylon',[21] but only to make England an auxiliary to the aggressive foreign policy of Cardinal Mazarin.[22]

All this might have taught public men a few lessons in the realities of sea-power, but the only one they seem to have learnt, at least in part, was its true financial cost. The Interregnum at least taught the English to pay taxes, and the political debates of Charles II's reign assumed a more realistic, or at least less unrealistic, estimate of the resources needed to make war at sea.[23] In all other respects England's experience of military dictatorship only entrenched the myths of sea-power. The failures of Cromwell's navy were swiftly forgotten, and its successes attributed to

[20] Thomas Gage, in *A Collection of the State Papers of John Thurloe*, ed. T. Birch (7 vols., 1742), III, 60.

[21] Thomas Gage, in *Thurloe State Papers*, ed. Birch, III, 61.

[22] Steven C. A. Pincus, 'Popery, Trade and Universal Monarchy: The Ideological Context of the Outbreak of the Second Anglo-Dutch War', *EHR*, 107 (1992), 1–29; John F. Battick, 'Cromwell's Diplomatic Blunder: The Relationship between the Western Design of 1654–55 and the French Alliance of 1657', *Albion*, 5 (1973), 279–98; Charles P. Korr, *Cromwell and the New Model Foreign Policy: England's Policy towards France, 1649–1658* (Berkeley, CA, 1975); Timothy Venning, *Cromwellian Foreign Policy* (1995); Hans-Christoph Junge, *Flottenpolitik und Revolution: Die Entstehung der englischen Seemacht während der Herrschaft Cromwells* (Stuttgart, 1980); Roger Crabtree, 'The Idea of a Protestant Foreign Policy', in *Cromwell, A Profile*, ed. Ivan Roots (London, 1973), 160–89; Blair Worden, 'Oliver Cromwell and the Sin of Achan', in *History, Society and the Churches: Essays in Honour of Owen Chadwick*, ed. Derek Beales and Geoffrey Best (Cambridge, 1985), 125–45; R. C. Thompson, 'Officers, Merchants and Foreign Policy in the Protectorate of Oliver Cromwell', *Historical Studies Australia and New Zealand*, 12 (1965–7), 149–65.

[23] James Scott Wheeler, *The Making of a World Power: War and the Military Revolution in Seventeenth-Century England* (Stroud, 1999).

virtue and godliness. In a striking witness to the English capacity to build an imaginary world, this military despotism came to be cited as a symbol of political liberty. All this was possible because sea-power, and the Navy in particular, was a subject in which every shade of opinion in Restoration England took pride. Here, and here alone, royalist and republican met on common ground. The Navy was a national concern, one on which every Englishman claimed an opinion. Things could be said about the Navy which could not be said about the state. It was impossible to speak openly in favour of the English Republic in the 1660s – but it was entirely acceptable to argue that the republican Navy had been successful because it had been virtuous and godly, where the Stuart Navy was neither. Right actions at home were the foundation of success abroad. As Charles II fought two wars against the Protestant Dutch, both of them in a context of resurgent royal authority, parliament reacted as it had to his father: when the king asked for money for the Navy, parliament rebuked his false sense of priorities by concentrating on suppressing the Catholics. During 1665 and 1666 it forced through the Irish Cattle Acts, and blamed the papists for the Great Fire. For want of the money the Commons were too busy and too suspicious to vote, the main fleet had to be laid up, opening the way for the Dutch raid on the Medway.[24]

The Third Dutch War, fought in alliance with Louis XIV, on a domestic policy of naked tolerance, initially without parliamentary support, still more strongly aroused all the old English nightmares of popery and tyranny. Parliament's reaction to naval disappointment was to suppress the king's Declaration of Indulgence and impose the Test Act. As always, the essential core of any truly English naval policy was Protestantism, and its most urgent application was in domestic, not foreign policy. Parliament was somewhat reassured by the partial hand-over of the Navy to opposition management in 1673, and by the anti-French alliance of 1678, but all the old paranoia broke out anew with the Popish Plot, and once again the Navy was at the heart of the political crisis because it was seen to embody all that was right or wrong with the nation. The failure to discover the Catholic officers and administrators, alleged to control the Navy, may be said to mark the moment at which the Exclusion Crisis passed its peak, and Charles II's decision to hand over much of the management of the Navy to the opposition in the Commons (and to send into exile his brother the former lord admiral) was perhaps the essential concession which permitted him to weather the storm. In all this the Navy's real connection with the political issues was at best tangential. Even if you believe, as some historians still do,[25] that Charles II genuinely

---

[24] Ronald Hutton, *The Restoration: A Political and Religious History of England and Wales, 1658–1667* (Oxford, 1985), 251–60; Miller, *Popery and Politics*, 103–5.
[25] Lenman, *England's Colonial Wars*, 206.

aimed at imposing a Catholic despotism, there is no doubt that the Navy
would have been of little direct help to him, and that he did nothing to
make it in the least responsive to such ambitions. But for contemporaries
the Navy's connections with liberty and Protestantism were so intimate
that any threat to either of them had to be seen as a threat to the Navy's
proper identity.[26]

The same arguments presented themselves with redoubled force under
James II. Here again most contemporaries believed that toleration and
tyranny were inseparably linked, and again some modern historians
agree.[27] Once again contemporaries assumed that the perversion of the
Navy must be an essential part of the king's wicked plans. In this case their
fears were not completely imaginary, in that there were a few real Catholic
sea officers, but their obsession with the Mediterranean squadron as a
nursery of papists proved to be the exact reverse of the truth.[28] Once
again the English view of the foreign world was hopelessly distorted.
'There were two inchanting terms', one of the bishops recalled, 'which
at the first pronounciation could, like Circe's intoxicating cups, change
men into beasts; namely, Popery, and the French interest. Which words,
if anyone did but slightly mention in the House of Commons, all serious
counsels were immediately turn'd into rage and clamour.'[29] The public
mind was obsessed with the risk that James II would crush Protestant
liberty with the aid of Louis XIV and Innocent XI, though in reality his
Most Christian Majesty was a declared enemy of the pope, and James II
was on indifferent terms with both of them. Meanwhile, all unnoticed by
the public, a real invasion was preparing in an entirely different quarter.

In many respects the Glorious Revolution sharply increased the gap
between myth and reality in English naval power. Charles II and James
II had known and cared a great deal about their Navy, so that during
their reigns it enjoyed strong and expert leadership. William III had a
clear sense of the strategic value of sea-power, but no personal interest in
ships. The Revolution settlement indirectly strengthened parliamentary
authority in matters financial, and it was natural for him to concede
the powers of admiralty to parliament. The Dutch constitution had

[26] Steven C. A. Pincus, *Protestantism and Patriotism: Ideologies and the making of English Foreign
Policy, 1650–1668* (Cambridge, 1996), 354–70, 410–29; J. D. Davies, 'The Navy, Parliament
and Political Crisis in the Reign of Charles II', *Historical Journal*, 36 (1993), 271–88; J. R.
Jones, *The Anglo-Dutch Wars of the Seventeenth Century* (1996); Miller, *Popery and Politics*, 125–31.

[27] W. A. Speck, 'Some Consequences of the Glorious Revolution', in *The World of William
and Mary: Anglo-Dutch Perspectives on the Revolution of 1688–89*, ed. Dale Hoak and Mordechai
Feingold (Stanford, 1996), 29–41, at 31–2.

[28] L. Gooch, 'Catholic Officers in the Navy of James II', *Recusant History*, 14 (1978), 276–
80; Peter Le Fevre, 'Tangier, the Navy, and its Connection with the Glorious Revolution of
1688', *MM*, 73 (1987), 187–90.

[29] *Bishop Parker's History of his Own Time*, trans. Thomas Newlin (1727), 379–80; this is
Samuel Parker, made bishop of Oxford in 1686.

taught him to regard admiralties as engines of disunity and inefficiency, irretrievably dominated by his republican enemies. His business was to avoid government and control power by acting in secret through a few trusted ministers. He despised the ignorant passions of members of parliament, which he regarded as God's punishment on England, but he permitted them to interfere in the detailed management of the naval war. Terrified by the apparent ease with which the Dutch had invaded in 1688, obsessed by the political treachery which it believed had been responsible, the House of Commons reacted to every naval defeat, and some victories, by impeaching the admirals responsible. It arbitrarily reduced the naval votes to punish want of success, and attempted to manage both operational deployments and warship design by legislation.[30]

The most striking evidence of the extent to which the parliaments of William III and Queen Anne were possessed by naval myth rather than naval reality is the great controversy between 'Gentlemen' and 'Tarpaulins' which was at its height during these years. Ostensibly this pitted the advocates of officers promoted from warrant rank or the merchant service, against those of officers chosen from gentlemen. Historians from Macaulay onwards have believed that this was a real debate about a real naval issue.[31] Once upon a time it had been. Charles II in 1660 had faced a serious political and practical problem, inheriting a Navy commanded entirely by sectaries and republicans, and without any established system for selecting and promoting officers. His success in resolving this issue is one of the great achievements of his reign. Well before his death the sea officers were becoming a united corps. There were still many quarrels amongst them, but they were the professional disputes of rivals for promotion and prize money, having little connection with politics and almost none with social origin.[32] This was still true after the Revolution. There was a new problem with political tensions amongst senior officers, which parliament with its obsessive conspiracy theories did all it could to make worse, but there were no significant social tensions,

[30] J. A. Johnstone, 'Parliament and the Navy, 1688–1714' (Ph.D. thesis, Sheffield University, 1968); T. J. Denman, 'The Political Debate over War Strategy, 1689–1712' (Ph.D. thesis, Cambridge University, 1985); *Archives ou correspondance inédite de la maison d'Orange-Nassau*, fourth series, ed. F. J. L. Krämer (3 vols., Leiden, 1907–9) III, 249–50, 509; John Ehrman, *The Navy in the War of William III, 1689–1697: Its State and Direction* (Cambridge, 1953), 311–20; Brian Lavery, *The Ship of the Line* (2 vols., 1983–4), I, 70–1.

[31] T. B. Macaulay, *The History of England from the Accession of James II* (Everyman edn, 4 vols., 1906), I, 225–8; Norbert Elias, 'Studies in the Genesis of the Naval Profession', *British Journal of Sociology*, 1 (1950), 291–309.

[32] J. D. Davies, *Gentlemen and Tarpaulins: The Officers and Men of the Restoration Navy* (Oxford, 1991); Bernard Capp, *Cromwell's Navy: The Fleet and the English Revolution, 1648–1660* (Oxford, 1989), 387–96.

and the rapidly expanding Navy of the 1690s provided good promotion prospects for all comers.[33]

The 'Gentlemen versus Tarpaulins' controversy was conducted by politicians, few of whom knew anything about the real Navy. The Navy mattered very much to them, and it was perhaps the only major national institution that everyone supported. The Church, the monarchy, parliament, the army – all these were intensely divisive in the 1690s. Only the Navy united the political world, and provided a common language of political rhetoric. It was a screen on which every party could project its own ideology – a blank screen, thanks to their ignorance of what it was really like. Those who supported the 'Tarpaulins' praised not only their superior skill, but even more their superior virtue; they were more English, more manly, more Protestant and more courageous than Frenchified courtiers, cruel, effeminate and cowardly. The advocates of gentlemen likewise invoked the virtues which only breeding conferred, and which contrasted with the brutish ignorance of the common men. In between there were other positions, notably Lord Halifax's famous *Rough Draught of a New Modell at Sea* of 1694, arguing for a combination of both characters.[34]

In all this the Navy provided the language of political debate, not the subject. To speak for the superior virtue of Tarpaulin officers was to praise the Cromwellian Navy, and by implication the republican cause. Thus the author of *An Enquiry into the Causes of our Naval Miscarriages*, a pamphlet of 1707, quoted 'an old Cromwellian captain' on the moral collapse allegedly brought about by the Restoration:

> Instead of the good Morals, and harmless Conversation of our Seamen in the Parliament-time, there was nothing but Cursing, Swearing, Damning, Sinking, and obscene nasty Discourse, to be heard on board our Fleet; so that it look'd more like the Suburbs of Hell, than a Christian Navy.

He did not literally mean that the recent successes of Forbin and Duguay-Trouin against Channel convoys had been made possible by an outbreak of bad language in the English Navy almost half a century before; he meant that naval, and therefore national, success sprang from the virtue which a godly, republican system generated.[35]

There was a tendency for parliamentarians to become somewhat less ignorant about the Navy during the course of the wars of King William

---

[33] David Davies, 'The English Navy on the Eve of War, 1689', in *Guerres Maritimes (1688–1713)* (Vincennes, 1996), 1–14; N. A. M. Rodger, 'Commissioned Officers' Careers in the Royal Navy, 1690–1815', *Journal for Maritime Research* [www.jmr.nmm.ac.uk] (July 2001), graphs 1.1, 2.1, 3.1, 6.1, 6.2.

[34] *The Works of George Savile, Marquis of Halifax*, ed. Mark N. Brown (3 vols., Oxford, 1989), I, 296–314; Robert E. Glass, 'The Image of the Sea Officer in English Literature, 1660–1710', *Albion*, 26 (1994), 583–99.

[35] Glass, 'The Image of the Sea Officer', 587–9.

and Queen Anne. The lapse of the Licensing Act in 1695 promoted the circulation of information and argument, some of it sound, and Queen Anne's desire to resign to parliament many decisions that William III had kept to himself encouraged a less irresponsible attitude.[36] Nevertheless the parliamentarians of the eighteenth century still thought naturally in terms of agreeable stereotypes, and many if not most would probably have agreed with Henry Pelham: 'My observation as to foreign affairs is, that the less one knows of them the better.'[37] Ignorant and credulous public men, informed or misinformed by ignorant and credulous journalists, were easily roused to xenophobia, and still obsessed by fears of popery and arbitrary government.[38]

An obvious example of this is the popular hysteria which forced Walpole's government into war with Spain in 1739. The public remained almost as convinced as Cromwell's government had been over eighty years before that Spain was wealthy, effete and vulnerable, though ministers were much better informed. A 'mad and vain nation... warmed and hardened by pride and prejudice',[39] identified with the traditional, patriotic myths of national naval superiority which dictated that a war against Spain must necessarily be easy, glorious and profitable. Pious, virtuous and blessed by God, English sea-power could not but be prosperous. It might cost money, but that money was in the nature of an investment which would yield a sure return. 'What we give towards the support of a War seems to be but a kind of Venture to the Sea, which may return again with great Profit which makes us Contribute with Alacrity towards the Charges of such a War.'[40] In the words of the title of a pamphlet of 1727, *Great Britain's Speediest Sinking Fund is a Powerful Maritime War, Rightly Manag'd, and Especially in the West Indies.*[41]

[36] Johnstone, 'Parliament and the Navy', 57–8 and 493–5; Denman, 'The Political Debate over War Strategy', 18–19; John B. Hattendorf, 'The Machinery for the Planning and Execution of English Grand Strategy in the War of the Spanish Succession, 1702–1713', in *Changing Interpretations and New Sources in Naval History: Papers from the Third United States Naval Academy History Symposium*, ed. R. W. Love, jr (New York, 1980), 80–95.

[37] To Lord Essex, 21 July 1735: Jeremy Black, 'British Neutrality in the War of the Polish Succession, 1733–1735', *International History Review*, 8 (1986), 345–66, at 358.

[38] J. C. D. Clark, *The Dynamics of Change: The Crisis of the 1750s and English Party Systems* (Cambridge, 1982), 11–12; Paul Langford, 'William Pitt and Public Opinion, 1757', EHR, 88 (1973), 54–80, at 58–9; J. R. Jones, *Britain and the World 1649–1815* (Brighton, 1980), 12–13; James T. Boulton, 'Arbitrary Power: An Eighteenth-Century Obsession', *Studies in Burke and his Times*, 9 (1968), 905–26; David Armitage, *The Ideological Origins of the British Empire* (Cambridge, 2000), 143–4, 173.

[39] Philip Woodfine, 'The Anglo-Spanish War of 1739', in *The Origins of War in Early Modern Europe*, ed. Jeremy Black (Edinburgh, 1987), 185–209, quoting at 185–6 the ministerial writer Henry Etough.

[40] Ruth Bourne, *Queen Anne's Navy in the West Indies* (New Haven, 1939), 20, quoting Dr James Drake, *An Essay concerning the Necessity of Equal Taxes* (1702).

[41] Daniel A. Baugh, *British Naval Administration in the Age of Walpole* (Princeton, 1965), 15.

The Cromwellian regime was now less fashionable, and the naval
virtues were once again evoked by references to the glories of Queen
Elizabeth's reign. Thomson and Arne united to remind the Opposition
of Britannia's glories, and to conjure up a future golden age in which
'Don Roberto' would be ejected from power, British sea-power restored
and Britons nevermore be slaves. The Navy, 'as essential to our Safety &
Wealth as Parliament or Magna Charta', was the guarantor of freedom,
virtue and conquest.[42] Those like Admiral Vernon whose victories gave
substance to these myths were immediately elevated to the status of
Protestant heroes.[43] Those who failed to do their duty by the myths of
sea-power, like Mathews, Lestock or Byng, were condemned to public
execration, if not execution.[44] Popular religious sentiment remained
strong, and anti-Catholicism was sharply revived by the 1745 Jacobite
rebellion, so that Protestantism, prosperity and naval mastery remained
closely connected.[45] From the 1750s, public attention tended to turn to
France rather than Spain, but sea-power was as ever the guarantor of all
that really mattered.

> All true Englishmen, since the decay of the Spanish monarchy, have ever taken it for
> granted, that the security of their religion, liberty and property; that their honour, their
> wealth, and their trade depend chiefly upon the proper measures to be taken from time
> to time against the growing power of France.[46]

The proper measures were of course naval, and by the end of the Seven
Years War sea-power was still more deeply entrenched as the supreme

[42] Philip Woodfine, *Britannia's Glories: The Walpole Ministry and the 1739 War with Spain*
(Woodbridge, 1998), quoting (at 235) the diplomat Sir Everard Fawkener; *idem*, 'Ideas of
Naval Power and the Conflict with Spain, 1737–1742', in *The British Navy and the Use of Naval
Power in the Eighteenth Century*, ed. Jeremy Black and Philip Woodfine (Leicester, 1988), 71–90;
Richard Harding, *Amphibious Warfare in the Eighteeth Century: The British Expedition to the West
Indies 1740–1742* (Woodbridge, 1991), 22–6.
[43] Gerald Jordan and Nicholas Rogers, 'Admirals as Heroes: Patriotism and Liberty in
Hanoverian England', *Journal of British Studies*, 28 (1989), 201–24; Kathleen Wilson, 'Empire,
Trade and Popular Politics in Mid-Hanoverian Britain: The Case of Admiral Vernon',
P&P, 121 (1988), 74–109.
[44] Bob Harris, '"American Idols": War and the Middling Ranks in Mid-Eighteenth
Century Britain', *P&P*, 150 (1996), 111–41, at 119–21; Nicholas Rogers, *Crowds, Culture and
Politics in Georgian Britain* (Oxford, 1998), 61–3.
[45] Jeremy Black, *Natural and Necessary Enemies: Anglo-French Relations in the Eighteenth Century*
(1986), 161; Colin Haydon, '"I Love my King and my Country, but a Roman Catholic
I Hate": Anti-Catholicism, Xenophobia and National Identity in Eighteenth-Century
England', in *Protestantism and National Identity: Britain and Ireland, c. 1650–c. 1850*, ed. Tony
Claydon and Ian McBride (Cambridge, 1998), 33–52; Armitage, *Ideological Origins*, 7–8.
[46] *The Fourth Earl of Sandwich: Diplomatic Correspondence 1763–1765*, ed. Frank Spencer
(Manchester, 1961), 7, quoting Israel Maudit, *Considerations on the Present German War*, 4th
edn (1761), 10.

symbol of the national character and virtue.[47] A generation later Admiral Keppel briefly attained the status of Protestant hero, not for having won a victory, but for having diverted the Navy from oppressing the Americans back to its proper role of fighting Catholics and defending English liberties. It was even insinuated that his enemy Admiral Palliser was a secret Catholic in league with the administration to subvert English freedom.[48]

Since liberty was a defining characteristic both of sea-power and of Britain, the methods used to man the Navy presented certain intellectual and moral inconsistencies which neatly illustrate the gap between myth and reality. For those professionally concerned with the efficiency of the Navy, the manning problem was a permanent nightmare. Seven times between 1696 and 1758 government bills were introduced into parliament which offered to move at least some way away towards methods more equitable and less arbitrary than the press. Only the first was enacted, and its failure reinforced prejudice against all plans of registration, however limited and voluntary. Liberty and the Navy were intimately associated, and the symbiosis of trade and sea-power provided the Navy's manpower by an automatic mechanism which required no government intervention. Consequently, there could be no manning problem; or if there appeared to be, it was only because of Walpole's malice and tyranny.[49] His 1740 scheme proposed, the Opposition claimed, 'not only to enslave, for the best part of their lives, upwards of 150,000 free born subjects, and to invest the crown with an absolute power over them; but also, thereby to give the crown a farther power of influencing of the

---

[47] Stephen Conway, 'War and National Identity in the Mid-Eighteenth-Century British Isles', *EHR*, 116 (2001), 863–93, at 884–6; Peter Krahé, *Literarische Seestücke: Darstellungen von Meer und Seefahrt in der englischen Literatur des 18. bis 20. Jahrhunderts* (Hamburg, 1992), 29–43; Juan A. Ortega y Medina, *El conflicto anglo-español por el dominio oceanico (siglos XVI y XVIII)* (Mexico City 1981); Geoff Quilley, '"All Ocean Is her Own": The Image of the Sea and the Identity of the Maritime Nation in Eighteenth-Century British Art', in *Imagining Nations*, ed. Geoffrey Cubitt (Manchester, 1998), 132–52.

[48] Rogers, *Crowds, Culture and Politics*, 122–51; Kathleen Wilson, *The Sense of the People: Politics, Culture and Imperialism in England, 1715–1785* (Cambridge, 1995), 256–8; *The Private Papers of John, Earl of Sandwich, First Lord of the Admiralty 1771–1782*, ed. G. R. Barnes and J. H. Owen (NRS, LXIX, LXXI, LXXV, LXXVIII, 1932–8), II, 191; A. M. W. Stirling, *Pages & Portraits from the Past, Being the Private Papers of Admiral Sir William Hotham, G.C.B. Admiral of the Red* (2 vols., 1919), II, 311; Stephen Conway, *The British Isles and the War of American Independence* (Oxford, 2000), 255–6.

[49] J. S. Bromley, 'Away from Impressment: The Idea of a Royal Naval Reserve, 1696–1859', in *Britain and the Netherlands*, VI: *War and Society*, ed. A. C. Duke and C. A. Tamse (The Hague, 1977), 168–88; Gillian Hughes, 'The Act for the Increase and Encouragement of Seamen, 1696–1710. Could it Have Solved the Royal Navy's Manning Problem?', in *Guerres Maritimes*, 25–34; Christopher Lloyd, *The British Seaman 1200–1860: A Social Survey* (1968), 173–93; Baugh, *British Naval Administration*, 234–40; Stephen Gradish, *The Manning of the British Navy during the Seven Years' War* (1980), 107–10.

elections throughout England'.[50] Genghis Khan, James II and the Spanish Inquisition were invoked to illustrate its horrors. The modest 1749 plan to establish a voluntary reserve of 3,000 men was denounced as intending 'to circumscribe public liberty, and augment the number of those, whom ministers desired to reduce to a state of slavery'.[51] Those who opposed reserve or registration schemes as a threat to the liberty of the subject were implicitly declaring that impressment was a lesser threat, or none at all, but perhaps understandably, they tended not to push their case to its logical conclusion. For the Wilkite and pro-American radicals later in the century who directly attacked impressment as an infringement of English liberties this graceful elision was not so easy. Taking impressment in isolation, their case almost made itself, but it presented difficulties when they fully subscribed to the traditional idea of British sea-power as a temple of Protestant liberty, and demanded that the Navy be mobilised at the same time as denying it an essential source of manpower. A figure like Granville Sharp neatly illustrates the contradictions. A leader of the City of London opposition to impressment during the American War, Sharp was also founding chairman both of the Anti-Slavery Society and later of the Protestant Union. There was nothing in the least contradictory, of course, in campaigning simultaneously for the emancipation of slaves and against that of Catholics. The suppression of Catholicism had always been regarded as an essential element of English liberty, and remained so for the popular radicals of the period. The difficulty for Sharp, and those who campaigned with him against impressment, was that the Navy also was so inseparably connected with English liberty that it was difficult to campaign against the tyranny of the press without appearing to be a friend of tyranny.[52]

Their solution lay not in explicit arguments, which might have been somewhat vulnerable, but in skilful insinuations that impressment,

---

[50] Lord Gage, in *The Parliamentary History of England*, ed. William Cobbett (36 vols., 1806–20), XI, 422.

[51] William Coxe, *Memoirs of the Administration of the Right Honourable Henry Pelham* (2 vols., 1829), II, 67, quoting Lord Egmont.

[52] John A. Wood, 'The City of London and Impressment 1776–1777', *Proceedings of the Leeds Philosophical and Literary Society*, 8 (1956–9), 111–27; Nicholas Rogers, 'Liberty Road: Opposition to Impressment in Britain during the American War of Independence', in *Jack Tar in History: Essays in the History of Maritime Life and Labour*, ed. Colin Howell and Richard J. Twomey (Fredericton, NB, 1991), 53–75; Bromley, 'Away from Impressment', 170–1; Prince Hoare, *Memoirs of Granville Sharp*, 2nd edn (2 vols., 1828); John Sainsbury, *Disaffected Patriots: London Supporters of Revolutionary America 1769–1782* (Gloucester, 1987), 134–9; Linda Colley, 'Radical Patriotism in Eighteenth-Century England', in *Patriotism: The Making and Unmaking of British National Identity*, ed. Raphael Samuel (3 vols., 1989), I, 169–87; Stephen Conway, 'The Politics of British Military and Naval Mobilization, 1775–83', *EHR*, 112 (1997), 1179–201; Conway, *British Isles*, 153, 255–6; Margarette Lincoln, *Representing the Royal Navy: British Sea Power, 1750–1815* (Aldershot, 2002), 66.

however the crown might try to justify it, was not really a method of manning the Navy at all.[53] The prints and engravings of the anti-impressment movement are a rich source of these ideas. In Gillray's celebrated 'The Liberty of the Subject' of 1779, for example, a press gang is discovered at work in a London square. To judge by the architecture and the clothes of the bystanders, the scene is somewhere in Mayfair, and we are meant to understand that the press gang is a threat, not to the poor and propertyless, but to people who matter, the sort who could afford to buy a one-shilling coloured print like this. The gang is in the process of seizing a tailor. Tailors were notoriously impotent, in every sense, and clearly outside the press-warrant's definition of 'Seamen, Seafaring Men and Persons whose Occupations or Callings are to work in Vessels and Boats upon Rivers.' To take a tailor, therefore, was both illegal and pointless: an arbitrary exercise of power which was of no service to the Navy, and which the patriot could oppose with a clear conscience. The print, in short, depicts an imaginary world which it was convenient for opposition radicals to believe in. Real impressment took place largely at sea. Press-gangs on shore did exist, but they were not promenading in Berkeley Square at noon, they were raiding the waterside pubs of Wapping and Shadwell at midnight. Nor were they illegally taking landsmen; they were selectively looking for the one category of manpower of which the Navy was critically in need: seamen, and above all topmen.[54]

Another imaginary world in which not only metropolitan radicals but all sorts of MPs devoutly wished to believe was that in which the Navy acted as an instrument to purify as well as to defend society, freeing it of 'idle and reprobate Vermin by converting them into a Body of the most industrious People, and even, becoming the very nerves of our State'.[55] Hence the regularity with which every naval bill, regardless of its other provisions, enacted means by which magistrates might despatch paupers and petty criminals into the Navy. This was more than a cynical exercise in reducing the poor rates, it represented a deep-seated feeling about the purifying and cleansing effect of righteous war which can be traced back to Protestant writers of the sixteenth century.[56] This was what ought to have been a function of a truly national force acting in a just cause, and

[53] The idea survives among American Marxists, for example, Jesse Lemisch's assertion that 'the navy pressed because to be in the navy was in some sense to be a slave'. J. Lemisch, 'Jack Tar in the Streets: Merchant Seamen in the Politics of Revolutionary America', *William and Mary Quarterly*, third series, 35 (1968), 371–407, at 383.

[54] N. A. M. Rodger, *The Wooden World: An Anatomy of the Georgian Navy* (1986), 164–82.

[55] Rogers, *Crowds, Culture and Politics*, 88, quoting a pamphlet of 1751 by 'Philonauta' (usually identified as Admiral Sir Charles Knowles).

[56] George, 'War and Peace in the Puritan Tradition', 499; J. R. Hale, 'Incitement to Violence? English Divines on the Theme of War, 1578 to 1631', in *Renaissance War Studies* (1983), 487–517, at 494, 498.

therefore, in the minds of public men, it was. In reality, though magistrates occasionally tried to exercise these powers, there was no provision to force the Navy to accept their offerings, and it was usually reluctant to do so.[57]

By the late eighteenth century, sea-power had been an essential part of the patriotic English self-image for over two centuries, and patriotism had always been the first resort of the opposition. Governments might be obliged to take some account of inconvenient facts, but oppositions could always triumph in the virtual reality of the English political imagination, in which sea-power was ever-victorious, in the right kind of war, against the right kind of enemy. A government which declined to fight such a war, like Walpole's in the 1730s, stood self-condemned as unpatriotic, cowardly and tyrannical. A government which accepted the challenge was doomed either to fail, demonstrating incompetence if not treachery, or to succeed, as Walpole's administration did in sending Vernon to attack Porto Bello in 1740, in which case the victory was immediately transformed in Opposition eyes into 'our honest admiral's triumph over Sir Robert and Spain'.[58] Governments, in short, could not win. As late as 1790, the Nootka Sound crisis aroused all the old anti-Spanish certainies so powerfully that the younger Pitt's government was driven by public opinion into claiming a right (to trade anywhere in Spanish territory regardless of Spanish law or policy) which it knew was indefensible, and which it expected would lead to war.[59]

The Navy was still, in the words of the *Gentleman's Magazine* in 1798, 'the sacred palladium of our laws, our religion, and our liberties, not to perish or be overthrown but with the downfal [*sic*] of Great Britain itself'.[60] Already, however, the moral and political value of sea-power was changing. In the Seven Years War the elder Pitt (with a little help from Frederick the Great) made the national myth work for the government. In the American War, the spectacle of Whig peers openly rejoicing at British naval defeats, and Whig admirals refusing to fight the French,

---

[57] Baugh, *British Naval Administration*, 160–1; D. Hay, 'War, Dearth and Theft in the Eighteenth Century: The Record of the English Courts', *P&P*, 95 (1982), 117–60, at 157; Gillian Russell, *The Theatres of War: Performance, Politics and Society, 1793–1815* (Oxford, 1995), 8; Clive Emsley, 'The Recruitment of Petty Offenders during the French Wars 1793–1815', *MM*, 66 (1980), 199–208; Rogers, 'Liberty Road', 70–1; Conway, *British Isles*, 37; Philip Woodfine, '"Proper Objects of the Press": Naval Impressment and Habeas Corpus in the French Revolutionary Wars', in *The Representation and Reality of War: The British Experience: Essays in Honour of David Wright*, ed. Keith Dockray and Keith Laybourn (Stroud, 1999), 39–60; Lincoln, *Representing the Royal Navy*, 79, 91; Bob Harris, 'Patriotic Commerce and National Revival: The Free British Fishery Society and British Politics, c. 1749–58', *EHR*, 114 (1999), 285–313, at 207, 302–3.
[58] Stanley Ayling, *The Elder Pitt, Earl of Chatham* (1976), 66.
[59] John M. Norris, 'The Policy of the British Cabinet in the Nootka Crisis', *EHR*, 70 (1955), 562–80.
[60] Quoted by Lincoln, *Representing the Royal Navy*, 99.

did a good deal to disgust public opinion and uncouple sea-power from the Opposition.[61] After the war, still aided by the folly of its opponents, and later by the violence of the French revolutionaries, the younger Pitt's government began to appropriate naval patriotism for itself. Anti-Catholicism, for so long an essential part of the English definition of liberty, began to wilt in the 1790s in the face of aggressive atheism. The Navy now became the 'characteristic and constitutional defence' of the country, as Wellington called it,[62] and its adoption as part of the political constitution of the state (as opposed to the moral constitution of the nation) marks a significant development. The nationalisation of patriotism changed the symbolic value of the Navy. Where formerly an abstract sea-power had embodied the national virtues, now sea officers and seamen in person were elevated from honest but somewhat comic figures of the stage, to the status of symbolic national heroes. Their plain, manly sincerity exemplified all that was truest in the English character, and contrasted with the disloyal, Frenchified effeminacy of the Whig aristocracy, and the atheistic republicanism of the radicals.[63] To the consternation of the old-fashioned, real seamen were allowed to walk in the 1797 procession organised by the government to give thanks for recent naval victories. Naval temples in which to celebrate the new national cult were proposed, and in some cases built. Naval monuments to the fallen heroes were erected at public expense.[64] Poets good and bad turned to the Navy – 'the scene of our Triumphs, the source of our Wealth, and the safeguard of our Empire', in the words of the Poet Laureate Henry Pye – for inspiration.[65] William Pitt had caught the Whigs bathing and stolen their clothes.[66]

Radical critics could no longer appeal to the easy certainties of the English naval myth, for Queen Elizabeth now belonged to the government. Naval warfare still came naturally to them as the language

[61] M. D. George, *English Political Caricature to 1792: A Study of Opinion and Propaganda* (Oxford, 1959), 163–6.

[62] John Ehrman, *The Younger Pitt: The Years of Acclaim* (1969), 313.

[63] Lincoln, *Representing the Royal Navy*, 2–6, 29–32; Gerald Newman, *The Rise of English Nationalism: A Cultural History, 1740–1830* (1987), 80–2, 92, 129–33, 194, 213–21; Paul Langford, *Public Life and the Propertied Englishman 1689–1798* (1991), 536–41; Emma Vincent Macleod, *A War of Ideas: British Attitudes to the Wars against Revolutionary France 1792–1802* (Aldershot, 1998), 185.

[64] Alison Yarrington, *The Commemoration of the Hero, 1800–1864: Monuments to the British Victors of the Napoleonic Wars* (1988), 7. The as-yet unpublished work of Dr Holger Hoock will also explore this theme.

[65] Lynda Pratt, 'Naval Contemplation: Poetry, Patriotism and the Navy 1797–99', *Journal for Maritime Research* [www.jmr.nmm.ac.uk] (Dec. 2000), 4.

[66] Linda Colley, 'The Apotheosis of George III: Loyalty, Royalty and the British Nation 1760–1820', *P&P*, 102 (1984), 94–129, at 128; Newman, *English Nationalism*, 36–82, 129–33, 230–1; Jordan and Rogers, 'Admirals as Heroes', 214–22; Russell, *Theatres of War*, 88; J. E. Cookson, *The British Armed Nation, 1793–1815* (Oxford, 1997), 215–17; Langford, *Public Life*, 536–41.

of political rhetoric, but they had to invent new myths of sea-power of their own. Thus, in the unpublished early version of his epic poem *Madoc*, finished in the same year as the naval procession of 1797, the young Robert Southey enriched English literature with a lengthy description of the (otherwise unrecorded) naval battles between Prince Madoc of Gwynedd and the Aztecs, in which the brutally efficient Welsh stand as figures for the Royal Navy; while the freedom-loving Aztecs, their piety and domestic virtues marred only by the occasional human sacrifice, represent the French republicans.[67]

Here we have come full circle, back to the original (and only genuine) British empire of Humphrey Llwyd and John Dee, in which Prince Madoc's most eminent descendant Elizabeth Tudor was to rule over the Welsh-speaking Indians of North America.[68] On this fantastic scene, we may draw this brief survey to a close. The English naval myth was by no means dead, but in its new guise as the property of the state it no longer represented a radical critique of reality. Much about it was still fictional, but henceforward the fictions were different, and in different service. Queen Elizabeth still had a long afterlife ahead of her, but for the historians of the nineteenth century she and the English seamen of her age were the private property of the Royal Navy.[69]

Much of the afterlife of Elizabethan sea-power in the seventeenth and eighteenth centuries can only be understood by carefully distinguishing the history of the real sea, and the sea as viewed from Westminster. There were connections between the two, of course. There was a good deal of correct information in the public domain, competing with much inaccuracy and fantasy.[70] There were men in public life with first-hand knowledge of the realities of sea-power, though their expertise often aroused as much suspicion as respect. In practice the degree of divergence between the reality of naval power, and the image of it as perceived by the political nation, varied at different periods, and on different issues. It did not vary in a random fashion, for the discrepancy was not simply caused by ignorance. Most public men were ignorant of the remote and highly technical world of the seamen, but the problem was not so much that they knew too little, but that they knew too much, or thought they did. 'The men of both these parties are alike in being open to conviction; but so many convictions have already got inside, that it is very difficult to find the openings.'[71] For centuries a set of simple, powerful and tenacious

---

[67] Pratt, 'Naval Contemplation'.

[68] Gwyn A. Williams, *Madoc: The Making of a Myth* (1979), 31–67.

[69] Cynthia Fansler Behrman, *Victorian Myths of the Sea* (Athens, OH, 1977).

[70] Clark, *The Dynamics of Change*, 10–13.

[71] F. M. Cornford, *Microcosmographia Academica, Being a Guide for the Young Academic Politician* (Cambridge, 1908), 4.

174

concepts occupied that part of the minds of English public men which was devoted to the sea, and left little room for inconvenient facts which could not be accommodated to the established image. English, later British, sea-power benefited essentially from a breadth and depth of public support which had no equivalent in any other naval power. Without that support it seems very unlikely that Britain would ever have risen to be a dominant trading and later industrial power – but it was not based on the rational analysis of accurate information. In many areas of history, the scholar needs to master the complex and technical world of real seafaring, but to understand policy and high politics we must put aside the inconvenient complications of the facts, to enter into the alternative reality of English sea-power as English politicians imagined it: a myth strong and simple, like all the best myths, with just enough truth to sustain credibility, and not too much to muddle or perplex the public mind.

Additional Note [2009]

This piece began life as my inaugural lecture as Professor of Naval History in the University of Exeter in 2002.

VII

THE VICTUALLING OF THE BRITISH NAVY
IN THE SEVEN YEARS WAR

In 1922 two schoolmasters at the Royal Naval College at Dartmouth published for the use of their pupils an edition of *Select Naval Documents* (1). It is a slim book, and the selection necessarily rigorous, but it is interesting as exactly representing contemporary opinion on what was essential in British naval history. One piece sufficed to illustrate the victualling of the Navy during the eighteenth century. It was a composite made up of a number of passages from a pamphlet of 1761 by William Thompson, *An Appeal to the Public in Vindication of Truth and Matters of Fact*. It reads, in part, as follows :

'That Mariners in the King's Ships have frequently put their 24 hours' allowance of salt provisions into their tobacco-boxes. That seamen in the King's Ships have made buttons for their Jackets and Trowses (sic) with the Cheese they were served with, having preferred it, by reason of its tough and durable quality, to buttons made of common metal ; and that Carpenters in the Navy-Service have made Trucks to their Ships' flagstaffs with whole Cheeses, which have stood the weather equally with any timber. That the Flour in the King's Ships has been devoured by weevils, and become so intolerably musty, and cemented into such hard rocks, that the men have been obliged to use instruments, with all their feeble power, to break and pulverise it before they could make use of it, as though, in a comparitive degree, they had been stubbing to pieces the ruins of an old fortification.

That their bread has been so full of large black-headed maggots and that they have so nauseated the thoughts of it, as to be obliged to shut their eyes to confine that sense from being offended before they could bring their minds to a resolution of consuming it.

That their beer has stunk as abominably as the foul stagnant water which is pumped out of many cellars in London at midnight hour ; and that they were under a necessity of shutting their eyes, and stopping their breath by holding of their noses before they could conquer their aversion, so as to prevail upon themselves in their extreme necessities to drink it' (2).

Students of British naval history will recognise here a number of cherished literary motifs, repeated by almost every writer on the subject (3) ; the meat shrunk to minute proportions, the cheese made into buttons, the bread full of maggots and weevils, the stinking beer, are all familiar friends, and with some notable exceptions (4), they are adopted now, as they were sixty years ago, as sufficient comment on the state of British naval victualling in the eighteenth century.

It is therefore worth examining William Thompson and his « truth and matters of fact » in more detail. He was a foreman cooper in the Pickle Yard of the Victualling Office in London, (5) who in 1744 approached his superiors with allegations of negligence and inefficiency in his department. At the same time complaints reached the Victualling Board from sea of some over-age provisions condemned, and the resulting investigation pointed again at the Pickle Yard. Thompson was one of those responsible, and in January 1744/5 he was dismissed. The fact that he was, in his own words, reputed a troublesome busy-body, no doubt did not help him (6).

There the matter rested for twelve years. Then, in 1757, Thompson published his first pamphlet, *The Royal Navy Men's Advocate,* in which he rehearsed the circumstances of his dismissal and vigorously attacked the sloth and corruption of the Victualling Office. It is not obvious why he had taken twelve years to bring himself to print, but the pamphlet is dedicated to Alderman Beckford, the leader of City opposition to the Newcastle administration then just losing power because, among other things, of its alleged mismanagement of the war at sea. It looks as though someone had found a use for Thompson's grievance. Next year he published *The Case of William Thompson,* which covered much the same ground as before, and in 1761 he followed it with the Appeal quoted above.

Having read these three works the reader may begin to feel, if he had not already suspected from the title, that there may be more, or rather less, to Thompson's statements than truth and matters of fact. Much of his writing is in a style of extravagant rhodomontade, of which a fair specimen is his description of his former employers, the Commissioners of the Victualling :

« Tinkers and Taylors, coachmen, Footmen, Cinder-Whenches and Coblers, all seated at a Board together, brooding wondrous addled things ; and whilst hatching, lo ! the vast Change of Time, assisted by Magick Art of Transmutation, these brightly illuminated, irradiated, sagacious, and once wonderful and much honoured terrible Things, after being well ground, brewed, backed, bled, pickled, salted, sifted, forged, mended etc..., were worked up into Animals, not much unlike the Academical Apes in the Print Shops » (7).

The factual claims which can be isolated from all this amount to three ; a statement of the abuses Thompson recollected from the 1740 s and presumed to be still current, some quotations from a Parliamentary enquiry in the reign of Queen Anne, and the claim that Admiral Boscawen supported him. Boscawen was certainly not an uncritical friend of the Victualling Office (8), but it is significant that the claim is advanced only in Thompson's third pamphlet, published just after the admiral's death. It was not made while he was alive to refute it.

The prudent historian, even if he knew nothing of the Victualling Office but what Thompson says, might well treat his claims with reserve. It is rather surprising that he continues to be quoted, sometimes with reservations, sometimes without (9). Happily we now have two important studies which give us a much more complete and accurate view of the victualling of the British Navy in the eighteenth century. Professor Baugh has explained in detail how the Victualling Office worked (10), and the late Professor Gradish has examined the victualling of the fleet during the Seven Years' War (11).

The Victualling Office was not the most prominent part of the naval administration, which embraced some of the largest industrial enterprises in the western world. But it was a substantial business. Its main establishment on Tower Hill covered six acres and employed more than seventy people (12). From there, and to a much lesser extent from other establishments and outside contractors, the Board issued provisions to the fleet in very large quantities. Eighty thousand men — the strength of the Navy for much of the Seven Year's War — required annually 16,640,000 lbs. of beef, or about 24,000 oxen, and 8,320,000 lbs of pork, or 80,000 hogs (13). This may have represented as much as 30 % and 55 % respectively of all the beasts traded in London, (14) which was by far the largest wholesale market in the three kingdoms. In the eight years 1750 to 1757 the Board issued to the fleet the following quantities of the chief items of diet :

Bread :	54,642,437 lbs.
Beer :	110,049 tuns.
Brandy :	351,692 gals.
Beef :	4,498,486 lbs.
Pork :	6,734,261 lbs.
Peas :	203,385 bus.
Flour :	6,264,879 lbs.
Suet :	809,419 lbs.
Raisins :	705,784 lbs.
Oatmeal :	138,504 lbs.
Vinegar :	390,863 gals.
Stockfish :	166,943 lbs.
Oil :	71,668 gals. (15).

By any standards this was a busy administration, crucially important for the success of the fleet. The Commissioners of Victualling who were responsible for it seem to have been in the main competent, diligent and honest (16). Many of them were former sea officers, and Lord Anson, who was First Lord of the Admiralty, with one short break, from 1751 to his death in 1762 was at pains to repel his civilian colleagues' attempts to introduce more of the political placement whom the previous administration had installed. As he wrote to the Duke of Newcastle in 1755 :

« I had the honour of your Grace's letter recommending Mr Whitmore to be a Commissioner of the Victualling in the room of Captain Cooper ; his lordship might as properly have asked to have made him a Captain of a Man of War, that branch having always been filled with a Seaman... this gives me an opportunity of observing to your Grace that instead of adding to the useless people that are already in that Office (if we should have a war with France) more people of business must be brought into it » (17).

The Commissioners included men well-known in the public life of the day, among them the philanthropist Jonas Hanway, appointed in 1762, an experienced administrator long acquainted with naval affairs, and a man of scrupulous honesty (18). The Victualling Board saw its job as the administration of the existing system as efficiently and economically as possible, and during the 1750s their standards rose steadily. They conducted experiments with new methods of curing, on the weight lost by meat in cooking, and on concentrated beer, among other subjects (20). They did not, however, take the initiative in issuing new foodstuffs. The Commissioners for Sick and Wounded Seamen were the medical authority of the Navy, and it was they who were expected to experiment with diet. During the Seven Years' War they tried a number of new issues, many of them with view to checking scurvy. Dried apples, issued complete with helpful recipes, was one which was abandoned after trial (21), but their most successful innovation was the 'portable soup', ancestor of many modern convenience foods. This was a beef broth dried in blocks, and made up (with vegetables if possible) to make soup for the sick (22). It rapidly became popular with the seamen and eventually became a standard victualling issue.

The only innovation in the Victualling Board's issues during the Seven Years' War, however, was the widespread issue of fresh meat and vegetables, which resulted from Admiralty rather than Victualling Board initiative (23). The Victualling Commissioners concentrated on the quantity and quality of the standard provisions. The table quoted above gives the amounts issued over eight years, and it includes also the amounts condemned by survey — that is to say pronounced unfit to eat on opening the cask by a panel of ship's officers (who had no interest in concealing any failures of the Victualling Office). The figures were as follows :

Bread :	0.3 %
Beer :	0,9 %
Brandy :	nil
Beef :	0,06 %
Pork :	0,03 %
Peas :	0,6 %
Flour :	0,3 %
Suet :	0,1 %
Raisins :	0,1 %
Oatmeal :	0,9 %
Vinegar :	nil
Stockfish :	7,9 %
Oil :	0,4 % (24)

Considering the limitations of contemporary technology and the hazards to which the full casks were exposed after issue, these figures are astonishingly low. Some of them would be creditable to a similar organisation in our own day.

These totals refer to victuals issued in England, the majority packed at Tower Hill, but the Board's business extended wherever the Navy sailed, and like all eighteenth-century administration, the further away it was from London, the more difficult to control. This was true of the Agent-Victuallers, the senior officers of the victualling yards at the home dockyard ports, for these were in some measure political appointees with local loyalties. The point was explained by Lord Sandwich in 1779 :

> « The Agent-Victualler's place at Portsmouth must go with the recommendation of the Borough, it has been long sollicited in that channel, and is destined to be given in that line, without which our interest there would be

at an end. This is the case of all most every Agent Victualler as it is a sort
of Employment to which Borough people may be raised without prejudice
to the Service » (25).

It was a political nomination which gained John Ommanney his place at
Plymouth, where we shall encounter him again (26). Nevertheless the Agent-
Victuallers were expected to live up to their masters' high standards, and the
Agent at Portsmouth was abruptly dismissed in 1757 for failing to do so (27).
The Board's correspondents in lesser ports were simply local merchants who
undertook to supply provisions at fixed prices whenever required (28). If they
proved unsatisfactory, replacements could usually be found. A more intractable
problem was presented by the contractors who largely supplied the squadrons
in the West Indies, chiefly from North America. Remote from the watchful eye
of the Board, they were free to indulge in a variety of sharp practices which it
was impossible to eradicate altogether (29).

The standard diet of the Navy in the eighteenth century may be
set out in a table, as it appeared in the printed *Instructions for the Sea Service :*

	Biscuit (1bs)	Beer (gals)	Beef (1bs)	Pork (1bs)	Peas (pts)	Oatmeal (pts)	Cheese (oz)	Butter (oz)
Sunday	1	1	—	1	1/2	—	—	—
Monday	1	1	—	—	—	1	2	4
Tuesday	1	1	2	—	—	—	—	—
Wednesday	1	1	—	—	1/2	1	2	4
Thursday	1	1	—	1	1/2	—	—	—
Friday	1	1	—	—	1/2	1	2	4
Saturday	1	1	2	—	—	—	—	—

This was for ships in home waters, but fresh meat, often accompanied by vegetables, was substituted for salt as often as possible when in port, or at sea within
reach of port. On overseas stations where some of the standard items were
impossible to obtain, substitutes were provided according to an elaborate table
which laid down, for example, that a pint of wine or half a pint of brandy or
rum equalled a gallon of beer ; four pounds of rice, a gallon of oatmeal ; a pint
of oil, a pound of butter ; two pounds of potatoes or yams a pound of bread ; a
quart of calavances (chick peas), three of oatmeal or a quart or pease, and
so on (31). Fruit was supplied as a substitute when it could be obtained (32).

For Englishmen of the day, no item of diet was so important as beef. A patriotic national mystique attended this most English of foods, symbol of liberty and prosperity. The subjects of foreign tyrants might be reduced to frogs' legs and snails, but Englishmen fed as befitted a free people. The Victualling Board took extreme care to buy only the best beef, and to pickle it with great care (33). Their standards may be illustrated at the cost of a small digression.

Ireland was a prolific producer of beef, pork and butter, which to protect English agriculture were excluded from England by the Cattle Acts. The Irish therefore exported much of their produce. In 1756 cattle and the products derived from them constituted 39 % of all Ireland's exports, and a large proportion of this went to France, some of it for the armed forces, much of it for the West India islands. France was reckoned to take a third of all Irish exports of beef, a seventh of its pork exports, and a fifth of its butter exports. Martinique was said to depend entirely on it (34). This made beef one of the prime strategic commodities of the age, and on the approach of war British governments always placed an embargo on the export of Irish foodstuffs. In order to supply an alternative market the Victualling Board was allowed, indeed encouraged, to buy in Ireland, and during the Seven Years' War (a time of rapidly rising prices in England) the Cattle Acts were firts suspended and at length repealed. In 1755 war was not yet declared, but in advance of an embargo (which followed the next year) the Lord Lieutenant of Ireland set about buying up shipments of foodstuffs destined for France. Among them was a large consignment of beef at Cork. Seeking to dispose of his acquisition, the Lord Lieutenant wrote to the Secretary of State, who wrote to the Admiralty, suggesting that the Navy should buy it. The Victualling Board was instructed to survey the beef, and reported that some of it was fit for naval use. The remainder, however, was *cow* beef. Never had the men of His Majesty's service been served so inferior an article as cow beef, and the Victualling Board (supported by the Admiralty) made it quite clear that it was not going to lower its standards to get the Lord Lieutenant of Ireland out of his difficulty. In this impasse, an act of God came to the aid of the British government. On 1st November 1755 a great earthquake destroyed the city of Lisbon. Christian Europe was appalled ; Protestant ally and Catholic coreligionary vied with the generosity of their aid. The first British convoy with relief supplies sailed within a month of the news being received, and among its cargoes was the entire consignment of cow beef. Thus, not for the last time, a British government disposed of an embarrassing food surplus by generously donating it to the needy overseas (35).

A good deal of Irish beef was indeed below the Navy's standards. Irish merchants opposing the 1741 embargo actually argued that they would be ruined by the impossibility of finding alternative markets, their beef being so bad that no one but Frenchmen would eat it (36). French seamen regarded captured British beef, even beef condemned as unfit to eat, as a great delicacy, and in default of that they chased rats to improve their diet (37).

The Victualling Board which was so careful to choose only the best beef and pack it well, naturally paid attention to turning over its stocks as quickly as possible. Well-pickled beef and pork in sound casks would keep up to five years (38), but in practice the Board never normally issued anything more than two years old. In 1773 a survey of the Victualling warehouses led to the remaining stocks from 1771 being sold at once (39). In the East Indies, at the end of a long and precarious line of supply, older meat was occasionally issued. The *Elizabeth* at Madras in April 1758 received a cask packed in London in October 1755, which when opened in May 1759 proved unfit to eat (40). But this was an extreme and unusual situation, and the East Indies was one of the parts of the world where fresh meat was difficult to obtain. A great deal of trouble was taken to find fresh beef, not only in home waters, but in every part of the world. In the West Indies arrangements were made to bring cattle from the highlands of the Orinoco (41), and even in India beef cattle were somehow obtained, though on the Mediterranean coast of Spain one captain was reduced, much to his disgust, to serving his men mutton (42). On the North American station in winter time ships were supplied with frozen beef (43).

When ships were in port, the cattle were usually slaughtered on the beach, so that the meat was extremely fresh. This was written into the ordinary contracts of victualling correspondents like Richard Cross, the Exeter butcher who undertook to provide 'good fat well-fed ox beef' in any quantity at forty-eight hours' notice, delivered in quarters into boats at Torbay (44). 'Any quantity' was not an idle provision ; in June 1759 Hawke brought the Western Squadron into Torbay and demanded 46,926 1bs. of beef from Mr Cross (45). It must have been quite an achievement for a butcher in a declining provincial city like Exeter to supply nearly seventy oxen at no notice.

Ships at sea received their fresh meat on the hoof, and astonishingly large numbers of cattle could be carried to sea. The *Somerset,* a third rate 64, sailed from Messina in October 1760 with provisions including sixty oxen (46), and in the following January the *Elizabeth,* a ship of the same size in the East Indies, was carrying seventy-one head of cattle — and, not surpisingly, running short of ffoder (47). These ships were in relatively friendly climates, but Sir Edward Hawke thought it quite reasonable that ships of the line sailing from Plymouth in winter should carry a dozen oxen and forty sheep each (48). By this means, and the use of specially-fitted victualling transports sent out to squadrons at sea, the great majority of British men of war received at least intermittent supplies of fresh meat. Only on long ocean passages was it necessary to subsist on salt meat alone.

A more difficult problem was the supply of cheese, another favourite food of British seamen. In the best circumstances cheese lasted only a few months, and the best cheese did not necessarily last the longest. Cheese and butter were supplied by contractors under warranty for six months, but a distribution system at the mercy of wind and weather often could not get the cheese to the men before the warranty was up, even in home waters, and cheese figured often in lists of provisions condemned (49). Traditionally the Navy bought Suffolk cheese, a hard, poor and cheap variety, but the most durable available. Defoe remarked that Suffolk was famous for producing the best butter and the worst cheese in England (50). It was to Suffolk cheese that William Thompson's stories of buttons carved of cheese referred, and whether his tales are true or no, it was often complained of. In 1758 Anson commanded the Western Squadron for the summer and had personal experience of its defects ; on his return to the Admiralty it was decided to buy no more from Suffolk, but to order Cheshire and Gloucester cheese instead. These were of much higher quality, and complaints about the cheese almost ceased. Even though two pounds of Cheshire cheese were issued as the equivalent of three of Suffolk, the change cost the Navy money, for the good cheese cost more than twice as much as the bad (52).

Besides fresh meat and better cheese there was a third important change in the seaman's rations during the Seven Years' War, vegetables. They were an increasing part of the eighteenth-century diet (53), and widely recognised as important to health, especially the prevention of scurvy. Anson, Boscawen and Hawke, the leading admirals of the day, were all enthusiasts for vegetables, and although they did not become part of the regular diet (that is to say that they were set against 'savings, of other foods) became a standard issue. Ships in port seem to have expected vegetables whenever they received fresh meat — indeed, one of the problems for the historian is that the two were usually subsumed in the phrase « fresh provisions », which certainly included fresh meat, but not necessarily vegetables also.

The real problem for the Victualling Board was supplying vegetables to ships at sea, and especially to the ships of the Western Squadron, cruising off Brest or in the Western Approaches. Unlike cattle, vegetables could not be sent out alive, and various experiments in preserving green vegetables enjoyed little success (54). Cabbages, onions, turnips, carrots and potatoes were sent out in large quantities (55), and sufficient survived the voyages to justify the effort, but the wastage was considerable. When westerly gales detained the 'vegetable vessels' in Plymouth Sound for weeks nothing could ensure a regular supply, even though the Victualling Board took the risk of sending transports unescorted (56). Shiploads of apples were also sent out from England (57), lemons and oranges were bought from passing Spanish merchantmen (58), and Hawke sent to Spain for onions and lemons for his squadron (59). The most effective solution to the problem of supplying the squadron with vegetables was found after the battle of Quiberon Bay, when a small island was occupied and cultivated to provide fresh vegetables (60), and in 1761 the much larger island of Belle Isle became available for the same purpose (61).

So far we have been describing a sophisticated and efficient administrative system responding with flexibility to the challenges of war. The seamen received as good, full and varied a diet as the limitations of technology allowed. This, at least, is what the evidence suggests, but many modern writers (with the notable exception of Professors Baugh and Gradish) still prefer to speak of lethargy, dishonesty and incompetence, and for support they always cite Hawke's complaints of 1759, especially his complaints about beer. This incident is worth studying in detail.

Beer was one of the most crucial of all victuals aboard ship. Apart from its supposed antiscorbutic properties (62), it was the only thing which the seamen normally drank, and by ancient tradition they might drink as much as they pleased. Their daily 'ration' of gallon was in practice simply an estimate of average consumption (63). Water was carried, of course, but usually only for cooking. Much of it was stowed in the 'ground tier' of casks where it formed part of the ballast, only to be started in an emergency. On long passages or on foreign stations seamen had to drink wine and water, or spirits and water, but in home waters they drank beer alone. The length of time a ship might spend at sea was effectively only as long as her beer lasted (64).

At a gallon a man a day, the quantities required were considerable, and of course were needed all the year round. This at once posed intractable problems, for eighteenth-century brewing was a highly uncertain art at any time, and never undertaken in the summer months. Ideally the Victualling Board would have brewed all it needed in the winter, in the same way that it packed all its meat in the winter, but the problem with beer was more difficult, because it kept far less well than meat. In wartime the demands of fleets at sea in the summer tended to force it to brew in summer. Moreover the strategic position complicated the Board's problems. Most of its fixed investment in buildings and equipment was on the Thames or near the eastern yards whose locations had originally been dictated by the requirements of the Dutch Wars. During the Seven Years' War the Western Squadron under Admiral Hawke developed the strategy of close blockade which was to characterize British naval policy for fifty years. This involved keeping large squadrons at sea in the Western Approaches winter and summer, based for the most part on the newest and smalled of the dockyards, Plymouth. It was also the newest and smallest of the victualling yards, inadequately equipped itself, and remote from the main centres of supply and manufacture. Plymouth, moreover, lay dead to leeward of the Western Squadron's station off Brest.

All this was a recipe for trouble, and it duly developed in the summer of 1759. The demands of the squadron obliged the brewer to brew during the summer, and the beer proved to go off very quickly. It seems clear that this proceeded from the weakness of contemporary brewing techniques, not from any failure of the staff. Neither John Ommanney the Agent-Victualler nor Captain Robert Pett, one of the Victualling Commissioners who was sent from London to investigate, could find any malpractice in the Plymouth brewhouse (65).

Admiral Hawke at sea, however, was impatient of excuses. He did not know or care about technical problems, and was inclined to blame everything on incompetence and corruption (66). Hawke was a great sea commander, calm and resolute in moments of crisis, but he never understood administration, and the petty vexation of daily life brought out the worst in him. Many of his complaints were quite unreasonable. On 2nd August he reproached the Victualling Board for not using their initiative and sending supplies without being asked ; on 18th September he informed them, in language verging on abuse, that because of their stupidity in sending supplies without being asked, the squadron was overstocked. On 2nd August, at sea off Ushant, he wrote to Ommanney demanding to know why his orders of 29th July had not been carried out — orders which Ommaney had probably not yet even received (67). Moreover Hawke was unduly influenced by his Secretary John Hay, an unprincipled schemer who deceived the admiral and dishonestly exploited his position (68). One of the main crosses the victualling authorities had to bear was innaccurate paperwork from Hawke's fleet — for which Hay was probably responsible. He sents lists of provisions without explaining if they represented stocks or requirements, he wrote tuns instead of butts in complaining about beer (thus doubling the quantity), and he constantly omitted to return the necessary receipts and accounts (69). He certainly had an interest in diverting the Admiral's wrath elsewhere, and may well be responsible for some of Hawke's unreasonable behaviour.

With the autumn the complaints about beer gave way to others over delay in sending any supplies at all. The problem here was the simple difficulty of leewardly and deep-laden merchantmen beating up against the westerly gales of autumn and winter. Ommanney, Pett, and Commissioner Hanway (70) did their best in preparing the transports, but they were powerless to alter the weather. They sailed transports unescorted, and loaded men of war with food in an effort to get supplies to the Western Squadron (71), but they did not, and clearly could not have overcome it altogether, and after the battle of Quiberon Bay, fought in a gale which dispersed yet another victualling convoy, the ships were short of fresh provisions for some weeks. In the long term the only, partial, answer to the problem of geography was to set up a victualling system based on

Irish ports, and later in the war experiments in this direction were undertaken (72).

It is quite clear from this episode that the Victualling Board was not infallible. It had no magic answers to the weaknesses of contemporary technology or the perverseness of wind and weather. Faced with novel problems, it did not at once find the perfect solutions. Viewing the evidence, however, it is difficult not to feel that some of what Hawke had to complain of was his own fault, and much of it nobody's. The failures which vexed his squadron in 1759 were the growing pains of a healthy system stretched by unprecedented demands, not, as has so often been suggested, the symptoms of sloth and corruption. In an age which expected much less than our own from even the most vital aspects of national administration, the Victualling Board stands out as a model of efficiency. Its success in a complex and demanding business was one of the foundations of the success of the Royal Navy in the Seven Years' War, and nothing illustrates this better than the state of Hawke's fleet on 20th November 1759, the day of his great victory. A squadron of over twenty sail had on that day not twenty men sick in the entire fleet.

> 'It is an observation, I think, worthy of record — that fourteen thousand persons, pent up in ships, should continue, for six or seven months, to enjoy a better state of health upon the watery element, than it can well be imagined so great a number of people would enjoy, on the most healthful spot of ground in the world' (73).

That observation goes as far in explaining British success in the Seven Years' War as all the gallantry and seamanship of the Navy.

Additional Note [2009]

Originally published in a minor French journal, which is difficult to find in France and impossible elsewhere, this short piece still seems to arouse interest.

NOTES

1 - H.W. Hodges & E.A. Hughes, *Documents* (Cambridge, 1922).

2 - Ibid. pp. 125-126.

3 - Sometimes, as with other motifs, in strangely altered forms : the 'beef carved into snuff boxes' mentioned by T.S. Ashton', Changes in Standards of Comfort in Eighteenth Century England', *Proceedings of the British Academy* XLI (1955) p. 175, is recognizably derived at several removes from Thompson.

4 - See *infra* nn. 8 & 10.

5 - Not to be confused with his namesake who was a Victualling Commissioner, 1729-1745.

6 - Thompson, *The Royal Navy Men's Advocate* (London, 1757) p. 14. All three of his pamphlets were published in London.

7 - *Ibid.* p. 34.

8 - Stephen Gradish, *The Manning of the British Navy during the Seven Years' War* (London, 1980) p. 143.

9 - E.g. Peter Kemp, *The British Sailor ; A Social History of the Lower Deck* (London, 1970) p. 125 (with reservations) ; Geoffrey Marcus, *Quiberon Bay* (London, 1960) p. 187 (without).

10 - Daniel A. Baugh, *British Naval Administration in the Age of Walpole* (Princeton, N.J., 1965) Ch. 8. See also his *Naval Administration, 1715-1750* (Navy Records Society Vol. 120, London, 1977) Sect. IX.

11 - *Op. cit.* n.8 *supra.*

12 - Baugh, *British Naval Administration in the Age of Walpole* pp. 31 & 55.

13 - Ibid. p. 407.

14 - Taking the figures of David MacPherson, *Annals of Commerce* (London, 1805, 4vv.) III, p. 350.
Other authorities give a larger total trade or smaller Victualling purchases : Peter Mathias, 'Agriculture and the Brewing and Distilling Industries in the Eighteenth Century', in

Mathias, *The Transformation of England* (London, 1979) pp. 254-255 (reprinted from the *Economic History Review* V (1952)) ; Sir William Beveridge *et al. Prices and Wages in England from the Twelfth to the Nineteenth Centuries* (London, 1939) p. 529.

15 - Gradish, *op. cit.* p. 144, quoting British Library (BM) Stone MSS 152 fo. 130. In the last line of Gradish's table 822 gals. should read 322 gals.

16 - *Ibid.* p. 145.

17 - BM Add. MSS 32852 fo. 485. Abbrevations have been expanded and punctuation slightly modified.

18 - J. H. Hutchins, *Jonas Hanway 1712-1786* (London, 1940).

19 - Gradish, *op. cit.* p. 140.

20 - *Ibid.* p. 153. Royal Commission on Historical Manuscripts, Du Cane MSS (No.61, 1905) p. 123, Victualling Board to Admiral Medley, 30th May 1746. Peter Mathias, 'Swords and Ploughshares ; The Armed Forces, Medicine and Public Health in the Eighteenth Century', in J.M. Winter, ed., *War and Economic Development* (Cambridge, 1975) p. 269.

21 - National Maritime Museum (NMM) : Hawke MSS HWK/10, Sick & Wounded Board to Admiral Hawke, 9th August 1757.

22 - Christopher Lloyd, *The British Seaman 1200-1860, A Social Survey* (London, 1968) p. 257. Gradish, *op. cit.* pp. 159-160.

23 - Gradish, pp. 161-163.

24 - *Supra* n. 15.

25 - Mulgrave Castle MS VI, 11/80, Lord Sandwich to Captain Lord Mulgrave, 7th October 1779. I am indebted to the Marquis of Normanby for permission to quote this document.

26 - Baugh, *Naval Administration 1715-1750,* pp. 32-34.

27 - Public Record Office (PRO) : ADM 1/924, Admiral Boscawen to Admiralty, 9th February 1757.

28 - Baugh, *Naval Administration in the Age of Walpole,* p.391.

29 - PRO ; ADM 1/236 fo. 259, Admiral Holmes to Admiralty, 23 rd July 1761.

30 - *Regulations and Instructions relating to His Majesty's Service at sea* (London, 1731 &c). Printed by Baugh, *Naval Administration in the Age of Walpole,* p. 375, and by many other authorities.

31 - PRO ; ADM 30/44 p.15.

32 - PRO ; ADM 7/745, Captain Palliser to Captain Hughes, 13th October 1760.

33 - PRO ; ADM 49/59 p. 36.

34 - John O'Donovan, *The Economic History of Live Stock in Ireland* (Cork, 1940) pp.106-111.

35 - Richard Pares, *War and Trade in the West Indies, 1739-1763* (Oxford, 1936) p. 428. PRO ; ADM 1/4120, Robinson to Admiralty, 27th August & 4th September ; Fox to Admiralty 26th September, 26th November & 30th November 1755, 4th March 1756. PRO ; PC 1/6 No. 59.

36 - O'Donovan, *op. cit.* p. 107.

37 - Adrien Carré, 'Eighteenth-century French Voyages of Exploration : General Problems of Nutrition with Special Reference to the Voyages of Bougainville and D'Entrecasteaux' in J. Watt, E.J. Freeman & W.F. Bynum, eds., *Starving Sailors ; The Influence of Nutrition upon Naval and Maritime History* (Greenwich, 1981) p. 75. Carré, 'Notes sur l'histoire de la medecine du travail et de l'ergonomie dans la Marine', *Revue d'Histoire Economique et Sociale* XLVII (1969) p. 273.

38 - Baugh, *Naval Administration in the Age of Walpole* p. 423.

39 - PRO ; ADM 30/44 p. 262.

40 - NMM ; Tiddeman MSS, TID/14 s.d. 2nd May 1759.

41 - PRO / Rodney MSS, PRO30/20/8 pp. 42-43. NMM : Douglas MSS, DOU/4 p. 53.

42 - David Erskine, ed., *Augustus Hervey's Journal* (London, 2nd. ed. 1954) p. 276.

43 - PRO ; ADM 1/482 fo. 146.

44 - NMM ; Hawke MSS, HWK/11, Victualling Board to Hawke, 21 st May 1759.

45 - Ruddock F. Mackay, *Admiral Hawke* (Oxford, 1965) p. 208.

52

46 - *Loc. cit.* n.32 *supra.*

47 - NMM ; TID/14, Captain Tiddeman to Captain Cowell, 1st January 1761.

48 - NMM ; HWK/14, Hawke to Commissioner Hanway, 4th November 1759.

49 - Not in the list on p.5, which deals with provisions packed or processed by the Victualling Board. Cheese came only from contractors.

50 - Daniel Defoe, *A Tour through England and Wales* (Everyman ed.) I, p.53.

51 - Gradish, *op. cit.* pp. 147-148.

52 - PRO ; ADM 30/44 p.15. Beveridge, *Prices & Wages* p. 576.

53 - Mathias, 'Swords and Ploughshares' p. 278 & n. 38.

54 - A.E. Bender, 'The History and Implications of Processed Food' in Watt et al., *Starving Sailors* p. 120.

55 - NMM ; HWK/14, Hawke to Admiralty, 14th August 1759.

56 - NMM ; HWK/11, Commissioner Pett to Hawke, 10th September 1759.

57 - NMM ; HWK/14, Hawke to Pett, 25th September 1759.

58 - Gradish, *op. cit.* p. 177.

59 - PRO ; ADM 1/92 fo. 344.

60 - Cecil Aspinall-Oglander, *Admiral's Wife* (London, 1940) p. 283.

61 - PRO ; ADM 1/91 fo.492.

62 - Gradish, *op. cit.* p. 156.

63 - Baugh, *British Naval Administration in the Age of Walpole* pp. 376-377.

64 - PRO ; ADM 1/90 fo.20v. ADM 1/92 fo.97.

65 - NMM ; HWK/11, Ommanney to Hawke, 10th August 1759. Gradish, *op. cit.* pp.157-158.

66 - NMM ; HWK/14, Hawke to Pett, 14th August 1759.

67 - *Ibid. s. d.*

68 - Mackay, Hawke pp.52, 86 & 198.

69 - NMM ; HWK/11, Pett to Hawke 24th August & 22nd September 1759 ; Ommanney to Hawke, 12th September 1759 ; Justice to Hawke 17th September. HWK/15, Hawke to Victualling Board, 15th December 1760.

70 - Captain Thomas Hanway, Commissioner of Plymouth Yard ; not to be confused with his brother Jonas.

71 - NMM ; HWK/11, Pett to Hawke, 10th September 1759. PRO ; ADM 1/802, Hanway to Admiralty, 25th & 28th December 1759, 1st January 1760.

72 - Gradish, *op. cit.* pp.168-169.

73 - James Lind, *An Essay on the Most Effectual Means of preserving the Health of Seamen in the Royal Navy* (London, 3 Vol. 1779), printed in C.C. Lloyd, *The Health of Seamen* (Navy Records Society Vol. 107, London 1965) p. 121.

VIII

Medicine, Administration and Society
in the Eighteenth-Century Royal Navy

There is nothing novel in the suggestion that much medical history is still cast in forms long since abandoned by professional historians. Fifteen years ago several contributors to EDWIN CLARKE's symposium Modern Methods in the History of Medicine (1) remarked on the need for modern attitudes to go with them, and agreed in linking the very old-fashioned historiography of the subject to the fact that so much of it had been written by doctors:

"Though this has provided many useful books and articles, it has also produced much positivistic Whig history, and many ahistorical judgements" (2).

Very much the same might be said of naval history, another backwater where survives that endangered species, the Whig interpretation of history. "The general tone of these works was largely defined in the nineteenth century when a facile view of progress was dominant" (3): that is certainly true of the medical history of the Royal Navy in the eighteenth century, and particularly of that erratic but monumental work Medicine and the Navy (4). This is medical history with the doctors in the foreground, the diseases next, the patients dimly in the background, and the general history and society of the period nowhere. It is a story of linear progress led by a succession of great men, medical heroes struggling against the sloth and obscurantism of the non-medical world.

I wish to suggest that this may not be the best way to understand the subject. It does not seem to me to be self-evident that the history of the medical profession encompasses all that we need to know about the history of medicine, and particularly not in the case of naval medicine in the eighteenth century, when the doctors were for a least three reasons ill-placed to make a decisive contribution to the health of seamen. In the first place the Navy was an organised and hierarchical society in which the medical men were a long way from positions of authority, and consequently unable to get things done except by persuasion. Moreover their powers of persuasion were much diminished by extreme fragmentation and internal divisions of their profession (5). The medical men were educated in an intellectual tradition which was in many cases actively unhelpful. Lastly, the most serious diseases in the Navy - scurvy, typhus and tropical fevers above all - were inaccessible to almost all the treatments offered by contemporary medicine and surgery.

The most senior doctors in the naval administration were the Commissioners for Sick and Wounded Seamen, commonly called the Sick and Hurt Board. They were available to advise the Board of Admiralty on medical questions if asked, but their chief function was to administer the naval medical service (6). They organised the naval hospitals and exercised a limited supervision over surgeons at sea, though until 1796 they neither examined nor appointed them (7). Their impact on naval medicine was considerable, but for the most part it was not medical, for they acted almost entirely as administrators and not as physicians. The most senior doctors actually having charge of patients were the physicians of the two great naval ho-

spitals at Haslar and Stonehouse, and those appointed to the larger overseas squadrons in time of war. Being physicians, and consequently belonging to the only one of the fragmented medical professions in England
which carried any considerable social or intellectual standing, they had
some chance to influence people who had to take decisions, but they were
in no position to take any themselves. The seagoing physicians were advisers to their commanders-in-chief, unable to give orders even to surgeons;
the hospital physicians were in effect the chairmen of committees of management, with a powerful say in the internal affairs of the hospitals, but
very little outside. In practice even the physicians' influence was often
weak, for most of them were licentiates rather than fellows of the Royal
College of Physicians, and many of them were Scotsmen, both of which circumstances placed them on the wrong side of an important social division
(8). When the Admiralty looked for the best medical advice, it tended to
look elsewhere (9). As for the surgeons who formed the great majority of
the naval medical men, they carried very little professional weight, least
of all among physicians (10).

The influence of doctors was therefore in inverse ratio to their practical acquaintance with naval diseases. This was the more unfortunate because most of them had been educated in the theoretical farmework of climatorial pathology, which located the causation and transmission of diseases in the air. This was not invariably a disadvantage: applied to tropical fevers, for example, the idea of the effluvium or miasma of the swamps
fitted sufficiently the real habits of the mosquito to reinforce the practical observations of naval men and provide useful advice (11). Applied to
typhus, the climatorial pathology had at least the virtue of encouraging
cleanliness (12). In the case of scurvy, however, it led the doctors hopelessly astray. For centuries seamen had observed that scurvy could be
prevented or cured by eating various things, lemons prominent among them
(13), and by the mid-eighteenth century there was something like a consensus among sea officers that it was a dietary disease, the key to which lay
in the seaman's food (14). In the medical profession the idea of deficiency diseases was still struggling for acceptance well into this century
(15). The result was that the observations of naval surgeons, and still
more of naval officers, were repeatedly discarded in favour of weighty
academic opinion (16).

Even if they had been better informed, however, the doctors could never
have had a leading rôle in preserving the health of seamen, because medicine and surgery had next to nothing to offer against the reigning
diseases in the Navy. With the important exception of the Jesuit's Bark
against malaria (17), there was simply no effective medical treatment
available against scurvy, typhus or tropical fevers. The prevention of
these illnesses was to an extent possible, but it was almost entirely a
matter of naval administration and discipline: of diet in the case of
scurvy; of cleanliness and isolation in that of typhus; and of the organisation of boatwork and landing parties in the tropics. The conquest of
scurvy - the only naval disease which was effectively eliminated, not merely contained, by the end of the eighteenth century (18) - was essentially a matter of public health, analagous to the conquest of cholera in nineteenth-century towns (19). It concerned naval administrators and senior
officers, and the doctors were useful only to the extent to which they
could offer relevant advice. In QUEEN ANNE's time PATRICK CAMPBELL published a work entitled 'Occasions of Sickness in Fleets and Ships of War which
come not within the verge of Physick or Surgery at Sea, but come wholly
under the Cognizance of Great Officers on Shore and Principal Officers at

Sea'(20). It is a fair description of the most serious naval medical problems of the century.

These considerations, it seems to me, prompt us to approach the evidence with different questions, and different assumptions, from those which have moved many writers on the subject. I do not pretend to have the answers to these questions, nor if I did would a brief paper suffice to present them, but there is time to point out some of the puzzles which would repay study, in particular concerning scurvy. We now know a great deal more than we used to about it, notably through the researches of SIR JAMES WATT, but there remain several unresolved problems. I wish to suggest that our understanding of the subject has been distorted by an undue concentration on JAMES LIND. Important and attractive though he is as an historical figure, it can be argued that he was largely irrelevant to the conquest of scurvy, or at least that his relevance was not what it has been supposed to be. I have elsewhere proposed that his famous controlled experiment may have occurred by accident (21): if it was intentional it presents an awkward problem, for there is nothing in his writings, his clinical practice or his career to suggest that he had any idea how - and still more why - to mount a controlled experiment or what to do with the results (22). He was a conventional empiricist, dedicated like very many other men of science in all professions, to the intelligent application of observation to practice, but I believe he was as much a stranger to the modern use of controls as almost all his contemporaries (23). He had remarkable gifts, but he applied them using methods typical of his day. His demonstration of the value of lemon juice - itself a commonplace known for centuries - was something on which he himself seems to have laid no extraordinary emphasis, either in theory or in practice.

The curious thing about JAMES LIND is the nature of his influence. It is not odd that he failed to impress his colleagues in the faculty: he was a man of diffident modesty, ill placed and ill-fitted to move the medical world, and he seems to have offended people of weight within it (24). He was a man who knew his limitations in a profession of gifted self-publicists (25). But he is said to have been highly respected in the Navy, and he was certainly cited with admiration by naval physicians both during his lifetime and after his death (26). We might therefore expect him to have had a significant influence on naval medicine during the twenty-six years (1758-1783) in which he was physician of Haslar. During the American War he was one of the most senior men in the naval medical service, and one would expect him to have been influential in it. Yet those years saw a disastrous resurgence in the very disease, scurvy, with which he is particularly associated. Even if one discounts his theoretical contribution, he was undoubtedly a noted clinician, and presided for a quarter of a century over the largest hospital in Europe. It seems strange that LIND was ignored when his opinion might have been most useful, only to be rediscovered by BLANE and TROTTER in his old age (27). The extent to which his views on scurvy had changed during his career, moving much further away from the truth than he had been in 1744, must certainly have had an unfortunate effect, and the disastrous influence of Captain COOK doubtless reinforced it, but there still seems to be more, or rather less, here than can plausibly be explained by our present knowledge (28).

We ought to ask, too, why scurvy had to be conquered twice. It is perfectly clear that it was eliminated as a serious problem during the Seven Years' War, re-emerged in terrible vigour during the American War, and was again overcome in the 1790s. The statistics for admissions per 1000 patients to Haslar Hospital give a simple index of its progress:

1759: Scurvy 119, Fever 393
1782: Scurvy 329, Fever 112
1796: Scurvy 74, Fever 257
1799: Scurvy 20, Fever 200 (29)

The disease was tackled during the Seven Years' War because LORD AN-SON's Board of Admiralty, convinced that diet alone could prevent it, went to immense trouble and expense to supply the principal squadrons, at sea as well as in port, with fresh meat and vegetables (30). We have to ask why LORD SANDWICH's Board was unable to do the same thing twenty years later. In part the answer may lie in strategic differences. HAWKE in 1759, like HOWE, COLLINGWOOD and DUNCAN in 1793-1795, was keeping the Western Squadron off Brest, within reach of British bases from which he could be supplied (31) During the American War the fleets were often cruising in the Bay of Biscay or on the coasts of America where fresh food was less easily come by (32). But it is difficult to believe that more could not have been achieved if the will had been there: RODNEY's squadron always received regular supplies of fruit, meat and vegetables, because he insisted (33). Why did not other flag officers apply the lessons they had learnt in the previous war? Are we to suppose they had forgotten them? Perhaps they had: In August 1780 LORD HAWKE wrote to his old friend and follower Admiral GEARY, then commanding the Channel Squadron, to commiserate with him on being forced to return to port with scurvy.

'I do not wonder at the men being so sickly upon so long a cruise. Six weeks is long enough in all conscience. Any time after that must be very hurtful to the men and will occasion their falling down very fast... I wish the Admiralty would see what was done in former times. It would make them act with more propriety, both for the good of officers and men' (34).

In former times, just over twenty years before, HAWKE himself had won his great victory of Quiberon Bay with that same squadron in perfect health after more than six months at sea. I should like to know what had gone wrong in the intervening years.

One answer may be that the techniques of replenishment at sea had been forgotten. Sea officers certainly did not forget the virtues of vegetables, and admirals continued to demand that their squadrons be supplied with them throughout the Revolutionary and Napoleonic Wars (35), up to the Admiralty Order of 1807 which confined them to the use of the sick (36). Only LORD St. VINCENT always disapproved of vegetables (37), as he disapproved of so many other naval traditions - was this another matter in which he dragged the Navy into the 'modern' world from the sloth and corruption of the eighteenth century? It is clear also that the second conquest of scurvy was achieved by fundamentally different means from the first: ANSON's Board of Admiralty had tried to eliminate it by making the seamen eat a healthier diet; LORD SPENCER's simply administered medicine. Was this difference of approach an historical accident, or does it reflect underlying changes in attitude to illness and cure? Was the Navy a pioneer in drug therapy?

It is worth asking also what rôle in all this was really played by SIR GILBERT BLANE. The conventional account it that he, the most influential of all naval physicians, was able 'to push through long-overdue reforms, such as the official issue of lemon juice in 1795' (38). Undoubtedly he was influential, and his ideas on scurvy were sound (sounder than LIND's in crucial respects, notably in preferring the raw juice of lemons and oranges to the boiled 'rob' (39)). But whom had he to convince? Apparently not the Sick and Hurt Board, which advised the Admiralty in May 1795, five months before BLANE joined the Board (40):

"From our own observations, and the experience of ages, we have been
led to consider fresh limes and lemons, or the juice of those fruits, properly prepared for keeping, as the most powerful antiscorbutic in nature,
and know of no instance in which (when administered genuine) it has failed
to cure the disease even in its most advanced stages, either on board ship
or on shore. It is also well ascertained that a certain proportion of lemon juice taken daily, as an article of seamen's diet, will prevent the
possibility of their being tainted with the scurvy, let the other articles
of their diet consist of what they will" (41).

The documents suggest that the adoption of lemon juice was well in
train before BLANE became involved. It is worth mentioning, moreover, that
within twelve months of his joining the Board, his quarrels with Dr. BLAIR
the First Commissioner had effectively paralysed its work (42), and that
not long after his retirement from it, it was abolished altogether, leaving uncleared accounts worth over £ 2,500,000, and a conviction in the
minds of senior officers that:

"The consequence of appointing men, educated for medicine and surgery,
without sufficient collateral help from others acquainted with accounts
and the general transaction of public business, has been... an immense ac-
cumulation of arrears... The habits of medical men are not formed for these purposes (administration), and coming late in life into a public office, they cannot be supposed to know the methods of accounts" (43).

These facts tend to raise queries about the real nature and effect of
BLANE's influence, and to suggest that in this as in other cases events
were moved by causes more complex than the unaided efforts of a few great
men.

It would be easy to prolong the list perplexities offered by our present accounts of eighteenth-century British naval medicine well beyond the
limits of my time or your patience, but I hope I have said enough to illustrate my thesis. My fundamental point is that we shall be in a better position to produce convincing explanations if we remember that in the naval
world at least, health, and even medicine, depended on the medical profession much less than the medical profession, for perfectly understandable
reasons, has been willing to recognize. We need a medical history of the
eighteenth-century Navy which puts the doctors in their proper place, and
that place, though honourable, was in many respects marginal.

Notes

(1) London, 1971
(2) MARIE BOAS HALL: History of Science and History of Medicine, in
ibid., p. 165. For similar comments, see idem p. 160, and CHARLES E. RO-
SENBERG: The Medical Profession, Medical Practice and the History of Medicine, ibid. pp. 23 & 27.
(3) R.S. ROBERTS: The Use of Literacy and Documentary Evidence in the
History of Medicine, ibid. p. 37; see als idem p. 45.
(4) Medicine and the Navy, 1200-1900, ed. J. KEEVIL, C.C. LLOYD &
J.L.S. COULTER (Edinburgh, 1957-63, 4 vols; Vol. 3, by LLOYD & COULTER,
covers the years 1714-1815).
(5) I. WADDINGTON: The Struggle to reform the Royal College of Physicians, 1767-1771: A sociological Analysis, Medical History XVII (1973) p.
107. BERNICE HAMILTON: The Medical Professions in the Eighteenth Century,
Economic History Review 2nd.S. IV (1951) p. 141.
(6) On the structure and functioning of the Sick & Hurt Board see DA-
NIEL A. BAUGH: British Naval Administration in the Age of Walpole (Prince-

ton, 1965) pp. 48-52, and LLOYD & COULTER, Medicine & the Navy, III, 3-10.

(7) Public Record Office, London (P.R.O.) MS ADM 99/51 p. 98.

(8) WADDINGTON: Struggle to Reform, pp. 113-121. HAMILTON: Medical Professions p. 143.

(9) N.A.M. RODGER: Le Scorbut dans la Royal Navy pendant la Guerre de Sept Ans, 1756-1763, pp. 455-456, in Alain Lottin, JEAN-CLAUDE HOCQUET & STEPHANE LEBECQ, eds., Les Hommes et la Mer dans l'Europe du Nord-Quest de l'Antiquité à nos Jours (Revue du Nord extra number, 1986).

(10) WADDINGTON: Struggle to Reform, p. 121.

(11)LLOYD & COULTER: Medicine & the Navy, III, 110-111.

(12) N.A.M. RODGER: The Wooden World: An Anatomy of the Georgian Navy (London, 1986) pp. 105-109.

(13) SIR JAMES WATT: Nutrition in Adverse Environments, I: Forgotten Lessons of Maritime Nutrition, Human Nutrition; Applied Nutrition 36A (1982) p. 35.

(14)RODGER: Scorbut pp. 459-461.

(15) R.E. HUGHES: GEORGE BUDD (1808-1882) and Nutricional Deficiency Diseases, Medical History XVII (1973) p. 127.

(16) RODGER: Scorbut, p. 456.

(17) LLOYD & COULTER: Medicine & the Navy, III, 334.

(18) Ibid. III, 183. Smallpox might be added, but neither the disease nor its cure were specifically naval.

(19) Eighteenth-century naval medicine has long been identified as a precursor of the modern public health movement: see, for example, SIR MALCOLM MORRIES: The Story of English Public Health (London, 1919) pp. 14 & 17-18; M.C. BUER: Health, Wealth and Population in the Early Days of the Industrial Revolution (London, 1926) p. 121. In his later years public health became BLANE's principal interest (LLOYD & COULTER, III, 47).

(20) LLOYD & COULTER: III, 77.

(21) RODGER: Scorbut, p. 458.

(22) R.E. HUGHES: JAMES LIND and the Cure of Scurvy: An Experimental Approach: Medical History XIX (1975) pp. 343-344.

(23)Among LIND's contemporaries who arguably did understand the principle of the control has been numbered Bishop BERKELY: see LESTER S. KING: The Medical World of the Eighteenth Century (Chicago, 1958) pp. 42-43. See also the sources cited in RODGER: Scorbut, p. 457 n. 10.

(24) A.P. MEIKLEJOHN: The Curious Obscurity of Dr. JAMES LIND: Journal of the History of Medicine IX (1954) pp. 305-309. LLOYD & COULTER, III, 91.

(25) His comment on the limits of scientific knowledge exemplifies some of his attractive qualities, but it was not the way to convince others: there are unquestionably certain limits prescribed to human researches beyond which, tho' fancy may take its flight, and theory make wide excursions, all is conjecture, obscurity, or profound darkness (Quoted in LLOYD & COULTER, III, 337).

(26) EDWARD IVES: A Voyage from England to India in the Year 1754 (London, 1773) p. 450. LLOYD & COULTER, III, 43.

(27) C.C. LLOYD, ed., The Health of Seamen; (Navy Records Society Vol. CVII, London, 1965) pp. 160, 178 & 280.

(28) KENNETH J. CARPENTER: JAMES LIND's Revised Views of Scurvy, 1773-1779, in this volume. On COOK, see SIR JAMES WATT: Medical Aspects and Consequences of COOK's Voyages, in ROBIN FISHER & HUGH JOHNSTONE, eds., Captain JAMES COOK and his Times (London, 1979).

(29) LLOYD & COULTER, III, 329; see also ibid. p. 170.

(30) N.A.M. RODGER: The Victualling of the British Navy in the Seven

Year's War', Bulletin du Centre d'Histoire des Espaces Atlantiques No. 2 (Bordeaux, 1985) p. 37.

(31) LLOYD & COULTER, III, 159.

(32) DAVID SYRETT: Shipping and the American War, 1775-1783 (London, 1970) p. 128.

(33) Letter-Books and Order Book of GEORGE, LORD RODNEY, 1780-1782 (New York Historical Society, 1932, 2 vols.) I, 205, 220-221; II, 599, 703 & 729.

(34) G.A.R. CALLENDER: With the Grand Fleet in 1780, Mariner's Mirror IX (1923) pp.292-293.

(35) LLOYD & COULTER, III, 149. CALLENDER, loc.cit. p. 291. P.R.O.: ADM 98/17 p. 245. Hundreds more examples could be offered.

(36) P.R.O.: ADM 98/24 p. 93ff. ADM 98/99 p. 63.

(37) LLOYD & COULTER, III, 168.

(38) LLOYD & COULTER, III, 46-47. LLOYD, Health of Seamen p. 133.

(39) LLOYD & COULTER, III, 132.

(40) P.R.O.: ADM 99/51 pp. 94-96.

(41) P.R.O.: ADM 98/17 pp. 137-138. The confusion between lemons and limes, which was to have such fatal effects later in the nineteenth century, is already present.

(42) P.R.O.: ADM 99/51 pp. 135ff. P.K. CRIMMIN: Admiralty Administration, 1783-1806 (London M.Phil.thesis, 1967) pp. 305-306. I am indebted to Miss CRIMMIN for this reference.

(43) SIR J.K. LAUGHTON, ed., Letters and Papers of CHARLES, LORD BARHAM (Navy Records Society Vols. XXXII, XXXVIII & XXXIX, London 1907-1910) III, 125-126. CRIMMIN: Admiralty Administration p. 307.

Additional Note [2009]

It is in many ways unfortunate that the history of naval medicine has been dominated by studies of scurvy, which killed very few people and had only a limited impact on operations, rather than the deadly fevers such as typhus and malaria. My own modest contributions have started from scurvy, but attempt to make some more general points. It is also regrettable that this most international of subjects is still too often studied by historians trapped within linguistic boxes. Though written in English, this piece and No.XI were published outside the English-speaking world, which has been enough to cloak them in total invisibility, and justifies re-issuing a preliminary sketch written more than twenty years ago.

Mobilizing Seapower in the Eighteenth Century

One factor sharply distinguishes the navies of the eighteenth century, both from the armies of that period and from the navies of our own day: they were largely demobilized in peacetime. The major navies were standing forces in that they possessed a permanent administration, a substantial infrastructure and a fleet of ships, but in time of peace few of the ships, and very few of the ships of the line, would be in commission. Maintaining a navy in any condition taxed the financial, technical and administrative resources of the eighteenth-century state to the utmost, and no country was wealthy enough even to contemplate keeping a large fleet at sea in peacetime. Not until the late nineteenth century did it become usual for modern warships to remain in permanent commission (in between refits) even when there was neither war nor rumour of war.

This simple fact affected every aspect of naval warfare. It meant that the first, and generally the most intractable difficulty facing any naval power going to war was not how to use its seapower, but how to realise it; how to transform a potential fleet into an actual instrument of victory. Success in this process made victory possible, and failure in it made defeat certain. Much of the naval and diplomatic history of the eighteenth century can be explained by the different methods of mobilization available to the naval powers, and the varied success with which they applied them on different occasions. Warfare in every age has depended heavily on logistics and finance, but the demobilized navies of the eighteenth century were especially dependent on administrative systems capable of setting in motion the huge and costly machine of naval power as swiftly and efficiently as possible.

The first essential of a fleet was of course ships, and above all the ships of the line on which the battle strength of every fleet depended. Because battleships took at least three years to build, often longer, a navy's strength until well into a major war consisted of those which had been built before it. Very few ships of the line, and hardly any of the first and second rates, were ever commissioned in time of peace, and it would be necessary to fit out virtually all the country's fleet at once. Dockyards were obliged to dock, inspect and repair scores of ships with the greatest urgency. The process imposed on them greater strains than they usually faced in the midst of war, for only the largest and most destructive of battles would be likely to bring into port so many ships needing attention at the same time. It was moreover a peculiarly difficult business to plan in advance. Anyone could forecast that mobilization would throw a great strain onto the yards, but exactly what, when and where, required knowledge of the condition of every ship. Every naval administration tried to keep the most accurate information on the state of its fleet (and on its potential enemies' fleets), but all found it impossible to arrive at the necessary accuracy. Even the number of ships available was usually doubtful, because whether a ship was capable of being made fit for service was very often a matter, not of absolute possibility or impossibility, but of whether the needful money and facilities could be made available. Many ships were abandoned because they were beyond economical or practical repair in the circumstances, not because restoration was technically impossible. Others, in other circumstances, received extensive repairs and were kept in service for very long periods. A ship like the *Victory* whose qualities made her the favourite of generations of flag officers, enjoyed a very long working life at a cost which would have been regarded as quite unjustified if applied to a less successful design.[1]

It was therefore a question of circumstance, judgement and even accident how many ships could be made ready for sea. What was certain is that no naval power ever commissioned all the ships it possessed, even if it wished to. There was always a proportion which proved upon inspection to be in too poor a condition to justify repair.[2] However carefully ships were looked after in reserve, their massive scantlings easily and often concealed decay. Frequently they were taken in hand for refit only for modest repairs to reveal unsuspected defects, and they in turn to lead on to further problems until the work was abandoned, or completed at a cost of time and money which would not have been accepted if it had been foreseen. Sometimes the reverse happened, when a ship accounted worn out was found upon inspection to be in a better condition than had been supposed.[3] All these factors made it very difficult to

---

[1]   Brian Lavery, *The Ship of the Line* (London, 1983–84, 2 vols), I, 101. For a comparison with the case of the Spanish *Santísima Trinidad* see José P. Merino Navarro, *La Armada Española en el Siglo XVIII* (Madrid, 1981), p. 348.

[2]   At the height of the American War of Independence Sir Charles Middleton, the Controller of the Navy, 'determined on a measure that had never before been attempted – and which was, to bring every ship in ordinary into service of some kind or other; to listen to no excuses, but to double or patch them up so as to make them equal to temporary and home services; and by reducing their masts and weight of metal, they served to the end of the war as part of the Western Squadron and made part of the fleet under Lord Howe which relieved Gibraltar'; Sir J.K. Laughton, ed., *Letters and Papers of Charles, Lord Barham, Admiral of the Red Squadron, 1758–1813* (London, 1906–11, Navy Records Society Vols. 32, 38 & 39), III, 28.

[3]   Public Record Office: ADM 7/659 (Minutes of Admiralty Visitation of the Dockyards, 1771), f. 42 gives an anecdote concerning the near-condemnation in the 1740s of the *Royal William* (1719–1813).

estimate what resources would be needed for mobilization, how many ships would emerge at the end of it, and when.

With frigates, and even more with sloops and smaller men-of-war, the problem was different. With their shorter working lives, but also short construction times, these ships were not economical to preserve in large numbers in peacetime reserve. To mobilize a balanced fleet therefore called for a large building programme, for which it was necessary to have the workmen, the materials, and the building slips. If the slips were to be available in the yards when they were needed, money and space had to be given up in peacetime, and when the crisis arrived, the same artificers would be needed both to refit line-of-battleships and build frigates. Private yards could take the strain only so far as the needs of the merchant fleet sustained sufficient yards with sufficient skills. Both building new ships and refitting those in reserve required large quantities of timber and other naval stores, most of which were as susceptible to decay as completed ships, and many of which had to be imported. Before any fleet could be mobilized, still more before it could be sustained on a war footing for any period of time, large stocks of these materials had to be built up and maintained. The process of mobilization, long in itself, therefore required long preparation before it could be set in train.

Other, equally intractable difficulties hindered navies from furnishing their ships with officers and men. By the eighteenth century all the major naval powers provided something like a permanent career for their commissioned officers, but of necessity the majority of them would be unemployed in time of peace. They might be put on half-pay and left at liberty to do what they pleased, so long as they did not leave the country without permission, which was the British system; they might be retained by the state and obliged to reside near a naval port, as in France.[4] In either case the officers were ashore, with few or no opportunities of practising their professional skills. This was a problem of commissioned officers, especially senior officers. Warrant officers in all navies were unlikely to be supported in peacetime unless actually employed, and unlikely to have the means to support themselves except by working at their trade. Commissioned officers might do the same – in Britain some lieutenants served in merchantmen in peacetime[5] – but captains and admirals were almost certain to stay ashore in peacetime except for those who might be needed for the few ships commissioned in time of peace. It was therefore

---

[4]   James Pritchard, *Louis XV's Navy, 1748–62: A Study of Organization and Administration* (Kingston & Montreal, 1987), pp. 59–61. On French officers in general see Michel Vergé-Franceschi, *Les Officiers Généraux de la Marine Française, 1715–74* (Paris, 1990, 7 vols).

[5]   N.A.M. Rodger, *The Wooden World: An Anatomy of the Georgian Navy* (London, 1986), p. 269.

usual for squadrons to assemble on the outbreak of war few of whose senior officers had been employed at sea for ten or fifteen years. However well they might originally have been trained, after years ashore they were bound to have half-forgotten their professional skills. The first duty of a flag officer appointed to command such a squadron was to relearn himself, and reteach his captains, how to handle ships in company, a process which took much time, and often involved an inordinate number of collisions. Since the line of battle as a fighting formation was much stronger in defence than offence, and could be turned to advantage only by a highly co-ordinated fleet, decisive battles between more or less equal forces were virtually unknown in the early phases of a war. The only obvious exception is the battle of Minorca in 1756, but here the battle itself was an indecisive skirmish, and the decisive strategic consequences flowed from Byng's needless withdrawal from the Mediterranean afterwards. The problem of re-training officers was one which eighteenth-century navies were slow to confront and slower still to solve, insofar as it was ever solved at all. The French navy organized some training cruises from the 1750s,[6] something which did not appear in Britain until 1772,[7] but in either case three or four ships of the line at sea for a few weeks could not do much to solve the problem.

With ratings, and to some extent warrant officers, the problem was the reverse. Senior officers were not scarce, but had to be re-taught their profession; seamen needed little instruction, but were very hard to find. Unable to afford to keep their fleets in commission in peacetime, the naval powers were equally unable to afford to pay seamen to lie idle. The number of seamen employed in peacetime was essentially the number of men who could find employment in the merchant fleet, for with a free market in labour, there was no incentive for a man to enter a trade in which he could not find work. In wartime every state intervened in the market in an attempt to find men for the navy, and no state found a satisfactory method. If wartime demand exceeded peacetime supply, which it usually did, there was no easy solution. Seamen took years to train, preferably from boyhood, and there was no possibility of improvising them in a few months to man a fleet as it mobilized. Those who could be found would need no particular training, but there were too few of them. This was for every navy the most severe limitation on its effective power, and shortage of manpower usually limited the number of ships which could be put into

---

[6]   Martine Acerra & Jean Meyer, *Marines et Révolution* ([Rennes] 1988), p. 43. Orville T. Murphy, *Charles Gravier, Comte de Vergennes: French Diplomacy in the Age of Revolution, 1719–1787* (Albany, 1982), p. 219. Jonathan R.Dull, *The French Navy and American Independence, A Study of Arms and Diplomacy 1774–1787* (Princeton, 1975), pp. 19 & 57.

[7]   Nicholas Tracy, *Navies, Deterrence and American Independence: Britain and Seapower in the 1760s and 1770s* (Vancouver, 1988), p. 38.

commission even when the logistical, technical and financial means existed to equip more.

It was in this area that the practice of the British navy differed most sharply from those of France and Spain. The *système des classes*, and its Spanish imitation the *matrícula del mar,* were viewed by British contemporaries as vastly superior to their own informal, not to say chaotic methods. In certain respects they were right, though it is clear today that at their best these systems did nothing to remedy the basic shortage of seamen in countries whose merchant fleets were smaller than that of Britain.[8] It has been calculated that the total number of seafarers employed in British ships was nearly 130,000 at the height of the Seven Years' War, and over 150,000 during the American War.[9] During the same period the number of skilled seamen (a more limited definition) enrolled in the French *classes* was not more than 60,000,[10] and in the *matrícula del mar* only 6,000.[11] The *système des classes* added not a single man to the total; what it could do was to recruit men up to a certain level of manpower, faster than the British practice of bounties backed by the press. In the words of the comte de La Luzerne, last French naval minister of the *ancien régime*, the system, 'nous a fourni des moyens de faire sortir nos flottes fort avant celles des Anglais, avantage important, et qu'il est même difficile d'évaluer'.[12] It was well understood on both sides of the Channel that France enjoyed an advantage in manning in the early stages of mobilization, so that if all other things were equal (which they seldom were) she could put a squadron of perhaps twenty or even thirty ships of the line to sea sooner than the Royal Navy could respond.[13] This was a transitory advantage, for the British, though slower, were drawing on a population of seamen so much greater than that available in France that

---

8   Jean Meyer, 'Les problèmes de personnel de la marine de guerre française aux XVIIe et XVIIIe siècles', in Alain Lottin, Jean-Claude Hocquet & Stéphane Lebecq, eds., *Les Hommes et la Mer dans l'Europe du Nord-Ouest de l'Antiquité à nos jours* (*Revue du Nord* extra number, 1986), pp. 107–124.

9   David J. Starkey, 'War and the Market for Seafarers in Britain, 1736–1792', in Lewis R.Fischer & Helge W. Nordvik, eds., *Shipping and Trade, 1750–1950: Essays in International Maritime Economic History* (Pontefract, 1990), pp. 25–42, App. I. These figures are better than those given in Rodger, *Wooden World*, p. 149.

10   T.J.A. Le Goff, 'Offre et productivité de la main-d'oeuvre dans les armements française au XVIIIème siècle', *Histoire Économie et Société* II (1983), pp. 457–473, Table 1.

11   Merino, *Armada Española*, pp. 85–86.

12   Quoted in Acerra & Meyer, *Marines et Révolution*, p. 31.

13   W.J. Smith, ed., *The Grenville Papers: being the Correspondence of Richard Grenville Earl Temple, K.G., and the Right Hon: George Grenville, their Friends and Contemporaries* (London, 1852–53, 4 vols), II, 172 (Egmont to George Grenville, 3 Dec 1763). Murphy, *Vergennes*, p. 263.

in time they could always commission more ships, but in the early stages of a war they ran the risk of a serious, even a crippling reverse.

The British answer to the *système des classes* was the guardships. These were ships of the line which lay at each of the dockyard ports, in commission without usually going to sea, with all their officers and part of their full crews. In theory they provided a defence of the yards against a surprise attack in peacetime, but no such attack was ever anticipated, and their real function was to provide a discreet measure of partial mobilization. Guardships received greater attention from the dockyards than ships in Ordinary (meaning in reserve): they were fully refitted and equipped for sea when they commissioned; thereafter they received a refit every three years known as 'triennial trimming', and were docked to clean their bottoms every few months. They were in principle capable of putting to sea at short notice, though not manned to more than half their wartime complement. The guardships could be used as an instrument of diplomacy and deterrence. To increase the number of guardships, or the complements of those already in commission, brought the Navy that much nearer mobilization, and made it that much more effective a threat. Every guardship commissioned was one fewer to fit out from Ordinary; every man added to a guardship's crew was one fewer to find on the outbreak of war. Done in secret it increased Britain's strength without alerting the enemy; done publicly it deterred attack.

The Falkland Island crisis of 1770 offers an example of the advantage the guardships gave; like the *système des classes*, though by a quite different mechanism, they permitted a limited squadron to be mobilized quickly. In June 1769 secret orders were given to increase their crews and to move them out of harbour into the roads, while two of them were sent to sea. Full mobilization was deliberately delayed until the autumn in order to take advantage of men freed by merchant shipping coming home for the winter. By the winter the British had gained a formidable lead and were able to dictate to France, which was all along treated as the principal in the affair.[14] Much the same happened in 1790 with the fleet mobilized against Spain over the Nootka Sound affair, with the difference that the Spanish fleet, then at the high point of its efficiency, began to mobilize first, and ran the British close in the speed with which they fitted out ships over the six months the crisis lasted.[15]

These affairs illustrate the strength but also the risks of early mobilization; a powerful instrument of coercion, but one which carried considerable risks of

---

[14]   Tracy, *Navies, Deterrence and American Independence*, pp. 77–99; and 'The Falklands Islands crisis of 1770; Use of naval Force', *English Historical Review* XC (1975), pp. 40–75.

[15]   Paul Webb, 'The Naval Aspects of the Nootka Sound Crisis', *Mariner's Mirror* LXI (1975), pp. 133–154.

precipitating war. In the aftermath of the Falkland Islands crisis it was decided to increase the establishment of guardships to twenty, and to double their crews, so that they could be ready to put to sea on a war footing in three or four weeks from receiving orders.[16] The king calculated that this force represented at least three months' start in mobilization.[17] So long as the political will and the money existed to keep up the guardships Britain had no need to fear being put at a disadvantage in mobilization. But unlike a permanent administrative machine such as the *système des classes*, an increase in the guardship establishment required a political decision, and consequently a united administration, resolved to deter even at the risk of war. The crisis of the mid-1770s found a British government by no means united, and anxious to avoid the risk of a European war until the American rebellion was safely extinguished. Consequently the efforts of Lord Sandwich, the First Lord of the Admiralty, to match French and Spanish mobilization, were weakened by colleagues who preferred appeasement, and when war finally broke out in 1778 the Royal Navy was not only distracted by its operations in America, but decisively behind in the mobilization race. It was not until August 1777 that the Cabinet finally agreed to full mobilization, by which time France and Spain combined had 64 ships of the line in commission against 43.[18]

All this has assumed that Britain and her potential enemies were undertaking essentially the same process when they mobilized. In practice until late in the century it would be more accurate to say that the British aimed to mobilize fully, and the French and Spanish only partially. British policy had been from the sixteenth century to commission the maximum number of ships, and keep them in commission as long as resources would permit. The French and Spanish navies preferred to fit out particular squadrons for particular services, replacing them with others, so that only a proportion of the ships and men available were in service at any time. This was a rational response to weaknesses of logistics and finance, and the wide dispersal of the dockyard ports; it also used to the best advantage an efficient but fragile system of recruitment. The problem was that it conceded to the enemy a permanent superiority in numbers. With the utmost strategic ingenuity it was difficult in these circumstances to face the

---

[16] Tracy, *Navies, Deterrence and American Independence*, p. 38.

[17] Sir John Fortescue, ed., *The Correspondence of King George the Third, from 1760 to December 1783* (London, 1927–28, 6 vols), II, 474.

[18] Daniel A. Baugh, 'Why did Britain lose command of the Sea during the War for America ?' in *The British Navy and the Use of Naval Power in the Eighteenth Century* (Leicester, 1988), ed. Jeremy Black & Philip Woodfine, pp. 153–156. Tracy, *Navies, Deterrence and American Independence*, pp. 129–148. Dull, *French Navy and American Independence*, pp. 51–84. H.M.Scott, *British Foreign Policy in the Age of the American Revolution* (Oxford, 1990), pp. 234–243.

British in battle on equal terms, and even more difficult to achieve worthwhile objectives without fighting. It was only in the American War of Independence that France seriously attempted once more to assemble a full battle fleet, as she had last done in the 1690s; in the past, said Maurepas, 'the loss of one or two squadrons undid us... but that will not be the case now'.[19] This was the last time France and Spain faced Britain in a naval war on something like equal terms. By the time the Revolution applied the spirit of the *levée en masse* to the fleet, numbers alone were powerless to redress its lost efficiency.

The difficulty of mobilizing seapower lies at the root of many aspects of naval strategy in the eighteenth century, and it had a marked impact on peacetime diplomacy. For Britain in particular, the fleet was the most powerful, often the only, diplomatic instrument available.[20] Its mere existance, in an efficient condition, might serve to persuade or deter, but if it failed to do so nothing could be achieved without at least partial mobilization. Naval mobilization – an 'armament', in the contemporary phrase – was essential to back a demand because unmobilized, with its ships, in the Admiralty's words, 'as useless as if they did not exist',[21] the Royal Navy would frighten nobody, and mobilized too late it might be a symbol of weakness rather than strength. There is an analogy to be drawn with the 'war of timetables' of 1914; like the Russian army, the British navy could deploy formidable strength, but it took a long time to do so. For this reason the British had compelling reasons to mobilize first, in spite of the risk that by doing so they would provoke war rather than prevent it.[22] Moreover the power which gained a decisive advantage in the mobilization race had a powerful temptation to use it quickly before the potential enemy caught up.[23] In such circumstances it took what Vergennes called 'a sublime effort of virtue'[24] to let the opportunity pass. The process of mobilization provided the means of deterrence but risked precipitating a war, in both cases because it was the first and most critical stage, not merely in starting, but in winning a war at sea.

It is arguable that mobilization is but one aspect of a larger problem which affected all eighteenth-century navies; their obsession with construction. Statesmen and admirals in every country concentrated on the number of ships

---

[19]   Tracy, *Navies, Deterrence and American Independence*, p. 153 (quoting in English).

[20]   Tracy, *Navies, Deterrence and American Independence*, p. 1.

[21]   Stephen Gradish, *The Manning of the British Navy during the Seven Years' War* (London, 1980, Royal Historical Society Studies in History No. 21), p. 29.

[22]   Walpole's reason for delaying preparations in 1739; see Richard Harding, *Amphibious Warfare in the Eighteenth Century: The British Expedition to the West Indies, 1740–1742* (Woodbridge, 1991, Royal Historical Society Studies in History No. 62), p. 24.

[23]   Scott, *British Foreign Policy in the Age of the American Revolution*, p. 147.

[24]   Dull, *French Navy and American Independence*, p. 84, quoting in English.

available on paper at the expense of more complex but more realistic measures of naval power. As a result they spent their resources on building more ships than they could usefully employ. The mere fact that no navy ever commissioned all its ships at once logically meant that a proportion of their building expense had been thrown away. In Britain, it has been powerfully argued,[25] the country consistently underinvested in the dockyards and built more ships than it could keep in repair, with the result that ships had shorter working lives, and had to be replaced more often, than ought to have been necessary. This in turn required needlessly high expenditure on building replacements, so reinforcing a vicious circle. A wiser distribution of expense would have achieved a fleet of the same effective size at lower cost – as it did in Spain.[26] The same argument might be applied to mobilization. Paying-off fleets in peacetime certainly saved money, but it entailed immense expenditure on the outbreak of war, and required all sorts of stocks and facilities to be maintained at a level sufficient to sustain the crisis of mobilization. The same fleet maintained in permanent commission would have had much higher running costs, but might well have required less investment in dockyards and magazines, because the load on them could have been spread evenly over the life of the ships. Moreover it ought to have been possible to develop the same power at sea with a smaller fleet. The necessity of mobilizing almost from nothing meant that it took a naval power two or three years to deploy her full strength, and many months to deploy any strength at all. The cost of this delay was as high in lost military opportunity as in money. How would Britain have fared in warfare against a naval power which kept, say, forty ships of the line in permanent commission, ready to go into action at short notice? In two years she could have produced a fleet decisively superior in numbers, if not in professional skill – but by then it might have been too late. We can never answer such questions, but they are certainly worth asking, because they highlight one of the most distinctive, and expensive, characteristics of the eighteenth-century way of warfare at sea. The maxim of Vegetius, *qui desiderat pacem, praeparet bellum*, was as well-known to peacetime statesmen in the eighteenth century as in the twentieth, and just as unattractive.

Additional Note [2009]

This is the original English text of an article which was published in a rather less than accurate French translation.

---

[25] By R.J.B. Knight; conveniently summarized in 'The Building and Maintenance of the British fleet during the Anglo-French Wars (1688–1815)', in Acerra, Merino & Meyer, *Les Marines de Guerre Européennes*, pp. 35–50.

[26] Merino, *Armada Española*, pp. 353–356.

THE NAVAL CHAPLAIN IN THE EIGHTEENTH CENTURY*

Few figures in the eighteenth-century Royal Navy were regarded as less important in their own day, and have attracted less notice from later historians, than
the chaplains. Gordon Taylor's pioneering history provides much valuable
evidence, but does not pretend to a systematic analysis.[1] The most scholarly
study of religion in the Navy remains unpublished, and is largely concerned
with the Evangelical revival.[2] Studies of naval chaplains in the seventeenth and
nineteenth centuries are also unpublished.[3] Other research on religion and the
seaman has concentrated on nineteenth-century missions, chiefly to merchant
seamen.[4] There is therefore scope even for a few preliminary observations on
the British naval chaplain in this period, and especially on the position of the
chaplain before the Evangelical revival had much affected public attitudes to
the relationship of a clergyman and his parishioners.

Scholars no longer dismiss the Church of England of the eighteenth century
as a spiritually moribund organization of pluralists and time-servers, but no
one would dispute that its position as an established church, part of the fabric
of civil society, compromised its ability, even at times its willingness, to preach
the Gospel with fearless independence. For various reasons naval chaplains
found it particularly difficult to carve out for themselves a spiritual role which
might fulfil their ambitions or occupy their time. Neither official nor popular
feeling in the Navy regarded a chaplain as important. The first edition of the
Regulations and Instructions relating to His Majesty's Service at Sea in 1731
failed to mention chaplains at all, nor did any subsequent edition until the
major revision of 1806.[5] The captain was enjoined 'to take Care that Divine
Service be performed twice a Day on board, according to the Liturgy of the
Church of England, and a sermon preached on Sundays unless bad Weather or
other extraordinary Accident prevent it', but there was no suggestion that a
clergyman would be needed to perform the duty.[6]

There would naturally be even less need if the duty were never performed
anyway. It is always difficult to prove a negative, but references to any sort of
divine service on shipboard between the end of Queen Anne's War in 1713 and
the American War sixty-five years later are exceedingly rare.[7] In 1734 Sir John
Norris wrote to his first-captain expressing the hope that 'the minister is aboard
and that there may be prayers twice a day for the people grow dissolute for
want of strict discipline', and the following year he ordered that 'the minister
preach every Sunday against swearing and debauchery, and give every man that
is guilty of it half a dozen drubs at the black stakes'.[8] A warrant officer writing
in 1743 had only once in his life heard prayers read aboard one of H.M. ships.[9]
Captain Charles Middleton claimed never to have met divine service performed
aboard ship in the sixteen years (1734-50) he served before he received his first
command.

As soon as I became a captain I begun reading prayers myself to the ship's company of
a Sunday and also a sermon. I continued this practice as long as I was in commission

and without a chaplain, and it never was omitted when I had one. I did not indeed venture to carry it further than Sundays, because the practice was confined to those days by the very few ships who had chaplains, when followed at all; and I should only have acquired the name of methodist or enthusiast if I attempted it.[10]

His nephew James Gambier (a post-captain of 1778) was accused of sectarianism for reading prayers in his ship.[11] In most of these cases, moreover, the services were held in port. A rare case of a service held at sea was on board Boscawen's flagship the *Torbay* off the American coast in 1755 – but that was in the wardroom, with the ship's company not invited.[12] The impression that divine service in the Navy virtually ceased for much of the century is confirmed by the absence of published sermons, in an age when printed sermons on every subject and occasion found a ready sale. In 1701 Philip Stubs issued *God's Dominion over the sea and the seaman's duty, consider'd in a sermon preached at Long-Reach on board [...] the Royal Soveraign*,[13] and he followed it in 1704 with another sermon preached on shipboard.[14] He was imitated by John Philips in 1709 with a sermon given aboard the *Chichester* in the Mediterranean.[15] Thereafter there was silence for seventy years.

It may have been somewhat less rare for prayers to be recited aboard merchant ships. A sailor writing in the 1770s of his youthful service in Queen Anne's time remembered 'prayers we had once a week if blowed hard; if little winds, knone'.[16] On his voyage to Lisbon in 1754 Fielding saw Sunday prayers 'read by a common sailor with more devout force and address than they are commonly read by a country curate, and received with more decency and attention by the sailors than are usually observed in a city congregation'.[17] On the other hand, when the diplomat Sir Gilbert Elliot took passage to Hamburg in a German ship in 1781, he was astonished to find the seamen singing psalms twice a day: 'different in all things from ours as sailors can be'. The English pilot disapproved: 'he says, it is very well to pray when a man is in the mind for it, but then he need not make such a noise, and *has no right to disturb the watch*'.[18]

When we first begin to encounter naval church services in the 1770s, they are almost all on board flagships, more often than not in port, and described in terms which suggest that public worship was a novelty arousing interest if not astonishment. In 1778 James Ramsay printed the first naval sermon to have been published since Queen Anne's time,[19] and he followed it in 1781 with what was probably the first book of sermons for use in the Navy.[20] One other sermon was printed in 1784;[21] like Ramsay's, it had been given aboard a flagship, at anchor, in thanksgiving for a remarkable deliverance, and both of them were printed at their authors' expense. The chaplain of Sir Chaloner Ogle's flagship in 1775 records that 'the duty of a clergyman was very seldom required of me while I was chaplain to the *Resolution*'. When one day the admiral did ask him to read prayers, and he ventured to suggest that he would be glad to do so more often, Sir Chaloner replied with something less than enthusiasm: 'At all events [...] I think it is right that these things should be done sometimes, as long as Christianity is on foot.'[22] This is a suspect recollection, from a man whose career was by no means so devoted to the gospel as his memoirs would suggest, but it is not implausible. When Benjamin Millingchamp joined Sir Edward Hughes's flagship the *Superb* in 1778, the captain, 'last Saturday [...] asked me if it was agreeable to read prayers and give 'em a sermon on the following day; said it was a very unusual thing in Harbour but hoped I had no objection'.[23] It was an even more unusual thing at sea, but no longer quite unknown. In May 1776 a passenger aboard Lord Howe's flagship the *Eagle* coming down Channel on her way to America,

was much pleased with the performance of divine service this morning, and the order and behaviour of the officers and ship's company upon the occasion. The Revd Mr O'Beirne our chaplain gave us a very solid and rational discourse, and I scarce ever saw one so well attended to in my life.[24]

In 1780 the chaplain of the *Royal George*, taking passage in the *Nonsuch*, 64, in search of his own ship, recorded two occasions on which the chaplain read prayers on Sunday, on one occasion while the ship was in chase.[25] This was notable, and certainly unusual, in that divine service was not laid aside when the ship was busy: in Hughes's flagship by 1782 'Divine Service [...] was grown quite a novelty in the *Superbe*, from the continual hurry and bustle unavoidable in war'.[26] It is also noteworthy that a ship as small as the *Nonsuch* bore a chaplain at all in a period when only a fraction of the ships in the Navy had one: there were twenty-two in service at the height of the 1770 mobilization over the Falkland Islands crisis, and the total had fallen to seventeen by 1777.[27]

The principal reason why only large ships usually bore chaplains was financial. A chaplain received the pay of an ordinary seaman, 17s 6d a lunar month net of fixed deductions, and unlike the ordinary seaman's his was not increased in 1797.[28] The main part of his income came from the compulsory deduction of fourpence a man a month from the wages of all on board. In a flagship with a complement of six or seven hundred men this yielded an income of £150 a year or more, which compared well with many curacies ashore, especially in the 1770s when their real value was falling behind inflation.[29] There was also some chance of prize money, the means by which John Deere, son of a petty squire from Glamorgan, allegedly amassed a fortune of £10,000 by the time of his death in 1764.[30]

This leads naturally to the question of why men chose to go to sea as naval chaplains, and what they did at sea in an era when even reading prayers was a rarity. There were two difficulties in the way of naval chaplains, if there were any such, who hoped to exercise the cure of souls: the officers, and the ratings. Officers, especially in the middle years of the century, were affected by the climate of indifference and anti-clericalism prevailing in the class from which they were largely drawn. The days were long gone when an officer might be dismissed the Service for blasphemy.[31] The awful havoc wrought by religious zealotry in the seventeenth century taught later generations to suspect anything like 'enthusiasm', by which they meant fanaticism.[32] The natural result was to emphasize the worldly conveniences offered by the Church of England, and there was no lack of divines ready to justify them. The 'extraordinary operation' of the Holy Ghost, Bishop Warburton declared, was no longer necessary 'now the profession of the Christian Faith is attended with ease and honour'.[33] George Grenville 'considered bishoprics of two kinds, bishops of business for men of abilities and learning, and bishops of ease for men of family and fashion'.[34] Men of godliness and prayer were not mentioned at all. In this climate of opinion a clergyman's first recourse was respectability rather than spirituality, and his immediate trial was the irreligious tone of wardroom life – if indeed he were admitted to the wardroom, for chaplains never slept there, and did not always mess with the commissioned officers. In 1758 one chaplain wrote an ironic poem lamenting his failure to secure that ultimate symbol of the status of a gentleman, access to the wardroom quarter-gallery (the officers' latrine).[35] The officers were the first object of most chaplains' complaints:

Nothing could be more shocking, and mortifying to me, or to any mind which possessed a particle of moral delicacy, or of intellectual improvement, than the manners, and conversation of the sea-officers. I speak of what they were, in general, almost half a century ago [in 1756]; I hope they are better now.[36]

Wardroom conversation inspired this memoirist to flights of sanctimony, 'I know by experience, that the clergyman who can endure it, must either have the invincible patience, and perseverance, of a missionary, or the profligacy of a CHARTRES.'[37] Edward Mangin's reflections in 1812 were more temperate, but essentially similar:

with a gentleman's education but without a sufficient income, my new undertaking had rather the air of desperation than of enterprise; and long accustomed to the society of the polite, the learned and the effeminate, I was now to dwell with those to whom not any of these epithets could possibly be applied.[38]

By 1812 these were perhaps old-fashioned views, and Mangin was clearly a jaundiced witness, temperamentally unsuited to the sea life. He thought the ship's company quite beyond the reach of rational religion:

To leave them unreproved and vicious, was possible; and I daresay it was equally possible to have transformed them all into Methodists, or madmen and hypocrites of some other kind: but to convert a man-of-war's crew into Christians would be a task to which the courage of Loyola, the philanthropy of Howard, and the eloquence of St. Paul united, would prove inadequate.[39]

Until late in the eighteenth century the summit of the average naval chaplain's ambition was to serve with 'that regularity and decency as may be of due service to the men and no discredit to my patrons'.[40] His difficulty was that he had nothing to do. His opportunities for preaching and teaching were non-existent for much of the century, and rare even by the end of it. Under the most sympathetic and active captain the best a chaplain could hope for was a few hours' work a week. The theology of the Church of England effectively denied him the opportunity to administer any sacraments (the occasional infant baptism excepted), unlike the Roman Catholic chaplains aboard French and Spanish men-of-war.[41] Communion services were apparently unknown before the 1840s,[42] and not all chaplains were in priest's orders anyway.[43] Not until 1812 were chaplains permitted to act as schoolmasters.[44] The duties laid upon the chaplain by the 1806 *Regulations and Instructions*, in addition to preaching and praying, were, in Mangin's view, few and impossible. He was to divert punishment from the guilty (hardly popular with the captain), visit the sick (which they regarded as an announcement of death), and rebuke profanity among the seamen (but not the officers).[45]

I could neither drink nor play at cards, etc. with such as indulged in these pastimes: to go among the crew, and discourse with them of religion and morality, I have already shown to be not very practicable [...] I accordingly felt myself most awkwardly situated, and fancied I was somewhat like a pet bear on board. I was fed, coaxed and stared at: – if in my den, forgotten; if at large, in every body's way; of no manner of use - and at best, endured![46]

This had long been the common lament of chaplains:

A Clergy man in a Man of War, if he wou'd assert the Dignity of his Character, is considered as a Nuisance, as a Damp to that Gaiety & Licentiousness which reigns without controll among the Sons of the Waves. Every thing he sees, & hears is an Insult on his Office – such swearing, such Obscenity, such contempt of every thing serious, & religious continually satiates you, that *believe* me, I am quite tired of a life so infernal, & daily invoke *Neptune* to expel me from his Dominions.[47]

Every chaplain had to find a way out of this dilemma. Mangin's was to quit the Service; more robust and experienced men found something useful to do, befitting their status and education. Since so many of them were serving in flagships, the most natural choice was to serve the admiral as some sort of a staff officer. John Lindsay, chaplain of the *Fougueux* during the Seven Years' War, exercised his talents as a hydrographer.[48] Nathaniel Cotton, chaplain of the *Princess Amelia*, flagship of the North American station, spent the winter of 1758-59 while his ship was frozen up in Halifax travelling between Rear-Admiral Durell and Governor Pownall, making arrangements for the forth-coming assault on Canada and recruiting seamen.[49] James Ramsay, a former naval surgeon lamed by a broken thigh, took orders and found a living in St Kitts, where his opposition to the slave trade made him so unpopular that he had to leave the island. He returned in 1778 as Rear-Admiral Barrington's chaplain, and established himself as intelligence officer for the Leeward Islands station.[50] As a man of letters, the chaplain was the natural choice to write a narrative of the campaign or expedition on which he had served, especially if the fortunes of war made it necessary to vindicate his patron's reputation.[51] Thus Cooper Willyams published *An Account of the Campaign in the West Indies in the year 1794*,[52] in an endeavour to repair the damage which Sir John Jervis and his colleague Lieutenant-General Sir Charles Grey had done themselves by their rapacious handling of prizes and booty.[53] In the Revolution-ary and Napoleonic Wars it was common for chaplains, or at least clergymen, to serve as admirals' secretaries.[54] On a less sophisticated level Laurence Halloran, chaplain to Lord Northesk's flagship the *Britannia* at Trafalgar (an impostor who falsely pretended to be in orders, and was later transported for fraud), made himself useful with his powerful voice repeating the captain's orders through a speaking-trumpet.[55]

One factor was common to almost all chaplains, that their service was essentially personal. They were followers of admiral or captain rather than full members of a ship's company, and however they filled their time, it was most often as part of the great man's retinue. The well-known Hogarth portrait of Captain Lord George Graham seated in his cabin in 1746 surrounded by his domestics, illustrates the point perfectly. William Burrows was officially the chaplain of the *Nottingham*, but here he appears with the captain's cook, his clerk, his black servant, his spaniel and his poodle.[56] Though we meet a chaplain killed in action attempting to rally the Marines,[57] the usual character of a clergyman at sea was essentially that of a domestic chaplain, and his duties, if any, were most often discharged in the household. In a 1793 Commons debate on chaplains for East Indiamen, one director of the Company whispered to a neighbour, 'I think a chaplain no bad thing, I shan't oppose it. He may always serve to make the grog, and will always be ready for a fourth at whist.'[58] If chaplains prospered in their careers, it was the fruit of loyal attendance upon an influential chief, or the lucky chance to pursue a more promising opening ashore, not a reward for service at sea. Thomas O'Beirne undoubtedly reached the see of Ossory (and subsequently Meath) upon the patronage of Lord Howe, and might equally have done so if neither of them had ever gone to sea. Robert Palk went to the East Indies as Boscawen's chaplain in 1747, but it was a timely transfer to the service of the East India Company which raised him in due course to be a baronet and M.P.[59]

Many chaplains in fact served only a short time at sea in the course of careers directed towards a good living ashore; indeed it was usual for the well-connected to go to sea leaving one or more livings in the hands of curates.[60] Nicholas Tindal, Admiral Wager's chaplain, was in 1740 simultaneously Chaplain of Greenwich Hospital, Rector both of Calbourne in the Isle of Wight and of Alverstoke, Hampshire, and chaplain to a regiment of Marines.[61] Nelson's clerical secretary Alexander Scott is described as 'establishing a record in long-distance pluralism', accompanying his chief to the Baltic in 1801 at the same time as he was incumbent of St John's, Jamaica. This convivial messmate, linguist, diplomatist and man of business, who went to sea with a harpsichord and a library of 650 volumes, typifies the more successful naval chaplain.[62] Others took refuge in the Navy from a variety of misfortunes. Debt was one of the commonest, as with William Plumbe in 1780:

Mr Plumbe has a very fine living in this neighbourhood but having been drawn into a litigation concerning his dues, & therein defeated, the costs are too heavy for him to discharge directly, wherefore the profits of his living are sequestered for that purpose.[63]

One clergyman went to sea in grief at the suicide of his wife; another to escape 'the claws of the Tygress' who was very much alive.[64] Thomas Seward was tutor to Lord Charles Fitzroy on the Grand Tour; when his patron died in Italy he joined a ship to get home.[65] The great astronomer Neville Maskelyne was appointed chaplain of the ship which took him to St. Helena to observe the transit of Venus in 1761.[66] Sometimes embassy or factory chaplains, clergymen going out to take up livings in the colonies and others in need of a free passage entered as chaplains for a single voyage,[67] and during the American War a number of loyalist clergy took refuge in the Navy as chaplains.[68]

Since chaplains were always personal followers of the captains or admirals they served, and since their functions were essentially practical and worldly, their appointments naturally followed the usual rules of influence and patronage which governed all promotion, naval, civil or ecclesiastical. Captains or admirals who desired to have a chaplain applied to the Admiralty naming their candidate. Their choice sometimes fell on a relative, always on a dependant or follower.[69] A chaplain might be the admiral's son[70] or brother. Sometimes the younger son of a clerical family, sent to sea to make his fortune, prospered while the eldest son failed to make a success of his destined career in the church. It was thus that both William Nelson and Arthur Hood served at sea under the patronage of their younger brothers.[71] Political activity often helped to establish or cement links with patrons. John Charles Bale, appointed chaplain of the *Hector* in 1776, had 'dedicated his mental faculty to convince the world of the legality of the several acts of the Corporation of Portsmouth'.[72]

In an age when incumbents of parishes, who had real duties to discharge, often delegated them to curates and enjoyed the revenues of their livings at a safe distance from their parishioners, it was not to be expected that naval chaplains would be unnaturally scrupulous to exercise their exiguous functions in person. For much of the century it seems to have been taken for granted that chaplains would usually be on leave. A Navy Board order of 1742 complained that

many clergymen have procured warrants from this Board to be Chaplains of His Majesty's ships fitting out for sea, without intention of proceeding to sea in them, or so much as appearing on board while they are fitting out, but get themselves discharged when their ships are ordered abroad, and others have been continued, as we are informed, on the ships' Books while the said ships have been employed in Foreign Parts, notwithstanding their residence in England, and have received their wages for the whole voyage, at the Pay of the ship.[73]

These strictures had little or no effect, and for much of the century chaplains continued to take it for granted that it was a gentleman's right to live ashore in civilized surroundings while his ship was at sea. 'A Chaplainship in the Navy', it was said in 1757,

is procured by interest. Now the same interest which enables a man to obtain this Office is sufficient also to get him excused from attendance on the duties of it, for a cruise or an expedition cannot be supposed to be extremely agreeable to a person who has had a liberal land-education.[74]

This was especially true of a voyage or expedition to the West Indies, a prospect which drove many officers of both services to resign or feign illness, preferring to risk their careers rather than their lives.[75] Orders to sail thither could be relied upon to remind chaplains of urgent private business ashore, or (for the more ingenuous), convince them that the climate of the Caribbean would not agree with them.[76]

The first serious attempts to change this attitude were made by Lord Sandwich, someone not normally thought of as a defender of the Church. As early as 1746, when he was still new at the Admiralty, he applied for leave on behalf of a chaplain, specifying that 'he has been constantly attending his duty & I assure you it is no Job to make his office a sinecure, as he is a very dilligent honest man'[77] – an assurance which most of his contemporaries would have regarded as unnecessary, if not quixotic. As First Lord of the Admiralty Sandwich was the enemy of chaplains who did not intend to go to sea with their ships:

I fear the attending in London upon a literary business and the duty of a sea chaplain are incompatible, especially as he can receive no pay but in consequence of his attending musters regularly on board his ship: if a fortnight's leave of absence would enable Mr Stockdale to finish his pamphlet, I could strain a point to make it easy to him; but I could not go any farther without subjecting you who recommended him, and myself who have appointed him, to a good deal of well-founded abuse.[78]

Stockdale was appalled: 'When you were so good as to apply for me for this Chaplainship, neither you nor I thought that in consequence of obtaining it I should be obliged to be near the ship or on board.'[79]

In three years in the guardship *Resolution* he had never been to sea, and he resigned rather than shift from his comfortable lodgings (opposite a brothel in Portsmouth) when she was mobilized. Ten years later, when Sandwich had been replaced at the Admiralty by Lord Howe, Stockdale spent an entire commission as chaplain to the flagship of the Mediterranean squadron living ashore at Gibraltar, and preaching occasionally when his ship touched at the port.[80] Sandwich took the same view of dockyard chaplains. When the Admiralty Board on their first visitation of the yards in 1749 arrived at Sheerness they found that Theodore Delafay the Chaplain of the Ordinary had been absent for over twelve months, and he was sternly ordered back to his duty.[81] Sandwich was later responsible for providing the first chapel ship at Chatham Dockyard.[82]

His motive was not religious zeal, for in his private opinions Sandwich was a representative of the sceptical indifference of his class and generation. Happy to employ known Papists in his private affairs,[83] he was not scandalized even when a Catholic priest was discovered to be secretly ministering to Irish patients in Haslar Hospital, and would have been content to ignore the whole affair had not the hospital Council, 'partly composed of North Britons who retain some of the spirit of their countryman Knox', discovered what was going on.[84] Nevertheless, Sandwich's efforts to improve the discipline of the Service, chaplains included, undoubtedly had some effect on their position. It is during the American War, when he was First Lord, that for the first time a few captains, like Philip Affleck, can be found referring (in letters to him) to the good effect a chaplain might have on their ships' companies.

As it is a happiness to have a clergyman of a moral and decent character, both for the oeconomy of the ship and as a companion, so does the contrary character (of which I have had the ill fortune to know some instances) destroy the whole comfort of a ship.[85]

Turning over into a new ship in 1775, John Jervis asked to take his three lieutenants and the chaplain, William Gardner:

I name the chaplain because he is respected by the officers and revered by the men; never goes out of the ship but to take his exercise and appears to have been at great pains to correct the morals of the people.[86]

This was a growing theme of thoughtful officers of the day; in Rear-Admiral Kempenfelt's words, 'religion is particularly necessary in the common people to preserve morals'.[87] He meant public religion as an aid to dutiful behaviour, not private conversion as a means to win souls for God. Kempenfelt was a man of real piety himself, but it was not something he thought he could or should communicate to his ship's company.[88]

The experience of the French Revolution, and still more the great mutinies of 1797, turned officers' attention very forcibly to the morals of their people, and caused many men whose serious thoughts did not have rest in heaven, to think about the importance of a good chaplain. This is the period when the naval Evangelicals begin to be influential, especially between 1804 and 1807 when James Gambier and Sir Charles Middleton were at the Admiralty, but it may be suggested that most officers were still more interested in discipline than personal conversion. 'There never was an era', wrote Captain John Duckworth in 1794, 'when the circulating of religion and morality appears more evidently necessary, especially among the lower orders of people, than at present.'[89] Divine service afloat was becoming less rare, and it is often associated with those, like Jervis, who cared more for discipline than vital religion. (In 1797 his second-in-command, Vice-Admiral Thompson, was removed for complaining that the commander-in-chief had profaned the Sabbath by hanging men during morning prayers on Sunday.)[90] In his flagship the *Boyne*,

The 25th December [1793], being Christmas Day, divine service was performed on the quarter-deck by the Chaplain, the crew appearing as on a Sunday, in clean trowsers and jackets: and here I must beg leave to mention, that I never saw more regularity and decorum in any place of worship than is invariably observed on board of his Majesty's ships of war.[91]

Regularity and decorum were certainly invariable in any ship under Jervis's command, and increasingly expected everywhere. On the Leeward Islands station a study of ships between 1784 and 1812 found that 40% held services aboard, while 18% received consignments of bibles from the Naval and Military Bible Society, at the officers' request, for distribution to the ships' companies.[92] We may perhaps think of the 40% as those who conceived of religion as an aid to authority, and the 18% as including those who also cared for the souls of their men. Unfortunately these figures tell us nothing about changes over this period, but it would be reasonable to guess that in both cases the frequency was increasing. It is certainly in the 1790s that naval sermons began again to find a market. Another book of sermons was printed in 1792,[93] and two years later a modest milestone was reached with the first published sermons to have been preached at sea.[94] In 1798 James Stanier Clarke, the future biographer of Nelson, issued *Naval Sermons preached on board His Majesty's Ship the Impetueux in the Western Squadron, during its services off Brest: to which is added a thanksgiving sermon for naval victories; preached at Park-Street Chapel, Grosvenor Square, Dec. 19 M,DCC,XCVII.*[95] This is a neat witness to the rising status of the naval chaplain and his duties, for it would be difficult to think of two less likely situations in which to find any of Clarke's predecessors of the 1740s or 1750s than preaching to the crew of a ship at sea, and to the congregation of a fashionable West End chapel.

During the nineteenth century a climate of moral and religious opinion was to develop which took the chaplain seriously, at least as an aid to good order and naval discipline, not infrequently as an instrument of personal conversion. For the eighteenth-century naval chaplain the fundamental problem was that the mood of the times and the circumstances of a warship left him few opportunities to discharge a genuinely spiritual role, or in many cases, any role whatsoever. Furthermore, naval chaplains were not often the best, and very seldom the luckiest men in their profession;[96] and the clerical profession itself tended to be the employment of last resort for an educated man who had failed to make a success of any other career. There must have been many men in the situation of William Peacock, though few expressed it with such brutal candour:

The idle unprofitable maner in which I have wasted many years past, & my total want of money, combine to render me disqualified for every kind of business, and because fit for nothing, I am going to follow the custom of the day, and take Orders [...]. I feel myself one of those destitute craving people, who are perpetually pestering Gentlemen in Power with their petitions; but are too insignificant to command attention, & too devoid of merit, to deserve any.[97]

Few naval chaplains were completely devoid of merit, but even at the end of the century, when the Service was increasingly concerned about the morals and discipline of the lower deck, the chaplain still tended to be largely devoid of a job, and it was inevitable that a profession with poor pay, little work and uncertain prospects, would have difficulty in attracting the best men. It was only with the development after 1812 of the Chaplain-Schoolmaster that the Navy found a useful and well-paid berth for clergymen afloat, and even then it is to be feared that the arrangement had as much to do with promoting the study of mathematics and establishing the decencies of public worship, as winning souls for God.

Additional Note [2009]

A preliminary sketch of a neglected and important class of men. There is a little more on seventeenth-century chaplains in *The Command of the Ocean*.

* I am indebted to Mr R. C. Blake and Dr Michael Duffy for helpful comments on a draft of this paper.

1. *The Sea Chaplains: A History of the Chaplains of the Royal Navy* (Oxford, 1978). It will be apparent from the notes how much I am indebted to this work. W. E. L. Smith, *The Navy and its Chaplains in the Age of Sail* (Toronto, 1961), is also scholarly and useful.

2. R. C. Blake, 'Aspects of Religion in the Royal Navy, *c.*1750-*c.*1870' (Southampton M.Phil. thesis, 1980).

3. W. F. Scott, 'The Naval Chaplain in Stuart Times' (Oxford D.Phil. thesis, 1935). J. Curry, 'English Sea-Chaplains in the Royal Navy (1577-1684)' (Bristol M.A. thesis, 1956). L. Davies, 'Royal Navy Chaplains, 1812-61' (Birmingham M.Phil. thesis, 1990).

4. Roald Kverndal, *Seamen's Missions: their origin and early growth* (Pasadena, 1986); and 'The 200th Anniversary of Organized Seamen's Missions, 1779-979', *Mariner's Mirror* 65 (1979), pp.255-63. Robert Miller, *From Shore to Shore: A History of the Church and the Merchant Seafarer* (Nailsworth, Gloucestershire, 1989). Alston Kennerley, 'British Seaman's Missions and Sailors' Homes, 1815-1970' (Plymouth Polytechnic Ph.D., 1989). Alain Cabantous, *Le Ciel dans la mer: Christianisme et civilisation maritime (xvi-xix siècle)* (Paris, 1990) ranges widely, but not widely enough to say much about the Royal Navy.

5. Taylor, *The Sea Chaplains*, p.230. Richard C. Blake, 'Transmission of the Faith and Transformation of the Fleet: the Religious Education of the Royal Navy 1770-1870', in *Foi chrétienne et milieux maritimes (XVe-XXe siècle)*, ed. by Alain Cabantous and Françoise Hildesheimer (Paris, 1987), pp.50-67, at pp.54-55.

6. Taylor, *The Sea Chaplains*, pp.170-71.

7. Blake, 'Transmission of the Faith', p.51.

8. G. Hinchliffe, 'Some letters of Sir John Norris', *Mariner's Mirror* 66 (1980), 77-84, at 79-80. I owe this reference to the kindness of Mr R. C. Blake.

9. John Bulkeley and John Cummin, *A Voyage to the South Seas in the Year 1740-41* (London, 1743), p.64.

10. *Letters and Papers of Charles, Lord Barham*, ed. by Sir J. K. Laughton (Navy Records Society, vols 36, 38 and 39, 1906-1910), II, 163.

11. *Memorials, Personal and Historical, of Admiral Lord Gambier*, ed. by Georgiana Lady Chatterton, 2 vols (London, 1861), I, 4.

12. Public Record Office [PRO]: ADM 1/90, f.278, E. Boscawen to the Admiralty, 8 July 1760.

13. London, with further printings in 1702, 1703 and 1706. For this reference and those to sermons which follow I am indebted to Mr Thomas R. Adams, who gave me sight of a draft copy of *English Maritime Books relatings to Ships and their Construction and Operation at Sea printed before 1801*, edited by himself and David W. Waters.

14. *Of Religious charity, and religious loyalty. A sermon preach'd June 4th, 1704. On board Her Majesty's capital ship the Royal Anne* (London, 1704). Stubs's *The Sea-assize; or, seafaring persons to be judged according to their works* (London, 1709) was apparently not given afloat.

15. *A Sermon preach'd on board Her Majesty's ship the Chichester, in the Bay of Sardinia, August 1 1708* (London, 1709).

16. *Ramblin' Jack, The Journal of Captain John Cremer, 1700-1774*, ed. by R. R. Bellamy (London, 1936), p.84.

17. Henry Fielding, *Journal of a Voyage to Lisbon in the Year 1754* (London, 1755), p.188.

18. Countess of Minto, *Life and Letters of Sir Gilbert Elliot, First Earl of Minto, from 1751 to 1806*, 3 vols (London, 1874), I, 57-58.

19. *A Sermon preached on board His Majesty's ship Prince of Wales, on the victory gained over the French fleet and army at St. Lucia, December 1778* (Basseterre, St Kitts, 1778).

20. *Sea Sermons; or A series of discourses for the use of the Royal Navy* (London, 1781).

21. P. Touch, *A Thanksgiving Sermon, preached at St. Lucia, the Sunday after the hurricane in October, 1780, on board His Majesty's ship Vengeance, Capt. Holloway and before Commodore Hotham* (London, 1784).

22. Percival Stockdale, *The Memoirs of the Life and Writings of Percival Stockdale*, 2 vols (London, 1809), I, 457.

23. Taylor, *The Sea Chaplains*, p.183.

24. *The American Journal of Ambrose Serle, Secretary to Lord Howe 1776-1778*, ed. by Edward H. Tatum, Jr (San Marino, California, 1940), p.2. Serle wrote and then deleted the second sentence.

25. National Maritime Museum [NMM]: JOD/23, 'Narrative of a fortnight's voyage', by Richard Vyvyan.

26. Taylor, *The Sea Chaplains*, p.183.

27. William L. Clements Library, Ann Arbor, Michigan: Shelburne Papers, vol. 141, no.47.

28. Taylor, *The Sea Chaplains*, p.167.

29. Paul Langford, *A Polite and Commercial People: England 1727-1783* (Oxford, 1989), p.261.

30. Philip Jenkins, *The Making of a Ruling Class: The Glamorgan Gentry 1640-1790* (Cambridge, 1983), p.37. Since Deere was warranted in 1701 his money must have been made in Queen Anne's War, if it was really made at sea; but a chaplain shared only as a petty officer, and the story arouses suspicion.

31. Smith, *The Navy and its Chaplains*, p.47, referring to a case of 1681.

32. W. A. Speck, *Stability and Strife: England 1714-1760* (London, 1977), p.105.

33. Langford, *A Polite and Commercial People*, pp.271-72. See also A. W. Evans, *Warburton and the Warburtonians: A Study in some Eighteenth-Century Controversies* (Oxford, 1932).

34. Langford, *A Polite and Commercial People*, p.262.

35. Taylor, *The Sea Chaplains*, p.170.

36. Stockdale, *Memoirs*, I, 333-34.

37. Stockdale, *Memoirs*, I, 340, and II, 258.

38. 'The Rev. E. Mangin, 1812', in *Five Naval Journals 1789-1817*, ed. by H. G. Thursfield (Navy Records Society, vol. 91, 1951), pp.1-39, at pp.7-8.

44

39. Thursfield, 'Mangin', p.14.

40. NMM: SAN/F/48/68, J. C. Bale to Sandwich, 9 July 1776.

41. Blake, 'Transmission of the Faith', p.51.

42. Blake, 'Transmission of the Faith', p.62.

43. Stockdale, *Memoirs*, II, 221.

44. F. B. Sullivan, 'The Naval Schoolmaster during the Eighteenth Century and the Early Nineteenth Century', *Mariner's Mirror* 62 (1976), 311-26, at 322. Taylor, *The Sea Chaplains*, p.233.

45. Thursfield, 'Mangin', p.9. Taylor, *The Sea Chaplains*, pp.230-31.

46. Thursfield, 'Mangin', p.22.

47. Clements Library, Ann Arbor: Miscellaneous Collection, R. Palmer to [T. Dampier?], 2 March 1772.

48. A. J. Marsh, 'The Taking of Goree, 1758', *Mariner's Mirror* 51 (1965), 121.

49. *The Grenville Papers: being the Correspondence of Richard Grenville Earl Temple, K. G., and the Right Hon: George Grenville, their Friends and Contemporaries*, ed. by W. J. Smith, 4 vols (London, 1852-1853), I, 305, N. Cotton to G. Grenville, 1 June 1759.

50. I. Lloyd Phillips, 'The Evangelical Administrator: Sir Charles Middleton at the Navy Board 1778-1790' (Oxford D.Phil. thesis, 1974), p.21.

51. The best-known example is *A Voyage round the World in the years MDCCXL, I, II, III, IV* by George Anson (London, 1748), though it is uncertain how far this was the sole work of the chaplain Richard Walter; see the edition by Glyndwr Williams (Oxford, 1974), pp.xxi-xxv. Less well known is [Thomas O'Beirne], *A Candid and Impartial Narrative of the Transactions of the Fleet under the Command of Lord Howe* (London, 1779).

52. London, 1796. I am indebted to Dr Duffy for this reference.

53. Michael Duffy, *Soldiers, Sugar and Seapower: The British Expeditions to the West Indies and the War against Revolutionary France* (Oxford, 1987), pp.106-14.

54. Taylor, *The Sea Chaplains*, p.206 gives a long list.

55. Taylor, *The Sea Chaplains*, pp.211 and 214.

56. The picture is now in the National Maritime Museum.

57. Taylor, *The Sea Chaplains*, p.157. Smith, *The Navy and its Chaplains*, pp.61-62.

58. Chatterton, *Gambier*, I, 219.

59. Sir Lewis Namier and John Brooke, *The History of Parliament: The House of Commons 1754-1790*, 3 vols (London, 1964), III, 245. I owe this reference to Dr Duffy.

60. Taylor, *The Sea Chaplains*, pp.210 and 219.

61. Taylor, *The Sea Chaplains*, p.151.

62. Taylor, *The Sea Chaplains*, pp.198-206.

63. NMM: SAN/F/24/95, B. Gascoyne to Sandwich, 30 September 1780.

64. Taylor, *The Sea Chaplains*, p.151. Clements Library, Ann Arbor: Miscellaneous Collection, Sandwich to [T. Dampier?], 23 September 1771. The unhappy husband was Richard Palmer.

65. Taylor, *The Sea Chaplains*, p.158.

66. Taylor, *The Sea Chaplains*, p.165. Derek Howse, *Neville Maskelyne. The Seaman's Astronomer* (Cambridge, 1989), pp.27-39.

67. Taylor, *The Sea Chaplains*, pp.152, 158 and 166.

68. Taylor, *The Sea Chaplains*, pp.172-77.

69. For example, Middleton's follower James Dods, for whom see NMM: SAN/F/10/104, SAN/F/14/20 and SAN/F/20/56, C. Middleton to Sandwich, 22 May 1777, 4 May 1778 and 17 August 1779.

70. NMM: SAN/F/8/7, J. Montagu to Sandwich, 7 March 1776.

71. Carola Oman, *Nelson* (London, 1947), pp.39, 42, 61, 64-66. PRO: ADM 1/1486, W. Brett to the Admiralty, 9 November 1755.

72. NMM: SAN/F/48/68, J. C. Bale to Sandwich, 9 July 1776; SAN/F/6/1, S. Hood to Sandwich, 1 January 1775.

73. Taylor, *The Sea Chaplains*, p.150, quoting PRO: ADM 7/676.

74. Taylor, *The Sea Chaplains*, p.170.

75. Duffy, *Soldiers, Sugar and Seapower*, p.343.

76. PRO: ADM 1/316, H. Linton to J. Brown enc in Brown to Sir J. Jervis, 13 November 1793; T. Puddicombe to E. Nugent enc in Nugent to Jervis, 25 November 1793. I owe these references to the generosity of Dr Duffy.

77. British Library Add. MSS 15957, f.3, Sandwich to G. Anson, 25 May 1746.

78. *The Private Correspondence of David Garrick* 2 vols (London, 1831), II, 173, Sandwich to D. Garrick [1776].

79. Garrick, *Private Correspondence*, II, 187, P. Stockdale to D. Garrick, 1 November 1776.

80. Stockdale, *Memoirs*, II, 102-109 and 247-48.

81. PRO: ADM 3/61, 5 July 1749.

82. NMM: ADM/B/186, Navy Board to Admiralty, 12 August 1772. PRO: ADM 7/660, f.63.

83. NMM: SAN/F/43a/65, C. Butler to Sandwich, 25 May 1791; SAN/F/43b/4, D. Murphy to Sandwich, 8 November 1759.

84. NMM: SAN/F/37a/34, R. Hudson to Sandwich, 5 December 1777. This must refer to the celebrated naval physician James Lind, who presided at the Council.

85. NMM: SAN/F/48//117, P. Affleck to Sandwich, 21 December 1778.

86. NMM: SAN/F/6/62, J. Jervis to Sandwich, 7 July 1775.

87. Laughton, *Barham Papers*, I, 308.

88. Blake, 'Transmission of the Faith', pp.51-52, implies that Middleton and Kempenfelt aimed at a real spiritual conversion of the seamen; the point is debatable, but it does not seem to me that the evidence carries us so far.

89. Blake, 'Transmission of the Faith', p.53.

90. *Private Papers of George, Second Earl Spencer*, ed. by Julian S. Corbett and H. W. Richmond (Navy Records Society, vols 46, 48, 58 and 59, 1913-1924), II, 410-11. *The Nagle Journal: A Diary of the Life of Jacob Nagle, Sailor, from the year 1775 to 1841*, ed. by John C. Dann (New York, 1988), p.211.

91. Willyams, *Campaign in the West Indies*, p.6, a reference I owe to Dr Duffy.

92. John D. Byrn, *Crime and Punishment in the Royal Navy. Discipline on the Leeward Islands Station 1784-1812* (Aldershot, 1989), p.105.

93. John Malham, *Sixteen sermons on the most interesting subjects to seamen, comprehending many important events in naval history* (London, 1792). Like Ramsay's book, this may have been directed less to chaplains than to pious or apprehensive captains who felt their men needed a sermon, but did not have a chaplain to preach it.

94. John James Fresselicque, *A Sermon of praise and thanksgiving to Almighty God, for the late victory obtained over the French fleet, on the 28th and 29th of May, and 1st of June; preached on board His Majesty's ship Bellerophon, at sea, on Sunday the 8th day of June, 1794* (Gosport, 1794). W. Griffith, *A Sermon, preached on Sunday, June 8th, 1794, on board His Majesty's ship Brunswick, Capt. John Harvey* (Portsea, 1794); the *Brunswick* was part of Howe's fleet and was certainly at sea on the 8th.

95. London, 1798.

96. Taylor, *The Sea Chaplains*, app.xi, shows no naval chaplain who rose to be a bishop between Thomas Ken (Bath and Wells, 1685) and Samuel Seabury (Connecticut, 1784); A. C. W. Rose (Dover, 1935) was the first naval chaplain to reach an English see since Bishop Ken.

97. NMM: SAN/F/48/121, W. Peacock Jr to Sandwich, 6 April 1779.

MEDICINE AND SCIENCE IN THE BRITISH NAVY OF THE EIGHTEENTH CENTURY

For many reasons it is still difficult to sketch the medical history of the Royal Navy in the eighteenth century. Though we possess many detailed studies and one massive (albeit somewhat uncritical) work of synthesis,[1] a great deal remains to be done. The bulk of modern research (my own included) has concentrated on the single problem of scurvy, to the virtual exclusion of all other aspects.[2] The fevers - the great killers of the age - notably typhus in European waters, malaria and yellow fever in the tropics, have been very little studied. Diseases not specific to seamen, such as smallpox, are even less discussed, though the naval vaccination campaign of 1800 was a notable early example of voluntary mass immunization.[3] Beyond diseases we have even less. Some work has been done on surgery in relation to wounds and burns;[4] but there is little on injuries, notably ruptures, the occupational injury of the top-man;[5] nor on venereal diseases, so common among seamen that they might almost be described as an occupational hazard.[6] Medical administration, and naval policy in relation to medical matters, have been very little studied. Even the naval hospitals, whose influence on public health policy and architecture is widely known, have received very little attention.[7]

There is, moreover, a general problem with many of the older, and not a few of the more recent studies which we do possess. Medical history was until twenty or thirty years ago the preserve of retired doctors, writing in a strongly positivist, Whig, intellectual framework. Theirs was emphatically a history of Progress, in which successive great men (invariably medical men) overcame reaction and indifference to advance the cause of medicine and humanity by the conquest of disease. It was a history in which the medical profession always occupied the foreground, with the diseases next in importance, the patient dimly visible in the background, and the general history of society nowhere.[8] Such an approach required the historian to identify a medical hero to personify and explain each period of history. For the Royal Navy in the eighteenth century the choice long ago fell on Dr James Lind, who has long been, and still often is, presented as the brilliant pioneer who invented the controlled experiment in 1746, demonstrated that citrus fruits cured scurvy, but failed to overcome the massed ranks of lay obscurantism in his lifetime, leaving his discovery as a legacy to another medical pioneer, Sir Gilbert Blane, who in the 1790s finally persuaded the Navy to adopt it.[9] In fact it is quite clear that Lind's famous experiment tested six different treatments at once with no control, and it has been argued that its structure arose largely by accident.[10] In Lind's own clinical practice as Physician of Haslar Hospital, 1758-1783, he employed citrus fruits among a wide variety of other traditional remedies, several of which his own work had shown to be useless; and it has been demonstrated that his thinking on the treatment of scurvy, never particularly clear, moved steadily away from the truth in the course of his long career.[11] We know now that most of the opposition Lind encountered came from physicians more influential than himself. Nevertheless he remains firmly ensconced as the patron saint of British naval medicine, and it is impossible to deal with the subject without referring frequently to him.

This is still so in spite of the striking rise over the last thirty years of a formidable and productive body of English-speaking medical historians (in Britain largely thanks to the support of the Wellcome Institute). These scholars have brought an admirable professional rigour and objectivity to their subject, and their work illuminates many aspects of it which were unknown to earlier generations. Nevertheless they remain «medical historians» in name and in fact, who define their subject largely in terms of the professional concerns of medical and scientific men. Theirs is still a history which puts medicine on the centre stage, even if the doctors are viewed with objectivity, and the perspective is enlarged to cover nurses, midwives and practitioners of every sort of healing art. Arguably it is an approach ill-equipped to make sense of the health of seamen in the eighteenth century. In the face of the maladies of the age, neither medicine nor surgery had much to offer. With the significant exception of Jesuit's bark against malaria, there was no effective medicine available against any common serious disease. The suppression of scurvy in the mid-century by the issue of fresh provisions,[12] and again in the 1790s by the mass dispensing of lemon juice; likewise the elimination of smallpox by vaccination, were essentially measures of public health conceived and implemented by naval administration rather than by doctors. Their true history will never be properly known until the naval administration of the period has been better studied.[13]

That administration was complex. The Board of Admiralty which stood at the pinnacle, and whose head, the First Lord, represented the Navy in Cabinet, was directly responsible only for naval discipline and the movements of ships, but it supervised and authorised the work of three other boards, each of which had something to do with naval medicine. The Navy Board administered the dockyards, built and maintained the ships. Among a mass of other responsibilities, it also appointed surgeons to ships, from among candidates examined by the Barber-Surgeons' Company of London (from 1745 the Surgeons' Company). Physicians were appointed by the Admiralty, but there were hardly any of them: one for each of the main naval hospitals, and in time of war sometimes one for each major overseas squadron. The Victualling Board was responsible for packing and issuing all naval victuals all over the world, but although it devoted much care and some experiment to doing so as efficiently and economically as possible, it did not regard itself as having any competence in nutrition. Finally the Sick and Hurt Board administered the naval hospitals and looked after prisoners of war of all services, but it had little to do with ships at sea, and though its members usually included a physician, it too was mainly an administrative rather than a medical or scientific body. Thus the naval administrative system provided no focus outside the Admiralty itself where medical or scientific opinion could be brought to bear on problems of health at sea.[14]

The medical world was still more divided. The surgeons who formed the great bulk of naval medical men had a very low status compared to physicians, very few of whom ever had the opportunity to encounter naval diseases, and the physicians themselves were disunited. The College of Physicians of London, the head of the medical profession at least in its own estimation, admitted to its fellowship only graduates of Oxford and Cambridge, educated in an exclusively theoretical syllabus based on the study of classical medical texts in their original languages, from which they emerged without having encountered actual patients.[15] Physicians educated abroad, notably in the medical schools of Edinburgh, Glasgow and Leiden, had had the opportunity to receive a professional training, partly based on actual clinical practice, which mixed medicine, surgery and midwifery, but their professional standing was inferior to that of the Oxford and Cambridge men, and the College of Physicians admitted them only as Associates. What was worse, most of them were not only trained abroad but foreigners themselves, usually Scotsmen like Lind and virtually all the naval physicians of the century, and consequently liable to prejudice and suspicion in England:

> Those who are Gentlemen by birth and education, are perhaps incapable of the servile Methods of insinuating Artifices made use of daily by the Foreign Gentry, whose Necessities to gain *Preferments* may be great, and whose compliances (probably the result of a low Education) no man of spirit can, or ever will condescend to submit to.[16]

A prominent minority, moreover, were Dissenters if not freethinkers in religion, and radicals in politics.[17] The consequence was that professional and social influence in the medical world was in inverse proportion to acquaintance with naval medicine and the diseases of seamen.[18]

All this does a great deal to explain, and has been cited to explain, the difficulties Lind faced in advancing his views on scurvy in opposition to those of more influential rivals.[19] His problems, however, were more than simply a reflection of his social standing, for there were real and important differences in scientific ideas which in Lind's day distinguished the Navy from much of the educated world ashore. These differing ideas were by no means confined to medicine, but the medical example clearly shows how they developed, and why they were significant. At the beginning of the century, the ideas of Hippocrates as elaborated by Galen were if anything more influential than ever in the medical world. The most prominent English physician of the recent past, Thomas Sydenham, and the outstanding European physician of that period, Hermann Boerhaave, were both powerful advocates of Galenic ideas, which taught physicians to explain disease in terms of the disturbed balance of the humours. It followed that every patient, and every day of his illness, were different, even if all should chance to suffer from the same illness, and only a skilled physician, daily observing his patient, could hope to prescribe remedies to restore the equilibrium of the humours.[20]

Unfortunately for the Navy, this was no help at all when men fell ill in their hundreds or thousands with not one physician on hand to treat them. What the Navy needed was what the Admiralty in 1693 asked the College of Physicians to provide: «a scheme of the severall species of Medicines, which in your opinion are most proper for the care of the sick and wounded men in the fleet», meaning a simple list of universal treatments appropriate to the common diseases, which could be put into the hands of the naval surgeons as a guide to treatment. The College of Physicians refused to provide one. Their objection was not only to allowing rude mechanicals to trespass in the domain of scientific medicine. According to Galenic principles, it was genuinely impossible to match treatments to diseases as such; they had to be judged for each individual patient according to the balance of his humours, by an expert physician.[21]

The result was an impasse. The medical establishment would not provide what the Navy needed, and had no effective alternative to offer. But the Navy's needs did not go away, and some physicians tried to meet them. Several doctors made themselves rich and famous as the authors of patent medicines designed to treat one, or more often many, specific maladies. Dr Cockburn's Electuary, Dr James's Powders, Dr Ward's Drop and Pill, were exceedingly popular in society at large as well as in the Navy, because they met a demand which the medical profession could not otherwise satisfy. The physicians objected to them in part because a respectable physician was a gentleman who was not supposed to engage in any trade, least of all the medicine trade which belonged to the humble apothecary. Above all, however, they objected to the principle of medicines, whoever sold them, which professed to treat any patient suffering from some specific condition, for according to Galenic principles, any such claim was necessarily fraudulent.[22]

Boerhaave and almost all medical men of the day also believed in the so-called «climatorial» pathology, which saw in corrupted air the cause, or at least the vector, of transmissable diseases.[23] This moreover was a medical theory which was widely dispersed and accepted by lay opinion, including by naval officers. It led them to pay great attention to cleanliness, because smells were regarded as the agents of disease. Sometimes (as with their obsession with rotting cheese) this was unhelpful, but in the main it was clearly salutary. Foreigners never failed to be impressed, if not horrified, by the fanatical attention to cleanliness which distinguished British ships and hospitals, and it must have played a real part in the steadily falling mortality and morbidity of the century.[24] The same idea encouraged them to fumigate or destroy the clothes of men suspected of carrying typhus.[25] It also suggested the wisdom of not anchoring to leeward of tropical swamps, within reach of the deadly effluvium (the «malaria»), and of not allowing boats' crews to sleep ashore.[26] Thus in 1762 Rodney contrasted Point-à-Pitre with Fort Royal:

> Guadaloupe has one good harbour, called Point Peter, capable of receiving the largest ships of war, but unfortunately it is situated to leeward of a continued and very extensive range of swampy land, which must ever cause it to be extremely unhealthy; whereas the carènage at Fort Royal, in Martinique, is to windward of the swampy ground, and never receives any bad effects from it.[27]

Though the true vector of neither typhus nor malaria was suspected, climatorial pathology was in these cases a helpful misunderstanding. It encouraged the development of ventilation, which was regarded as the answer to typhus, scurvy, smallpox and other illnesses, and it led to the design of Stonehouse Hospital, the first in the world to be built on the pavilion system, which provided the maximum possible circulation of air, and incidentally isolated the different wards.[28] In the case of scurvy, in the other hand, it persuaded most physicians, Lind included, that damp or salt air must be the real cause of the malady. None of the numerous remedies he advocated and used were, in his opinion, anything more than palliatives. Only the smell of the land could effect a true cure.[29] For the same reason it followed that land scurvy, endemic and well-known in many parts of Europe, had to be a different disease.[30]

In the mid-century, new theories became popular among scientists and doctors, which challenged and modified the old principle of the humours. Iatromechanists explained the workings of the body by analogy with the physical laws of the universe, as they were coming to be understood, treating it as a delicate and complex engine whose machinery had to be restored to equilibrium. For the iatrochemists it was the new science of chemistry which provided the key to illness, which was seen in terms of processes such as fermentation which disturbed the balance of the humours.[31] It was this theory which was advocated by Lind's rival Dr John McBride, and by the eminent physician Sir John Pringle who was President of the Royal Society. The reason why McBride's wort was more acceptable to the scientific and medical establishment as a remedy for scurvy than Lind's orange juice, was not just that he was plausible and well-connected while Lind was an obscure Scotsman. Much more important was the fact that McBride had a coherent explanation of why his remedy worked, presented in terms of the best current scientific theory, whereas Lind had nothing but an incoherent mass of observations.[32] Indeed, he openly admitted the limits of his understanding: «there are unquestionably certain limits prescribed to human researches beyond which, tho' fancy may take its flight, and theory make wide excursions, all is conjecture, obscurity, or profound darkness».[33] Then, as now, this was no way to win respect in the medical profession.

What was worse, Lind's observations were not simply unconvincing, but inherently disreputable. Medical science, whether Galenic, iatrochemical or iatromechanist, was truly scientific, as the eighteenth century understood it. It was argued *a priori*, on the basis of the best authorities, which was the only intellectually respectable approach. A doctor who attempted to generalise from observation or experiment sinned both against the basic premise of Galenic medicine, that every patient was different; and against the basic premise of contemporary science, that understanding flowed from abstract logic applied to first principles. Lind was openly practising the empirical approach, and by so doing identifying himself as an «empiric» - that is, in the medical language of the day, a quack.[34] But he was not alone. He represented, in fact, what was by the 1760s an established intellectual method, springing from Enlightenment attitudes to the natural world. It was particularly common in the Navy, that most modern and intellectually adventurous of professions. Experiment and observation were at the heart of an approach which assumed that understanding would come through the amassing of facts.[35] There was nothing distinctively medical about this way of thinking and working; many examples of it can be found in naval (and non-naval) thinking and administration;[36] but in adopting it Lind was taking a line which in his day carried more credibility among naval men than it did among doctors. Its real weakness was precisely that the controlled experiment had not been invented: people were not in the habit of trying to isolate individual causes and effects. Instead they collected information, the more and more diverse the better, and swamped themselves in a mass of fact and fancy which they had no means of sorting into the true and the false, the relevant and the irrelevant.[37] Lind's own writings give a vivid impression of this creative but incoherent spirit of enquiry, and his practice as Physician of Haslar

Hospital was an excellent example of it. He was, for instance, a pioneer in the collection of medical statistics - but the figures themselves are so vague and haphazard as to be practically useless. He was a pioneer, too, in collecting standard information about every patient and his case, but he does not seem to have understood how this information might have been analysed to show patterns of disease or the effectiveness of different treatments.[38]

Nevertheless, it was this way of thinking about problems, medical and non-medical, which was steadily gaining in intellectual respectability during the eighteenth century. Whatever might be its weaknesses, it was at least a direct attempt to answer the real problems of the Navy. Moreover by the end of the century the empirical approach could justly claim some real successes, notably against scurvy and smallpox, which did much to strengthen its intellectual pretensions. An Act of Parliament in 1698 allowed former members of the armed forces the right to practice a trade without having to follow the apprenticeship or training prescribed by guilds and corporations, and another in 1749 specifically applied this right to surgeons. Many doctors used these provisions to enter the medical profession by way of a few years' service afloat. Naturally they were influenced by the intellectual climate of the Navy, and returned to the shore ready to disseminate empiricist ideas among their colleagues and clients.[39] By the years of the Revolutionary and Napoleonic Wars, the intellectual world was ready to listen to doctors like Sir Gilbert Blane who openly advocated empirical methods, and backed their arguments with medical statistics.[40]

Neither orthodox science nor orthodox medicine yet had much to offer in preserving the health of seamen, but the empricists did. Their success laid the foundations for the public health movement of the nineteenth century, of which Blane has sometimes been seen as the founder.[41] In essence they applied to problems of public health an intellectual approach which was not specifically medical, and required no specialised medical knowledge. It called only for a logical mind and a systematic method. It was quite irrelevant to the personal relationship of physician and patient which was integral to traditional medicine; it was a mechanistic strategy for massed attack on a mass problem. Inherently it was a strategy for the administrator rather than the doctor, for the man with control over the community rather than the man with access to arcane knowledge. It was the child of admirals and naval administrators, the men with real power in the Navy, the men who could impose systematic measures to preserve the health of seamen. The doctors could not have done this; those in the Navy were not in positions of power over the Service as a whole, and those influential outside were not for most of the century prepared to admit such an approach as respectable or honest. In any case, the diseases which affected the Navy were not accessible to the medical knowledge of the day. The eighteenth-century Navy was thus the laboratory in which many of the ideas were worked out which in time fuelled the nineteenth-century public-health movement, and the Navy's suppression of scurvy and smallpox can be seen as rehearsals for the conquest of cholera.

Any true history of eighteenth-century naval medicine has to be one in which the rôle of the medical profession is in many respects marginal. It must in part be a history of medical knowledge gained by demolishing, or at least circumventing the power of the medical establishment. In some countries, notably Spain, naval medicine was consciously used as a tool of government policy to break up the monopolies of the traditional medical corporations.[42] In England it was more a matter of a free market in ideas by which the empiricists were able to outflank the establishment by demonstrating the power of their ideas in practice. In doing so they not only showed that one method of problem-solving was more effective than another; they showed that civil authority could do more than medical learning. The elegant logic of science finally gave way to the vulgar utility of empiricism.

NOTES

1 J.J. Keevil, C.C. Lloyd & J.L.S. Coulter, *Medicine and the Navy, 1200-1900* , Edinburgh, 1957-63, 4 vols; Vol.III, by Lloyd and Coulter, covers 1714-1815.

2 The literature on scurvy is enormous: among the latest contributions the most valuable is undoubtedly Kenneth J. Carpenter, *The History of Scurvy and Vitamin C*, Cambridge, 1986. Less useful are Francis E. Cuppage, *James Cook and the Conquest of Scurvy*, Westport, Conn., 1994; Luigi L. Barbieri, «Breve storia dello scorbuto e della vitamina C», *Quaderni Internazionali di Storia della Medicina e della Sanità* II, 1993, pp.67-79; Irene Knaut, «Geschichte der Krankenheitsbezeichnung Skorbut», Free University of Berlin, Faculty of Dentistry doctoral thesis, 1984; Eleanora C. Gordon, «Scurvy and Anson's Voyage round the World: 1740-1744. An Analysis of the Royal Navy's Worst Outbreak», *American Neptune* XLIV, 1984, pp.155-166.

3 Lloyd & Coulter, *Medicine and the Navy* III, op. cit., pp.348-352. R.W. Jones, «The Royal Navy and the spread of vaccination», *Journal of the Royal Naval Medical Service* LXXIII, 1987, pp.204-206.

4 Sir James Watt, «The Injuries of Four Centuries of Naval Warfare», *Annals of the Royal College of Surgeons of England* LVII, 1975, pp.3-24; idem, «The Burns of Seafarers under Oars, Sail and Steam», *Injury* XII, 1980, pp.69-81; idem, «The Surgery of Sea Warfare from the Galley to the Nuclear Age», *Proceedings of the Royal Society of Medicine* I, 1981, pp.1-15.

5 Lloyd & Coulter, *Medicine and the Navy*, III, op. cit., pp.352-354.

6 N.A.M. Rodger, *The Wooden World: An Anatomy of the Georgian Navy*, London, 1986, App.X.

7 Axel Hinrich Murken, «Zur Geschichte der europäischen Marinelazarette - Ihr Einfluss auf das Krankenhauswesen des 19. Jahrhunderts», in *Geschichte der Schiffahrtsmedezin: Verhandlung des Symbosiums aus Anlass des 60. Geburtstages von Flottenarzt d.R. Professor Dr.med. Hans Schadewaldt*, ed. Heinz Goerke, Coblenz, 1985, pp.93-117. Jacques Tenon, *Journal d'observations sur les principaux hôpitaux et sur quelques prisons d'Angleterre (1787)*, ed. Jacques Carré, Clermont-Ferrand, 1992.

8 N.A.M. Rodger, «Medicine, Administration and Society in the Eighteenth-Century Royal Navy», in *IX Deutsch-Französisches Symposium zur Geschichte der Schiffahrts- und Marinemedizin*, ed. Hans Schadewaldt & Karl-Heinz Leven, Düsseldorf, 1988, pp.126-132, citing at pp.126 comments by various contributors to *Modern Methods in the History of Medicine*, ed. Edwin Clarke, London, 1971. Cuppage's *James Cook and the Conquest of Scurvy* is very much in this tradition. Cf Colin Jones & Laurence Brockliss, *The Medical World of Early Modern France*, Oxford, forthcoming, Introduction. I am greatly indebted to Professor Jones for allowing me to consult this book before publication.

9 Sir James Watt, «James Lind (1716-1794)», *University of Edinburgh Medical Journal* XXXI, 1983, pp.37-39. J.H. Baron, «James Lind would not have approved», *The Lancet*, 1982 i,1313. Surgeon-Lieutenant M.S. Smith, «The diagnosis and treatment of scurvy: an historical perspective», *Journal of the Royal Naval Medical Service* LXXII, 1986, pp.104-106.

10 R.E. Hughes, «James Lind and the Cure of Scurvy: An Experimental Approach», *Medical History* XIX, 1975, pp.342-351. Rodger, «Medicine, Administration and Society», p.128.

11 Kenneth J. Carpenter, «James Lind's Revised Views of Scurvy», in Schadewaldt & Leven, *Geschichte der Schiffahrts- und Marinemedizin*, pp.108-111.

12 N.A.M. Rodger, «Le Scorbut dans la Royal Navy pendant la Guerre de Sept Ans», in *Les hommes et la mer dans l'Europe du Nord-Ouest de l'Antiquité à nos jours*, ed.Alain Lottin, Jean-Claude Hocquet & Stéphane Lebecq, *Revue du Nord* extra number, 1986, pp.455-462; & «The Victualling of the British Navy during the Seven Years' War», *Bulletin du Centre d'Histoire des Espaces Atlantiques* No.2, Bordeaux, 1985, pp.37-53.

13 Rodger, «Medicine, Administration and Society», op. cit.

14 The standard authority on British naval administration is Daniel A. Baugh, *British Naval Administration in the Age of Walpole* , Princeton, 1965; see also his *Naval Administration 1715-50* , Navy Records Society, Vol.120, 1977.

15 Cf the Paris Medical Faculty, as described by Jones & Brockliss, *The Medical World of Early Modern France*, Introduction.

16 Bernice Hamilton, «The Medical Professions in the Eighteenth Century», *Economic History Review* 2nd.Ser.,IV, 1951, pp.143.

17 David Harley, «Honour and property: the structure of professional disputes in eighteenth-century English medicine», in *The Medical Enlightenment of the Eighteenth Century*,ed. Andrew Cunningham & Roger French, Cambridge, 1990, pp.138-164. B. Keith-Lucas, «Some Influences Affecting the Development of Sanitary Legislation in England», *Economic History Review* 2nd.Ser.,VI, 1953-54, pp.291.

18 I. Waddington, «The struggle to reform the Royal College of Physicians, 1767-1771: a sociological analysis», *Medical History* XVII, 1973, pp.107-121. B.Hamilton, «Medical Professions», op. cit., p.141.

19 A.P. Meiklejohn, «The Curious Obscurity of Dr James Lind», *Journal of the History of Medicine* IX, 1954, pp.304-310.

20 Arnold Zuckerman, «Scurvy and the Ventilation of Ships in the Royal Navy: Samuel Sutton's Contribution», *Eighteenth-Century Studies* X, 1976-77, pp.222-234.

21 Harold J. Cook, «Practical Medicine and the British Armed Forces after the Glorious Revolution», *Medical History* XXXIV, 1990, pp.13-15.

22 Cook, «Practical Medicine...», op. cit., pp.1-26.

23 James C. Riley, *The Eighteenth-Century Campaign to avoid Disease*, London, 1987, pp.16-26.

24 N.A.M. Rodger, *Wooden World*, op. cit., pp.105-109. Lloyd & Coulter, *Medicine and the Navy* III, op. cit., pp.72-73.

25 Tenon, *Journal d'Observations*, op. cit., pp.182-183. James Lind, *An Essay on... Preserving the Health of Seamen in the Royal Navy*, London, 5th ed., 1779, pp.29-31.

26 Lloyd & Coulter, *Medicine and the Navy* III, op. cit., pp.110-111 & 334. Lind, *Health of Seamen*, op. cit., pp.55-58.

27 W.J. Smith, ed., *The Grenville Papers: being the Correspondence of Richard Grenville Earl Temple, K.G., and the Right Hon: George Grenville, their Friends and Contemporaries*, London, 1852-3, 4 vol), vol. II, p.11.

28 Lloyd & Coulter, *Medicine and the Navy* III, op. cit., p.72-73. Zuckerman, «Scurvy and the Ventilation of Ships», op. cit. Riley, *Eighteenth-Century Campaign*, op. cit., p.99 & 106-107. Tenon, *Journal d'Observations*, op. cit., pp.7 & 12. Murken, «Zur Geschichte der europäischen Marinelazarette», op. cit., pp.95-110. P.D. Pugh, «History of the Royal Naval Hospital, Plymouth», *Journal of the Royal Naval Medical Service* LVIII, 1972, pp.78-94 & 207-226.

29 James Lind, *A Treatise of the Scurvy*, ed. C.P. Stewart & D.Guthrie, Edinburgh, 1953, pp.73-76 & 84-85. Carpenter, *Scurvy*, op. cit., pp.57-63.

30 R. Elwyn Hughes, «The Rise and Fall of the *Antiscorbutics*: Some Notes on the Traditional Cures for *Land Scurvy*», *Medical History* XXXIV, 1990, pp.52-64.

31 Zuckerman, «Scurvy and the Ventilation of Ships», op. cit., pp.226-227. Jones & Brockliss, *The Medical World of Early Modern France*, Introduction.

32 William M. McBride, «*Normal* Medical Science and British Treatment of the Sea Scurvy, 1753-75», *Journal of the History of Medicine* XLVI, 1991, pp.158-177. Sir James Watt, «Medical Aspects and Consequences of Cook's Voyages», in *Captain James Cook and his Times*, ed. Robin Fisher & Hugh Johnston, London, 1979, pp.129-157.

33 Lloyd & Coulter, *Medicine and the Navy* III, op. cit., p.337.

34 Cook, «Practical Medicine and the British Armed Forces», op. cit., p.13.

35 Riley, *Eighteenth-Century Campaign*, op. cit., pp.54-69. Peter Mathias, «Who Unbound Prometheus ? Science and Technical Change, 1600-1800», in *Science and Society, 1600-1800*, ed.Mathias, Cambridge, 1972. Idem, «Swords and Ploughshares: the armed forces, medicine and public health in the late eighteenth century», in *War and Economic Development*, ed. J.M. Winter, Cambridge, 1975. Lester S. King, *The Medical World of the Eighteenth Century* , Chicago, 1958, pp.42-43. Jones & Brockliss, *The Medical World of Early Modern France*, Introduction.

36 Rodger, «Le scorbut», op. cit., p.457, n. 10.

37 Riley, *Eighteenth-Century Campaign*, op. cit., pp.72-73. Cf the comparable situation in French military and naval medicine of this period described by Jones & Brockliss, *The Medical World of Early Modern France*, Ch.11.

38 Ulrich Troehler, «Towards Clinical Investigation on a Numerical Basis: James Lind at Haslar Hospital 1758-1783», *Actas XXVII Congreso Internacional de Historia de la Medicina*, Barcelona, 1981, pp.414-419.

39 Cook, «Practical Medicine and the British Armed Forces», op. cit., pp.8 & 15. Hamilton, «Medical Professions», op. cit., p.151.

40 Sir Gilbert Blane, *Select Dissertations*, London, 1822; see also the extracts from this and other publications of Blane's in *The Health of Seamen*, ed. Christopher Lloyd, Navy Records Society, Vol.107, 1965, pp.175-211. Lloyd & Coulter, *Medicine and the Navy* III, op. cit., pp.46-47. Cook, «Practical Medicine and the British Armed Forces», op. cit., p.25.

41 Sir Malcolm Morris, *The Story of English Public Health*, London, 1919, pp.14 & 17-18. M.C. Buer, *Health, Wealth and Population in the Early Days of the Industrial Revolution*, London, 1926, p.121.

42 Mikel Astrain Gallart, «La formacion teorica y practica de los cirujanos de la Armada Española en el siglo XVIII», *Quaderni Internazionali di Storia della Medicina e della Sanità* II, 1993, pp.43-58. *Seis impresos relativos al establecimiento y gobierno de diversos hospitales navales españoles des siglo XVIII (1748-1781)*, ed. David Marley, Mexico City, 1983.

XII

Weather, Geography and Naval Power in the Age of Sail

The tyranny of lines on a map distorts historians' understanding of the realities of warfare in the age of sail. Half-remembered school atlases marking steamer tracks and air routes as straight lines across the empty oceans persuade modern scholars that distances can be measured simply by laying a ruler across a map. Maps themselves commonly mark the sea as an unbroken expanse of blue stretching from coast to coast, as indeed it seems when viewed from a cliff or an aeroplane, revealing nothing of the shoals and tides which in reality constrain the movements of ships in coastal waters.

Shoals and tides are with us yet, but in the age of sail there were two more equally fundamental factors which limited the free movements of sailing vessels. The first of these was the extreme difficulty of making progress against the wind. For practical purposes no ship[1] could point higher than six points (67½°) off the wind, to which must be added at least another point of leeway to arrive at distance made good. This meant that it was always difficult and often impossible to win any ground to windward without a favourable tide or current. Added to the strain on crew and gear of constant beating, this meant that ships did not normally attempt to work to windward for any considerable distance except in emergency. Usually they awaited a fair wind; one on or abaft the beam was best for most ships, but a following wind was perfectly satisfactory. This gave an enormous strategic importance to those anchorages, safely and easily entered, and cleared when the wind shifted, in which shipping might anchor to await a fair wind.

By the far the most important of these in the British Isles was the Downs off Sandwich (see Map 1, p.180), the focal anchorage used by the shipping of London, East Coast ports and most of the North Sea ports when waiting for an easterly wind; control of this anchorage alone helped England to control the deep-sea commerce of the Netherlands, Denmark and other countries to the eastward. In the words of James II, 'our situation proper to command all trades going through our seas to and from the northern parts of the world, and the plenty and quality of our ports, are the principal real advantages above our neighbours'.[2] In a dead calm or light airs, ships might make progress by working the tides: drifting with the favourable stream and anchoring at the turn of the tide. This was often done during the Anglo-Dutch Wars (1652–74), mostly fought in summer in the Narrow Seas (the upper part of the Channel and the south-western corner of the North Sea), and it was the means by which the Allied fleet withdrew after the defeat of Beachy Head in 1690, but the time and effort required to weigh anchor by manpower ruled it out in deeper water.

The great difficulty of beating to windward not only imposed numerous delays, and forced ships to make passages by roundabout routes in search of fair winds, but made all approaches to the land, or shoal water, inherently dangerous. The nightmare of every seaman under sail was the lee shore, for if the wind blew towards the land there were many circumstances in which there was grave danger of shipwreck. At night or in thick weather a ship might be on or very near the coast before being aware of it, and unable to claw off. It was easy to become 'embayed'; trapped between two headlands neither of which the ship could weather. Then the anchors were the only hope, but in an onshore gale they were not likely to hold. Even if the wind were blowing offshore and the coast could be closed in relative safety, the wind might shift much faster than the ship could gain an offing. For all these reasons seamen constantly sought sea room, and regarded any approach to the land as their most dangerous moment. Unfortunately it is impossible to make port without approaching the land, and all sorts of naval operations repeatedly called for warships to put themselves in harm's way by working close inshore.

Navigational conditions, interacting with national traditions of warship design, had a large effect on the course of the Dutch Wars. The Straits of Dover, the Thames Estuary and the south-western quarter of the North Sea are shoal everywhere and much of the area is occupied by sands which dry or break at low water, and could not be crossed even at high water by the larger ships of the English fleet. Very few of these shoals were marked, and in wartime those buoys which existed might be removed or misplaced. Even if the sky were clear, observations accurate to 20 or 30 miles were useless in an area where the pilot often needed to know his whereabouts to within a few cables.³ In any case it was pointless attempting to plot positions on charts which were grossly unreliable. In 1673 Sir John Narborough found the Dogger Bank laid down between 24 and 36 miles too far south and the charted soundings everywhere erroneous.⁴ With the exception of the cliffs of Kent and the Blackness and Whiteness (Capes Gris Nez and Blanc Nez) east of Calais, the coasts surrounding the southern North Sea are low-lying, and the best seamarks are windmills and church steeples visible no more than ten miles off at best.

In these waters local knowledge and constant sounding were the pilots' only recourse, and out of sight of land they were frequently mistaken. English ships often ran aground through mistaking their positions in familiar waters. At the Battle of the Kentish Knock in 1652 two of Admiral Robert Blake's ships went aground on that shoal. The *Prince Royal* was lost on 3 June 1666, during the Four Days' Battle, when she ran on the Galloper. In 1682 on his passage to Scotland the Duke of York nearly lost his life when the *Gloucester* was wrecked on the Leman Bank off Yarmouth.⁵

MAP 1
THE THAMES ESTUARY

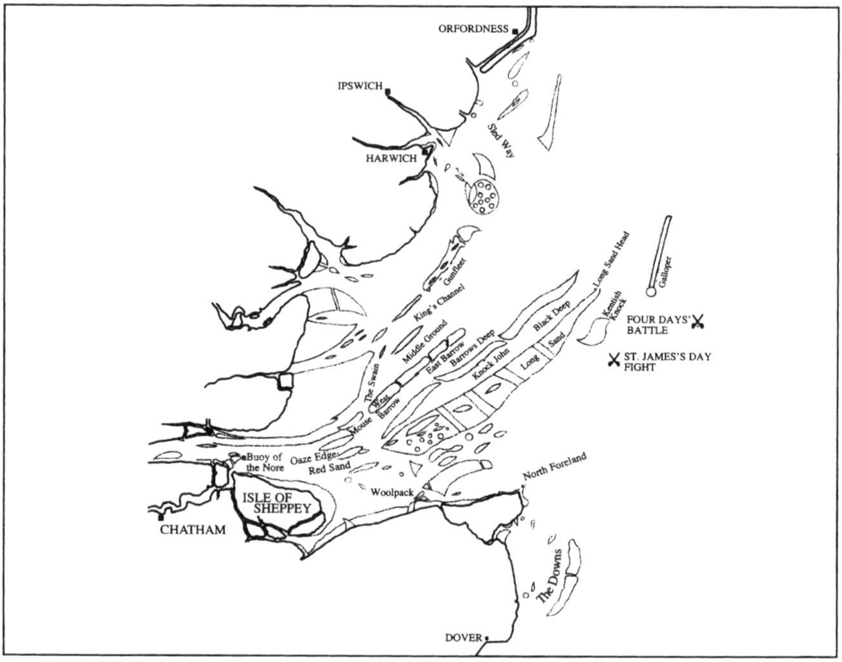

Source: J.R. Powell and E.K. Timings (eds.) *The Rupert and Monck Letter Book, 1666* (London: Navy Records Society Vol.112, 1969) facing p.288.

For both sides the strategic situation was dominated by the navigation of their coasts, and the approaches to their ports. The Thames Estuary, which looks like a large expanse of open water on a land map, is actually open only to small craft at high water in good weather. Most of the estuary is filled with sands which form a pattern of ridges separated by narrow channels, lying roughly parallel with the Essex shore. The King's Channel, the nearest to that coast, was until modern times the usual deep-water channel. It extends roughly north-east and south-west, from the Nore at the junction of Thames and Medway, to the anchorage north of the Gunfleet shoal and east of the Naze. The outer anchorage of a fleet sailing from the Thames was the Gunfleet. From here it could sail northward, keeping to seaward of the Shipwash; or southward, rounding the Long Sand Head and keeping outside the Kentish Knock; or eastward, towards the Dutch coast, avoiding the Inner Gabbard and the Galloper which partially block that course. Here too the resources of the small naval yard at Harwich were available. The Gunfleet was safe in most weather conditions, and covered the mouth of the Thames, but the shoals to the north and south-east made it difficult to clear the anchorage on an easterly wind.

The Barrows Deep, parallel to the King's Channel and just to the south, was surveyed in 1666 and occasionally used[6] (for which reason the Dutch plan in 1673 to bottle up the English fleet in the Thames by sinking blockships in the narrowest part of the King's Channel would probably not have worked)[7] but the only other common entrance to the Thames was parallel to the Kentish shore, through Queen Elizabeth's Channel and over the Kentish Flats. This was practicable for small and medium-sized ships, including all but the largest merchantmen, and was the obvious choice for ships bound to the westward down-Channel. Ships of the line, however, could only take this passage in charge of an expert pilot who was confident of finding one of the 'holes' where a big ship could anchor at low water, or with a leading wind, in charge of one who would risk making the whole distance between the Nore and the North Foreland on a single tide. Prince Rupert, the boldest navigator of all the admirals of his day, took the *Royal Sovereign* over the Kentish Flats in 1673. Sir Phineas Pett, asked what Trinity House would make of such rashness, 'answered that he believed they would say his Highness was mad, whereto the Prince replied, "I believe so too"'.[8] It was out of the question to take a whole fleet that way.

For English fleets of the period, the first strategic question which presented itself was usually whether to stay at the Gunfleet or to move. Southwold Bay 25 miles north was completely open to the eastward, so that a fleet could conveniently sail for the Dutch coast with any suitable wind. It was equally open to Dutch attack, as the Anglo-French fleet discovered in May 1672. The major dilemma, however, was usually whether to shift to the Downs, the only position from which the Straits of Dover could be covered. The strategic danger of using the Downs was that the mouth of the Thames was left open. The tactical danger was that the anchorage itself was a trap. The Downs is formed by the Kentish coast to the west, and the Goodwin Sands to the east. Its southern entrance is easy, but the Gull Stream to the north is narrow and big ships can only pass it in single file, so that no squadron could escape that way in a hurry. With a southerly or south-westerly wind a squadron lying in the Downs might be trapped by an enemy entering from the southward. This was exactly how Admiral Maarten Tromp gained his crushing victory over the Spaniards in 1639, and neither the Dutch who had won the battle nor the English who had witnessed it ever forgot the lesson.

Tromp spent much of the First Dutch War vainly attempting to repeat his triumph, but the English were extremely wary of risking large squadrons in the Downs. The same considerations recurred in 1688, when the Downs would have been the perfect anchorage from which to watch the Straits of Dover and intercept William III's fleet, whether he chose to go down Channel, as in the event he did, or if he had gone north, as he was expected to do. No 'Protestant Wind' could have prevented the English fleet from sailing from there. Its great disadvantage was that it would have exposed the fleet to being trapped by a surprise attack, which was no doubt why Sir Roger Strickland and his Council of War chose the Gunfleet. James II initially preferred a position midway between the two, just south of the Kentish Knock, and it would have been well for him if he had kept to that resolution and not allowed the fleet to return to the Gunfleet.[9]

The Dutch were equally constrained by geography. Political history and commercial logic dispersed their naval resources among widely separated ports, whereas the four principal English dockyards were all on the Thames or Medway. Ships from the Zuider Zee ports of Amsterdam, Hoorn and Enkhuizen (also Harlingen in Friesland) had a long and tricky passage to their advance anchorage of the Marsdiep, inshore of the island of Texel. Amsterdam, moreover, was a bar harbour, and big ships could not cross the bar (the Pampus), which limited the size of warships which could be contributed by the richest of the provincial admiralties. Rotterdam, the other major naval port of Holland, could float bigger ships, but its tortuous channels to the open sea issued either by the Goereese Gat between the islands of Goeree and Voorn, or by the Brouwersgat north of Schouwen.[10] That is to say that though Amsterdam and Rotterdam are only 30 miles apart by land, their respective harbours were about 300 miles apart by sea, and their advance anchorages on the North Sea 100 miles apart. The last major naval port, Flushing in Zealand, had deep water and easy access to the open sea, but was further south still. This meant that the first problem of the Dutch admirals was to unite the scattered units of their fleet before the enemy could attack them in detail.

Most often they tried to do so off the southern ports. Partly this was because they lay nearer to England there, partly it was because several of the greatest Dutch admirals (notably Michiel De Ruyter and the Evertsen family) were Zealanders themselves who knew these waters best,[11] but chiefly it was because the coast here is screened by a considerable number of scattered offshore banks which make the movement of any fleet hazardous unless it is perfectly familiar with the waters. This was the key to De Ruyter's brilliant handling of the 1673 campaign, when his fleet operated in and around the area known as the Schoonvelt off the mouth of the Western Scheldt, which covered the coast on which the allies threatened a landing. This is sufficiently open water to allow free movement of the Dutch fleet, near enough to the Scheldt and the Brouwersgat for easy escape if necessary, but surrounded by scattered shoals which made the English and French extremely cautious of approaching.[12] By contrast the coast of North Holland is open, and an enemy fleet might have trapped the Dutch against the land, as Admiral Adam Duncan did at Camperdown in 1797.

When everything depended on expert pilotage, fleets of warships were remarkably cautious in enemy waters, even though on both sides during the Dutch Wars there were numerous seamen who had been accustomed in peacetime to trade there. Partly this was because warships, especially English warships, were so much bigger and deeper than merchantmen that an ordinary pilot's experience was not very useful. There must have been hundreds of Dutch pilots who knew the Thames intimately, but the great majority were no doubt accustomed to using the Kentish Flats. In 1653 the Dutch admirals refused to consider entering the Thames, and when Jan De Witt, Grand Pensionary of Holland, sent the Dutch fleet into the Thames in 1667 De Ruyter and his colleagues were extremely reluctant to risk their ships in the unknown waters of the King's Channel. Only political authority overrode the seamen's professional objections and made possible the Medway attack.[13]

The Glorious Revolution overturned the strategic situation as completely as the political. England's geographical and strategic situation in the Dutch Wars was highly favourable,

> when (like an eagle's wings extended over her body) our coast surrounded theirs for 120 leagues from Scilly to the Maas in Holland one way, and as many from the Orcades thither the other way; and the wind blowing above three-quarters of the year westerly on the coast of England, made all our cape-lands and bays very good roads for ships to anchor at ...[14]

War with France forced the Royal Navy to operate down Channel and to the westward, in waters with which it was not so familiar, and where it lacked bases. English ships, especially the bigger ships of the line, had been designed to carry the maximum broadside into battle in shallow, enclosed waters with no considerable fetch, where most gales could be ridden out at anchor. In the deep and open waters of the lower Channel and the Western Approaches they had to face onshore storms and seas sweeping off the open Atlantic which they could not beat into. Dutch ships were still less adapted for these waters. Instead of the friendly weather shores the English had enjoyed during the Dutch Wars, all the coasts were dangerous lee shores. In these circumstances it was considered 'a mighty boldness to advance with the Grand Fleet further westward of the Isle of Wight than the *Soveraigne* had been knowne to have been, since the time of her built'.[15] Commanding the Allied fleet after the victory of La Hogue (Barfleur) in 1692, in summer weather 'fitting only for Laplanders to be at sea with', Admiral Edward Russell felt that

> no fleet of ships, being so many in number, nor of this bigness, ought to be ventured at sea but where they may have room enough to drive any way for eight and forty hours, or where they may let go an anchor and ride. In the Channel six hours with a change of wind, makes either side a lee shore ...[16]

In order to appreciate the real difficulties of operating down-Channel, or anywhere across the open oceans, from bases on the Thames and Medway, it is necessary to understand the weather system of the British Isles, where the prevailing winds are westerly or south-westerly throughout the year. This means that ships sailing from ports in the English Channel, or coming down the Channel from the North Sea, are likely to face long delays while waiting for a favourable wind. The same is generally true of ports in the Bristol Channel and Irish Sea, though it is rather easier to clear Scottish ports on a north-westerly course. Easterly or north-easterly winds are commonest in the spring, between January and May, which was an important reason why major military expeditions, and those foreign trades which followed an annual cycle, usually planned to sail during these months.[17] At the cost of preparing in mid-winter, often in hard frosts produced by the same high pressure which generated the easterly winds, this gave the best prospects of getting clear of the British Isles without undue delay, of reaching the Caribbean or North America early in the campaigning season, and in the case of the West Indies, of achieving some success before the onset of the hurricane months of September and October made those waters deadly for men and ships. For ships bound to the East Indies a departure early in the year was essential in order to reach the Indian Ocean during the season of the South-West Monsoon, May to October. At all seasons, but especially in winter, a succession of depressions blows in from the Atlantic over the British Isles or to the north. These cause the prevailing wind to veer northerly as they pass, which gives other opportunities for ships to work down Channel. It seems also to have been the case that winter easterlies were relatively more common (and the winters harder) at periods in the late seventeenth and late eighteenth centuries.[18]

Nevertheless, in every age the prevailing westerlies severely disadvantaged English ports, and none more so than London, which is almost the furthest from the open Atlantic of any major British seaport. What was worse, the axis of the Thames Estuary and that of the English Channel are almost the same, so that ships sailing from London and bound down Channel needed first a westerly and then an easterly wind, or the reverse for the homeward passage. No steady wind would serve. Indeed the Thames itself twists so much that 'there is only one point of the compass that the wind can be at, which will carry a ship from Sea-Reach into the Pool without making a board'.[19] It was this which made the anchorage of the Downs so important, for it could be entered from the Thames Estuary round the North Foreland, and from the Channel round the South Foreland, while the anchorage itself was large enough to shelter hundreds of sail, protected from westerlies by the land, and from easterlies by the Goodwin Sands. It was the great focal point for much of the trade of London and many North Sea ports in the age of sail, for in westerly winds ships lay here, sometimes for weeks, waiting their chance to get up the Thames or down the Channel. If the wind shifted easterly, many hundreds of ships would make sail at once and the great anchorage would empty in a few hours.

As soon as the main fleets began to operate down-Channel, they left the pilotage waters of the Narrow Seas and faced the other great challenge to the navigator under sail: the impossibility, before the mid-eighteenth century, of fixing longitude. In principle it had been possible from the late

Middle Ages to fix a ship's latitude by observation of the altitude of a heavy body – usually the the Pole Star at dawn or the sun at noon – and most English navigators could do so in practice by the late sixteenth century. By the mid-eighteenth century a good observer with a good instrument could fix his latitude to within about ten miles, but this was an ideal figure. Errors of scores or even hundreds of miles were still common, and of course no observations were possible when the sky was overcast or the horizon obscured, that is, on the majority of days in the year around the British Isles.[20]

Moreover the best latitude position without longitude only answers half the navigator's question. Since the earth is symmetrical about its polar axis and in constant rotation, the problem of fixing the longitude of any point on the earth's surface relative to any other is the same as determining the difference of local time between the two. Several methods of doing so were theoretically available, and in the 1750s two became practicable more or less at the same time. The Göttingen astronomer Tobias Mayer published in 1755 tables which for the first time described the complex and irregular motions of the moon with sufficient accuracy to permit the calculation of longitude by lunar distances; that is, by inferring the rotation of the earth by measuring the movement of the moon against fixed stars. This called only for three straightforward observations with standard instruments, but the calculations were extremely lengthy and difficult. The Reverend Neville Maskelyn, the Astronomer Royal, reduced the time needed from about four hours to only half an hour with the publication of the *British Mariner's Guide* of 1763, followed by the first *Nautical Almanac* in 1767. The mathematics remained demanding, but they were immediately adopted into the curriculum of the schools which trained boys for careers at sea, and 'lunars' became the standard method of determining longitude well into the nineteenth century. The method allowed a good navigator to fix his longitude to better than one degree.[21] Even so, large errors of longitude remained normal. Vice-Admiral Lord Howe's squadron crossing the Atlantic in 1776 got 300 miles out of their reckoning in spite of taking a lunar halfway across.[22]

The rival method was the chronometer, perfected by John Harrison in the 1760s after 30 years of work, and soon imitated by other watchmakers in England and abroad. An instrument which can keep accurate time at sea over long periods permits an easy comparison between local sun time (so long as the sun can be observed) and the fixed or mean time of some datum meridian of longitude, the difference between the two representing the observer's easting or westing from the datum. For British navigators, and eventually for the whole world, the longitude of Greenwich Observatory was this datum. The accuracy required is considerable; to fix longitude to half a degree after a six-week voyage (a fast transatlantic passage) the chronometer must lose or gain no more than three seconds a day.[23] Before Harrison no-one had been able to make a clock which would keep accurate time in a constantly moving ship, subject to damp and rapid changes of temperature. The chronometer is a simple method of fixing longitude, and eventually it became the normal method, but initially chronometers were too expensive for many masters to buy them; 60 guineas in the 1780s, or between two and four months' salary for a master in the Navy. Even the Royal Navy did not begin to issue official chronometers until early in the nineteenth century, and ships in home waters did not receive them until the 1840s.[24]

Before the 'discovery of the longitude', all ocean navigation was a combination of observation of the latitude component, and dead-reackoning for the longitude. When the sky was obscured and observations impossible, dead-reckoning had to serve for both, until the development of radio aids to navigation in the twentieth century. Dead-reckoning is simply an estimation of the ship's progress from a given point of departure whose position is known, measuring speed by casting the log, recording courses steered by the compass, and adding a guess for leeway and drift. In the best circumstances it cannot be relied on for more than a few days. Admiral Lord Dartmouth's squadron sailed from Plymouth for Tangier on 23 August 1683 and on 10 September sighted the Burlings, a group of islands on the coast of Portugal. Of 12 officers of the flagship who were keeping a reckoning, the best was 75 miles out of his reckoning, and some were over 200 miles out. Moreover the different charts aboard the flagship disagreed widely on the position of Portugal, there being over 50 miles between the longitudes given for Cape Finisterre (see Map 2, p.188).[25]

The impossibility of fixing longitude made it a matter of great uncertainty when any ship making a passage involving much easting or westing – which in practice means any ocean passage – would actually make the land. One aspect of this uncertainty was question of fixing the length of a degree of longitude. The diameter of the earth, and hence the length of a degree of latitute and the length of the nautical mile (one minute of arc of latitude, conventionally reckoned as 6,080 feet) was measured with good accuracy in 1669–70.[26] Since the meridians of latitude converge at the poles, the length of a degree of longitude varies from nothing at the poles to 60 nautical miles at the Equator. For accuracy the navigator has to recalculate the length of the degree of longitude continuously. In practice

MAP 2

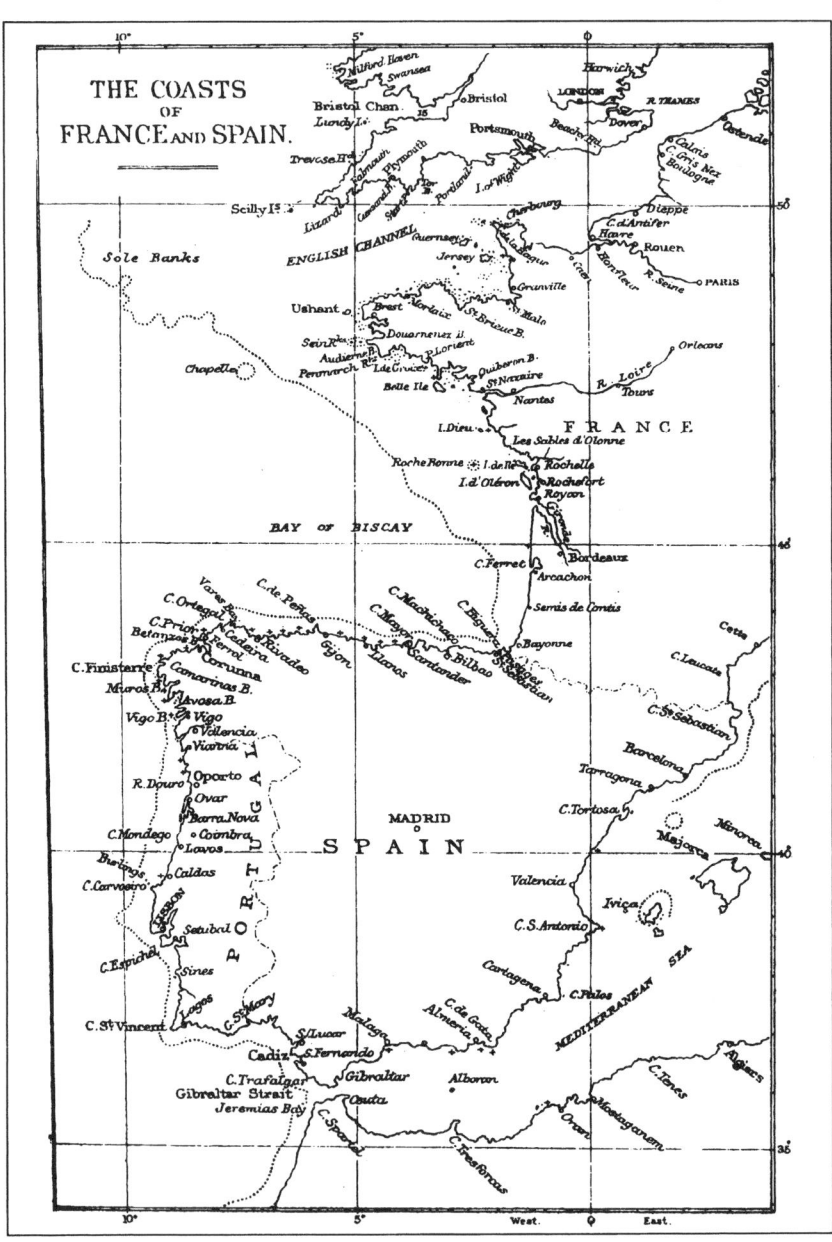

Source: J. Leyland (ed.) *The Blockade of Brest* (London: Navy Records Society Vols.14–15, 1899) pp.1 and 176.

English navigators preferred approximation. For convenience they kept 60 miles to the degree, but reduced the mile to some conventional figure, most often 5,000 feet.[27] This is roughly correct for Lat. 35°, but progressively too small as the ship approaches the Equator. On transatlantic voyages from England to America a ship would make virtually all her westing south of 35°N.

Even when the traditional measures were known to be inaccurate, navigators preferred to 'sight land after they sought it', in order to be forewarned of danger.[28] They had additional reason to do so since the longitude even of entire continents was laid down wrongly on the charts until the late eighteenth century (nor could the average navigator afford to replace his expensive charts with the latest editions at frequent intervals), and it would have been dangerously misleading to plot the ship's position accurately on a chart which misplaced the land. Thus in 1755 HMS *Winchester* on passage to Barbados, 'by allowing only forty-two feet to a glass of thirty seconds, overrun her reckoning by near a hundred leagues between Madeira and this island'.[29] Moreover the same log-line was used on all courses, so this deliberate inaccuracy was liable to affect dead-reckoning of latitude as well unless the navigator remembered to apply a correction.

Uncertain of their own longitude and that of the land, mariners making an ocean passage, say across the Atlantic, would usually try and make the land by getting into the latitude of a good landfall and running their easting or westing down (cautiously, at night or in thick weather) until they made landfall. The ideal port for oceanic trade in the pre-longitude era was one lying roughly midway along a coast trending north and south, with high land inshore and deep water offshore, the entry to the port itself marked by a prominent peak visible at a great distance – in a word, Lisbon. No other European seaport was as easy to find after a long ocean passage, but the ports on the Atlantic coast of Andalusia are nearly as satisfactory, for Cape St Vincent is a good landfall from which it is easy to make Seville, Cadiz and the rest. This alone is a powerful explanation for the lead taken by the Portuguese and then the Spaniards in oceanic navigation. By contrast, English ports in general, and London in particular, are exceptionally difficult to reach under sail from the open sea.

In wartime, the desirability of closing the coast along a parallel of latitude was an important strategic factor, because it made the course of friendly or hostile shipping predictable. In the sixteenth century French and English pirates cruised off Cape St Vincent waiting to surprise inward-bound Spanish ships from the West Indies, knowing that the 'Indies trade' was a legal monopoly of the port of Seville, and the 'Cape of Surprises', as

Spanish seamen nicknamed it, was their only likely landfall.[30] Others lay in the Azores to catch the same ships earlier in their voyages. In eighteenth-century wars French privateers from Martinique or Guadaloupe would cruise in the latitude of Barbados, 50 or 100 miles to windward, waiting for British ships bound into the Caribbean to swim into their jaws. More difficult landfalls like the French Atlantic or the English Channel ports, which could not safely be approached on a parallel of latitude, were more dangerous to make but less vulnerable to enemy interception.

There was a particular problem in finding islands in the open sea, for having got into their latitude, the navigator might not know which way to turn. This was the situation of Commodore George Anson's squadron in 1741. Having struggled round the Horn, in a desperate condition with men dying daily of scurvy, they made the latitude of their intended landfall in the Juan Fernández Islands, guessed that they were west of the island, and did not discover their mistake until they sighted the coast of Chile. This error cost them 11 days in finding the island, and the lives of between 70 and 80 men.[31] The easiest island landfalls were those in the trade wind latitudes, where the weather is reliably clear for much of the year, and a stationary cloud hangs over the islands which may be visible 100 miles or even more. Hence for example St Helena, though small and very remote, was relatively easy to find, and early established itself as a popular way-station on the long passage home from the East Indies (though in 1696 Commodore Thomas Warren spent weeks vainly searching for it and eventually had to put back to Rio de Janeiro with 77 men dead of scurvy).[32] For British ships, Madeira and the Canary Islands served the same function on westward transatlantic voyages, the high peaks of Madeira and Teneriffe being especially easy to find. In the same way Spanish ships homeward bound from the Caribbean often called in the Azores.

In both cases the islands lay more or less directly on the usual sailing routes, for the wind and current systems of the North Atlantic are broadly circular. With only minor variations over the year, the winds blow from the north on the coast of Portugal, north-easterly around Madeira and the Canaries, and thence easterly across the southern part of the North Atlantic (roughly between 30°S and 10°S) and into the Caribbean basin (see Map 3, p.192). Off the Bahamas they blow south-easterly then southerly and south-westerly along the coast of North America, and so westerly back across the North Atlantic and across the British Isles. The currents, generated by the winds, follow the same pattern, the northerly drift of the Gulf Stream flowing at two or three knots out of the Florida Strait and up the American coast being especially powerful.[33] For this reason the natural and normal route from European ports to North America traced a great arc to the southward, sometimes as far south as the Cape Verde Islands (15–16°N), and thence across the Atlantic and up the coast.

Modern writers often speak of the Atlantic as being 3,000 miles wide, because that is the actual distance on a great circle course from the Bishop's Rock to Nantucket Light, such as a modern ocean liner might follow. The real distance for a sailing vessel following the usual course to New York is at least 1,000 miles longer, and the Scillies are 400 miles by sea from London.[34] The total distance under sail is 50 per cent greater, and the real difficulties of the passage are completely overlooked.

The strategic importance of the West Indies is likewise obscured. To the modern eye the Caribbean appears to be marginal to the American War of Independence, whereas in the real terms of sailing passages, the islands lay on the easiest direct route from Europe to North America. Hence the strategic importance, but also the navigational danger, of the Bahamas, a great area of low-lying reefs and islands lying on the western edge of the normal route. Further north many ships bound for the middle or northern colonies were lost on the Carolina Banks, for they had to pass not far off this most dangerous coast, unmarked and invisible from a distance, with no good idea of their longitude.

The Atlantic wind system gave the Spaniards a huge advantage in settling the Caribbean basin, for the transatlantic passage from Seville and back is swift and easy. Since both winds and currents set westward across the Caribbean, all shipping entered through the Windward Islands. Spanish ships generally gathered at Havana and left through the Florida Strait, continuing up the coast past Cape Hatteras before picking up the westerlies to blow them home across the central North Atlantic to the Azores and so on, due east for Cape St Vincent. The navigation was simple, predictable, and consequently dangerous in wartime. The early English colonies in Roanoke and Virginia were partly inspired by the hope of establishing privateer bases within easy reach of homeward-bound Spanish shipping.[35] In the seventeenth century Spain conceded a much more serious strategic advantage in permitting the French and English to settle the Windward Islands, and hence in due course to control the entrance to the Caribbean. This was the strategic function of the British Leeward Islands squadron (which in spite of its name covered the Windward Islands as well), as established in the 1740s. It was necessarily a distinct force from the Jamaica squadron to leeward, for though all ships bound for Jamaica passed through the Lesser Antilles, the reverse passage was impossible. Ships leaving Jamaica beat through the Mona Passage into the Atlantic, or ran to leeward,

MAP 3
THE CARIBBEAN

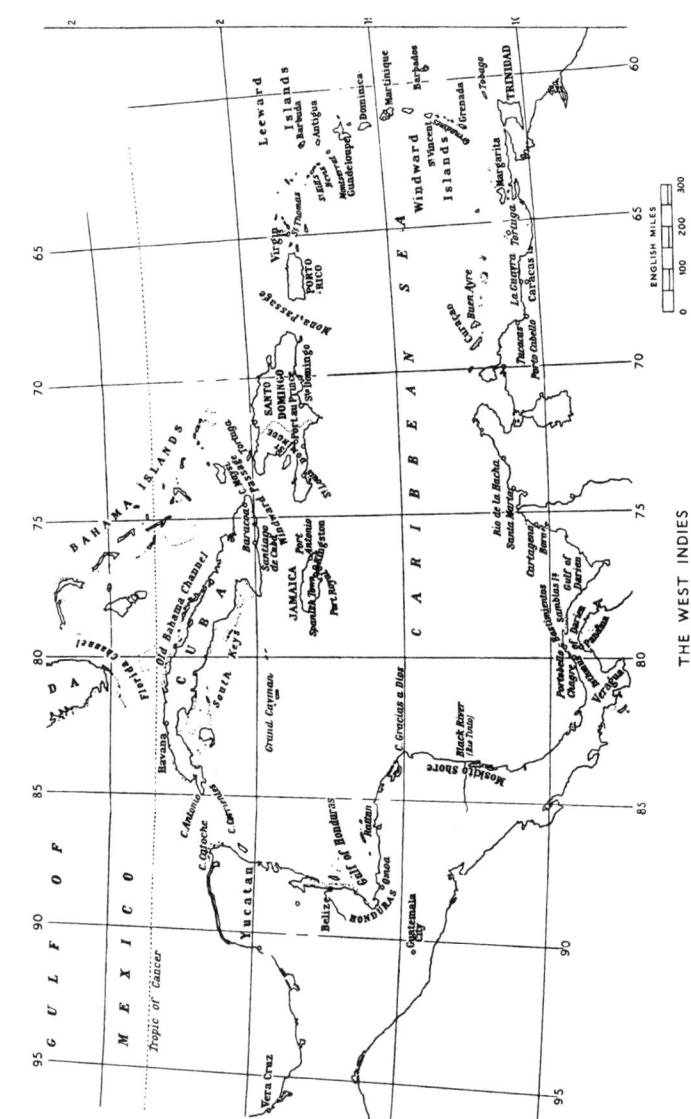

THE WEST INDIES

Source: Bryan Ranft (ed.), *The Vernon Papers* (London: Navy Records Society 1958) endpaper.

rounded Cape Corrientes and beat up the north coast of Cuba (where the current is favourable though the wind is not) and so through the Florida Strait. In the eighteenth century the quickest passage normally available from Jamaica to Barbados (a distance of just over 1,000 miles by steamer) was via London or New York.

Just as the wind and current systems favoured the Spaniards in the Caribbean, they favoured the Portuguese in the South Atlantic. The early Portuguese explorers found favourable winds and currents to work down the coast of Africa and into the Bight of Benin. To return they had to learn to make the 'leap' out into the open Atlantic and so north to the Azores or thereabouts to pick up the westerlies to carry them home. This was not so easy, but it was the essential school of deep-sea navigation which made possible all subsequent oceanic voyaging. From the Bight of Benin along the African coast southwards both wind and currents were adverse, but there was another and better way, by crossing the Atlantic and striking south-westward, across the belt of calms around the Equator, and so down the coast of Brazil. Portuguese settlement of Brazil (and Dutch rivalry for it) followed naturally from the fact that it was on the way to the Far East. On the coast of Brazil, as over most of the South Atlantic, the South-East trades blow throughout the year, providing an easy passage down to the latitude of Rio de Janeiro or even the River Plate, where a ship may pick up the westerlies which blow all round the world in high southern latitudes, often with great force. These blew a ship easily down to the Cape of Good Hope, though it was a surprisingly difficult landfall to make. A small error of latitude to the north would put a ship ashore, or drive her northward up the coast; too far to the south and she missed the Cape altogether, without being aware of the fact in the absence of a precise longitude.

Some ships voyaging to the East deliberately risked scurvy and passed well south of the Cape to continue across the Indian Ocean. Others took the trouble to heave-to and take a sounding with a deep-sea lead, a process which took several hours, but gave the most reliable indication of the proximity of land: 'This sounding served the purpose of correcting our reckoning as much as though we had seen the land.'[36] Returning from the East, ships rounding the Cape had an easy run up the South Atlantic before the South-East Trades before rejoining the North Atlantic wind system north of the Equator.

For British ships inward bound from the Atlantic, the prevailing westerlies obviously served very well, but from the navigational point of view the approaches of the Channel were difficult. There are no safe landfalls which might be approached by a vessel unsure of her longitude.

The Scillies are protected by a screen of reefs to the west and south-west, unmarked and unlit before the nineteenth century, on which any ship approaching them risks being wrecked before having the chance to verify her position. Until well into the eighteenth century, the islands were laid down 15 miles or more to the north of their true position on English charts.[37] Moreover there is a variable northerly set, the Rennell Current, across the mouth of the Channel after south-westerly gales, which was not described until 1793 and cannot be predicted without good knowledge of the weather in the area over the previous month – unavailable to inward-bound shipping in the days before wireless.[38] It was this current which drove Admiral Sir Cloudesley Shovell's squadron onto the Scillies in 1707.[39] It is impossible to run into the Channel on a parallel of latitude, for a course due east clearing the Scillies by ten miles (an exceedingly small margin even with a good observation) leads straight onto the Casquets reef off Alderney.[40] Ushant at the southern mouth of the Channel is a rather less dangerous landfall than the Scillies, but only so long as the navigator approaches in daylight with a good idea of his position. For anyone unsure of his whereabouts western Brittany is one of the most perilous coasts in the world.

The only possible entry to the Channel is on a NW or WNW course aiming initially, not for a landfall which might be identified, but for the right area of open water. In these circumstances, and every circumstance 'in soundings' (within the 100-fathom line, on the Continental shelf), the navigator placed great reliance on the lead. Armed with tallow, it not only gave him the depth but a sample of the bottom, and a line of soundings might give him a good idea of his whereabouts. Precise knowledge of the composition and smell of the bottom was one of the most precious skills of the pilot, and often the key to the survival of a ship running into the Channel, unsure of her position after weeks at sea.[41] Captain Richard Rooth of the *Bear*, homeward bound from Jamaica in 1655, hove to on 29 August to sound with the deep-sea lead, getting 70 fathoms, 'sandy with cockle shells and small dark grains like mustard seeds'. Next morning early he sounded again and found 63 fathoms with small pebbles and 'brandy sand', which he interpreted as putting him 15 leagues SW of the Lizard. At 8 o'clock he sounded again, and reckoned himself 7 leagues SW; one hour later he raised the Lizard 5 leagues to the north-east. With luck and judgement, the lead might yield a perfect landfall like this; yet even a careful seamen like Rear-Admiral Sir John Narborough in 1673 might very easily mistake:

> the soundings also deceived men in their depth and ground, for the same depth is 5 leagues SW from Scilly as is 5 leagues W from Scilly,

and the ground fine white sand in many places; also, heave the lead three times one after another as fast as you can, and you will find the ground to differ every cast; sometimes sand and sometimes sand and stones &c will come up in the tallow, which deceiveth men.[43]

Narborough was lucky to disentangle himself from the Bishop and Clerks. Ten years later Lord Dartmouth on his passage home from Tangier found himself in similar uncertainty:

Strange the disagreement in so fair weather with so fair a wind immediately upon a fair observation and clear sounding at 65 fathoms and 49°34′ latitude, among our navigators about the entrance into our Channel, my lord and Mr Phillips being very positive we were shot to the Eastward of Scilly, while Sir W. Booth with the master and mates were of opinion we were yet to the westward, and one part of them apprehensive of our running upon the French coast, and the other upon the English ...[44]

The intention of the English navigator would be to make a landfall somewhere along the South Coast of England. In many ways this was relatively easy, for there is a succession of prominent headlands: the Lizard, the Dodman, Rame Head, Bolt Head or Tail, the Start, Portland Bill, St Alban's Head, Anvil Point and finally St Catherine's Point on the Isle of Wight, each of which is fairly easy to identify in clear weather and safe to approach from the south-west. Many of them, moreover, have practicable anchorages on their eastern side, sheltered from the prevailing westerlies.[45] The danger in making this coast by night or in poor visibility, however, was in becoming embayed on the windward side of one of these headlands. This was how HMS *Ramillies* was wrecked in Hope Cove in 1760 when the master mistook his landfall in thick weather and she was unable to weather Bolt Tail.[46] There was also a danger to ships sheltering in one of the anchorages on the south-easterly side of these headlands if the wind backed (unusual but always possible), for all of them are exposed to easterly or south-easterly winds. Torbay, throughout the eighteenth century the usual advance anchorage of the Channel Fleet, was capacious and safe in most circumstances, but notoriously a deathtrap if the wind blew up and backed suddenly easterly. Lord Howe very nearly lost the entire fleet when this happened on 13 February 1795.[47]

Having once made a landfall on the English coast, the ship bound up Channel had a relatively simple task of working along the coast. For French navigators the situation was more difficult, especially in wartime when they could not safely hug the English coast. No ship having made landfall at

Ushant and bound up-Channel, would choose to coast the north coast of Brittany, for not only is the coast itself dangerous, with numerous offshore reefs and islands, and a dead lee shore if the wind veers northerly (as it regularly does), but it also leads straight into the great bight enclosed by the Côtentin Peninsula and occupied by the Channel Isles and their numerous outlying reefs and shoals.[48] To add to their dangers the bight collects the flood tide coming up Channel, leading to a large tidal range (nearly 40 feet in places) and violent tidal streams (up to eight knots in the Race of Alderney). Combined with frequent fog, these dangers provided an effective defence for St Malo, the great privateer base of the late seventeenth-century wars, which enemy warships were reluctant even to approach, but they forced ships bound for Norman ports over towards the English shore of the Channel. Ships bound to the westward from Dieppe or Le Havre were likewise forced north towards the English shore by the Côtentin Peninsula.

Naval historians have often remarked how French fleets entered the Channel reluctantly and seldom, and how strangely ignorant French sea officers were of these neighbouring waters.[49] Much of the explanation lies in navigational conditions which tended to force ships into English waters. This was compounded by the French tradition of building warships of very deep draught, so that French ships of the line were unable to enter any French Channel ports, until the artificial harbour of Cherbourg, begun by Louis XIV, was finally completed by Napoleon III.

Nevertheless the French began their naval wars against England in 1689 with the enormous advantage of a major naval base directly to windward at the mouth of the Channel. They could and should have used the advantage of Brest to dominate the Western Approaches, cut off British and Dutch trade, and support James II in Ireland. The British were slow to appreciate their new position, and it was not primarily their efforts which prevented the French from exploiting their situation. It took the British nearly 60 years before they learned to make best use of the prevailing winds and the geography of the English Channel. It is not going too far to say that the Western Squadron, as developed in the years 1746 and 1747, was the key to British naval supremacy for over a century. Its essential principle was to keep the main fleet cruising for much or even all of the year in the Western Approaches to the Channel. Far enough in the offing to avoid the worst navigational dangers of lee shores, the fleet was placed to answer all Britain's most essential strategic requirements at once.

If France or Spain mounted an invasion attempt, the fleet to cover it would have to sail from Brest or some port to the southward, and pass directly to leeward of the Western Squadron. Transports might sail from ports in Brittany or Normandy, but without a fleet to escort them they could safely be left to local forces in the Channel. The Western Squadron was well placed to blockade, or at least watch, all the French Atlantic ports, and to intercept warships and merchantmen clearing or entering the Bay of Biscay. Its cruising ground equally covered the passage of most important British overseas trades, excepting those to the Baltic.[50]

All this was made possible by the intelligent exploitation of the prevailing westerlies, plus the fact that Britain's naval and colonial rivals, France and Spain, lay near at hand. Success in dominating the waters of Western Europe translated progressively into dominance of the whole world, as the enemy was cut off from his forces overseas. Only once did the system fail, during the American War, when the British forgot what had given them victory in two previous wars and sent their main fleets overseas, beyond the reach of effective direction or proper maintenance, where campaigns were reduced to aimless blunderings and their results to chance. They never made the same mistake again, and the Western Squadron (under various names) remained the basis of British naval superiority until the rise of major naval powers outside Europe in the later nineteenth century finally undermined its foundations.[51]

This was not in the least inevitable. The hard facts of geography favoured England in its wars against the Netherlands, but against France the British had few natural advantages. The western winds were available to all, and might have served France or Spain as well as they did Britain if these nations had seized their potential. France was better placed to exploit them, and the Spaniards actually planned to establish a western squadron to dominate the Channel in 1574, though circumstances frustrated the attempt.[52]

As a base for oceanic trade and expansion across the world, English ports were for the most part ill placed, and London especially so. Easy access to the Atlantic wind systems goes far to explain how Portugal and Spain took an early lead in oceanic voyaging; but the French, especially Normans from the Channel ports, were not far behind them in spite of substantial disadvantages, and they in turn were followed by the English and Dutch from a still worse position. Naval strategy was necessarily dominated by weather and geography, but it was not in the least predetermined. Britain's eventual success can be explained in terms of a prolonged process of learning how to exploit the favourable, and overcome the unfavourable, aspects of the situation. None of this was inevitable, and not much of it is intelligible to the historian who ignores the real world of winds and currents, navigation and pilotage.

NOTES

1. Virtually all men of war of any size, and all merchantmen engaged in deep-sea trade, were ship-rigged, and it is in any case something of a myth that fore and aft rigged vessels can point higher.

2. J.R. Tanner (ed.) *Samuel Pepys's Naval Minutes*, Navy Records Society [hereafter NRS] Vol.60 (London: NRS 1925) p.38.

3. The cable is one-tenth of a nautical mile, conventionally reckoned equal to 100 fathoms or 200 yards.

4. R.C. Anderson (ed.) *Journals and Narratives of the Third Dutch War*, Navy Records Society Vol.86 (London: NRS 1946) pp.122 and 132.

5. P.M. Cowburn, 'Christopher Gunman and the Wreck of the *Gloucester*', *Mariner's Mirror* 42 (1956) pp.113–26 and 219–29.

6. J.R. Powell and E.K. Timings (eds.) *The Rupert and Monck Letter Book, 1666*, Navy Records Society Vol.112 (London: NRS 1969) pp.41–2 and 90.

7. J.C.M. Warnsinck, *Admiraal De Ruyter: De Zeeslag op Schooneveld Juni 1673* (The Hague: Nijhoff 1930) pp.3–6.

8. Tanner, *Pepys's Naval Minutes* (note 2) p.112.

9. Clyve Jones, 'The Protestant Wind of 1688: Myth and Reality', *European Studies Review* 3 (1973) pp.201–21; Brian Tunstall (ed.) *The Byng Papers*, NRS Vols.67, 68 and 70 (London, 1930–32) Vol.I, p.xxxii. Charles II also preferred to avoid the Downs in 1666: Powell and Timings, *Rupert and Monck Letter Book* (note 6) p.55.

10. G. Asaert *et al.* (eds.) *Maritieme Geschiedenis der Nederlanden* (Bussum: De Boer 1976–78, 4 vols) II, pp.83–4 and III, pp.69–72.

11. Contrast the opinion of the Hollander Witte de With, in Johan Elias, *Schetsen uit de Geschiedenis van ons Zeewezen* (The Hague: Nijhoff, 1916–30, 6 vols) Vol.III, p.51.

12. Anderson, *Third Dutch War* (note 4) pp.29–44. Warnsinck, *Admiraal De Ruyter* (note 7) pp.32–42.

13. S.R. Gardiner and C.T. Atkinson (eds.) *Letters and Papers relating to the First Dutch War, 1652–1654*, NRS Vols.13, 17, 30, 37, 41 and 66 (London: NRS 1899–1930) Vol.III, p.236. Johanna K. Oudendijk, *Johan de Witt en de Zeemacht* (Amsterdam: Noord-Hollandsche, 1944) pp.181–5. C.A. van Waning and A. van der Moer, *Dese Aengenaeme Tocht: Chatham 1667* (Zutphen: De Walburg 1981) pp.25–30.

14. Gardiner and Atkinson, *First Dutch War* (note 13) Vol.I, pp.31–2.

15. Michael Duffy, 'Devon and the Naval Strategy of the French Wars 1689–1815', in idem *et al.* (eds.) *The New Maritime History of Devon* (London: Conway Maritime Press 1992–94, 2 vols) Vol.I, pp.182–91, at p.182.

16. Philip Aubrey, *The Defeat of James Stuart's Armada, 1692* (Leicester UP 1969) p.140. Duffy, 'Devon and the Naval Strategy of the French Wars' (note 15) p.182.

17. Peter Allington *et al.*, 'Shiphandling and Hazards on the Devon Coast', in *New Maritime History of Devon* (note 15) II, pp.14–24, at p.14.

18. J.L. Anderson, 'Climatic Change, Sea-Power and Historical Discontinuity: The Spanish Armada and the Glorious Revolution of 1688', *The Great Circle* 5 (1983) pp.13–23; H.H. Lamb, *Climate, History and the Modern World* (London: Methuen 1982) pp.50–1.

19. William Spavens, *The Narrative of William Spavens, a Chatham Pensioner* (London: Chatham 1998) p.97.

20. N.A.M. Rodger, *The Wooden World, An Anatomy of the Georgian Navy* (London: Collins 1986) p.47; E.G.R. Taylor, *The Haven-Finding Art: A History of Navigation from Odysseus to Captain Cook* (London: Hollis & Carter 1956) pp.216–17. C.J. Sölver and G.J. Marcus, 'Dead Reckoning and the Ocean Voyages of the Past', *Mariner's Mirror* 44 (1958) pp.18–34.

21. Derek Howse, *Greenwich Time and the Longitude* (London: Philip Wilson 1988); this is the 2nd ed. of *Greenwich Time and the Discovery of the Longitude* (London: OUP 1980) pp.57–71.

22. Edward H. Tatum Jr (ed.) *The American Journal of Ambrose Serle, Secretary to Lord Howe 1776–1778* (San Marino, CA: Huntington Library 1940) pp.26–7.

23. Howse, *Greenwich Time* (note 21) pp.71–8. David W. Waters, *The Art of Navigation in*

   England in Elizabethan and Early Stuart Times (London: Hollis & Carter 1958) p.58.
24. Howse, *Greenwich Time* (note 1) pp.71–8.
25. Edwin Chappell (ed.) *The Tangier Papers of Samuel Pepys*, NRS Vol.73 (London: NRS 1935) pp.126–7.
26. Taylor, *Haven-Finding Art* (note 20) pp.236–7.
27. Waters, *Art of Navigation* (note 23) pp.58–66; G.B.P. Naish, 'The "Dyoll" and the Bearing-Dial', *Journal of the Institute of Navigation* 7 (1954) pp.205–8; see particularly the comment by W.E. May on p.208. Taylor, *Haven-Finding Art* (note 20) pp.224–30.
28. Waters, *Art of Navigation* (note 23) pp.64–6; Spavens, *Narrative* (note 19) p.103.
29. Rodger, *Wooden World* (note 20) p.53. This equates to a mile of 5,040 ft. or a degree of just under 50 nautical miles, about right for Madeira in 33°N, but eight miles too short for the parallel of Barbados in 13°N. A 51ft knot to a 30-sec. glass equates to a true nautical mile.
30. Huguette and Pierre Chaunu, *Séville et l'Atlantique, (1504–1650)* (Paris: Colin 1955–59, 8 vols in 11) Vol.VIII, i, p.267.
31. Glyndwr Williams (ed.) *A Voyage Around the World by George Anson* (London: OUP 1974) pp.109–10.
32. Robert C.Ritchie, *Captain Kidd and the War against the Pirates* (Cambridge, MA : Harvard UP 1986) p.77.
33. Boyle T. Somerville (ed.) *Ocean Passages for the World* (London: Admiralty 1923 ed.); James Clarke, *Atlantic Pilot Atlas* (London: Adlard Coles 2nd ed. 1996). Note that winds are described by the direction from which they blow, currents by the direction to which they set, so a southerly wind goes with a northerly current.
34. Somerville, *Ocean Passages* (note 33) pp.80 and 347.
35. John C.Appleby, 'War, Politics, and Colonization, 1558–1625', in Nicholas Canny (ed.) *The Oxford History of the British Empire Vol.I: The Origins of Empire, British Overseas Enterprise to the Close of the Seventeenth Century* (Oxford: OUP 1998), pp.55–78, at p.64.
36. Spavens, *Narrative* (note 19) p.41.
37. D.W. Waters, 'The English Pilot: English Sailing Directions and Charts and the Rise of English Shipping, 16th to 18th Centuries', *Journal of Navigation* 42 (1989) pp.317–54, at p.342.
38. Waters, *Art of Navigation* (note 23) pp.267–8. Allington, 'Shiphandling' (note 17) p.15.
39. G.J. Marcus, 'Sir Clowdisley Shovel's Last Passage', *Journal of the Royal United Service Institution* 102 (1957) pp.540–8; W.E. May, 'The Last Voyage of Sir Clowdisley Shovell', *Journal of the Institute of Navigation* 13 (1960) pp.324–32.
40. The Bishop Rock is in 49°52′ N, the Casquets in 49°43′N.
41. Allington, 'Shiphandling' (note 17) pp.15–16.
42. John F. Battick (ed.), 'Richard Rooth's Sea Journal of the Western Design, 1654–55', *Jamaica Journal* 5/4 (1971) pp.3–22, at p.21.
43. Anderson, *Third Dutch War* (note 4) p.287.
44. Chappell, *Tangier Papers* (note 25) p.248.
45. Carrick Roads in the lee of the Lizard, Mevagissey Bay in the lee of the Dodman, Cawsand Bay in the lee of Rame Head, Start Bay and Torbay in the lee of the Start, Portland Bay in the lee of the Bill, Swanage Bay in the lee of Anvil Point, and the Solent behind the Isle of Wight.
46. Rodger, *Wooden World* (note 20) p.46.
47. Duffy, 'Devon and the Naval Strategy of the French Wars' (note 15) p.186.
48. Allington, 'Shiphandling' (note 17) p.16.
49. E.g. A.Temple Patterson, *The Other Armada: The Franco-Spanish Attempt to Invade Britain in 1779* (Manchester UP 1960) p.28.
50. Michael Duffy, 'The Establishment of the Western Squadron as the Linchpin of British Naval Strategy', in idem (ed.) *Parameters of British Naval Power, 1650–1850* (Exeter UP 1992) pp.60–81; H.W. Richmond, *The Navy in the War of 1739–48* (Cambridge UP 1920, 3 vols) Vol.III, pp.6–8, 20–3, 82–4, 226–9; B.McL. Ranft (ed.) *The Vernon Papers*, NRS Vol.99 (London: NRS 1958) pp.436–7, 441, 451–2, 459; A.N. Ryan, 'The Royal Navy and the Blockade of Brest, 1689–1805: Theory and Practice', iu Martine Acerra, José Merino and Jean Meyer (eds.) *Les marines de guerre européennes, XVII-XVIIIe siècles* (Paris: Presses

de l'Université de Paris-Sorbonne 1985) pp.175–93; Daniel A. Baugh, 'Great Britain's "Blue-Water" Policy, 1689–1815', *International History Review* 10 (1988) pp.33–58.

51. N.A.M. Rodger, 'Sea-power and Empire, 1688–1793', in P.J. Marshall (ed.) *The Oxford History of the British Empire Vol.II, The Eighteenth Century* (Oxford: OUP 1998) pp.169–83.

52. Magdalena de Pazzis Pi Corrales, *La otra Invencible, 1574: España y las potencias nórdicas* (Madrid: San Martin 1983).

XIII

Form and Function in European Navies, 1660–1815[1]

Anyone who has even a brief acquaintance with British naval history of the seventeenth and eighteenth centuries will be familiar with the accepted truism that British warships were inferior to their French and Spanish opponents, because British shipwrights remained wedded to craft traditions, while their Continental rivals were men of education who applied mathematics and science to the solution of their problems. This judgement, ultimately derived from the well-known histories of Charnock and Fincham,[2] continued to figure in standard textbooks until recently, and is still repeated by non-expert writers. It flattered, and sometimes still flatters, a range of agreeable prejudices. It fitted the eighteenth-century upper classes' admiration for France as the home of social glamour and prestige. It expressed British sea officers' conviction that as men of honour they were both morally and practically superior to civilian technicians; it magnified their courage and judgement when they won, and excused their failures when they lost. According to this received opinion, the incompetence of British designers was made up, in part by the skill of British captains, who captured enemy prizes of superior quality which the Royal Navy preferred to its own ships, in part by the widespread practice of copying French designs in British yards.[3]

It is not difficult to find contemporary sources which give the appearance of confirming these judgements. In 1747, for example, Captain Philip Sausmarez complained to the Admiralty that the Navy Board refused to offer more than

[1] An earlier version of this paper appeared in English in *In het kielzog. Maritiem-historische studies aangeboden aan Jaap R. Bruijn bij zijn vertrek als hoogleraar zeegeschiedenis aan de Universiteit Leiden*, ed. Leo Akveld et al. (Amsterdam, 2003), pp. 85–97.

[2] John Charnock, *History of Marine Architecture* (London, 1801, 3 vols). John Fincham, *A History of Naval Architecture* (London, 1851). Fincham was writing in support of a campaign to establish a government school of naval architecture in Britain; he needed to demonstrate that the lack of such an establishment had had bad effects in the past.

[3] Daniel A. Baugh, *British Naval Administration in the Age of Walpole* (Princeton, 1965), pp. 251–253, summarizes the 'woeful story' in respect of his period; D.K. Brown, *Before the Ironclad: Development of Ship Design, Propulsion and Armament in the Royal Navy, 1815–60* (London, 1990), pp. 10–14, discusses the theme in a later one; but the authoritative treatment is now Larrie D. Ferreiro, *Ships and Science: The Birth of Naval Architecture in the Scientific Revolution, 1600–1800* (Boston, Mass., 2007).

£6 a ton for his prize the *Mars*, niggardly behaviour which he attributed to a 'secret reluctance & jealousy of admitting French Men of War into our Service, whereby so visible an advantage in sailing is discover'd on their side as probably may not be agreable, and is dayly experienced in the *Ambuscade* and *Amazon*'.[4] These two were recently captured French frigates, and Sausmarez was certainly not alone in his opinion of them. Two months later Vice-Admiral Anson wrote from his flagship in the Western Approaches to the Duke of Bedford, First Lord of the Admiralty,

> As all our Frigates sail wretchedly I intreat your Grace that an order may be immediately sent from your Board to the Navy Board to direct Mr Slade the Builder at Plymouth to take off the Body of the French *Tyger* with the utmost exactness, and that two Frigates may be order'd to be built with all possible dispatch; of her dimensions and as similar to her as the Builders Art will allow; let Slade have the building of one of them.[5]

A generation later in 1791, the prospectus of the new Society for the Improvement of Naval Architecture claimed that,

> It is also but too well known to all who have any skill in Naval Architecture, that the theory is not so well understood as it deserves; and that the French, actually surpassing us in this most important art, have derived many advantages from this superiority in time of war.[6]

In spite of these and other suchlike quotations, there are three things wrong with the traditional view. The first is that it tends to explain how France and Spain won the naval war against Britain – which is not what we need to explain. In the century from 1714 more than half of all French warships (ships of the line and frigates) ended their careers sunk or captured, and the proportion rose steadily. In just over twenty years of warfare from 1793 to 1815, the French built 133 ships of the line and 127 frigates; and lost 112 and 126 respectively to enemy action or stress of weather. On average they lost a ship a month for twenty years.[7] At first sight this does not look like the result of superior design.

The second difficulty is that the traditional view is demonstrably false as a statement of fact. Though there were particular problems with British designs

---

⁴   Sausmarez MSS, Sausmarez Manor, Guernsey: undated draft [13 Feb 1746/7].

⁵   Woburn Abbey, Bedfordshire: MSS of the 4th Duke of Bedford Vol. XVI, f. 73, 17 Apr 1747.

⁶   National Maritime Museum: MID/8/1/38.

⁷   Martine Acerra, *Rochefort et la construction navale française, 1661–1815* (Paris, 1993, 1 vol in 4) III, 589 & 598. Martine Acerra & Jean Meyer, *Marines et Révolution* (Rennes, 1988), p. 99.

in one specific period (the 1740s and 1750s), the general assertion that all British designs were bad and all French or Spanish were good is completely untenable. The work of specialists, particularly Brian Lavery[8] and Robert Gardiner,[9] who have examined the subject in recent years, has given us a detailed knowledge of the evolution of British warship design which leaves no room for the traditional stereotype. Lastly, even if it were defensable in the light of the evidence, it would still be deeply unsatisfactory as an understanding of the past. To divide ships into 'good' and 'bad' is hopelessly simplistic. Real ships, then as now, cannot be meaningfully described as 'good' or 'bad' in the abstract, or even in comparison with foreign ships; they can only be good or bad at discharging particular functions.

The point may perhaps be made more clearly via an excursion into the twentieth century. Modern warships are the product of a design process which may be conceived of in three stages. First is the level of national policy. Governments formulate foreign policy; they take a view of the outside world which implies a judgement about when, whom and in what circumstances it might be necessary to fight. They must also judge what income it is proper or possible to devote to defence. This policy is then taken by the naval staff and developed into a requirement for certain numbers of ships of different types, intended to meet the requirements of the policy laid down by government. Finally the resulting 'staff requirements' are passed to the naval architects to design the actual ships. This is an idealised concept: in real life the design process is more untidy, and the last two stages are usually more like a dialogue between the staff and the naval architects, both parties referring to existing designs as a guide to what might be achieved on a given tonnage, for a given price. For this reason, and because of the immense complexity and difficulty of naval architecture even in the age of computers, designs still tend to be developed from existing ships even in response to new strategic requirements.[10]

---

[8]   Brian Lavery, *The Ship of the Line* (London, 1983–84, 2 vols).

[9]   Robert Gardiner, 'Frigate Design in the Eighteenth Century', *Warship* Nos. 9–12 (1979), pp. 3–12, 80–92 & 269–277; *Idem, The First Frigates: Nine-Pounder and Twelve-Pounder Frigates, 1748–1815* (London, 1992); *Idem, The Heavy Frigate. Eighteen-Pounder Frigates: Vol. I, 1778–1800* (London, 1994); *Idem, Frigates of the Napoleonic Wars* (London, 2000).

[10]   D.K. Brown, *Warrior to Dreadnought: Warship Development 1860–1905* (London, 1997), pp. 198–199. *Idem, Nelson to Vanguard: Warship Design and Development, 1923–1945* (London, 2000), pp. 187–192. *Idem,* 'What is a "Good Design"?', *Naval Review* LXXV (1987), pp. 308–314. Eighteenth-century design methods are described by Ferreiro, *Ships and Science*; Lavery, *Ship of the Line* II, 7–17; Jean Boudriot, *Le vaisseau de 74 canons* (Grenoble, 1973–77, 4 vols), I, 18–35; and Jean Boudriot & Hubert Berti, *Les vaisseaux de 50 et 64 canons: Étude historique 1650–1780* (Paris, 1994), pp. 34–58.

A successful warship design is one in which all three stages succeed; an unsuccessful one may be the result of failure at any stage. If government misconceives the country's situation, it may build the wrong fleet to face the wrong enemy. No amount of ingenuity by the naval staff or the naval architect will make up for this, and the problem is especially acute because warships often are, and sometimes were in the seventeenth and eighteenth centuries, in service fifty years or more after the date of their original conception. The successful policy, and the successful staff requirement, is an act of prophecy. The most successful designs are often the most balanced and flexible ones, the most adaptable to unexpected circumstances. The question to ask of a warship design is not primarily whether it is better or worse than its foreign contemporaries, for it will almost always be found that the foreign ship, even if superficially similar, is designed to meet significantly different requirements. The useful questions are whether the policy rightly predicts the strategic requirements of the future; and whether the designs efficiently meet them. Strategic requirements, of course, spring partly from circumstances which may be anticipated but cannot be controlled; and partly from policy choices. A government may blunder; it may commit its country to a war for which it had not prepared. In this case ships may fail to do what they had not been designed to do. The fault lies with the policy-makers rather than the naval architects.

All these considerations apply, at least in principle, to the seventeenth and eighteenth centuries. Though there were few institutions resembling a modern naval staff,[11] though the documents do not often allow us to see ships designed in conscious response to anticipated requirements, the proper question to ask of any design is whether it efficiently met the imperatives of an intelligently-conceived policy. There is no reason to think that British ships should have been the same as French or Spanish ones, unless one supposes that the strategic situations of the three countries were the same. This in fact is implicitly what many naval historians do assume: that the Bourbon powers, and subsequently Revolutionary and Imperial France, built their navies, and had to build their navies, to mount a frontal challenge to Britain for command of the sea, so that the opposing fleets may be considered as mirror images of one another. Command of the sea was the only thing worth striving for, it is assumed, and Britain was the only enemy worth mentioning: the historical function of the French and Spanish navies was therefore to provide the Royal Navy with suitable opponents. It is not in the least obvious, however, either that this was

---

[11]   A notable exception is the Danish navy's *Konstruktionskommission*, established in 1739 to regulate warship design, on which see Hans Christian Bjerg & John Erichsen, *Danske orlogsskibe 1690–1860* (Copenhagen, 1980, 2 vols), I, 133.

always the policy of the Bourbon powers, or that circumstances forbade them to adopt any other. We need to ask what really were the grand strategies of France and Spain at different periods, and whether the designs of their ships corresponded to the policies they adopted.

So far we have been considering warship design in isolation, as though it were the only factor which determined success or failure in naval war. The three-stage conceptual process of ship design, however, may equally be applied to the 'design' of entire navies and their component parts. Navies as a whole existed to meet the requirements of foreign policy; like their ships they were, or ought rationally to have been, adapted to fight when, whom and in what circumstances policy suggested. The nature of systems of command and administration, of recruitment and training, of victualling and supply, the location and equipment of dockyards and bases, can all be tested against this criterion. Of course in real life navies reflect the governments and societies which create them, and are shaped by many forces other than the dictates of rational policy,[12] but it is still reasonable and helpful for the historian to ask if the structure of the navy matched the policy of the country.

Taking these concepts as a guide, and using warship design as a key to unlock the strategies of different navies and countries, we may return to the seventeenth and eighteenth centuries. The first point to make is that warship design was competitive, and constructors constantly compared their ships with those of rivals at home and abroad, looking for ideas to borrow. In France and the Netherlands, so much less centralised in naval administration than Britain, these comparisons were often internal, between the rival traditions of the Mediterranean and Atlantic yards of France, and the five admiralties of the United Provinces, but everywhere they were also international. In England, for example, Sir Anthony Deane, as reported by Samuel Pepys, based the design of the 3rd-Rates ordered in 1677 on the French *Superbe*.[13] At Rochefort, however, where the *Superbe* had been built, Deane was regarded as the finest designer of the age, and his ships were held up as models to be copied – though as usual Toulon and Brest disagreed.[14] Colbert sent his son the Marquis de Seignelay on a lengthy reconnaissance or espionage trip to learn everything he could about

---

[12] Jan Glete, *Navies and Nations: Warships, Navies and State Building in Europe and America, 1500–1860* (Stockholm, 1993, 2 vols), I, 158.

[13] *Samuel Pepys's Naval Minutes*, ed. J.R. Tanner (Navy Records Society [NRS] Vol. 60, 1926), p. 241.

[14] Daniel Dessert, *La Royale: vaisseaux et marins du Roi Soleil* (Paris, 1996), p. 144. René Mémain, *La marine de guerre sous Louis XIV: Le matériel, Rochefort, arsenal modèle de Colbert* (Paris, 1937), pp. 537–539. *Deane's Doctrine of Naval Architecture, 1670*, ed. Brian Lavery (London, 1981), pp. 11–14.

the English and Dutch navies, and their shipbuilding in particular.[15] He was immediately followed on a similar mission by Pierre Arnoul, whose 'Remarks'[16] are equally full of admiring comments on the practice of the English and Dutch. These were amongst the earliest of a series of more than a dozen major French espionage missions designed to reveal the secrets of English naval architecture, which extend throughout the eighteenth century. Among the most important were those of Blaise Geslain, master shipwright of Brest, in 1729, and of his successor Blaise Ollivier in 1737.[17] The French navy, like the British, studied enemy prizes and commissioned them into its own service. After the victory of Vigo in 1703, for example, the Admiralty ordered its experts to 'survey and view the French prizes, and give an account of what they observe in them that may be of advantage to H.M. service when other ships shall be built.'[18] But when the Comte de Saint-Pol Hécourt took the *Salisbury* in the same year, her lines were taken off and circulated to all the French yards as a model. Discarding his previous ship, Saint-Pol took command of the *Salisbury*, and led to sea a squadron consisting almost entirely of English prizes.[19]

All the European navies engaged in similar borrowings. In wartime they studied prizes; in peacetime they fished in the international market for warship designers. In 1727 the Admiralty of Amsterdam secured the services of three English shipwrights, with whose help it adopted 'English-style' designs – though naturally Rotterdam and Zealand declined to follow suit.[20] In 1748 the Marques de Ensenada, preparing to reform Spanish naval construction, sent Don Jorge

---

[15]   *Lettres, Instructions et Mémoires de Colbert*, ed. Pierre Clément (Paris, 1861–82, 8 vols in 10) III, ii, 318 ff., prints Seignelay's 'Mémoire concernant la marine d'Angleterre'.

[16]   *Beschieden uit Vreemde Archieven omtrent de Groote Nederlandsche Zeeoorlogen 1652–1676*, ed. H.T. Colenbrander (R.G.P. k.s. Vols 18–19, The Hague, 1919), II, 7–73.

[17]   [Blaise Ollivier], *18th Century Shipbuilding: Remarks on the Navies of the English & the Dutch...* trans. & ed. David H. Roberts (Rotherfield, East Sussex, 1992), pp. 25–30 (this work prints both the original French report and an English translation). Sylviane Llinares, *Marine, propulsion et technique: l'évolution du système technologique du navire de guerre français au XVIIIe siècle* (Paris, 1994, 1 vol in 2), I, 99–110 & II, 348–352.

[18]   *Queen Anne's Navy: Documents concerning the Administration of the Navy of Queen Anne, 1702–1714*, ed. R.D. Merriman (NRS Vol. 103, 1961), pp. 68–69. J.H. Owen, *War at Sea under Queen Anne, 1702–1708* (Cambridge, 1938), p. 28.

[19]   Henri Malo, *La Grande Guerre des corsaires: Dunkerque (1702–1715)* (Paris, 1925), pp. 15–16.

[20]   J.R. Bruijn, 'Engelse scheepsbouwers op de Amsterdamse Admiraliteitswerf in de achttiende eeuw: enige aspecten', *Medelingen van de Nederlandse Vereniging voor Zeegeschiedenis* No. 25 (September 1972), pp. 18–24. A.J. Hoving & A.A. Lemmers, *In Tekening Gebracht: De achttiende-eeuwse scheepsbouwers en hun ontwerpmethoden* (Amsterdam, 2001), pp. 13–32 & 142–143. Hans Vlot, '"Bevonden het een weergaloos schip": Willem van Wassenaer en de Rotterdamse marinescheepsbouw in de achttiende eeuw,' *Tijdschrift voor Zeegeschiedenis* XXVI (2007), pp. 3–16.

Juan on a major mission of industrial espionage to England. He returned with both information and a considerable number of shipwrights and artificers for the Spanish yards. English or Irish shipwrights became master shipwrights of Cadiz, Havana, Cartagena, Guarnizo, and Ferrol.[21] Throughout the eighteenth century the Danish navy, undoubtedly the world leader in technical intelligence, systematically collected copies of secret warship designs from every admiralty in Europe.[22]

What seems to have been rare if not completely unknown in any navy was the literal copying of complete designs. Though statesmen and sea officers, impressed by foreign ships and ignorant of naval architecture, sometimes ordered ships to be built after the lines of a prize, it was in practice difficult if not impossible to do so. British hulls, for example, were more heavily constructed than French, so that a ship built in a British dockyard to the exact lines of a French design would displace more and float deeper. To maintain the same draught and freeboard, the British designer would have to adjust the lines, and so the ship would no longer be the same. In such cases the British designer might allow his superiors to believe that he had 'copied' a French design, or he might attempt to educate them in the complexities of naval architecture.[23] Besides the lines, many other aspects of a foreign design would be changed to reflect British practice and requirements. The result might be a ship greatly influenced by foreign models, but it was never a slavish copy. Even prizes were usually significantly altered. The ships were always re-rigged and re-armed, and the holds (especially of frigates) were rebuilt to give increased stowage to allow for prolonged cruising. The hanging of the decks, the siting of hatchways and magazines, the stowage of boats and booms, the position and design of pumps and capstans were often changed. These alterations produced substantially different ships.[24]

---

[21] José P. Merino Navarro, *La Armada Española en el Siglo XVIII* (Madrid, 1981), pp. 49–53 & 100–102. Rolf Mühlmann, *Die Reorganisation der Spanischen Kriegsmarine im 18. Jahrhundert* (Cologne & Vienna, 1975), pp. 68–74. Antonio Lafuente & José Luis Peset, 'Politica cientifica y espionaje industrial en los viajes de Jorge Juan y Antonio de Uluoa (1748–1751)', *Mélanges de la Casa de Velázquez* XVII (1981), pp. 233–262. Juan Carlos Mejías Tavero, *Los navíos españoles de la batalla de Trafalgar: del astillero a la mar* (Madrid, 2004), pp. 35–41. José Ignacio Gonzalez-Aller Hierro, 'El navio de tres puentes en la Armada Española', *Revista de Historia Naval* III (1985), No. 9, pp. 45–77, at pp. 54–55. Public Record Office: SP 42/35 ff. 48–49.

[22] Bjerg & Erichsen, *Danske orlogsskibe.*

[23] *British Naval Documents 1204–1960*, ed. John B. Hattendorf et al. (NRS Vol. 131, 1993), pp. 491–493. Lavery, *Ship of the Line*, I, 206.

[24] Gardiner, *Heavy Frigate*, pp. 108–111. Brian Lavery, *The Arming and Fitting of English Ships of War 1600–1815* (London, 1987).

All this traffic was inspired by the search for improved design, but it was also influenced by politics and fashion. When Ensenada fell from power his anglophile policy fell with him, and the French constructor François Gautier was imported to reform Spanish warship design along French lines; the naval architecture of the Family Compact.[25] In Sweden the eclipse of Gilbert Sheldon by Frederick Henry Chapman,[26] often understood in naively positivist terms as a triumph of science and progress over ignorance and reaction,[27] in reality had everything to do with Swedish politics: it was the triumph of the 'Hat' party over their rivals the 'Caps'. Chapman was unquestionably a talented designer, as well as a talented self-publicist,[28] but the alleged superiority and more 'scientific' character of his ships, compared to Sheldon's, rests on partisan reports by his supporters.[29] In Britain the real problems of the 1740s and 1750s gave a generation of sea officers a naive faith in the superiority of French warships which led Lord St.Vincent and Lord Barham to foist some unsatisfactory designs on the Navy long after most other officers had discarded French fashions. Experience of these ships, plus the designs of the exiled French engineer Jean-Louis Barallier, finally eliminated any remaining British enthusiasm for French naval architecture. By the time of the Napoleonic Wars the majority of captured French warships were either hulked or commissioned only as troopships.[30]

All these international influences affected the ways in which navies responded to their situations, but they should not have affected their underlying policies, and in the absence of explicit statements for posterity, ship designs ought to

[25] Mühlmann, *Der Spanischen Kriegsmarine*, pp. 75–79. Merino Navarro, *La Armada Española*, pp. 55–59 & 348. Mejías Tavero, *Los navíos españoles*, pp. 55–59. José María Blanco Nuñez, 'Material naval en el siglo XVIII: Las pruebas de Mazarredo', in *De la Paz de París a Trafalgar (1763–1805): El acontecer bélico y sus protagonistas* (Madrid, Centro Superior de Estudios de la Defensa Nacional, 2005), pp. 81–107, at pp. 89–95.

[26] Or Fredrik Hendrik af Chapman; both men were Swedes of English descent.

[27] *Svenska Flottans Historia*, ed. S.A. Svensson (Malmö, 1942–45, 3 vols), II, 340–358. Daniel G. Harris, *F.H. Chapman: The First Naval Architect and his Work* (London, 1989), pp. 105–135.

[28] His folio of plans *Architectura Navalis Mercatoria* (Stockholm, 1768), which in spite of its title includes warships, made him the best-known naval architect in Europe.

[29] Jan Glete, 'Bridge and Bulwark: The Swedish Navy and the Baltic, 1500–1809', in *In Quest of Trade and Security: The Baltic in Power Politics 1500–1990*, ed. Göran Rystad, Klaus-Richard Böhme & Wilhelm M. Carlgren (Stockholm, 1994–95, 2 vols), I, 9–59, at 20–22 & 33. Ferreiro, *Ships and Science*, p. 246.

[30] Of 38 French ships of the line captured between 1793 and 1815 exactly half (19) served as such in the Royal Navy: Rif Winfield, *British Warships in the Age of Sail 1793–1817: Design, Construction, Careers, Fates* (London, 2005), pp. 8–108. For frigates see Gardiner, *Frigates of the Napoleonic Wars*, pp. 16–18, 29–32 & 87–94.

be one of the best keys we have to reveal what their strategic priorities were. In England Charles II at least seems to have been aware that the form of ships ought to be dictated by their function. Considering the 1677 programme,

> His Majesty proceeding to discourse of the burthen of the ships... declaring his opinion and pleasure that the principal consideration to be had as to the size of the ships be the pitching upon such dimensions as may render them by their force and build most capable of performing the service they are designed for...[31]

Though the service is not here specified, the king was undoubtedly thinking of the recent battles of the Dutch Wars. Charles's favourite shipbuilder was even clearer:

> Sir A[nthony] D[eane] says that no one shape of a ship can in general be said to be the best; for every distinct use requires a different shape, and the skill lies only in building best for the particular use designed, which differs as your purposes for this or that depth of water, for speed, for strength, for weight of guns, for number of men, for calm or rough seas, for short or long voyages, for stowage of goods, and many other circumstances, as fewness of hands to sail with, bearing sail, etc. [32]

Policy in France at this date was by no means so coherent. The early years of Colbert's new navy produced a chaos of competing styles. The unhappy experience of the Dutch war led to a drive for uniformity, but no-one could agree on the best pattern. Colbert, so obsessed with standardization, wanted to standardize on the impossible: he wanted high freeboard combined with shallow draught and low upperworks; he wanted ships which were faster, more powerful, more weatherly, more seaworthy and above all, more heavily and gloriously decorated than any others; and he wanted them built more quickly, using less timber, at less cost, to last longer, without maintenance. His method was as usual to issue orders that it should be so; and as usual, it was not.[33] As the first generation of Colbert's ships needed replacement in the 1690s, the great influence of the Marquis de Tourville and his favourite shipwright, the Neapolitan Biaggio Pangallo, imposed a measure of uniformity. Pangallo stood for long, deep hulls designed to carry their main deck batteries well clear of

---

[31]   *A Descriptive Catalogue of the Pepysian Manuscripts...*, ed. J.R. Tanner (NRS Vols. 26, 27, 36 & 57, 1903–23) IV, 415, quoting Papys's Admiralty Journal for 5 May 1677. Cf. Frank Fox, 'The English Naval Shipbuilding Programme of 1664', *Mariner's Mirror* LXXVIII (1992), pp. 277–292.

[32]   *Samuel Pepys's Naval Minutes*, ed. Tanner, pp. 9–10.

[33]   Jean-Claude Lemineur, *Les vaisseaux du Roi Soleil* (Nice, 1996), pp. 37–66. Dessert, *La Royale*, pp. 22–29 & 128–155. Mémain, *Rochefort*, pp. 537–539 & 645–699. Etienne Taillemite, 'Les problèmes de la marine de guerre au XVIIe siècle', *XVIIe Siècle* Nos. 86–87 (1970), pp. 21–37; *Idem*, Colbert, législateur de la Marine Royale', *Revue Maritime* 380 (1983), pp. 44–70.

the water, and to make high speed. The result was a fleet of big, powerful, handsomely decorated and extremely costly ships of very deep draught, which could not enter any French Channel port, and only one or two on the Atlantic coast.[34] With this fleet Louis XIV went to war against England and the Netherlands, the two naval powers whose home waters it was unable to enter. There are two explanations for the glaring mismatch between the fleet that Colbert and Seignelay built, and the strategy that Louis XIV adopted. Either the fleet was meant for the Mediterranean and had never been intended to fight the maritime powers;[35] or the fleet was meant for prestige, and no coherent thought had been given to how and where it was going to fight anybody.[36] Meanwhile Colbert had built his new model dockyard, Rochefort, on a river too shallow to admit any French ship of the line without great difficulty and danger. In the first twenty-five years of its operation five ships of the line were wrecked in the Charente, after which Pontchartrain ordered nothing larger than a fourth-rate to use the yard.[37] If Louis XIV's foreign policy meant anything, his navy should have been designed to fight the Dutch, with small ships of the line capable of being based at Dunkirk, and numerous cruisers to attack Dutch trade, but when war broke out in 1690, neither were available.

The English navy at the same date faced an abrupt transformation of its strategic situation. The fleet of Charles II had been successfully developed to meet the requirement of the Dutch Wars.[38] It consisted largely of battleships designed to carry the maximum broadside into action in the sheltered and shallow waters of the southern North Sea, where gales can be ridden out at anchor, and all operations were within a few days' sail of bases admirably distributed along the weather shore. The unexpected war with France forced English admirals for the first time to operate in the deep and open waters

---

[34]   Patrick Villiers, 'Marine de Colbert ou Marine de Seignelay. Victoire de Barfleur et progrès technique', in *Guerres Maritimes (1688–1713)*, (Vincennes, 1996), pp. 173–96, at 183–186. Lemineur, *Les vaisseaux du Roi Soleil*, pp. 59–84. *Idem*, 'La marine de Louis XIV: une marine nouvelle de conception française', in *L'invention du vaisseau de ligne (1450–1700)*, ed. Martine Acerra (Paris, 1997), pp. 29–37. Mémain, *Rochefort*, pp. 703–707. J. Delarbre, *Tourville et la marine de son temps* (Paris, 1889), pp. 286–293. R.C. Anderson, 'Comparative Naval Architecture, 1670–1720', *Mariner's Mirror* VII (1921), pp. 38–45, 172–181 & 308–314. J.P. Hemingway, 'The work of the Surveyors of the Navy during the period of the establishments : a comparative study of naval architecture between 1672 and 1755' (Bristol Ph.D. Thesis, 2002), p. 71.

[35]   Jean Meyer, *Béveziers (1690): La France prend la maîtrise de la Manche* (Paris, 1993), p. 52.

[36]   Dessert, *La Royale*, pp. 132–139. Philippe Masson, *Histoire de la Marine* (Paris, 2nd edn 1992, 2 vols), I, 71–72 & 104.

[37]   Mémain, *Rochefort*, pp. 33–52, 259 & 976–877. Acerra, *Rochefort* I, 32–36. Dessert, *La Royale*, p. 113.

[38]   Frank Fox, *Great Ships: The Battlefleet of King Charles II* (London, 1980).

of the lower Channel and the Western Approaches, where they had to face onshore storms and seas sweeping off the open Atlantic which they could not beat into. Dutch ships were still less adapted for these waters. Instead of the friendly weather shores the English had enjoyed during the Dutch Wars, all the coasts were dangerous lee shores. In these circumstances, it seemed 'a mighty boldness to advance with the Grand Fleet further westward of the Isle of Wight than the *[Royal] Soveraigne* had been known to have been, since the time of her built' (52 years before).[39] The allied fleet was as unsuitable to intercept French ships sailing to Ireland as Tourville's was to push up the Channel.[40] Moreover the English navy had few cruisers, and much of the action of the war came to turn on the defence of allied convoys against French raiding squadrons.[41]

The English reaction was in some respects commendably fast. Numbers of new ships were ordered, extensive works were put in hand at Portsmouth, and a completely new dockyard was established at Plymouth to support squadrons operating to the westward.[42] But though the size and composition of the Navy changed in response to the new situation, the designs of the ships changed more slowly, and of course many older ships continued long in service. The worst designs were the small 80-gun ships built in the 1690s under the terms of an Act of Parliament which dictated both the number of guns and the quite insufficient size of 1,100 tons.[43] In the 1720s and 1730s change was still impeded by a political climate in which Parliament was unwilling to grant money for new construction, but happily financed 'rebuilding', which in practice meant new ships built more or less to the lines of the old. The very success of Walpole's government in maintaining a large fleet in reserve over nearly thirty years of peace paradoxically hampered the introduction of new designs, and so did a conservative and long-lived Surveyor of the Navy, Sir

---

[39]   Michael Duffy, 'Edmund Dummer's "Account of the General Progress and Advancement of His Majesty's New Dock and Yard at Plymouth", December 1694', in *The Naval Miscellany Vol. VI*, ed. M. Duffy (NRS Vol. 146, 2003), pp. 93–147, quoted at p. 121.

[40]   N.A.M. Rodger, 'Weather, Geography and Naval Power in the Age of Sail', *Journal of Strategic Studies* XXII (1999), No. 2/3, pp. 178–200.

[41]   David Davies, 'The English Navy on the Eve of War, 1689', in *Guerres Maritimes (1688–1713)*, (Vincennes, 1996), pp. 1–14. A.N. Ryan, 'William III and the Brest Fleet in the Nine Years War', in *William III and Louis XIV: Essays 1680–1720 by and for Mark A. Thomson*, ed. Ragnhild Hatton & J.S. Bromley (Liverpool, 1968), pp. 49–67.

[42]   John Ehrman, *The Navy in the War of William III, 1689–1697* (Cambridge, 1953), pp. 428–435. Jonathan G. Coad, 'The Development and Organisation of Plymouth Dockyard, 1689–1815', in *The New Maritime History of Devon*, ed. Michael Duffy et al. (London, 1992–4, 2 vols), I, 192–200.

[43]   Lavery, *Ship of the Line* I, 54–68. Ehrman, *Navy*, pp. 625–632. *The Sergison Papers*, ed. R.D. Merriman (NRS Vol. 89, 1950), pp. 80–84.

Jacob Acworth. The result was that the fleet which went to war in 1739 was in many respects still marked by the requirements of the Dutch Wars. British ships were small, powerfully-armed for their size but cramped, slow, leewardly and unsuited for the prolonged open-ocean cruising which the new war soon called for.[44] Moreover they faced the French and Spanish navies both of which had been rebuilt over the previous twenty years virtually from nothing. The comparison between the new enemy warship types and the older British ones produced widespread dissatisfaction amongst British officers, the echoes of which continue to influence historians to-day.[45]

There is no doubt that the rebuilding of the Spanish navy begun by Patiño and continued under Campillo and Ensenada sprang from consideration of Spain's strategic position as the possessor of two overseas empires, in Italy and America. The function of the navy was to protect the empires' lines of communication by patrol and convoy escort. It was meant to be strong enough to hold a balance of power between its two major potential enemies, France and Britain, but it was not intended for a frontal attack on either.[46] Ensenada's objective was a fleet sufficient 'mantener la paz sin claudicar y poder ejercer una neutralidad vigilada.'[47] Both the navy and the ships Spain developed were in most respects well-suited for this task. The ships were excellently built and very long-lived, large and comfortable for long-distance cruising, but lightly armed

---

[44]   Lavery, *Ship of the Line*, I, 64–71. *Idem*, 'The Rebuilding of British Warships 1690-1740', *Mariner's Mirror* LXVI (1980), pp. 5–14 & 113–127. Rif Winfield, *The 50-Gun Ship* (London, 1997), pp. 25–45. Daniel A. Baugh. 'Sir Charles Wager, 1666–1743', in *Precursors of Nelson: British Admirals of the Eighteenth Century*, ed. Peter Le Fevre & Richard Harding (London, 2000), pp. 100–126, at 119–124.

[45]   Hattendorf, *British Naval Documents*, pp. 483–490.

[46]   Pablo Emilio Perez-Mallaina Bueno, *Política Naval Española en el Atlántico 1700–1715* (Seville, 1982), pp. 397–407 & 442–443. Antonio Béthencourt Massieu, *Patiño en la política internacional de Felipe V* (Valladolid, 1954), pp. 21–24. Jeremy Black, 'Anglo-Spanish Naval Relations in the Eighteenth Century', *Mariner's Mirror* LXXVII (1991), pp. 235–258. J.R. McNeill, *Atlantic Empires of France and Spain: Louisbourg and Havana, 1700–1763* (Chapel Hill, 1985), pp. 52–57. Geoffrey J. Walker, *Spanish Politics and Imperial Trade, 1700–1789* (London, 1979), pp. 94–113. José Cervera Pery, *La Marina de la Ilustración (Resurgimiento y crisis del poder naval)* (Madrid, 1986), pp. 57–70. Jean McLachlan, 'The seven years' peace and the West India policy of Carvajal and Wall', *English Historical Review* LIII (1938), pp. 457–477. Agustín Ramón Rodríguez González, *Tragalgar y el conflicto naval Anglo-Español del siglo XVIII* (Madrid, 2005), pp. 127–138. Ivan Valdez Bubnov, 'Naval Power and State Modernisation: Spanish Shipbuilding Policy in the Eighteenth Century' (Cambridge Ph.D. thesis, 2005), pp. 100–124 & 154–163. Enrique Manera Regueyra, 'La defensa del Imperio: Carlos III', in *España y el mar en el siglo de Carlos III*, ed.Vicente Palacio Atard (Madrid, 1989), pp. 405–414.

[47]   Federico F.de Bordejé y Morencos, 'El inmovilismo táctico en el siglo XVIII', *Revista de Historia Naval* XIV (1996), 52, pp. 45–66, at p. 65.

for their size. The dockyards and infrastructure were developed to keep pace with the growth of the fleet. A dry dock was built at La Carraca near Cadiz in the 1750s. Two (the first in the Mediterranean) followed at Cartagena in 1754, two more at Ferrol in the 1760s, and in the 1780s three more at Cadiz.[48]

The French navy, like the Spanish, was rebuilt from a very low ebb, beginning about 1730 under the direction of the Comte de Maurepas. The new fleet was based on a range of new standard types of original conception. The cruisers were of a completely new class called frigates; small two-deckers with an unarmed lower deck. Although the first French frigates were fragile and lightly armed, the type soon developed into the classic cruiser of the sailing navies: fast, seaworthy, capable of long-range operations, and carrying an increasingly powerful armament which could be fought in any weather. By the end of the American War frigates were being built with a main battery of 18-pdrs, equivalent to the lower deck of a small ship of the line. Frigates were a major innovation, and the striking overall superiority of the first French frigates to the small cruisers of the Royal Navy was one reason for the discontent of British officers in the 1740s. What is unfortunately unclear is whether the frigate was a private inspiration of Blaise Ollivier at Brest, or the consequence of policy decisions taken by Maurepas at Versailles.[49]

The new French ships of the line were built to different designs by the different yards, but in a standard range of classes which must be the result of central direction. There were virtually no three-deckers, which had formed more than a third of the French fleet in the 1690s; the battle-fleet was composed of large two-deckers.[50] This alone makes it clear that Maurepas was not planning to fight fleet battles, for it was univerally understood that the concentrated

---

[48]   McNeill, *Atlantic Empires of France and Spain*, pp. 52–65. José Ignacio Gonzalez-Aller & Hugo O'Donnell, 'The Spanish Navy in the 18th Century', in *Battle of St.Vincent 200 Years*, ed. Stephen Howarth (Shelton, Notts, 1998), pp. 67–83, at 67–68. Enrique Manera Regueyra, 'La epoca de Felipe V y Fernando VI', in *El buque en la Armada Española*, ed. E. Manera Regueyra (Madrid, 1981), pp. 169–200. Carlos Moya Blanco, 'La arquitectura naval en el siglo XVIII', ibid., pp. 233–255. Cesáreo Fernández Duro, *Armada Española desde la unión de los reinos de Castilla y de Aragón* (Madrid, 1895–1902, 9 vols), VI, 378–381. Merino Navarro, *La Armada Española*, pp. 352–356. *Idem*, 'Graving Docks in France and Spain before 1800', *Mariner's Mirror* LXXI (1985), pp. 35–58. Blanco Nuñez, 'Material naval', pp. 87–88. Pascual O'Dogherty, 'La Construcción Naval en la Península', in *España y el mar*, ed. Palacio Atard, pp. 93–118, at pp. 112–118.

[49]   Gardiner, *First Frigates*. Jean Boudriot & Hubert Berti, *The History of the French Frigate 1650–1850*, trans. David H.Roberts (Rotherfield, East Sussex, 1993), pp. 68–137.

[50]   Acerra, *Rochefort*, I, 216. Martine Acerra & André Zysberg, *L'essor des marines de guerres européennes (vers 1680–vers 1790)* (Paris, 1997), pp. 65–69. One three-decker was begun but accidentally burnt on the stocks. I am grateful to Dr Michael Duffy for pointing out the significance of the absence of three-deckers.

power of the three-decker would be decisive in close action. The new standard third-rate mounted 74 guns, with a lower deck battery of twenty-eight 36-pdrs and a main deck battery of thirty 18-pdrs.[51] One of these new 74s, the *Invincible*, was captured in 1747, and caused a sensation in the Royal Navy. Though she was by no means the largest in her class (the *Magnanime*, taken next year, was considerably bigger) she was 50% larger in tonnage than the standard British 70-gun third-rate, and fired a broadside 75% heavier.[52] It is not surprising that British captains rated her as better than their own ships; and of course none were louder in the praise of French prizes than those who had taken them, and were trying to sell them to the Navy Board for the best possible price.

The differences between these British and French ships arose overwhelmingly from the difference of size. Naval architecture is a question of balance: if two competent designers build rival ships of the same tonnage and type, one can only gain a marked advantage in any one quality, such as speed or armament, by sacrificing the others. Even a modest increase in size, however, permits a significant improvement in quality all round, and a 50% increase ought to translate into overwhelming superiority. But increased size naturally means increased cost. British naval agitation to match or copy French designs was not so much a technical as a political campaign, directed at Parliament, to finance bigger and more expensive ships.[53] This campaign was substantially successful, and by the Seven Years' War the Royal Navy was in the process of transformation to a superficially French-style line of battle based on 74-gun third-rates, and a cruising force of 12-pdr frigates. These new designs, better armed and much better adapted for long-range cruising, helped the Royal Navy to the oceanic, all-weather operations which were increasingly called for.

But there remained important differences between British and French warships. British ships continued to be somewhat smaller in tonnage and shorter, but much more heavily timbered and fastened. Their rig and lines performed best in going to windward, and in heavy weather. They were built to stand the strain of prolonged sea-time at all seasons, they were stored for long cruises, and they were built to fight. They were also built to last; relatively cheap to construct and maintain, they were the rational choice of the navy which meant to surpass its enemies both in numbers and in stamina.[54] Their rig, masts,

---

[51]   Boudriot, *Le vaisseau de 74 canons*, describes the type in exhaustive detail.

[52]   1793 tons burthen by English measure, against 1130 to 1230 tons; 838 lb. broadside (*livre de Paris*, equivalent to 905 lbs avoirdupois) against 522 lbs. Brian Lavery, *The Royal Navy's First Invincible* (Portsmouth, 1988).

[53]   Gardiner, *Frigates of the Napoleonic Wars*, pp. 139–141.

[54]   Gardiner, *Frigates of the Napoleonic Wars*, pp. 87–98 & 131–141. Peter Goodwin, *The Construction and Fitting of the Sailing Man of War, 1650–1850* (London, 1987).

sails, cordage, blocks, pumps, cables, steering gear, and fittings of every kind were greatly superior in design and quality.[55] French ships of all classes were lightly built of inferior timber, fastened with nails instead of trenails, but their very long hulls were highly stressed in a seaway. In fine weather these 'battle-cruisers' with their long hulls and taunt rigs were fast off the wind, but their performance fell off rapidly when close hauled, or when wind and sea rose.[56] What was worse French designers seem to have had something of an obsession with reducing the depth and weight of the hull, which made their ships light and buoyant, but directly weakened resistance to hogging, sagging and racking strains. A warship, one constructor wrote about 1763,

> ...doit être supérieure pour la marche et ordinairement on lui sacrifie tout pour cet avantage; on le fait plus léger de bois pour le rendre plus flottant et lui conserver une belle batterie; on s'applique moins à y appliquer les liaisons fortes, solides et multipliées, parce que le jeu de toutes les parties facilite la marche... En partant de ce principe, on doute que les constructeurs du roi s'exposent à entreprendre de bâtir des vaisseaux qui n'auraient pas toutes les qualités qui demande un vaisseau de guerre: ils craindraient de perdre leur réputation, car, pour eux, c'est le comble de la gloire que de faire des vaisseaux qui aient une belle batterie et qui marchent supérieurement.[57]

Successive senior officers of the dockyards complained about the results.[58] As the comte de Rocquefeuille put it to the minister in 1771:

> Je ne puis m'empêcher, Monseigneur, de dire en général que M.M. les constructeurs des ports subalternes font tous des ouvrages de charlatan; ils font des bâtiments fort

---

[55]　Llinares, *Marine, propulsion et technique*, I, 99–142 & 177–201; II, 351–352. D.K. Brown, 'The Form and Speed of Sailing Warships', *Mariner's Mirror* LXXXIV (1998), pp. 298–307; & *idem*, 'The Speed of Sailing Warships, 1793–1840; an Examination of the Evidence', in *Les empires en guerre et paix, 1793–1860*, ed. Edward Freeman (Vincennes, 1990), pp. 155–194, argues that hull lines made an insignificant difference to speed, and that the rig, cleanness of bottom and skill of the captain were more important. Ferreiro, *Ships and Science*, rates the constructors' contribution somewhat higher.

[56]　Llinares, *Marine, propulsion et technique*, I, 156–168. Acerra & Meyer, *Marines et Révolution*, pp. 74–75. Acerra, *Rochefort*, II, 388–398. Gardiner, 'Frigate Design', pp. 83–92. *Idem, First Frigates*, pp. 93–117. Boudriot & Berti, *French Frigate*, pp. 130–137. On French timber see P. W. Bamford, *Forests and French Sea Power 1660–1789* (Toronto, 1956). The apt analogy with the battle-cruiser is from Glete, *Navies and Nations*, I, 247.

[57]　Geneviève Beauchesne, *Historique de la construction navale à Lorient de 1666 à 1770* (Vincennes, 1979), pp. 137–138. Note Ollivier's comments on the excessive depth of British, and the excessive draught of French ships: *Shipbuilding*, pp. 113, 136 & 161.

[58]　James Pritchard, 'From Shipwright to Naval Constructor: The Professionalization of 18th-Century French Naval Shipbuilders', *Technology and Culture* XXVIII (1987), pp. 1–25, at p. 14.

légers, fort longs et fort mal liés parce qu'ils sacrifient tout à la marche, et qu'ils sont bien certains de l'obtenir par là.

C'est la première campagne qui donne la réputation aux bâtiments et aux constructeurs. Voilà tout ce qu'on veut. Je n'en excepte pas même le sieur Groignard dans les vaisseaux et frégates qu'il a faites à Lorient et ailleurs, et que nous avons été obligé de relier, tout de nouveau icy, à grand frais, pour les mettre en état de faire de secondes campagnes où ces bâtiments perdent leur marche précédemment vantée.[59]

In close action French ships with their light scantlings were a death trap. Moreover they had high building costs, high maintenance costs and short working lives.[60] This made dockyards, and above all the dry docks themselves, critically important, but as late as 1750 the French navy had built only four dry docks, of which one had been abandoned and the other three did not work properly.[61] Its first fully functional dry docks, the Formes de Pontaniou at Brest (one double and one single) were not completed until 1756, and they were not deepened to take a three-decker until the 1780s. The French navy was therefore forced to rely on the cumbersome method of heaving down, which imposed severe strains on the hull, and often damaged it permanently.[62] By the 1780s France had seven graving docks at least partly functional, or one for every ten ships of the line. The British and Spanish navies at the same date had one for every 7.5 battleships, and the British were planning a large increase in the number of docks.[63] To build costly ships with short lives and high maintenance costs, and to invest in building rather than repair, was a rational choice only for a navy with deep pockets and low building costs – but there is no doubt that finance was the weakest point of the French navy, and that France's hectic participation in the naval arms race of the 1780s directly contributed to the

---

[59]   Jean Mascart, *La vie et les travaux du Chevalier Jean-Charles de Borda (1733–1799): Épisodes de la vie scientifique au XVIIIe siècle* (Lyon, 1919), pp. 390–391.

[60]   Acerra, *Rochefort*, III, 552–585. Acerra & Zysberg, *L'essor des marines de guerre*, pp. 79–85.

[61]   The original stone dock at Rochefort was abandoned as too small. The double dock, finished in 1728 after nearly 40 years' effort, was inaccessible to ships unable to get up the Charente. The Fosse de Troulan at Brest was impossible to drain completely because a stream fell into it and its sill was below low water level.

[62]   Bernard Cros, 'Les formes de Pontaniou dans l'arsenal de Brest, 1683–1818', *Neptunia* 162 (1986), pp. 34–44 & 163 (1986), pp. 24–33. Mémain, *Rochefort*, pp. 112–151. Ollivier, *Shipbuilding*, pp. 21–23 &112–118. Acerra, *Rochefort*, I, 51–70 & 81–90; III, 552–555 & 567–573.

[63]   Acerra & Zysberg, *L'essor des marines de guerre*, p. 84. Jonathan Coad, *The Royal Dockyards 1690–1850: Architecture and Engineering Works of the Sailing Navy* (Aldershot, 1989), pp. 91–99.

fall of the old régime.[64] Whereas other navies with limited budgets, such as those of Spain and Sweden, rationally planned to save money in the long run by building a fleet which would last, and looking after it properly, France did the opposite.

It seems reasonable to connect the designs of Maurepas' new fleet with France's then foreign policy and his expressed priority for colonial trade.[65] As an ally of Britain and a rival of Spain, France needed a small fleet of individually well-armed ships designed for fast ocean passages in the trade-wind latitudes. For the protection of French trade, for convoy escort and small expeditionary forces, the new ships were well suited. The French preference for pursuing the mission rather than fighting the enemy, so often repeated during the eighteenth century, and so often derided during the twentieth, makes some sense in the context of operations against the Spanish empire.[66] Unfortunately, however, Maurepas' new policy (if that is what it was) was scarcely launched before the ambitions of Louis XV (supported by Maurepas himself) precipitated France into war against the Maritime Powers just as Louis XIV's had done. A succession of rulers and ministers then involved France in a succession of naval wars against Britain without making any significant changes in the structure of the French navy or the design philosophy of its ships. Only in one of these wars, the War of American Independence, did France come close to imposing the sort of fluid, unpredictable, long-range strategy, with a maximum

---

[64] McNeill, *Atlantic Empires of France and Spain*, p. 61. J.C. Riley, *The Seven Years War and the Old Regime in France: The Economic and Financial Toll* (Princeton, 1986), pp. 170–176, *Idem, International Government Finance and the Amsterdam Capital Market, 1740–1815* (Cambridge, 1980), pp. 104–112 & 174–176. Richard Bonney, 'The Eighteenth Century. II. The Struggle for Great Power Status and the End of the Old Fiscal Regime' in *Economic Systems and State Finance*, ed. R. Bonney (Oxford, 1995), pp. 315–390, at 343–347. Glete, *Navies and Nations*, I, 276–277. François Crouzet, 'The sources of England's wealth: some French views in the eighteenth century', in *Shipping, trade and commerce: essays in memory of Ralph Davis*, ed. P. L. Cottrell & D.H. Aldcroft (Leicester, 1981), pp. 61–79 at 61–64. James Pritchard, *Louis XV's Navy, 1748–1762: A Study of Organization and Administration* (Kingston, Ontario & Montreal, 1987), pp. 187–205.

[65] Maurice Filion, *Maurepas: ministre de Louis XV (1715–1749)* (Montreal, 1967), pp. 49–50, 101–148 & 157–172. *Idem*, 'La crise de la marine française, d'après le mémoire de Maurepas de 1745 sur la marine et le commerce', *Revue d'Histoire de l'Amérique Française* XXI (1967), pp. 230–242. Acerra, *Rochefort*, II, 236. Acerra & Zysberg, *L'essor des marines de guerres*, pp. 65–69. Jean Meyer & Martine Acerra, 'La marine française vue par elle-même (XVIIe–XVIIIe siècles)', in *Guerres et Paix 1660–1815* (Vincennes, 1987) pp. 231–243 at pp. 231–235. James Pritchard, *Anatomy of a Naval Disaster: The 1746 French Expedition to North America* (Montreal & Kingston, 1995), pp. 19–22.

[66] R.V.P. Castex, *Les Idées Militaires de la Marine du XVIIIme siècle: De Ruyter à Suffren* (Paris, 1911), pp. 30–43. François Caron, 'La stratégie navale au temps de la marine à voile', in *La lutte pour l'empire de la mer: histoire et géostratégie maritimes*, ed. Hervé Coutau-Bégarie (Paris, 1995), pp. 163–195.

of movement and a minimum of fighting, which best suited French warships – and that was thanks to British miscalculations which were never repeated.[67] Far from rethinking its philosophy, the French navy of the 1780s decided that it had reached perfection, and adopted a standard range of designs to which it remained committed until the 1830s – by which time they were entirely obsolete.[68]

In Spain the naval policy of Patiño and Ensenada was abandoned on the accession of the anglophobe Carlos III, and the Spanish navy too was committed to naval wars against Britain for which it was structurally ill-suited.[69] In Spain, however, the naval leadership was not complacent about the quality and suitability of its ships. Immediately after the American War, the most talented Spanish admiral of that generation, Don José de Mazarredo, organised a series of comparative trials of different designs, and a new chief constructor, Don José Romero Fernández de Landa, began building a new fleet designed for war against Britain.[70] This fleet was centred on eight big, heavily-armed three-deckers which the British regarded as the finest warships of the age. The *Príncipe de Asturias* and *Santa Ana*, Collingwood's 'Spanish perfections', were the most powerful ships present on either side at Trafalgar.[71] Whether or not Spain was wise to abandon its succesful policy of neutrality and commit itself to the Family Compact,[72] Spanish naval policy was logically and successfully adapted to face the new strategic situation, as far as Spanish resources permitted.

Though at several periods (notably 1779–81) the French and Spanish fleets combined were superior in numbers to the Royal Navy, the French navy, unlike

---

[67] Orville T. Murphy, *Charles Gravier, Comte de Vergennes: French Diplomacy in the Age of Revolution, 1719–1787* (Albany, 1982), pp. 263–269. Jonathan R. Dull, *The French Navy and American Independence: A Study of Arms and Diplomacy, 1774–1787* (Princeton, 1975), pp. 97–98. N.A.M. Rodger, 'Sea-power and Empire, 1688–1793', in *The Oxford History of the British Empire Vol. II, The Eighteenth Century*, ed. P. J. Marshall (Oxford, 1998), pp. 169–183, at 180–181.

[68] Llinares, *Marine, propulsion et technique*, I, 171–192. Acerra, *Rochefort*, II, 361–366. Acerra & Zysberg, *L'essor des marines de guerres*, pp. 75–77. Acerra & Meyer, *Marines et Révolution*, pp. 66–72. Mascart, *Borda*, pp. 482–483.

[69] Enrique Manera Regueyra, 'El apogeo de la Marina Española (Carlos III y Carlos IV)', in Manera Regueyra, *El buque en la Armada Española*, pp. 201–232.

[70] Blanco Nuñez, 'Material Naval', pp. 95–107. Rodríguez González, *Trafalgar*, pp. 226–227. Gonzalez-Aller Hierro, 'El navio de tres puentes'.

[71] *The Despatches and Letters of Vice Admiral Lord Viscount Nelson*, ed. Sir N.H. Nicolas (London, 1844–45, 7 vols), VII, 239. The older Spanish first-rates *Rayo* and *Santísima Trinidad* were also present.

[72] The question is examined by Maria Victoria López-Cordón Cortezo, 'Entre Francia e Inglaterra: intereses estratégicos y acuerdos políticos antecendentes de Trafalgar', in *Trafalgar y el mundo atlántico*, ed. Agustin Guimerá, Alberto Ramos & Gonzalo Butrón (Madrid, 2004), pp. 19–60.

the Spanish, remained the wrong sort of navy, with the wrong sort of ships, for the kind of war it needed to fight to defeat Britain at sea. The result was lost battles, providing the Royal Navy with numerous prizes, many of which were commissioned into British service. The political value of making up one's fleet with enemy prizes was immense, and the Royal Navy enjoyed having squadrons full of French and other foreign names (as indeed it still does; at this day there are three British warships in service named after Louis XIV).[73] They made up for the relatively slow building rate of the Royal Navy, whose dockyards by the end of the eighteenth century devoted almost their entire effort to maintenance, and they were worth having at a suitable price, which was usually less than half the price per ton which the Navy Board would pay for British-built ships.[74]

We must conclude that the real differences between the structure and ship design of the major navies was not one of quality but of suitability. Between the 1720s and 1740s both French and Spanish fleets were reconstructed to match a new foreign policy, resulting in new and impressive ships. At the same period the British fleet was checked in its still incomplete process of adaptation to the new Atlantic strategy required by war with France. For both France and Britain, however, the 1740s were a turning point. The British were shocked into completing the evolution of an oceanic fleet, and arrived at a design philosophy which served them well and in the end gained them the mastery of the seas. The French then, and the Spaniards later, changed their policy, but only Spain adjusted her warship designs accordingly. The result was a succession of wars in which France deployed the wrong sort of squadrons, of the wrong sort of ships. By the 1760s the form and function of the Royal Navy were in reasonable balance, but a gap had opened which was never bridged, between the structure the French navy had adopted, and the policy it was called upon to execute.

Additional Note [2009]

This is the original English text of an article published in French, which itself is a revised version of something originally issued in English, but by a Dutch publisher.

---

[73] *Invincible, Vigilant, Superb*. On the origin of these names see Martine Acerra, 'La symbolique des noms de navires de guerre dans la marine française, 1661–1815', *Histoire, Economie et Société* XVI (1997), pp. 45–61; and Philippe de Villette-Mursay, *Mes campagnes de mer sous Louis XIV*, ed. Michel Vergé-Franceschi (Paris, 1991), pp. 43–47.

[74] Glete, *Navies and Nations*, II, 383–386. R.J.B. Knight, 'The Building and Maintenance of the British Fleet during the Anglo-French Wars (1688–1815)', in *Les Marines de Guerre Européennes, XVII–XVIIIe siècles*, ed. Martine Acerra, José Merino & Jean Meyer (Paris, 1985), pp. 35–50. P. L.C. Webb, 'The Rebuilding and Repair of the Fleet, 1783–93', *Bulletin of the Institute of Historical Research* L (1977), pp. 194–209.

Navies and the Enlightenment

It is something of a commonplace amongst naval historians that the navies of the eighteenth century were, in Jean Meyer's words, 'the spearhead of the Enlightenment'.[1] Navies in general, and the French navy in particular, have been held up as examples of a scientific culture, and there are obvious reasons why they should be.[2] At the heart of the Enlightenment was an intellectual project to replace ignorance, superstition and tradition with precise knowledge, and above all precise measurement. Mathematics was the favoured language of the Enlightenment, because figures expressed and defined what words often obscured and concealed. Numbers were objective; words were subjective. Numbers belonged to the scientist; words belonged to the poet, and all too often to the churchman. The fundamental design of the Creator – whom most Enlightenment thinkers were prepared to admit as a theoretical principle, however distasteful they found organized religion in practice[3] – was expressed in the mathematical order underlying the apparently haphazard forms of nature. Navigation and exploration were perfect expressions of the Enlightenment's ideals: they applied mathematics and astronomy to measure and define the world, to master space and time. They constituted an ideal example of that characteristic Enlightenment objective, a 'system'; meaning an intellectual and preferably mathematical framework in which to classify and regulate a subject. The untidy, the irregular and the haphazard were inherently unscientific and unenlightened. That which could be reduced to order, classified and standardized, was an expression of man's intellectual mastery of his world. The natural order, it was believed, had to be fundamentally orderly, and the function of the philosopher was to clear away the rubbish of centuries in order to expose its underlying perfection.[4]

Originally published in *Science and the French and British Navies 1700–1850* (Greenwich, 2003). Reprinted by permission of the National Maritime Museum.

Sea officers and naval officials of all sorts are indeed, at first glance, ideal representatives of the new type, displaying many of its characteristics; including mathematics, freemasonry,[5] science, sexual licence[6] and anti-clericalism. Not only navigation and astronomy but also naval architecture, naval tactics, naval medicine and various aspects of naval administration offer examples of the characteristic intellectual approaches of the age. Nevertheless, when the picture is examined in more detail, many accepted simplicities begin to dissolve. Navies were not in practice such perfect exemplars of the Enlightenment spirit as they at first sight appear, nor was the influence of the Enlightenment itself the unambiguous benefit which has been presented by the Positivist tradition of history. Moreover there were considerable differences between the French and British navies,[7] and considerable divergences over time.

It is important to understand from the start that mathematics was not an intellectually or socially neutral language. The mathematics of the 'philosopher' was pure mathematics: geometry, algebra, calculus. It was pure because it was abstract, uncontaminated by vulgar practicalities. It was scientific because it was essential to true science, that process of pure reasoning *a priori*, deriving universal truths from first principles, which Cartesianism prescribed. In social terms, this was the mathematics of the gentleman; one fully qualified for philosophy because he had no necessity to earn a living. It was very different from the vulgar utility of what in English was called 'mixed mathematics', the working calculations of men who had to work: men like bankers, tradesmen, excise officers – and navigators.[8] Duhamel du Monceau, whose *Eléments d'architecture navale* of 1754 was explicitly a handbook of practical engineering ('purement pratique, et même élémentaire') rather than of 'sublime speculation', was condemned by his peers for exactly this reason: in France, at least, practicality was not intellectually respectable.[9] Condorcet dismissed experimental physics as 'physicaille', parlour tricks, unworthy of the serious scholar.[10] Whereas in Britain the application of practical mathematics to actuarial principles led directly to the resilient forms of national debt which sustained the British war effort over a hundred years of conflict, in France the state was crippled, and eventually destroyed, by an irrational and costly system of self-amortising public debt which owed its survival solely to the fact that it had never been subject to mathematical analysis.[11]

The duality of pure science versus impure practicality, the leisured gentleman versus the working professional, was central to the ambiguous situation of sea officers, who very much wanted to be seen to belong to the first world but in practice belonged to both. It was also a point in which British and French officers differed significantly in their attitudes. All sea officers were gentlemen in principle and in France they were supposed to be gentlemen by birth. The education provided to the *gardes de marine* was intended to be one entirely appropriate to the gentleman officer. It laid a heavy stress on theoretical mathematics, particularly after the introduction of Etienne Bézout's *Cours de mathématique* in 1765, and it laid an even heavier stress on fencing and dancing. The educational scheme was an Enlightenment 'system', regulated in the nicest detail. (The 1775 regulations even prescribed how the caretaker was to clean the blackboards.) In practice, however, the scheme never worked properly. Officers emerged from the *gardes de marine*, after ten years or more of what was meant to be unbroken instruction, with a very imperfect theoretical education and almost no practical experience.[12] Moreover, skill in navigation was socially ambiguous. The association with astronomy carried prestige: the association with warrant officers and pilots definitely did not. Though the navigation of French warships depended largely on their skills, the *maître pilotes* ('a class of men incapable of perfection, blind slaves of prejudice and routine', in Fleurieu's words[13]*) were disregarded by the officers of the *grand corps*. In practice, relatively few French officers mastered such technicalities of oceanic navigation as lunar distances, and very few indeed cared to be too closely involved with the despised business of coastal pilotage – which was one of the reasons why French warships were so reluctant to enter the Channel.[14] The quality of French charts reflected this disdain. The Dépôt des Cartes, sometimes cited as an example of France's scientific advantage, was still reprinting the *Neptune françois* of 1693, from the original plates, eighty years after its first publication. Though French military engineers had long been accustomed to triangulated surveys, and in Britain Murdoch Mackenzie had pioneered the same technique for sea charts in the 1740s, the *Neptune françois* was an untriangulated chart which grossly deformed the coast of France. Brest, to name but one port of some interest to the French navy, was laid down thirty-five miles out of position.[15] In practice, the Enlightenment's determination to replace error and tradition with precise measurement was somewhat selective.

---

* 'Une classe d'hommes incapables de perfectionner, esclaves aveugles des préjugés & de la pratique.'

The disasters of the Seven Years War discredited a generation of French officers, and successive ministers tried to renew the officer corps by drawing on officers and civilian advisers from other backgrounds. At the age of thirty-three, the Comte d'Estaing was transformed overnight from a Lieutenant-General to a Rear-Admiral; Bougainville made his voyage round the world in the substantive rank of Colonel of Infantry. Bigot de Morogues came from the Artillery, Borda and Monge from the Engineers. Bourdé de Villehuet, Surville, Thévenard and Marion-Dufresne were officers of the Compagnie des Indes; Beaussier de l'Isle was a former warrant officer. Duhamel du Monceau was a by training a botanist and Pingré a theologian. What recommended them as candidates to transform the navy, was their scientific achievements. The officers of the Compagnie des Indes were the élite of French scientific navigators.[16] Bougainville was not transferred to the navy because of his distinguished fighting record as an infantryman but because, at twenty-two, he had published a work on integral calculus.[17] At the same period others like Verdun de la Crenne and Fleurieu who were already sea officers were promoted on account of their scientific distinction, not their war service.

This primacy of theory over practice, and of science over technology, was characteristic of France in the eighteenth century.[18] It was a natural product of the Cartesian approach, and even after Newton became popular in the 1740s, his ideas served more as a symbol of man's mastery of nature than as a guide to scientific method. In France the instinctive reaction to any problem was to seek the underlying system which would explain it. The philosopher-mathematician alone was qualified for the task, and by tracing the fundamental machinery of nature he demonstrated his superior intellectual and social standing.[19] 'Tracing' is the precise word, for geometry was a form of pure mathematics, and those whose subject could be expressed in geometrical terms enjoyed the highest scientific standing. Siege warfare was thus the most rational form of land war, replacing the untidy brutality of battle with the neat angles of ravelin and salient, and the military engineers who presented the spectacle of royal power in this perfect theatre of war were the most scientific of officers.[20] Writers on naval tactics, aspiring to the same status, expressed their subject in the same way by the use of complex diagrams closely modelled on contemporary editions of Euclid: these bore very little relation to the messy simplicity of real naval tactics, and the writers themselves had little experience of real battles,[21] but they carried an intellectual credibility which reality could never have done. Geometry produced perfect systems, and systems were the magic key to the most intractable problems.[22]

The best example of this approach is naval architecture. It is still possible to encounter histories influenced by a naïve Positivism, in which the French government's investment in scientific research is said to have led automatically to better French warship design.[23] This is sometimes illustrated by the changing titles of the shipbuilders. In France *maîtres charpentiers* became *maîtres constructeurs* and then simply *constructeurs*, before advancing to *ingénieurs-constructeurs* and finally becoming known as *architectes navales*, whereas in Britain warships were still being designed in the mid-nineteenth century by persons styled 'master shipwrights'.[24] The retention of a name drawn from the vulgar tongue, it is implied, must obviously indicate an unlettered craftsman confined to traditional rules, while a name derived from Latin must bespeak logic and education, and one based on Greek marks the summit of enlightened science.[25] Perhaps it is still necessary to point out that the different titles of shipbuilders tell us something about their social status but nothing whatever about their working methods.

This is not the place to offer more than a sketch of eighteenth-century French warship design but in outline it may be said that, from the 1730s until well into the nineteenth century, French ships of the line and frigates were large and, in particular, very long ships for their rate. Though they often drew more water than their British counterparts, their hulls were actually shallower in proportion. This fact, together with the virtual absence of lodging knees, meant a lack of longitudinal strength and a tendency rapidly to break their sheer. Lightly built and fastened with nails rather than trenails, they had high maintenance requirements and short working lives. Their rig was exceptionally taunt (lofty). All these features were directed to producing high initial speed, off the wind in fair weather, the quality on which constructors' reputations were judged.[26] Successive senior officers of the dockyards complained about the results.[27] As the Comte de Roquefeuil put it to the Minister in 1771:

> I cannot prevent myself, My Lord, from saying that in general the dockyard constructors are all frauds: they build ships which are very light, very long and very weakly fastened, because they sacrifice everything to speed and that is the way to get it.

The first cruise gives the ship and her builder their reputation. That is all they are interested in. I do not even exclude the ships of the line and frigates that M. Groignard has built at Lorient and elsewhere, which we have had to rebuild here at great expense for a second commission, by which time they have lost all their boasted speed.[28] *

This was the real problem of French naval architecture: the ships, in some ways impressive, were poorly adapted to France's strategic situation and especially to a war against Britain.[29]

French ministers and French shipwrights were not wholly indifferent to this issue. Throughout the eighteenth century they mounted repeated espionage missions designed to reveal the secrets of British warship design.[30] In general, however, they remained convinced that the real source of improvement lay not in learning from the enemy, nor from experience, but from science. It was a fundamental article of the Enlightenment faith that the philosopher was entitled and obliged to correct the work of the craftsman – and this, indeed, was part of the official duties of the French Académie Royale des Sciences.[31] As philosophers, gentlemen and mathematicians, its members were necessarily superior to mere practical experience. Thus Roquefeuil's remedy for the evils he identified was to recommend Borda as Inspector-General of Naval Construction: '[He] is *one of the most able geometers*, and I know no-one who seems better able to explain and perfect ship design, and to advise and enlighten you on the subject.'† He had already recommended Borda for this position in 1766: 'He would at first be just an inspector, but he would soon be in a position to correct, then direct and perfect the designs.'‡ Roquefeuil admitted that some practical experience might be desirable,

---

* 'Je ne puis m'empêcher, Monseigneur, de dire en général que M. M. les constructeurs des ports subalternes font tous des ouvrages de charlatan; ils font des bâtiments fort légers, fort longs et fort mal liés parce qu'ils sacrifient tout à la marche, et qu'ils sont bien certains de l'obtenir par là.

C'est la première campagne qui donne la réputation aux bâtiments et aux constructeurs. Voilà tout ce qu'on veut. Je n'en excepte pas même le sieur Groignard dans les vaisseaux et frégates qu'il a faites à Lorient et ailleurs, et que nous avons été obligé de relier, tout de nouveau icy, à grand frais, pour les mettre en état de faire de secondes campagnes où ces bâtiments perdent leur marche précédemment vantée.'
† 'M. le Chevalier de Borda de l'Académie des Sciences *est un des plus habile géomètres*, et je ne connais personne qui me paraisse plus capable d'éclaircir et de perfectionner la partie en construction et de vous donner des avis et des lumières sur cet objet.'
‡ 'Il n'aurait d'abord qu'un emploi d'examen; mais se trouverait bientôt en état de corriger, puis de diriger et de perfectionner ces mêmes constructions.'

specifically three or four weeks at the Ecole de Construction in Paris, but the thirty-three-year-old army engineer was chiefly qualified, in his patron's eyes, to 'direct and perfect' the shipbuilders because he was already one of the most distinguished geometers of his generation.[32]

This attitude was wholly typical of eighteenth-century France. However else they differed, French ministers were all convinced that it was the duty of officers and philosophers to correct the vulgar errors of the shipwrights, by the application of pure mathematics.[33] Some of this effort was devoted to hydrostatics, a subject in which a good deal of ground had already been cleared by the seventeenth-century Dutch mathematician Simon Stevin and others, and which yielded the important definition of the metacentre by the Swede, Chapman, and the Frenchman, Bouguer.[34] This was of some real utility to shipbuilders, though it did not stop French ships of the line being built which were too tender to carry sail.[35] Much more effort, however, was devoted to the prestigious subject of hydrodynamics and above all to the problem of determining the resistance of a hull moving through water. Twenty-three out of forty-eight prize subjects proposed by the Académie Royale des Sciences between 1720 and 1787 were on naval topics and resistance was the most popular of them.[36] Though some practical experiments were undertaken, this was above all a matter of pure theory and pure mathematics applied by metropolitan intellectuals, deriving its status precisely from its remoteness from actual shipbuilding or seafaring. The most eminent of these theorists was Leonhard Euler, author of the *Scientia Navalis* of 1749. Swiss by birth, resident in St Petersburg and publishing in Latin, he secured his scientific reputation by keeping himself and his work as far away as possible from any connection with real shipbuilding. A writer who begins his work by solemnly explaining to his readers that ships are intended to float was not addressing practical men.[37] Since all these theorists ignored the existence of skin friction, which we now know to constitute virtually the whole of resistance at the speeds of which these ships were capable, their work was completely valueless to the designer.[38] Some of it, indeed, was positively mischievous: Euler and Bossut won the Académie's 1761 prize with an essay arguing that the problem of pitching would be solved by loading the ships' ends to the maximum, precisely the worst possible proposal.[39]

At the time this did little harm, because in practice neither philosophers in Paris nor ministers in Versailles had much control over the constructors in the yards. One or two French naval ministers (notably Castries) even seem to have had an awareness that competition between the designers of different yards might be useful. What most ministers and all philosophers sought, however, was perfection, and the expression of perfection was a system. It was Borda (appointed, ironically enough, by Castries, with the intention of avoiding any one designer's system) who finally achieved it with the imposition of Sané's designs in the 1780s. Sané was a naval architect of talent but what really recommended him was that he was a young man in need of a patron and prepared to do what he was told. Since Borda was incapable of designing a ship himself he needed Sané to do the technical work, while he imposed the overall plan and took the credit for the perfect system. Perfection having been attained there was no more need of change, so French warship design ossified.[40]

In Britain the influence of Enlightenment ideas on the Navy was significantly moderated and diffused by the different nature of society and government. Scientific activity took place across a wider spectrum of society, and was much more connected with practical and even commercial objectives than in France. Newtonian rather than Cartesian ideas predominated and they were the ideas of the practical, deductive, English-speaking Newton of the *Opticks*, rather than the speculative Newton of the *Principia Mathematica*, whose rebarbative Latin was more praised than read.[41] Though the prevailing tone in high society for much of the eighteenth century was one of scepticism towards religion – and public religion was almost unknown in the Navy between 1715 and the 1790s[42] – Enlightenment thinkers did not target the Church as a citadel of reaction, as they did in France. This was partly because the Church of England had few defences and partly because, in Britain, religion remained an important component of social and scientific debate. In a more pluralistic society, differences of philosophy and of religion overlapped. Newton's heterodox disciple William Whiston, for example, was attacked for religious and scientific views which seemed equally erratic: he was at once a Latitudinarian and a Longitudinarian.[43] For many moralists and patriots, irreligion and speculative philosophy were connected with effeminacy and moral degeneracy, all imported from France to corrupt the upper classes. Manly English qualities were associated with the God-fearing and hard-working middle classes, and those gentlemen who chose to imitate their virtues. 'Systems' seemed to have threatening absolutist connotations: English liberties were expressed by initiative and invention.[44] The French Revolution and the notoriously radical political (and religious) views of English scientists like Priestley, only reinforced the association in the public mind between philosophy and subversion, algebra and atheism.[45] Pure, abstract science was therefore suspect; but practical thinking, applied to real problems, was regarded as admirable.

Britain, or rather England, seems to have been at its most 'French' in the late seventeenth and early eighteenth centuries, when Newton and Wallis worked on resistance, and Halley was commissioned as a captain in the Navy to undertake voyages to chart magnetic variation and the tidal streams of the Channel.[46] Later in the eighteenth century the state did not lose interest in science but it was more often sponsored indirectly, by 'Establishment' or quasi-state bodies like the Royal Society and the Board of Longitude in co-operation with the Navy and private interests, for motives practical and commercial rather than speculative.[47] Observations occupied a large place in these researches and even such eminent men as Nevil Maskelyne, the Astronomer Royal, were expected to go to sea in person to conduct them. The experimental method was understood in theory[48] and sometimes applied in practice by naval administrators. The Navy Board conducted controlled experiments on anti-fouling compounds and ventilators, among other things.[49] The Victualling Board experimented with different methods of curing meat and investigated its loss of weight in cooking.[50] The Sick and Wounded Board conducted trials of patent medicines and, in 1795, recommended the general isssue of lemon juice on the basis of experiments.[51]

The 'modernity' of all this should not be exaggerated. Most experiments were uncontrolled and such major decisions as the adoption of copper bottoms were based on scanty observations and a great deal of wishful thinking.[52] The characteristic approach of the age seems to have been to collect all sorts of information more or less at random, in the hope that it would prove useful. At Haslar Hospital, for example, James Lind was a pioneer in collecting medical statistics, but his information was disorganized and he seems to have had no clear idea of how to exploit it.[53] Medicine, moreover, was a subject dominated by Cartesian thinking until late in the century. Medical and scientific prestige attached, very much in the French style, to the product of pure reason applied from first principles, or at least derived from the classical authors read in the original languages, by educated gentlemen (which in the medical context meant English, not Scottish, physicians). In medical parlance the word 'empiric' indicated a charlatan, and a doctor who, like Lind, openly flirted with the experimental method was automatically condemned in the eyes of his peers. This changed towards the end of the century, when a more pragmatic and deductive approach became acceptable, and naval physicians – in particular Trotter and Blane – collected statistics and laid the foundations both of epidemiology and of public health.[54]

Medicine was not the only subject in which practical experience could be overriden by the prestige of theory. In the 1750s, for example, Dr Gowin Knight, with the backing of the Royal Society, successfully established himself as the Navy's expert on compasses and secured the adoption of an azimuth compass which he had designed (and patented), and which promised significant advantages. Unfortunately his very hasty trials did not reveal that the instrument was too flimsy for practical use. But here, too, the empiricists subsequently took over and by the end of the century such questions were being settled by co-operation between the professionals concerned; seamen and instrument makers. It is noteworthy that several instrument makers became Fellows of the Royal Society, something which would have been socially unthinkable in France.[55]

Perhaps the most characteristic 'scientific' activities in eighteenth-century England were joint operations conducted by gentlemen and craftsmen. Captain John Bentinck, for example, an officer and a gentleman (indeed, a Count of the Holy Roman Empire), developed his improved design of chain-pumps in co-operation with the civilian engineer William Coles.[56] The merits of the Bentinck-Coles chain-pumps, more than twice as efficient as French pumps, were soon reported to Versailles. However, in spite of inviting Coles to France, Sartine was unable to overcome the institutional barriers to innovation and French ships continued to sail, and on occasion to sink, with pumps of the old pattern. It was the same story with the Taylor block-making machinery, whose advantages the efficient French naval espionage network did not fail to report. In spite of the fullest information, including examples of the machines themselves, the Taylor system was not made to work in a French dockyard until 1795, more than thirty years after it had been adopted in Britain. Soon afterwards the Royal Navy moved on to the vastly superior machine tools designed by the French exile, Marc Brunel.[57] Episodes like this help to explain why British ships were, by common consent, very much better fitted with every sort of rig and equipment than their French counterparts.[58]

The English taste for practice over theory, and technology rather than science, lowered the psychological barriers which made the gentleman officer hestitate to master the skills of the navigator. Nevertheless, the professional standards of British officers rose only slowly. The loss of Sir Clowdisley Shovell in 1707 reveals deplorable practical navigation in the officers of his squadron and gross inaccuracy in the manuals they were using.[59] Though the social gulf between lieutenants and masters was much smaller in British than French ships, and British commissioned officers do not seem to have felt the same repugnance as their French counterparts towards coastal pilotage, as a matter of practice they did not care to navigate along the coasts of the British Isles (the approaches to the dockyard ports not excepted), without the assistance of a pilot as late as the 1760s.[60] It seems to have been only during the Revolutionary and Napoleonic Wars, and in part as a result of the prolonged inshore operations which these called for, that British officers became really skilled inshore navigators. Though there were officers who distinguished them-selves in scientific circles, the bulk of them were essentially experts in the practice of their profession, ignorant even of relevant facts known to philosophers, such as magnetic deviation, and unaware of the risks of stowing iron objects in or near the binnacle.[61]

In naval architecture, as in other areas, the British showed their preference for technology over science. There was a traditional sense of the essential connection between function and design, clearly expressed by Sir Anthony Deane in the seventeenth century[62] and well understood in the eighteenth.[63] In Britain, as in France, ships were designed by experts brought up in the trade, frequently the sons of shipbuilders before them, but there was a much weaker sense that they ought to be supervised by metropolitan theorists. Though British ship designers, like British professionals in comparable subjects such as architecture and engineering, continued to learn their business by apprenticeship until well into the nineteenth century, and though they were expected to spend a period working with their tools to understand the fundamentals of shipwrightry, the training they received in the mould lofts and drawing offices of the dockyards seems to have been in most respects as sophisticated as anything available in France.[64] The crisis of eighteenth-century British warship design occurred in the War of the Austrian Succession (1740–48) when the Navy encountered French and Spanish ships of new classes which were 50% or more larger than their British counterparts. The problem was one of size, not quality, and it was the product of institutional and political circumstances which had tended to arrest the development of British warship design since the end of the War of the Spanish Succession thirty years before. Neither the problem nor the solution had much to do with the skills of the constructors or the influence of scientific ideas; it was a question of persuading Parliament to finance larger classes of ships.[65] The chief exception to this is the frigate, which really was an important innovation in design adopted from France, but as far as the evidence goes its conception was due to the private genius of the constructor Blaise Ollivier at Brest, and certainly not to the input of any scientific ideas by Parisian intellectuals.[66]

Nevertheless, the mid-century crisis in British warship design had an important consequence in persuading a generation of sea officers and civilians that French and Spanish design was superior to British. The conviction helped to inspire a revival of the idea of model tests, directed as in France at the fashionable problem of resistance. Such tests had first been attempted in England by the engineer Sir Henry Sheres in the 1680s.[67] In the 1760s further model trials were mounted by the Society of Arts.[68] These trials precede those undertaken in 1777 by Borda, d'Alembert, Condorcet and Bossut in France, and by Chapman in Sweden in the 1790s,[69] and it is significant that they were sponsored by a body explicitly devoted, not to science, but to the practical improvement of arts and manufactures. A more French approach was adopted by the Society for the Improvement of Naval Architecture, founded in 1791 on a prospectus proclaiming that, 'It is also but too well known to all who have any skill in Naval Architecture, that the theory is not so well understood as it deserves; and that the French, actually surpassing us in this most important art, have derived many advantages from this superiority in time of war'.[70] This Society was patronized by men of social and scientific eminence, and undertook experiments of considerable sophistication. They yielded nothing of practical value to the shipbuilder, however, and the Society soon faded away as French-inspired pure science fell out of fashion.[71]

It is clear that both the British and the French navies of the eighteenth century embodied Enlightenment values to some extent, but they did so in different ways, reflecting the different societies to which they belonged. In France abstract Cartesian ideas expressed by pure science and mathematics predominated, whereas in Britain the dominant culture was Newtonian, deductive and pragmatic. To what extent the differences can be attributed to varying intellectual influences, as opposed to the different natures of the societies on which they played, is a matter of interpretation. Indeed, some caution if not scepticism is in order in assessing the real influence of the Enlightenment, even on navies, whose 'modern', technical and industrial character seems to make them such obvious candidates. Astronomy was essentially involved in the solution of the longitude problem, but with this important exception pure science was generally ineffectual on both sides of the Channel, and the limited practical contribution it made to naval affairs was largely to darken counsel and retard the advance of knowledge. Not until the nineteenth century did most of the relevant sciences reach the stage at which they could make a practical contribution of real value. Only a small proportion of officers in either navy were directly involved in exploration or any other 'scientific' activity.[72] In the long run the most decisive intellectual change over the century was surely the rise of a deductive, inventive culture, which in time led on to the technical and industrial revolutions and the diffusion of the experimental method. In this Britain led the way but it seems doubtful that the Enlightenment can be made primarily responsible. In historical tradition, the Enlightenment has been seen very much in the nineteenth-century mould as the record of a small number of great men, most of them great Frenchmen.[73] If this is just, it is hard to rate the Enlightenment as a dominant influence on the Royal Navy or on English society, except in the very indirect sense that the French Revolution subsequently changed everybody's mental and political world. Even in France, where matters naval occupied a prominent place in the discourse of Enlightenment thinkers, it was largely an imaginary navy to which they referred. Naval technology figures prominently in the *Grande encyclopédie*, but it is the obsolete technology of the seventeenth century, deployed for symbolic rather than practical value. Panckoucke's *Encyclopédie méthodique marine* of 1783–87 was up to date with its information but it was condemned by Bézout and others for adding nothing to theory.[74] From the point of view of the majority of French sea officers, administrators and constructors, many Enlightenment ideas appeared as irrelevancies if not as threats. They were proposed by the new officers intruded from other services, whose presence was so much resented. In time, the Enlightenment came to be indelibly connected with political and moral ideas which were deeply unpopular in Britain from the 1790s and out of favour in the France of the Restoration. The navies of the eighteenth century were certainly complex organizations, dependent on the mastery of advanced technology, but they had been that for centuries before the Enlightenment was thought of. Its direct impact on the navies of the day, as opposed to its indirect, long-term influence on the societies which sustained them, seems in truth to have been rather limited.

Notes

1. 'Le fer de lance des Lumières'; quoted in Michel Vergé-Franceschi, 'Un enseignement éclairé au XVIIIe siècle: l'enseignement maritime dispensé aux gardes', *Revue Historique*, 278 (1986), 29–55 (p. 30).

2. Martine Acerra and Jean Meyer, *Marines et Révolution* (Rennes, 1988), 118. Philippe Masson and José Muracciole, *Napoléon et la Marine* (Paris, 1968), 15. Etienne Taillemite, *L'histoire ignorée de la Marine Française* (Paris, 1988), 263–67. Peter Mathias, 'Who Unbound Prometheus? Science and Technical Change, 1600–1800', in *The Transformation of England* [collected papers] (London, 1979), at pp. 50–51. Richard Harding, *The Evolution of the Sailing Navy, 1509–1815* (Basingstoke, 1995), 88. *España y el ultramar hispánico hasta la Illustración: Jornadas de Historia Naval, No. 1* (Madrid, 1989). José Cervera Pery, *La Marina de la Ilustración (Resurgimiento y crisis del poder naval)* (Madrid, 1986), 201–04. María Dolores Higueras Rodríguez, 'Desarrollo de la Armada española en el siglo XVIII: institucionalización de la ciencias náuticas', *Revista de Historia Naval*, 6 (1988), 21, pp. 19–35. Ricardo Arroyo, 'Les enseñanzas de náutica en el siglo XVIII', *Revista de Historia Naval*, 12 (1994), 46, pp. 7–30.

3. Roy Porter, *The Enlightenment* (Basingstoke, 1990), 32–36. Thomas Munck, *The Enlightenment: A Comparative Social History 1721–1794* (London, 2000), 8. William Doyle, *The Old European Order, 1660–1800*, 2nd edn (Oxford, 1992), 174–75. Thomas L. Hankins, *Science and the Enlightenment* (Cambridge, 1985), 1–3, 16.

4. Olivier Chapuis, *À la mer comme au ciel: Beautemps-Beaupré et la naissance de l'hydrographie moderne (1700–1850)* (Paris, 1999), 24–30. Norman Hampson, 'The Enlightenment in France', in Roy Porter and Mikuláš Teich (eds), *The Enlightenment in National Context* (Cambridge, 1981), 41–53 (pp. 41–42). Jan Golinski, 'Astronomy', in John W. Yolton *et al.* (eds), *The Blackwell Companion to the Enlightenment* (Oxford, 1991), 44–45. Roy Porter, *Enlightenment: Britain and the Creation of the Modern World* (London, 2000), 53–54, 149, 214 and 354. Azar Gat, *The Origins of Military Thought, from the Enlightenment to Clausewitz* (Oxford, 1989), 27.

5. Naval freemasonry is a very obscure subject. It certainly existed but what little

evidence I have seen suggests that in the Royal Navy at least it may have been most common among junior and warrant officers, and used by senior officers mainly as a convenient entrée into good society in foreign ports. See, for example, Henry Sadler, *Thomas Dunckerley, His Life, Labours and Letters* (London, 1891); Philip Jenkins, *The Making of a Ruling Class: The Glamorgan Gentry, 1640–1790* (Cambridge, 1983), 64; David Erskine (ed.), *Augustus Hervey's Journal* (London, 1953), 144; W. G. Perrin and Christopher Lloyd (eds), *The Keith Papers* (NRS; vols 62, 90 and 96, 1927–55), I, 416; J. H. Lepper, 'Freemasonry and the Sea', *Transactions of the Manchester Association for Masonic Research*, 36 (1946), 54–74. A case of freemasonry among French privateersmen is mentioned by Henri Malo, *Les corsaires: mémoires et documents inédits* (Paris, 1908), 155–56.

6. Roy Porter, 'Mixed Feelings: the Enlightenment and sexuality in eighteenth-century Britain', in Paul-Gabriel Boucé (ed.), *Sexuality in eighteenth-century Britain* (Manchester, 1982), 1–27.

7. And of course other navies, but in the context of a paper prepared for a Franco-British conference, I concentrate on these two.

8. Hankins, *Science and the Enlightenment*, 11–12, 20–21 and 2–29. Keith Thomas, 'Numeracy in Early Modern England', *Transactions of the Royal Historical Society*, 5th s. 38 (1987), 103–32. John Brewer, *The Sinews of Power: War, Money and the English State, 1688–1783* (London, 1989), 228–30. Patricia Fara, *Sympathetic Attractions: Magnetic Practices, Beliefs, and Symbolism in Eighteenth-Century England* (Princeton, 1996), 21, 123–24 and 145.

9. James Pritchard, 'From Shipwright to Naval Constructor: The Professionalization of 18th-Century French Naval Shipbuilders', *Technology and Culture*, 28 (1987), 1–25 (pp. 16–19). H. L. Duhamel du Monceau, *Elémens de l'architecture navale, ou traité pratique de la construction des vaisseaux*, 2nd edn (Paris, 1758), vi.

10. Hankins, *Science and the Enlightenment*, 47.

11. Geoffrey Holmes, *The Making of a Great Power: Late Stuart and Early Georgian Britain 1660–1722* (London, 1993), 259–61. James C. Riley, *International Government Finance and the Amsterdam Capital Market, 1740–1815* (Cambridge, 1980), 104–12. Idem, *The Seven Years War and the Old Regime in France: The Economic and Financial Toll* (Princeton, 1986), 170–76.

12. Roger Hahn, 'L'enseignement scientifique des gardes de la marine au XVIIIe siècle', in René Taton (ed.), *Enseignement et diffusion des sciences en France au XVIIIe siècle* (Paris, 1964), 547–58. Vergé-Franceschi, 'Un enseignement éclairé'.

13. Chapuis, *Beautemps-Beaupré*, 47 and 147.

14. Chapuis, *Beautemps-Beaupré*, 29–30, 47, 72, 136–37, 147 and 150. Acerra and Meyer, *Marines et Révolution*, 75 and 118.

15. Chapuis, *Beautemps-Beaupré*, 101–28.

16. Philippe Haudrère, 'Les officiers des vaisseaux de la Compagnie des Indes: un corps d'élite dans la Marine Française du XVIIIe siècle', *Histoire, Economie et Société*, 16 (1997), 117–24.

17. Michel Vergé-Franceschi, *Marine et Education sous l'Ancien Régime* (Paris, 1991), 258–61. Jean Mascart, *La vie et les travaux du Chevalier Jean-Charles de Borda (1733–1799): Épisodes de la vie scientifique au XVIIIe siècle* (Lyon, 1919), 286. Chapuis, *Beautemps-Beaupré*, 136–37.

18. Cf. A. R. Hall, *Ballistics in the Seventeenth Century* (Cambridge, 1952), 163–64.

19. Hankins, *Science and the Enlightenment*, 9–10. Gat, *Origins of Military Thought*, 26–27.

20. Ken Alder, *Engineering the Revolution: Arms and Enlightenment in France, 1763–1815* (Princeton, 1997), 33–34. Hankins, *Science and the Enlightenment*, 11–12.

21. The principal seventeenth- and eighteenth-century writers on naval tactics were Hoste (a Jesuit naval chaplain), Bigot de Morogues (an artilleryman turned sea officer), Bourdé de Villehuet (of the Compagnie des Indes), du Pavillon (an infantryman turned sea officer), Verdun de la Crenne, Grenier and d'Amblimont (all sea officers) and Clerk of Eldin (a merchant). None of them ever commanded a fleet.

22. Michel Depeyre, *Tactiques et stratégies navales de la France et du Royaume-Uni de 1690 à 1815* (Paris, 1998), 263–88. N. A. M. Rodger, 'Image and Reality in eighteenth-century Naval Tactics', *MM*, 89 (2003), 280–96.

23. For example, Daniel G. Harris, *F. H. Chapman: The First Naval Architect and his Work* (London, 1989), 11–18; Daniel A. Baugh, *British Naval Administration in the Age of Walpole* (Princeton, 1965), 251–53.

24. Pritchard, 'Shipwright to Naval Constructor'. Martine Acerra, 'Les constructeurs de la marine (xviie–xviiie siècle)', *Revue Historique*, 273 (1985), 283–304.

25. Martine Acerra and André Zysberg, *L'essor des marines de guerres européennes, 1680–1790* (Paris, 1997), 121–30. Martine Acerra, *Rochefort et la construction navale française, 1661–1815*, 4 vols (Paris, 1993), II, 433–70. Jean Boudriot and Hubert Berti, *The History of the French Frigate 1650–1850*, trans. David H. Roberts (Rotherfield, East Sussex, 1993), 36–37.

26. Acerra and Meyer, *Marines et Révolution*, 74–75. Sylviane Llinares, *Marine, propulsion et technique: l'évolution du système technologique du navire de guerre français au XVIIIe siècle*, 1 vol. in 2 (Paris, 1994), I, 99–102. Jean Meyer, 'L'évolution de la guerre marine et de son matérial (1650–1815)', in Martine Acerra, José Merino and Jean Meyer (eds), *Les Marines de Guerre Européennes, XVII–XVIIIe siècles* (Paris, 1985), 123–46 (pp. 141–45). J. Bourdé de Villehuet, *Le Manoeuvrier, ou Essai sur la Théorie et la Pratique des Mouvements du Navire et des Évolutions Navales* (Paris, 1765), 190–92.

27. Pritchard, 'Shipwright to Naval Constructor', 14.

28. Mascart, *Borda*, 390–91.

29. Argued in more detail in N. A. M. Rodger, 'Form and Function in European Navies, 1660–1815', in Leo Akveld *et al.* (eds), *In het kielzog: Maritiem-historische studies aangeboden aan Jaap R. Bruijn bij zijn vertrek als hoogleraar zeegeschiedenis aan de Universiteit Leiden* (Amsterdam, 2003), 85–97.

30. [Blaise Ollivier], *18th-Century Shipbuilding: Remarks on the Navies of the English & the Dutch ...*, trans. and ed. by David H. Roberts (Rotherfield, East Sussex, 1992), 25–30.

31. Hankins, *Science and the Enlightenment*, 171–73. J. R. Harris, *Industrial Espionage and Technology Transfer: Britain and France in the Eighteenth Century* (Aldershot, 1998), 561–562. Robin Briggs, 'The Académie Royale des Sciences and the Pursuit of Utility', *Past and Present*, 131 (1991), 38–88.

32. Mascart, *Borda*, 144, 147 and 391.

33. René Mémain, *La marine de guerre sous Louis XIV: Le matériel, Rochefort, arsenal modèle de Colbert* (Paris, 1937), 697–99.

34. Gerhard Timmerman, *Das Eindringen der Naturwissenschaft in das Schiffbauhandwerk*

(Munich, 1962), 15. Harris, *Chapman*, 74–83. Brian Lavery, *The Ship of the Line*, 2 vols (London, 1983–84), II, 23. Llinares, *Marine, propulsion et technique*, I, 154–56. Jean Boudriot, *The Seventy-Four Gun Ship: A Practical Treatise on the Art of Naval Architecture*, trans. by David H. Roberts, 4 vols (Rotherfield, East Sussex, 1986–88), I, 30–33.

35. Llinares, *Marine, propulsion et technique*, I, 158. Patrick Villiers, *Marine Royale, Corsaires et Trafic dans l'Atlantique de Louis XIV à Louis XVI*, 2 vols (Dunkirk, 1991), II, 695–96.

36. Llinares, *Marine, propulsion et technique*, I, 91–92.

37. 'Primo enim omnes naves ad natandum aptae esse debent, in hocque ipsa navium essentia continentur: …': Leonhard Euler, *Scientia Navalis seu Tractatus de construendis ac dirigendis Navibus*, 2 vols (St Petersburg, 1749,) II, 2.

38. John Fincham, *A History of Naval Architecture* (London, 1851), xiii and xlvi–xlix. Jean Boudriot and Hubert Berti, *Les vaisseaux de 50 et 64 canons: Étude historique 1650–1780* (Paris, 1994), 11–13 and 23–27. Mascart, *Borda*, 83–90. C. Truesdell, 'Euler's Contribution to the Theory of Ships and Mechanics', *Centaurus*, 28 (1983), 323–35. Pritchard, 'Shipwright to Naval Constructor', 16–17. Timmerman, *Das Eindringen der Naturwissenschaft*, 27–28. Meyer, 'L'évolution de la guerre marine', 129–36. David K. Brown, 'The Form and Speed of Sailing Warships', *MM*, 84 (1998), 298–307.

39. Llinares, *Marine, propulsion et technique*, I, 154–56.

40. Acerra, *Rochefort*, II, 361–66. Meyer, 'L'évolution de la guerre marine', 124–33. Acerra and Meyer, *Marines et Révolution*, 66–72. Mascart, *Borda*, 481–83.

41. Jan Golinski, 'Science, experimental' and 'Scientific method' in Yolton (ed.), *The Blackwell Companion to the Enlightenment*, 476–78. Antoine Picon, 'Technique', in Michel Delon (ed.), *Dictionnaire européen des Lumières* (Paris, 1997), 1025–30. Fara, *Sympathetic Attractions*, 15–21. Porter, *Enlightenment: Britain*, 134–42. Porter, 'The Enlightenment in England'. John Ehrman, *The Navy in the War of William III, 1689–1697: Its State and Direction* (Cambridge, 1953), 14–18.

42. N. A. M. Rodger, 'The Naval Chaplain in the Eighteenth Century', *British Journal for Eighteenth-Century Studies*, 18 (1995),33–45.

43. Fara, *Sympathetic Attractions*, 25–27 and 99. Successor to Newton's mathematical chair at Cambridge, Whiston was evicted from it in 1710 for his religious views. His eccentric later contributions to the longitude problem nevertheless instigated the Longitude Act of 1714.

44. [John Brown] *An Estimate of the Manners and Principles of the Times*, 2 vols (London, 1757–58). Gerald Newman, *The Rise of English Nationalism: A Cultural History, 1740–1830* (London, 1987), 80–82, 92, 151, 194, 213–21. Porter, *Enlightenment: Britain*, 215.

45. Newman, *English Nationalism*, 230–31. Fara, *Sympathetic Attractions*, 130–31. B. Keith-Lucas, 'Some Influences Affecting the Development of Sanitary Legislation in England', *Economic History Review*, 2nd. s. 4 (1953–54), 290–96 (p. 291).

46. Lavery, *Ship of the Line*, II, 14–17. Alan Cooke, *Edmond Halley: Charting the Heavens and the Seas* (Oxford, 1998), 256–90.

47. Daniel A. Baugh, 'Seapower and Science: The Motives for Pacific Exploration', in Derek Howse (ed.), *Background to Discovery: Pacific Exploration from Dampier to Cook* (Berkeley, Calif., 1990), 1–55. Margaret Deacon, *Scientists and the Sea, 1650–1900: A Study of Marine Science*, 2nd edn (Aldershot, 1997) 189–90. Constantine John

Phipps, *A Voyage towards the North Pole Undertaken by His Majesty's Command 1773* (London, 1774). Derek Howse, *Nevil Maskelyne, The Seaman's Astronomer* (Cambridge, 1989). David Mackay, 'A Presiding Genius of Exploration: Banks, Cook, and Empire, 1767–1805', in Robin Fisher and Hugh Johnston (eds), *Captain James Cook and his Times* (Seattle, 1979), 21–39. Idem, *In the Wake of Cook: Exploration, Science and Empire, 1780–1801* (London, 1985), 5–11. John Gascoigne, *Science in the Service of Empire: Joseph Banks, the British State and the Uses of Science in the Age of Revolution* (Cambridge, 1998), 24–33.

48. By Bishop Berkeley: Lester S. King, *The Medical World of the Eighteenth Century* (Chicago, 1958), 42–43.

49. TNA: PRO ADM 95/17, pp. 58, 68, 69, 82, 91 and 216; TNA: PRO ADM 106/2082, 29 July 1772.

50. Historical Manuscripts Commission, no. 61, *Report on the Manuscripts of Lady Du Cane* (1905), 123. Daniel A. Baugh (ed.), *Naval Administration, 1715–1750* (NRS; vol. 120, 1977), 441–42. TNA: PRO ADM 30/44, pp. 60–61.

51. R. D. Merriman (ed.), *The Sergison Papers* (NRS; vol. 89, 1950), 221–22. TNA: PRO ADM 98/17, pp. 137–39. P. K. Crimmin, 'The Sick and Hurt Board and the health of seamen, *c.* 1700–1806', *Journal for Maritime Research* (www.nmm.ac.uk/jmr), Dec. 1999.

52. R. J. B. Knight, 'The Introduction of Copper Sheathing into the Royal Navy, 1779–1786', *MM*, 59 (1973), 299–309. John E. Talbott, *The Pen and Ink Sailor: Charles Middleton and the King's Navy, 1778–1813* (London, 1998), 45–60.

53. Ulrich Troehler, 'Towards Clinical Investigation on a Numerical Basis: James Lind at Haslar Hospital, 1758–1783', *Actas XXVII Congreso Internacional de Historia de la Medicina* (Barcelona, 1981), 414–19.

54. Peter Mathias, 'Swords and Ploughshares: the armed forces, medicine and public health in the late eighteenth century', in J. M. Winter (ed.), *War and Economic Development: Essays in Memory of David Joslin* (Cambridge, 1975), 73–90. Harold J. Cook, 'Practical Medicine and the British Armed Forces after the "Glorious Revolution"', *Medical History*, 34 (1990), 1–26. J. J. Keevil, C. C. Lloyd and J. L. S. Coulter, *Medicine and the Navy, 1200–1900*, 4 vols (Edinburgh, 1957–63), III, 41–46. N. A. M. Rodger, 'Medicine and Science in the British Navy of the Eighteenth Century', in Christian Buchet (ed.), *L'homme, la santé et la mer* (Paris, 1997), 333–44. Michael Bartholomew, 'James Lind and Scurvy: a Revaluation', *Journal of Maritime Research*, Jan. 2002. Gilbert Blane, *Observations on the Diseases of Seamen*, 3rd edn (London, 1799), xvi–xvii. Kenneth J. Carpenter, *The History of Scurvy and Vitamin C* (Cambridge, 1986), 40–96.

55. Fara, *Sympathetic Attractions*, 17, 70–88. (See also p. 33, n. 32 below.)

56. Brian Lavery, *The Arming and Fitting of English Ships of War, 1600–1815* (London, 1987), 72–8. Peter Goodwin, *The Construction and Fitting of the Sailing Man of War, 1650–1850* (London, 1987), 138–42. Thomas J. Oertling, *Ships' Bilge Pumps: A History of their Development, 1500–1900* (College Station, Texas, 1996), 56–73.

57. Llinares, *Marine, propulsion et technique*, I, 135–42. Harris, *Industrial Espionage*, 439–48, rates the French success with the Taylor system rather higher.

58. Llinares, *Marine, propulsion et technique*, I, 99–142 and 177–201; II, 351–52.

59. W. E. May, 'The Last Voyage of Sir Clowdisley Shovel', *Journal of the Institute of Navigation*, 13 (1960), 324–32.

60. N. A. M. Rodger, *The Wooden World: An Anatomy of the Georgian Navy* (London, 1986), 48–49.
61. Fara, *Sympathetic Attractions*, 86.
62. J. R. Tanner (ed.), *Samuel Pepys's Naval Minutes* (NRS; vol. 60, 1926), 9.
63. John B. Hattendorf *et al.* (eds), *British Naval Documents, 1204–1960* (NRS; vol. 131, 1993), 493–95.
64. Picon, 'Technique'. Lavery, *Ship of the Line*, II, 17–25. Ollivier, *Shipbuilding*, 139–44. Robert Gardiner, *Frigates of the Napoleonic Wars* (London, 2000).
65. Gardiner, *Frigates*, 139–41.
66. Robert Gardiner, *The First Frigates: Nine-Pounder and Twelve-Pounder Frigates, 1748–1815* (London, 1992). Boudriot and Berti, *The French Frigate*, 68–137.
67. Lavery, *Ship of the Line*, II, 14.
68. Basil Harley, 'The Society of Arts' Model Ship Trials, 1758–1763', *Transactions of the Newcomen Society*, 63 (1991–92), 53–71.
69. Timmerman, *Das Eindringen der Naturwissenschaft*, 27–28. Fredrik Henrik af Chapman, *Architectura Navalis Mercatoria* (Stockholm, 1768; repr. New York, 1968, with the addition of part of his *Tractat om Skepps-Byggeriet* (1775) as trans. by James Inman, 1820), 81–83. Harris, *Chapman*, 168–69.
70. NMM MID/8/1/38.
71. A. W. Johns, 'An Account of the Society for the Improvement of Naval Architecture', *Transactions of the Institution of Naval Architects*, 52 (1910), 28–40. John Charnock, *History of Marine Architecture*, 3 vols (London, 1801), III, 386–402.
72. Cf. Thea Roodhuyzen, *In Woelig Vaarwater: Marineofficieren in de jaren 1779–1802* (Amsterdam, 1998), 36–37, for a similar view of Dutch officers.
73. Porter, 'The Enlightenment in England', 3–4. Recent surveys like Hankins, *Science and the Enlightenment*, still adopt this approach.
74. Llinares, *Marine, propulsion et technique*, I, 86–89.

XV

Commissioned Officers' Careers in the Royal Navy, 1690–1815*

Introduction

Anyone who has ever investigated the social history of the Royal Navy in the eighteenth century, and particularly the history of its officers, will have encountered a surprising lack of basic information. Although we possess an alphabetical list of the commissioned officers of the Navy, lately re-issued by the Navy Records Society,[1] there is no printed source which can tell us how many officers there were in the Navy at any time. The question of how the Navy was manned presents the modern historian (as it presented the contemporary naval administrator) with many difficulties, but at least the number of men serving in particular years is easily discovered.[2] Though personal information about officers is much more plentiful than about men, with statistics the situation is reversed. There is no means of knowing whether the supply of officers in each rank matched the demand, and whether the relationship between supply and demand changed over time. We have no quantitive information as to when and at what stages in their careers officers were promoted. As a consequence we cannot tell precisely how the commissioned officer corps as a whole developed, and we have no context in which to place the careers of individuals. We cannot exactly tell if, or how, particular officers were lucky or unlucky in their careers, because we cannot say what were the normal expectations of officers of their generation.

This paper is an attempt to sketch some preliminary answers to these basic questions. Although there are records of officers' commissions from 1660, the years 1660 to 1689 have been omitted because the structure of rank and the concept of seniority were so loose that it is not possible to analyse career

---

[1]   *The Commissioned Sea Officers of the Royal Navy, 1660–1815*, ed. David Syrett & R.L. DiNardo (Navy Records Society Occasional Publications Vol. 1, 1994). This is a new edition of a compilation originally issued in typescript by the National Maritime Museum in 1954.

[2]   Christopher Lloyd, *The British Seaman 1200–1860: A Social Survey* (London, 1968), pp. 286–289.

* Reprinted by permission of the National Maritime Museum, Greenwich.

progression statistically in any realistic fashion. After 1815 better Admiralty record-keeping, and the official *Navy List*, provide evidence of much greater detail and accuracy, but that is material for another study. This paper rests on sketchy research into unsatisfactory primary sources, for the most part inaccurate, incomplete and inconsistent. The resulting statistics are far from reliable, and should certainly not be used as more than a general indication of trends, but they do provide at least an elementary impression of sea officers' careers, which helps to make sense of much that is already known in British naval history, and to point to some topics of future investigation.

Occasional attempts have already been made to measure the size of the commissioned officer corps. We know that the 1715 peace establishment provided for seventy ships in commission, requiring 70 Captains and 98 Lieutenants out of totals of 258 and 359 respectively.[3] We are told that there were 367 Lieutenants in 1739, 640 in 1748, 880 in 1763, 1,349 in 1783, and 3,270 in 1813.[4] A Parliamentary return of 1833 offered the following figures:

Table 1

1784	2,230 officers, of whom	567 (25%) were serving afloat
1800	3,168	1,892 (60%)
1810	4,549	2,007 (44%)
1816	5,868	880 (15%)
1784	1,499 Lieutenants, of whom	397 (26%) were serving afloat
1792	1,441	260 (18%)
1800	2,120	1,439 (68%)
1810	3,097	1,538 (50%)
1816	3,994	670 (17%)

Source: Naval Promotions (HC 1833 XXIV p. 279) p. 282. In the context it is clear that 'officers' here means commissioned officers, but it is not stated whether the figures were taken at one particular date in each year or averaged over twelve months.

---

[3]   *Queen Anne's Navy: Documents concerning the Administration of the Navy of Queen Anne, 1702–1714*, ed. R.D. Merriman (Navy Records Society [NRS] Vol. 103, 1961), p. 315. *Naval Administration 1715–1750*, ed. Daniel A. Baugh (NRS Vol. 120, 1977), pp. 43–45.

[4]   Daniel A. Baugh, 'The Eighteenth-Century Navy as a National Institution, 1690–1815', in *The Oxford Illustrated History of the Royal Navy* ed. J.R. Hill (Oxford, 1995), pp.120–160, at p. 120. H.W. Richmond in *Johnson's England: An Account of the Life and Manners of his Age*, ed. A.S. Turberville (Oxford, 1933, 2 vols), I, 59.

This tells us that most officers were unemployed in peacetime, which will surprise nobody familiar with the period, but it also suggests that the proportion of officers employed during the Napoleonic War was low and falling. This does not seem natural, and raises some important questions which it is impossible to answer without comparable figures for earlier wars. Another set of figures covering the Napoleonic War allows us to compare the number of officers with the number of ships and the total tonnage of the Navy between 1805 and 1815.

Table 2

	1803	1804	1805	1806	1807	1808	1809	1810	1811	1812	1813	1814	1815
FO	132	123	149	161	159	161	176	170	181	187	201	209	219
Capts	668	673	639	617	693	700	689	725	753	777	802	798	824
Cdrs	413	409	422	416	502	501	543	608	558	566	602	628	762
Lts	2480	2457	2472	2437	2728	2912	3036	3114	3071	3163	3268	3285	3211
Tot	3693	3662	3682	3631	4082	4274	4444	4617	4563	4693	4873	4920	5016
Line	111	115	116	120	123	126	127	124	124	120	124	118	109
All	388	423	543	590	657	673	728	699	657	623	610	637	554

Source: William Laird Clowes, *The Royal Navy: A History from the Earliest Times to the Present* (London, 1897–1903, 7 vols) V, 9–10. The categories are flag officers, captains, commanders, lieutenants, total officers, ships of the line, and all ships. Clowes gives no indication of the sources of his figures, nor how they were compiled.

This table roughly agrees with the 1833 Parliamentary return's figures, and suggests some questions of its own. The increase in the total number of officers over these twelve years is more or less proportional to the increase in the total number of ships of all sizes, though the number of ships of the line actually fell slightly over the same time. Was this characteristic? Why did the proportion of Commanders rise so much faster than that of Captains or Lieutenants? Why did the Navy need more admirals than battleships? In the seventy years from 1743 to 1813 the tonnage of the Navy increased by rather less than three times,[5] and the number of flag officers by twenty-five times.

---

[5]   Jan Glete, *Navies and Nations: Warships, Navies and State Building in Europe and America, 1500–1860* (Stockholm, 1993, 2 vols), II, 551–553.

These fragmentary figures raise more questions than they answer, and they conceal a critical problem. All of them are cast in terms of the total number of officers of a given rank at a given date, and the unwary reader might naturally assume that these were officers 'on the Active List', in modern parlance; available to serve. Unfortunately for the historian, there is no doubt that some officers remained on the official lists even though they were no longer fit to serve.[6] An unknown, and probably variable proportion of the officers listed in the tables above, and in all other figures deriveable from the Admiralty's official lists, were not in practice available for service. The true supply of officers was less than it appears to be, by a factor which it is extremely difficult to estimate. This is the crux of the statistical problem which this paper addresses, for it is impossible to analyse any trends or developments without at least a rough idea of the number of officers who were really available for service.

Rank Structure

First it is necessary to offer a brief sketch of the commissioned officers' ranks and their development over the century and a quarter of this study.[7] At the summit stood the admirals. There were eight flag officers' ranks: Admirals of the White and Blue, Vice-Admirals and Rear-Admirals of the Red, White and Blue. Until 1743 there was in principle only one officer of each of these ranks By that time the Navy was acutely short of admirals, and as soon as George II was persuaded to allow a multiplication of flag officers, their numbers increased rapidly. The growing complexity and scale of naval warfare required ever more flag officers at sea, and as operations came to be carried on in all seasons, with very prolonged cruises and blockades (especially during the Great Wars against France), the physical strain on admirals, and the rate at which they had to be relieved, seem to have increased. Above the eight admirals' ranks there might be an Admiral of the Fleet (very seldom still active), and in 1805 the rank of Admiral of the Red was created. For the purposes of this study all flag officers have been lumped together.

Below them were two, later three permanent ranks. Captains were always known in the eighteenth-century as 'Post Captains', because the title of 'Captain'

---

[6]   Daniel A. Baugh, *British Naval Administration in the Age of Walpole* (Princeton, 1965), pp. 102–108.

[7]   This sketch is based on Michael Lewis, *England's Sea-Officers: The Story of the Naval Profession* (London, 1939), pp. 177–224; Merriman, *Queen Anne's Navy*, pp. 309–335; Baugh, *Age of Walpole* pp. 127–146 and *Naval Administration*, pp. 35–88; N.A.M. Rodger, *The Wooden World; An Anatomy of the Georgian Navy* (London, 1986), pp. 16–19; & *Naval Records for Genealogists* (H.M.S.O., 2nd edn. 1988; 3rd edn. PRO 1998), pp. 13–20.

was given to all officers who commanded ships ('commanders', in contemporary parlance) regardless of their rank. They reached this rank, or 'took post', by virtue of their first commission to command a 'post ship', meaning one of the 5th Rate or larger (6th Rate from 1713), for in this period only admirals held rank in the Navy as a whole, independent of appointments to a named ship. Since admirals were promoted only from the top of the Captains' List, it was crucial to an officer's career to take post as young as possible. One of the simplest and most telling indicators of an officer's professional fortunes is his age on reaching post rank, or the time elapsed since his first commission as Lieutenant.[8]

Captains might hold the temporary rank of Commodore. The word was borrowed from the Dutch in the seventeenth century, and initially referred to the senior officer for the time being of any group of ships not in the presence of an admiral. Initially in the Downs only, and later elsewhere, the senior Captain present would hoist a broad pendant and assume the title of 'Commodore' until some more senior officer appeared.[9] In the eighteenth century the Commodore evolved into two distinct quasi-ranks, often called Commodore 'with a captain' and 'with a pendant', and formally distinguished in 1805 as First and Second Class Commodores. The Commodore with a flag-captain was a Captain appointed by the Admiralty as commander-in-chief of a squadron or station, and was for all practical purposes (including pay and uniform) a temporary Rear-Admiral. The Commodore with a pendant (i.e. with a pendant alone) was a senior Captain ordered by his commander-in-chief to hoist a broad pendant and command a detached squadron or a division of the fleet; for example when an admiral commanding a squadron large enough to be divided into the traditional three divisions found himself with only one junior flag officer, he would order the senior Captain to hoist a pendant and command the rear division. Such a Commodore commanded his own ship and received no extra pay. In principle a Commodore could be chosen from anywhere in the Captains' List, and during the Seven Years War Lord Anson used the rank with some freedom to obtain active commanders-in-chief who were not yet senior enough to be made admirals, but it was regarded as impossible for a Commodore to command Captains senior to himself, and as

---

[8]   Baugh, *Age of Walpole*, pp. 132–135 prints a table giving the seniority in post rank of admirals made between 1739 and 1748. This is interesting, but it is largely a measure of the length of the captain's list, and hence the varying prospects of different generations, for which purpose ten years is too short a period to show any significant variation. What distinguished officers of any given generation was how quickly they joined the bottom of that list.

[9]   *A Descriptive Catalogue of the Naval Manuscrits in the Pepysian Library*, ed. J.R. Tanner (NRS Vols. 27, 27, 36 & 57, 1903–23) II, 400 & 111, 98. *Three Sea Journals of Stuart Times*, ed. Bruce S. Ingram (London, 1936), p. 120.

a rule the Commodore was near the top of the Captains' List and on his way to becoming a Rear-Admiral. For the purposes of this study Commodore, as a temporary rank, has not been distinguished from Captain.

Below Post-Captain came another quasi-rank, that of Master and Commander. These officers were originally the commanding officers ('commanders', in the language of the time) of small men of war of the 6th Rate and below, which were not allowed Masters for navigation purposes. In social terms the officers' entry and training system instituted in the 1670s envisaged that this rank would be occupied by men of humble birth, from the lower deck or the merchant service, who would normally rise no further. Meanwhile young gentlemen would enter the Navy under royal patronage as 'Volunteers per Order', and proceed in due course to become Lieutenants and so directly to Post-Captain. This was very similar to the system which the French navy adopted at this period, and retained until the 1790s. In the English service, however, practice never corresponded to the letter of the regulations. Though on a strict construction the Lieutenants' examination was open only to Volunteers, in practice it was open to all, and in 1702 the regulations were altered to admit as much. Royal patronage, so valuable under Charles II and James II, who knew and cared a great deal about their Navy and its officers, proved to be less useful after 1688. Fewer than half of the Lieutenants promoted during Queen Anne's reign had been Volunteers.[10] Candidates of all social origins soon discovered that it was the protection of senior officers which would best advance their careers, and the Volunteer per Order scheme was abandoned altogether in 1733. The great majority of young would-be officers now advanced under a regime of informal patronage which took no official account of their social status, and the original idea of two parallel officer streams, one starting and rising higher than the other, largely disappeared except for the important fact that it was still possible to be promoted directly from Lieutenant to Post-Captain. Well into the eighteenth century, lucky or well-connected officers still passed directly to post-rank, while older men with less successful careers rose no further than the command of a sloop or fireship – that is, to the rank of Master and Commander. Over time, however, attitudes and practice evolved, and it became more and more normal for all officers to spend at least a short time commanding a sloop before they took post. In 1746, when sloops were allowed Masters, the rank was renamed simply 'Commander', though the old form remained current long afterwards.[11] An Admiralty order of 1757 forbade overseas commanders-in-chief to promote Lieutenants into post vacancies if

10   Baugh, *Age of Walpole*, p. 98.
11   Public Record Office [PRO]: ADM 7/678 No. 8, Order in Council of 27 Mar 1746.

there were any Commanders available – to the disgust of at least one admiral: 'as I should be most exceedingly chagrin'd, at being the Instrument of Promotion, to anyone whose only merit was being a commander, & even that far above his Deserts.'[12] The process reached its logical conclusion in 1794 when Commander became a formal rank and the only channel of promotion to Post-Captain. One significant anomaly remained even then: all Commanders were still captains of sloops (and therefore addressed as 'Captain'), though they were frequently much younger and less experienced than the first Lieutenants of line-of-battle ships who were now unequivocally their juniors. It was not until 1827 that the first Lieutenants of big ships were raised to the rank of Commander.

Meanwhile, throughout the period we are studying, Lieutenant remained the basic commissioned rank. All officers, whatever their origins, had to pass an examination in seamanship in order to qualify for it, and they had to prove that they had served a minimum period of sea time. From 1677 this time was three years, of which one year had to have been spent in the rating of midshipman. In 1703 the requirement was increased to four years, two of them as a midshipman or master's mate, and in 1729 the total sea-time was increased to six years, which it remained. The regulations were ambiguous on whether all this time had to be served in the Navy, but in 1745 the Admiralty officially declared that service in merchant ships was acceptable for the four years of 'non-rated' time.[13] Throughout our period, the minimum qualifying age for a Lieutenant's commission remained twenty.[14] Some candidates, however, are known to have received their commissions younger, while others were much older, so that the date of a Lieutenant's commission can only very roughly be used as a proxy for age.[15] This is unfortunate, for the Admiralty kept no consistent records of officers' ages, and consequently we lack a very important piece of evidence for assessing their careers.

Two other titles should be mentioned because they might appear to the modern reader to be commissioned officers' ranks: lieutenant-commander and sub-lieutenant. 'Lieutenants-commander' or 'lieutenants in command' were the captains of men-of-war too small to be commanded by Commanders. Though sometimes styled 'Captain' like other commanding officers, they were not officially regarded as being in any sense distinct from other Lieutenants. There is no connection with the rank of Lieutenant-Commander, created in 1914 by

---

[12]   PRO: ADM 1/306, Rear-Admiral T. Frankland to the Admiralty, 16 Jun 1757.

[13]   Baugh, *Age of Walpole*, pp. 101–102.

[14]   The qualifying age applied to the commission, not the examination, which could legally be sat under the age of twenty.

[15]   N.A.M. Rodger, 'Lieutenants' Sea-Time and Age', *Mariner's Mirror* LXXV (1989), pp. 269–272.

re-classifying Lieutenants of eight years' seniority and above. 'Sub-lieutenant' was a term officially used between 1804 and 1814 for midshipmen and master's mates who had passed the Lieutenant's examination but had not yet been promoted, and who served as watchkeeping officers of gunboats, schooners and other small vessels which were allowed no commissioned officer except the Lieutenant in command. Sub-lieutenant in this sense was an appointment, not to be confused with the rank instituted in 1860.

Seniority and Half-Pay

The key to understanding the development of officers' careers, and the limitations of the records which we have to use to study them, lies in two apparently rather technical issues which are closely related: half-pay and the concept of seniority. The Navy of the Restoration already felt a need to distinguish the relative authority of officers, but the structure of rank was as yet extremely fluid, and successive appointments did not imply any permanent status. It was perfectly possible for an officer to serve in successive seasons as Lieutenant, Captain, second Lieutenant, first Lieutenant, Master and Commander, first Lieutenant and Captain, as one Thomas Berry did.[16] In this situation career progression was in the mind, but still situations often arose in which officers' relative authority had to be determined, and naval opinion divided between the advocates of seniority in rank, and those of the size of ship as determining factors. If a number of ships met, which Captain should take overall command: the one with the oldest commission, or the one commanding the largest ship, who would tend to be socially and perhaps professionally the most eminent ? 'How it is come to pass I know not', Samuel Pepys wrote in 1675,

> but... I find there hath been wanting to this day a clear determination how commanders are to behave themselves in reference to precedence, and giving command one to the other when they chance to fall in company (as it often happens) without any warrant from the lord admiral giving the command to some one of them, the want whereof hath three or four times within my knowledge begot very much ill-blood and some disorder to the king's service.[17]

Pepys applied his methodical genius to assembling a seniority list, but after years of effort the result was still unsatisfactory, as he warned Lord Dartmouth in 1688: 'though this may guide you very much, yet it is liable to as many defects as there may be gentlemen in the fleet, whose first commissions have happened

---

16   Lewis, *Sea-Officers*, p.70.
17   *Pepysian Manuscripts*, ed. Tanner, III, 147, to Sir T. Allin, 16 Dec 1675.

to be granted to them by Admiralls or Commanders in Chief at sea.'[18] In 1691 the Admiralty made a further attempt to compile an official seniority list, but disputes continued to occur. The following year Captain David Lambert of the *Breda* came into Spithead with a broad pendant flying as senior officer, to find Captain George Meese of the *Ruby* flying one already. 'Captain Lambert, it appears, expected to have had his post from the date of his Commission in 1664, since when, till he came into the *Newcastle*, he has never been in the Service.'[19] Such disputes were especially sharp when so many officers had recently been appointed on political grounds after long absence from the Navy or no previous service at all. As late as 1715 the Admiralty was still ordering officers to obey those senior to themselves in terms which suggest that the idea was not yet universally understood or accepted.[20]

The first grants of half-pay were made in 1668 and 1674, unequivocally as a reward to admirals, Commodores and Captains who had served in the wars just ended. The 1694 establishment followed a similar line, granting half-pay to all Post-Captains, plus the first Lieutenants and Masters of the first three rates, who had served in the war then in progress. After the war, however, the 1700 establishment referred not only to previous services but to the intention 'to have always a Competent Number of Experienced Sea-Officers, supported on Shore... within reach to answer any sudden or immergent Occasion.' To this end officers in receipt of half-pay were not to go abroad or accept other public employment. At the same time half-pay was granted only to the first fifty Captains and the first hundred Lieutenants: an explicit reference to established seniority, now regulated by the first printed seniority list; and an implicit acknowledgement that half-pay was still a reward for past services, since the most senior officers were the least likely to be useful in a future war.[21] The peace establishment of 1713 for the first time awarded half-pay to all Captains and Lieutenants who 'stand fair to be employed when there shall be occasion.'[22] This seemed to fix it unequivocally as a retainer for future services – but the pay itself was on a sliding scale descending with seniority, which implied the

[18]   Historical Manuscripts Commission [HMC] No. 20, *Manuscripts of the Earl of Dartmouth* (1887–96, 3 vols), I, 162.

[19]   John Ehrman, *The Navy in the War of William III, 1689–1697: Its State and Direction* (Cambridge, 1953), pp. 452–457. HMC No. 17 *House of Lords MSS 1692–1693* (1894), p. 240, E. Russell to Admiralty, 6 Aug 1692.

[20]   *The Byng Papers...*, ed. Brian Tunstall (NRS Vols. 67, 68 & 70, 1930–32), III, 134–135.

[21]   *The Sergison Papers*, ed. R.D. Merriman (NRS Vol. 89, 1950), pp. 265–270, 278–282 & 345–361. Baugh, *Age of Walpole*, pp. 103–104. Ehrman, *The Navy in the War of William III*, pp. 457–461.

[22]   Merriman, *Queen Anne's Navy*, pp. 327–329.

opposite. In practice the elements of retainer and reward were inextricably mixed throughout the eighteenth century. Half pay was granted to officers who had served in the previous war and witheld from those who had not. In 1721, for example, Captain Wentworth Paxton's petition for half pay was refused, 'he having been many years out of England, declined going Master and Commander of one of his Majesty's ships to the West Indies, and not having served the last War, as required by the Establishment.'[23] Officers were retained on the list who were known to be incapable and even insane because no other support for their old age was available. Though pensions for wounds and good service might be granted by Admiralty order to individual senior officers, which in some, though not all, cases covered their retirement from active service, no regular superannuation scheme for any commissioned officers existed until in 1738 an allowance was granted to thirty of the most senior Lieutenants – which by no means sufficed to remove all the elderly.[24] During the Napoleonic War the Admiralty introduced an official sub-category of 'unserviceable' officers to the Lieutenents' List, though it is doubtful even then if the remainder were all available for service. In 1747 the Admiralty introduced a scheme for senior Captains whereby those not selected for active flag rank received a nominal promotion to the rank of 'Rear-Admiral without distinction of squadron'. In effect this was a disguised form of compulsory retirement scheme, but the 'yellow admirals' retired on a Rear-Admiral's half-pay.[25] The intent of the 1747 scheme was to stop the complaints of Captains passed over for promotion. It did nothing to eliminate the many elderly or unfit Captains who had not yet risen to the top of the list. Retirement pensions in the modern style, granted to all officers who had reached a certain age or length of service, did not come in until the mid-nineteenth century.

Sources

This paper is based on two types of sources, which approach the subject as it were from two bearings, in the hope of getting a better 'fix' on it. The first source is the list of *Commissioned Sea Officers* (henceforward abbreviated to *CSO*), recently re-edited by Professors Syrett and DiNardo, and printed by the Navy Records Society. From this a 10% sample has been taken of all officers

---

[23]   PRO: ADM 3/33, 25 Apr 1721, *ex inf.* Professor Daniel Baugh.

[24]   Baugh, *Age of Walpole*, pp. 104–107.

[25]   N.A.M. Rodger, *The Insatiable Earl: A Life of John Montagu, Fourth Earl of Sandwich, 1718–1792* (London, 1993), pp. 33–34. Baugh, *Age of Walpole*, pp. 136–137.

whose first commissions as Lieutenants fell between 1690 and 1815.[26] The basic information available in this source is the dates of officers' successive first commissions in each rank. This sample therefore has the great merit of providing good information of the calendar dates of officers' promotions. [Graphs 1.0–1.3]. From it it is possible to construct graphs showing, amongst other things, the career progression of each year's intake of new Lieutenants. In practice the annual samples are too small to be statistically useful, and the graphs have been worked out for five-yearly 'generations' from 1740 to 1814, with a one-year analysis for the exceptional year of 1815. The first fifty years of the study, where the overall numbers of officers are small and the records particularly inadequate, have been divided into two twenty-five year generations, 1690-1714 and 1715–1739. For each generation, the information is presented for fifty years from the date of first commission; the assumption being that too few officers to be statistically meaningful were still professionally active more than fifty years after their first commissions [Graphs 2.1–2.14]. In addition to dates of promotion, *CSO* records some dates of superannuation, removal from the list, and death. With the addition of this information graphs have been constructed showing the 'fates' of each generation; meaning the progressive removal over time of officers from the Lieutenants' List by promotion, retirement or death [Graphs 3.1–3.14].

In using these graphs, especially the Fates, it is important to be aware of the limitations of the source. *CSO* is based on official records which themselves were inaccurate. Particularly before 1715, it is clear that much information never reached the Admiralty, and some of what it had was contradictory or erroneous. In spite of several attempts, the Admiralty never succeeded in keeping up a complete address list, and could make contact with the officer corps as a whole only by inserting advertisements in the newspapers. The spelling of surnames was sometimes variable, the recording of christian names haphazard, and persons of the same or similar surnames were apt to be confused. The dates on which officers disappeared from the lists are not consistently recorded, nor would they be easy to interpret if they were present, since names could be removed in peacetime only to re-appear on the outbreak of war. Dates of Lieutenants' superannuation are recorded in some, but probably not all cases. The dates of Captains' 'promotion' to 'yellow admiral' are recorded, and have been treated for the purposes of this study as retirement in Captain's rank. Dates of death are probably complete only for those who died in service.

---

[26]   The sample consists of all the names on every tenth page, omitting only a handful of officers whose first, Lieutenant's, commission was not recorded.

As a consequence the recording of 'Fates' is incomplete. A glance at the graphs will show that a proportion of each generation is unaccounted for even after fifty years. If the records were complete, that should represent officers who were still available to serve in the rank of Lieutenant; in practice we can take it for granted that Lieutenants of fifty years' seniority were effectively retired if not effectively dead. The 'Fate' of the 1690–1714 generation [Graph 3.1] appears to show that 50% were still available to serve after fifty years, while only 27% were known to have died. Undoubtedly the reality was that virtually all these officers were retired, and many more than 27% were already dead. Only 15% of the 1755–59 generation were unaccounted for after fifty years, and 75% were dead [Graph 3.5]. This seems to have been the summit of Admiralty Office efficiency. By 1810–14 nearly a third of the officers were unaccounted for after fifty years, and only 40% were known to have died [Graph 3.13]. Perhaps average longevity had increased in half a century, and length of service certainly had, but we must still suspect that part of the difference represents failures in record-keeping. Another way to express this variation in the rate, or apparent rate, of wastage of generations of Lieutenants is to plot the 'half-life' of each, meaning the number of years taken for half the generation to be removed from the list [Graph 6.2].

The information deriveable from *CSO* about the dates and circumstances in which officers left active service is therefore incomplete, but it is not useless. Assuming that the fact of death or superannuation, if recorded, is in most cases correct, the graphs of 'Fate' provide at least a floor. They tell us for any particular year that at least a certain proportion of each generation had been removed from the Lieutenants' List by promotion, retirement or death. The shape of the graphs for each generation show us a minimum rate of wastage or turnover, and give us at least some idea of how the Navy's 'rate of consumption' of officers varied over time. Moreover the figures can be corrected by assuming that officers ceased to be available for service at any given seniority, and used to provide an estimate of the notional stock of officers which ought to have been available [Graphs 4.1–4.3]. This in turn can be compared with figures calculated from actual lists of ships and officers in order to select the most plausible assumption of the average length of time an officer remained available for service [Graphs 5.1–5.2].

Two fundamental points need to be stressed about the information derived from *CSO*. Because it has not proved possible to recalculate the information for each officer on the basis of his promotions to Commander or Captain, all *CSO* information is based on seniority in Lieutenant's rank, or as a commissioned officer. This has the advantage of providing a common base with which to compare all careers, but the disadvantage that it cannot be directly compared with information derived from Commanders' or Captains' Lists, which are arranged in order of seniority in those ranks. Nor is it easy to use the *CSO* information to compare over time the careers of, say, Captains in terms of seniority in post rank. Moreover the common base of the *CSO* information in terms of first commission has to serve as a proxy for the officers' dates of birth, which in most cases we do not know. If we had a means of knowing their dates of birth, we could make much more secure assumptions about how long on average they were available to serve, and make more realistic assessments about the shape of average careers. As it is we may legitimately assume that few lieutenants were younger than about eighteen, so that once more we have some kind of floor, but on present information it is impossible to guess what was the mean age at first commission, nor how it may have changed over time.

The second essential point to understand about the *CSO* information is that it looks forward. Being based on the start of officers' careers, its base years or 'generations' are traced forward in time over fifty years. Though it can be used to make inferences [Graphs 4.1–4.3 and 10.1–10.3] about the number of officers notionally available in any given year, it is essentially different from a printed *Navy List*, which shows the officers in service in a given year with their seniority in their current ranks, and hence looks backward to provide partial information about their previous careers. In the case of Lieutenants directly, Commanders and Captains indirectly, such a list can be compared with the *CSO*, showing what their real seniority was, and hence controlling estimates of how long they might notionally be expected to serve [Graphs 5.1–5.2, 10.1–10.3].

This brings us to the other main category of evidence used in this study: original Admiralty records now in the Public Record Office, and printed Navy Lists. Three classes of records have been used, of which the first are the printed seniority lists of officers now in the class ADM 118. These lists of officers in order of seniority were printed by the Admiralty for internal use. Some of them were then annotated to form the basis for half-pay lists by striking out the names of officers not eligible for half pay. It would be convenient for the historian if one could assume that those not on half pay were serving on full pay, but unfortunately there are not a few officers on the list who were receiving neither, and a few who were in a sense receiving both. Half-pay was not legally tenable in conjunction with other public employments. In practice many of those holding naval civil employments (notably Commissioners of the Admiralty, Navy and Victualling) were dispensed from the regulation and allowed to continue drawing half pay in addition to their salaries; but other civil employments, for example under the Customs or Ordnance Boards, did disable their holders from drawing half pay, without necessarily disabling them from future service, or causing them to be struck off the lists. Officers with leave to travel abroad, to serve afloat in merchant ships or foreign navies, forfeited their half pay during their absence but were restored on their return. It follows that though those on half pay were certainly not serving afloat, the remainder were not necessarily on full pay. The same reasoning applies to the Half Pay Lists themselves (ADM 25), which are definitive as far as they go, but give a complete picture only in conjunction with the corresponding Full Pay Lists (ADM 24), which do not survive before 1795.

Another important documentary source is the monthly compilations known as List Books (ADM 8), in which the Admiralty recorded the command or station of every ship in commission together with other information including the names of her captain and (up to 1808) her lieutenants. From these lists it is possible to calculate the Navy's requirement for commissioned officers, assuming that every appointment was filled.[27] In practice there were always some vacancies, and the seagoing Navy normally employed less than 100% of its requirement. Up until the mid-century it was largely true that employment on full pay was only as an officer of one of H.M. Ships in commission. Progressively thereafter there grew up a number of officers' shore employments on full pay. These included the officers of the Impress Service and the Sea Fencibles, the Lieutenants commanding signal stations and semaphore towers, and the Transport Agents (the last not strictly a shore employment since they served afloat, though they did not belong to any of H.M. Ships). To them it is realistic to add the captains of some old yachts, no longer in seagoing condition, which were retained on the lists specifically in order to provide sinecure employments.[28] By the time of the Napoleonic Wars these shore employments accounted for a significant fraction of the total officers: 21 Captains and 29 Commanders in 1800, out of 195 and 293 respectively on full pay.[29] Some of these shore employments, such as the Lieutenants of semaphore towers, were regarded as suitable for disabled officers, while the Impress Service by the time of the Great Wars seems to have been largely filled with older officers who were presumably regarded as unfit, or at least less fit, for sea service. Shore employments introduce another element of ambiguity to the statistics, particularly

---

[27]　Some degree of uncertainty, amounting perhaps to a margin of error of 5% plus or minus, is introduced by the Admiralty's then lack of information about the current situation on foreign stations, and the difficulty now of knowing the proper establishment of such vessels as troopships and receiving ships which did not conform to the normal establishments.

[28]　For the case of Captain Sir Alexander Schomberg, who commanded the *Dorset* yacht in the service of the Lord Lieutenant of Ireland from 1771 to his death in 1804, see HMC No. 19, *Manuscripts of the Marquess Townshend* (1887), pp. 410–411; and G.W. Place, 'Parkgate and the Royal Yachts: Passenger Traffic between the North-West and Dublin in the Eighteenth Century', *Transactions of the Historic Society of Lancashire and Cheshire* CXXXVIII (1988), pp. 67–83. As a Captain of 1754 still more or less at sea in the nineteenth century, he had a unique record.

[29]　*Steel's Navy List*, June 1800.

in including employments on full pay for officers who were unfit to go to sea, and might in an earlier age have been effectively retired.

Finally, from the 1790s, it is possible to replace, or at least supplement, the Admiralty records with a publication drawn from them, *Steel's Navy List*.[30] This private (and less accurate) forerunner of the official *Navy List* provides monthly lists of ships in commission and lists of officers in order of seniority, with an indication of the ships or employments of those on full pay. It can therefore be used to provide totals of officers employed and unemployed at any given date, broken down by their seniority. This makes it possible to compile 'snapshots' of the officer corps at given dates, looking backwards to see the seniority of those serving and not serving [Graphs 7.4–7.6, 8.1-8.2, 9.4, 11.1–11.2]. It also makes possible comparison of those actually serving of different seniorities, with those 'predicted' from *CSO* [Graphs 5.1–5.2].

Timing of Promotions [Graphs 1.0–1.3]

The evidence drawn from these sources has been presented chiefly in the form of graphs. The experienced eye can deduce, or guess, much from them which would be difficult or impossible to learn from the raw data on which they are based. One of the most basic lessons is that promotions almost stopped in peacetime. There was no regular progression in naval careers, but a succession of feast and famine. On a major mobilization, including those such as 1726–28, 1733-35, 1770 and 1790 which did not lead to war, very large numbers of officers (especially Lieutenants) received commissions in a short period. On a single day, 22nd November 1790, over 150 Lieutenants received their first commissions – a concentration of officers with the same seniority which later caused such trouble that their seniorities were redistributed over 13th to 22nd November.[31] The rate of promotions then tended to decline during a war; the peaks of 1744 and 1762 represent the outbreak of war against France and Spain respectively, extending fighting which was already in progress. In 1782–83 there occurs a new phenomenon: a very large peak of promotions in the closing year of a war, when peace was clearly imminent. It is hardly possible to doubt that this is the work of Lord Keppel, First Lord in the Whig administration which took office in May 1782. The new government was committed to making peace, at least with the Americans. It was also committed to rewarding its own people. Contemporaries remarked on Keppel's advancement of his allies, many

---

[30]   *Steel's Original and Correct List of the Royal Navy*, first issued in March 1780; there are slight variations in the titles of the early issues.

[31]   PRO: ADM 118/84, note against that date.

of whom had not served during the war, and Graph 1.2 provides striking visual evidence of it.[32] Another Whig First Lord, St.Vincent, followed the precedent in 1802. His relatively modest promotion consisted largely of Captains and Commanders, but the extraordinary promotions of 1814–15 added nearly a thousand Lieutenants to the list. Many of them were never employed again, but continued to draw half-pay until the first retirement schemes of the 1840s began to thin their ranks.

The same picture of promotions virtually confined to wartime can be shown from the opposite perspective – looking backwards from fixed points in time, with the help of two graphs [Graphs 11.1–11.2] derived from *Steel's Navy List* for July 1792, shortly before the outbreak of the French Revolutionary War, and July 1800, not long before its end. Both graphs show all Captains, Commanders and Lieutenants then listed, arranged by seniority in those ranks, and it is at once obvious that there had been heavy promotions in wartime, and on occasions of peacetime mobilization (above all the Nootka Sound Armament of 1790), but almost no promotion in other peacetime years.

The simple fact that promotions scarcely occurred outside periods of general mobilization was the most important factor shaping naval careers. The Navy seldom had the right number of officers, and never for any length of time. In the opening years of a war there was a severe shortage of officers of all ranks, and promotion was rapid. Before the end of the war, supply had matched if not exceeded demand, though in wartime turnover, and consequentially promotion, remained steady. With the coming of peace and demobilization, the Navy always had far more officers than it could employ, and promotions almost ceased. Over the years of peace, the numbers of officers steadily declined as illness, age and death took their toll, and disappointment drove others to seek a living elsewhere. When the Navy next mobilized, the numbers still willing and able to serve were always insufficient, and so the cycle began again.

For this reason the single most important factor governing an officer's prospects in the Navy was his date of birth. The ideal was to be born about twenty years before the outbreak of a major war, to contrive (in spite of the small number of H.M. Ships in commission) to get the qualifying sea time in peacetime, and to pass for Lieutenant just as the war broke out – ready to profit from the acute shortage of officers of all ranks. Luckiest of all were a handful of officers, usually influential as well as able, who managed to gain promotion in peacetime, and were ready at the outbreak of war on the very crest of the

---

[32]   Rodger, *Insatiable Earl*, pp. 305–306. John A. Davies, 'An Enquiry into Faction among British Naval Officers during the War of the American Revolution' (Liverpool, MA thesis, 1964) pp. 270–272.

advancing wave of promotions. Unluckiest were those who entered during a war and were qualified for Lieutenant at the end of it, but failed to gain their commissions before the peace left them as unemployed midshipmen for ten or fifteen years. At higher seniority, there were unlucky Lieutenants and Commanders in the same situation, poised for promotion, but forced to wait through long years of peace – by the end of which many of them were too old for further service.

A good illustration of the system is provided by an analysis, made on the occasion of George III's visit to Portsmouth in 1773, of the service records of the officers of the two flagships *Barfleur* and *Dublin*.[33] Ten years after the end of the Seven Years' War, the five lieutenants of the *Barfleur* had between fourteen and seventeen years' seniority. The first three lieutenants of the *Dublin* had between eleven and fourteen years' seniority, and a total of seventy-five years' naval service between them. Only one lucky young man, Lieutenant John Manley, Fourth of the *Dublin*, had been promoted in 1770 during the major mobilization over the Falkland Islands crisis. Perfectly positioned to profit from the promotion boom of the American War, young Manley reached post rank in October 1782 just as it ended, and in due course died a Vice-Admiral. The two First Lieutenants, though promoted Commander on the occasion of the king's visit, did not have such successful careers.[34] Amongst the young gentlemen of the two ships, the disappointments of peacetime were even more marked. There were twelve young men on the two quarter-decks, with between seven and eighteen years' service each, who had already passed for Lieutenant, and eight more who had exceeded the qualifying sea-time (more than doubled it in four cases). Three of these twenty were promoted on the occasion of the king's visit, and thirteen more achieved commissioned rank after the outbreak of war, between 1775 and 1781, by which time they had accumulated an average of nearly seventeen years' service each. Two of those who had already passed appear never to have been promoted. Yet these were lucky persons in all respects except their dates of birth; employed in guard ships which were much sought-after berths, in several cases noted as possessing influential patrons. Their only fault lay in having been born at the wrong time.

---

[33]   National Maritime Museum [NMM]: SAN/F/4/66–67.

[34]   William Halstead died a Commander in 1778; James Reid reached Captain in 1776, but had risen no further when he died in 1798.

Promotion Prospects

The importance of being born at the right time can be seen in a graph [Graph 6.1] which expresses the promotion prospects of each generation of Lieutenants in terms of the proportion reaching Commander, Captain or Admiral. The luckiest cohort was the small peacetime generation of 1765–69; only nine officers in the sample, but six of them were promoted. The generation of 1770–74, which included the 'Spanish Armament' of 1770, was larger (a sample of seventeen) and almost as lucky; slightly fewer promotions overall, but not less than one third reached flag rank. By contrast only 22% of the much larger number (sample 41) of Lieutenants of 1745–49, made in the latter part of a long war, received any promotion at all. Least lucky of all on this measure were the Lieutenants of 1815, of whom only 12% were ever promoted. The same tendencies are expressed in a different way in another graph [Graph 6.2] which again shows the proportion of each generation reaching Commander and Captain, but plots against these columns two measures of the speed of promotion: the 'half-life' of each generation, and the mean length of time it took those who reached post-rank to advance from Lieutenant to Captain. In each case the small peace-time generations produce results too erratic to justify plotting, but it is obvious that the early-war generations have better prospects than those promoted later. The figures for the 'half-life' of Lieutenants' generations – roughly a measure of the speed with which the list was turning over – vary in a range from seven years (1790–94) to sixteen (1760–64 and 1780–84). Those for seniority in commissioned rank on being made post vary in the range from nine years (1755–59 and 1800–04) to fifteen (1760–64, 1765–69 and 1780–84). Both lines break right out of their traditional ranges towards the end of the Napoleonic War. Between 1805 and 1815 the 'half-life' of a generation increased from 12 to 36 years, and the time taken to reach post-rank (for those who did) rose from 9 to 20 years. These figures suggest that a longstanding relationship between supply and demand had completely broken down.

The promotion prospects of each generation can be analysed in more detail by plotting their promotions over time from first commission. [Graphs 2.1–2.14] The first of the 'grand generations', the Lieutenants of 1690-1714 [Graph 2.1], shows a slow rise. It took 23 years before 30% of this generation were promoted, and the eventual total was only 33%. The 'grand generation' of 1715–35 [Graph 2.2] did strikingly better: in fourteen years over half of them had been promoted, and one eighth reached flag rank. Undoubtedly this contrast is explained by the fact that the 1690–1714 Lieutenants spent the latter part of their careers in a time of general peace, while the 1715–35 Lieutenants started in peacetime and then enjoyed the professional opportunities of ten years of war, 1739–48. These two grand generations each span 25 years, too long a period to see any more detailed effects, but the later, five-year generations, allow one to observe promotions at a higher magnification. The 1740–44 Lieutenants [Graph 2.3] passed through two distinct periods of promotion separated by a plateau; up to eight years' seniority, then from fourteen to twenty. Clearly these are two successive wars (the Austrian Succession and Seven Years' Wars), to which can be added a third (the American War) for the lucky two who became Admirals with 34 and 35 years' seniority in commissioned rank. 42% of this generation, first commissioned early in a war, were promoted as least as far as Commander. In the next, late-war generation, 1745–49 [Graph 2.4] only 22% rose so far. In this graph a prominent 'spike' of promotion, both to Commander and Captain, at around nine years' seniority, clearly represents the outbreak of the Seven Years' War. The 1755–59 generation [Graph 2.5], well-positioned early in a war, enjoyed a fairly steep rise in promotions until the end of the Seven Years' War at around seven years' seniority, followed by a plateau until at around twenty years' seniority the American War produces a second, smaller, promotion boom. Presumably by then there were few officers still active to benefit from the new war, or perhaps they were crowded out by the competition of younger men. 39% of this generation were promoted at least to Commander.

It can be seen that up to this period the rank of Commander was a brief stepping-stone to post-rank for many officers, and the final achievement of a relatively small number, mainly promoted late in their careers. We may guess that this latter group was disproportionately made up of older men who had reached commissioned rank from warrant rank or the merchant service. The next early-war generation, 1775–79 [Graph 2.7] did better, with a total of 46% promoted, including no less than 11% reaching flag rank. Their steep rise in promotion for the first six years represents the opportunities of the American War, followed between twelve and 20 years' seniority by the French Revolutionary Wars. By contrast the 1780-84 generation [Graph 2.8] enjoyed only a tiny initial promotion at the end of the American War, then nothing until a steady advance between seven and eighteen years' seniority as the French Wars lifted their prospects. Eventually 33% were promoted, but their rise was inevitably slow. Ten years later the 1790–94 generation [Graph 2.9] enjoyed brilliant careers. The period began with the full mobilization of the Nootka Sound Armament, followed by the Ochakov crisis and the outbreak of the French Revolutionary War. Fuelled by this demand, over half this generation had been promoted within nine years.[35]

---

[35]   A number appear to have been promoted directly from Lieutenant to Captain, which was no longer possible, but undoubtedly they had in fact spent a few months commanding a sloop

By this date Commanders are more numerous, relative to Captains, but their promotions still show the characteristic two-stage pattern, with a large initial promotion of high-flyers moving swiftly on to post-rank, and a smaller late promotion of Lieutenants around twenty years' seniority who go no further. The officers of 1795–99 [Graph 2.10] did well, but significantly less well; it took sixteen years of almost continuous war before half this generation had been promoted. In the next generation, 1800–04, [Graph 2.11] only a third were ever promoted. These were the first years in which Commanders outnumbered Captains. The two distinct groups of young and older Commanders are still identifiable, but the late promotions are now much more numerous. The implication is that the typical Commander of the Napoleonic War was a middle-aged officer with no further prospects. The lucky young men who commanded a sloop for a few months or years on their way to greater things still existed, but they were proportionately less numerous than in earlier years. What the graph cannot show, but seems very likely, is that the two groups (insofar as they were employed at all) commanded different sorts of ships: the dashing young men taking the cruisers, the glory and the prize-money; the middle-aged taking the troop-ships which became so prominent a feature of the Navy List in these years.

Promotion for this generation continued to rise steeply up to fourteen years' seniority. The next generation, 1805-09, [Graph 2.12] had a similar steep rise, but only for eight years (until the end of the war), by which time a quarter had been promoted, followed by another 10% spread over a further twelve years, and then virtually nothing. For the final wartime generation, 1810–14, promotion for a lucky few (16%) was fairly swift in the first six years [Graph 2.13]. Another 9% advanced over the next eleven years, and that was that until a lucky handful of officers reached flag rank in old age. Fewer than 30% of this generation were ever promoted, but even they were fortunate compared to the extraordinary promotion of 1815 [Graph 2.14]: almost a thousand Lieutenants for whom there was no employment in wartime, made when peace and demobilization was already in sight. Analysis would presumably show that these were long-serving passed midshipmen, many of them no doubt former sub-lieutenants, making the leap to gentility and half-pay as a reward for sacrificing their youth to a service which had nothing more to offer them. Fewer than 12% of this group were ever promoted, after extraordinarily long waits.

---

before advancing to post rank – too short a period to show up on graphs cast in terms of whole years.

Careers and Fates [Graphs 3.1–3.14]

Graphs showing officers' successive promotions give a good idea of how career prospects varied over time, but a more realistic sense of the Navy's supply of officers can be gained by adding the available information about deaths, superannuation and other forms of retirement. Of these death is by far the most consequential. As early as 1690–1714, [Graph 3.1] a period for which the official records underlying *CSO* are particularly sketchy, it can be seen that by 25 years' seniority, death and retirement together have removed more Lieutenants from the list than promotion. The more complete records of later generations show a surprisingly high mortality rate. One third of the 1745–49 generation [Graph 3.4] were dead within twelve years of receiving their commissions, when the great majority were presumably still young men. What had killed them is not possible to say, but from the seniority, most these deaths must have been in peacetime, and there does not seem in any of these graphs to be an identifiable steepening of the curve of deaths over seniorities corresponding to war years. This would suggest that neither bloody wars nor sickly seasons had a marked effect on promotion prospects. What is perceptible is a secular decline in the rate of deaths. By the end of the century [Graphs 3.10–11] it was over twenty years before one third of the Lieutenants had died, and by 1805-09 [Graph 3.12] it was almost thirty years.

It is possible to use the 'fates' of each generation of Lieutenants to calculate how many officers of each rank might notionally have been available at any one time. The calculation can be made assuming any desired figure (not exceeding fifty years) for the mean working life of an officer. Graphs 4.1–4.3 show the results assuming Captains, Commanders and Lieutenants available to serve for a range of seniorities up to forty years from their first commissions. (Note that all three are cast in terms of seniority in commissioned rank; not, for those officers, seniority in Commander's or Captain's rank). These are purely notional calculations of how many officers might have been available on certain assumptions, but they clarify possibilities. In particular they show that it is statistically of little importance what length of career one assumes for Lieutenants and Commanders beyond about fifteen years, for the maximum number of officers older than that who might have been available is too small to make a major difference to the population. Middle-aged or elderly Captains might have been available in sufficient numbers to make a real difference, but these graphs show that the bulk of junior officers in the Navy had to be drawn from young men, or at least those who had received their first commissions within not more than fifteen years, because natural wastage had removed too many of the older men.

Supply Notional and Actual

From these theoretical calculations we can proceed to others derived from actual lists of officers. Graphs 7.1–7.5 are taken from actual Captains' Lists for selected years (1745, 1748, 1759, 1795 and 1800). They amply confirm what we have already seen, that virtually all promotions took place in wartime (plus periods of peacetime mobilization), and that the majority of officers on the lists had been recently promoted. (Note that these graphs are in terms of post-rank). All these graphs are for wartime years, and in the early graphs, the majority of listed officers were also serving, but there is a significant development over time. In 1745 and 1748 [Graphs 7.1–7.2] the unemployed captains were predominantly the most senior, and presumably the most elderly. In later years unemployment is more evenly distributed, and the proportion of Captains unemployed steadily increases until by 1800 it has reached 50%. This is a striking figure. It can only mean either that the Captains' List at the end of the century included many more of the elderly and unfit than it had formerly done; or that the Navy was producing many more Captains than it could consume. Since the officers most recently promoted (and hence presumably the youngest and fittest) were amongst the least likely to be employed, the only plausible conclusion is that the Navy was promoting considerably more Captains than it could employ. Graphs 8.1–8.2 demonstrate something similar for Commanders. In 1800 and 1810 there was heavy, and growing unemployment, and in 1810 it was especially severe among the most recent promotions.

For Lieutenants the same conclusions can be drawn from Graphs 9.1–9.4, derived from Lieutenants' Lists for 1745, 1748, 1759 and 1810. In the 1740s, at war after thirty years of peace, the Navy depended overwhelmingly on Lieutenants who had recently been promoted, and most of those listed were also serving. By 1759 a significant proportion of the Lieutenants remained on the list from the previous war, and among these older men unemployment was higher. The natural explanation must be that they were less fit to serve, and the implication would be that there was more or less full employment among those who were fit. In 1810, however [Graph 9.4] the picture was completely different.[36] Half the Lieutenants were unemployed, and the most recent promotions were the least likely to be serving. This can only mean that the supply of fit officers greatly exceeded the demand.

These figures showing the number of officers actually listed at particular dates can be set against those derived from *CSO* to suggest how long in

---

[36]   But comparison with Table 3 suggests that *Steel's Navy List* had failed to record a number of recent Lieutenants' appointments.

reality officers' active careers actually lasted. Graph 5.2 shows the number of Lieutenants actually listed for selected years set against the predicted supply of seniority up to five years. The fit is reasonably good for the eighteenth century, and confirms that Lieutenants actually available to serve were predominantly the youngest and most recently promoted men. A mean figure of about five years' seniority, as suggested by this graph, agrees quite well with the observed range of actual seniorities of Lieutenants serving in selected years. [Graphs 9.1–9.3] The same agreement is expressed in a different form in Graphs 10.1–10.3, showing the Lieutenants' List for three selected years, 1745, 1748 and 1759, giving the seniority of those listed, those serving, and those 'predicted' from *CSO* to be available. Though the 'predicted' numbers greatly exceed those really listed, the shape of the curves matches perfectly, which confirms that *CSO* can be used to 'predict' the supply, at least of Lieutenants, with the help of a realistic estimate of the average length of an officer's active service. The relationship between prediction and reality seems to remain good for the 18th century: that is, that the number of Lieutenants actually available matches the figure suggested by *CSO* on the assumption that the mean active career of a Lieutenant throughout the century was about five years. This relationship breaks down about 1800 as the number of Lieutenants listed begins to exceed by a large margin the number predicted. The two sources can now be reconciled only by assuming that the mean active career of the Lieutenants (and presumably also their average age) were rapidly increasing.

Graph 5.1 attempts a similar exercise with captains, plotting those actually listed in selected years with those which might be predicted from *CSO* on the assumption that Captains had a mean of thirty years' service in commissioned rank – equivalent to saying that the average captain was fifty years old, if we could assume that all Lieutenants were promoted at twenty. In addition this graph includes a line representing the growth in the total tonnage of the Navy. There is a rough fit between all three measures until near the end of the Napoleonic War, when the supply of captains suddenly exceeds the requirement.

Supply and Demand

The information which all these graphs provide about the supply and demand of officers can be supplemented by a table giving figures for selected years. The 'requirement' here is to officer the seagoing Navy, but those 'serving' include shore appointments as well. Many of the figures in different columns come from different sources, and may not have been calculated on a consistent basis, but they are all true figures, and presumably more accurate than the graphs derived from the 10% sample of *CSO*.

Table 3

	Captains			Commanders			Lieutenants		
	Listed	Required	Serving	Listed	Required	Serving	Listed	Required	Serving
1690		109			58			202	
1705		144			69			354	
1710		141			68			321	
1720	196			35			382		
1737	176			35			389		
1745	246	151	151	103	53	51	598	457	439
1748	266		172	106		60	656		509
1758	272	190	199	145	69	78	759	610	607
1760	315	209	218	148	73	72	935	693	701
1762		222			93			724	
1778	307	173		98	84		1060	675	
1780	339	215		182	91		948	875	
1782	410	232	250	202	101	115	1231	933	807
1790	411			174			1309		
1792	499	48		166	34		1431	222	
1795	413	249	285	191	83		1762	1189	
1800	545	291	262	373	141	149	2039	1445	
1802	664	89		412	57		2546	596	
1805	643	239	338	435	154	221	2512	1483	1795
1810	728		299	537		238	3058		1848

Sources: 1690: ADM 8/2; 1705: ADM 8/9; 1710: ADM 8/11; 1720: ADM 118/1; 1737: ADM 118/1; 1745: ADM 8/24, ADM 118/2; 1748: ADM 118/3; 1758: ADM 8/33, ADM 118/5; 1760: ADM 8/35, ADM 118/6; 1762: ADM 8/38; 1778: ADM 8/54, ADM 25/95, ADM 118/26; 1780: ADM 8/56, ADM 25/99, ADM 118/29; 1782: ADM 8/58, ADM 118/31–32; 1790: *Steel's Navy List* August 1790; 1792: ADM 8/68, *Steel's Navy List* July 1792; 1795: ADM 8/71, ADM 118/48, *Steel's Navy List* July 1795; 1800: ADM 8/80, *Steel's Navy List* June & July 1800; 1802: ADM 7/678 No.27; 1805: ADM 8/90, ADM 118/71; 1810: ADM 118/84, *Steel's Navy List* June 1810.

During the 18th century, according to this table, the proportion of Captains serving varied between a low of 61% of those listed (1745 and 1782) and a high of 73% (1758). Over the same period Commanders serving ranged from 49% of those listed (1745 and 1760) to 57% (1782). The least proportion of Lieutenants serving was 65% of those listed in 1782, and the greatest proportion was 80% in 1758. Consistently over the whole century, Lieutenants were most likely to be employed, and Commanders least likely. This makes sense so long as supply and demand were roughly in balance, for Lieutenants were presumably the youngest and fittest officers. Commanders suffered because the number of Commanders' commands in the Navy was always less than half the number of post ships. However quickly lucky officers passed through the rank, it was diffficult to find commands for all the Commanders who sought them. The more it became usual, and in the end compulsory, for the future Captain to have passed through the rank of Commander, the greater the liklihood that Commanders would have to be promoted, not because they were needed in that rank, but solely to assure a supply of Captains for the future. It is also possible that the low rate of employment reflects the presence of numbers of elderly Commanders, but it is hard to believe that the mean age of Commanders can have been higher than that of post Captains, who have consistently higher rates of employment.

The figures for the early 19th century show the same abrupt change as the graphs. Between 1795 and 1800 Captains serving fell from 69% to 48% of those listed, and had reached 41% by 1810. Commanders serving were only 40% of those listed in 1800, but recovered to 51% in 1805, before falling again to 44% in 1810. Lieutenants were the least, or latest, affected by the trend: 71% were serving in 1805, which was within the historic range, but by 1810 the proportion had fallen to only 60%.

The obvious conclusion from these tables and graphs, taken together, is that the Navy's 'boom and bust' promotion cycle remained in overall balance during the eighteenth century. Irrational and inefficient though it undoubtedly was, in the long term it provided approximately the right number of officers, and erected no insuperable barriers to selecting the best – though the fact that promotion prospects varied so widely must have meant that in some generations talent was scarcer and better rewarded than others. About the end of the century, however, something went badly wrong. In the 1790s the supply of Commanders and Captains began to outstrip the Navy's requirements, and ten years later the supply of Lieutenants did the same. The development was sudden; much too sudden to be explained by demographic change. No doubt it was true then, as it had long been, that some of those on the list were effectively retired, and possibly that proportion was growing, but it is very difficult to believe that it can have been growing so fast.

The phenomenon of unemployed Captains and Commanders during the Great Wars, particularly the Napoleonic War, and of officers promoted for gallantry but obliged to wait several years for a command, will be familiar to all who know the memoirs and correspondence of the period. These figures are not a complete surprise, but they provide striking confirmation of the reality and extent of the problem. In the year of Trafalgar barely half the Captains and Commanders on the list were actually serving. Graphs 7.1–7.2 and 8.1–8.2 confirm that unemployment was highest among the most recently promoted. It cannot be explained by a growing proportion of the elderly or sickly; it must be the result of excessive promotions.

Contemporaries were clearly aware of the problem. In 1797 Lord Spencer, the First Lord, explained to Lord St.Vincent that 'all the frigates we have coming forward are nearly engaged, and the town of London, as well as Portsmouth and Plymouth, swarm with young captains who on every account ought to be employed, but whom I am, for want of ships for them, under the necessity with great regret to keep in idleness.'[37] When St.Vincent himself succeeded Spencer in 1801, he announced publicly that there would be no further promotions of Commanders or Captains until appointments could be found for existing officers. 'The system is undoubtedly just and highly honourable to him,' commented the *Times*, 'but if the Noble Lord can pursue such a rigorous and impartial line of conduct for a long continuance, it will be more than any of his Predecessors have been able to accomplish.'[38] 'The list of Post Captains and Commanders so far exceeds that of ships and sloops,' St.Vincent told Keith in September 1801, 'I cannot, consistently with what is due to the public and to the incredible number of meritorious persons of those classes upon half pay, promote except upon very extraordinary occasions, such as that of Lord Cochrane and Captain Dundas, who have the rank of Post Captain; nor can I confirm any of the appointments made by Commanders-in-Chief upon foreign stations, except the vacancies are occasioned by death or the sentences of Courts Martial.'[39] In spite of this rigour, the problem grew worse rather than better. In the middle of the Napoleonic War, officers were taking command of ships who had been long enough ashore to have forgotten their profession;

---

[37] *Private Papers of George, second Earl Spencer* (NRS Vols 46, 48, 58 & 59, 1913–24), ed. Julian S. Corbett & H.W. Richmond, II, 390. It is convenient to call him St.Vincent, though Jervis's new earldom had not yet been gazetted two months after the battle which had earned him the title.

[38] *Letters of Admiral of the Fleet the Earl of St.Vincent whilst First Lord of the Admiralty, 1801–1804*, ed. David Bonner Smith (NRS Vols. 55 & 61, 1922–27), I, 313.

[39] Smith, *St.Vincent Letters*, I, 222.

something hitherto confined to the outbreak of war after years of peace. In January 1808, for example, Captain Thomas Brodie took command of the new frigate *Hyperion*. Although a Captain of 1802, Brodie 'had not had his foot on board a ship since he was a lieutenant,' (as one of his officers recorded), 'and was consequently "rather rum in his nauticals", as the common phrase went respecting him.'[40]

Promotion during the Napoleonic War

The statistics on which this study is based show us what had happened, but they cannot tell us how. It is nevertheless possible to offer some plausible guesses, which further research must confirm or deny. Firstly it is necessary to point out that would-be officers began their careers as young gentlemen under the patronage of captains and other officers, and that the Admiralty had no official knowledge of them until they presented themselves for examination as Lieutenant. Even then it did not directly control the examination (which was conducted by the Navy Board at home, and by panels of Captains convened by commanders-in-chief abroad), and no attempt was ever made to limit the number who were examined, or who passed. The first stage of the commissioned officer's career was altogether out of official control, and there was no possibility of imposing any mechanism to match supply to demand. The Admiralty was not formally under any obligation to commission any more of these young gentlemen as Lieutenants than there was employment for, but one can understand that the presence of numerous qualified candidates created at least an expectation of advancement, if not a sense of entitlement.

In the century starting 1690, the Royal Navy fought five major wars, but none of these wars lasted longer than ten years, and none of the intervening peaces was shorter than five years. Overall, there were more years of peace than war. The regular alternation of war and peace allowed the promotion system to retain a long-term balance, oscillating wildly about a steady trend. In 1793, however, began a period of twenty-three years of almost continuous warfare. Moreover the Nootka Sound Armament of 1790, and the lesser but still significant activity over the Dutch crisis in 1787 and the Ochakov affair in 1791, had filled the Navy List with new officers before the Great Wars began. In 1790 a full-scale mobilization succeeded by a period of peace allowed the Admiralty secretariat to overhaul the half-pay lists, striking out large numbers of officers who had not responded to the proclamation calling for their

---

[40]   *Eyewitness to Trafalgar: Thomas Huskisson RN, 1800–1808*, ed. D.B. Ellison (Royston, 1985), p. 99. Brodie was a Commander of February 1801.

services.[41] As a result, the lists on the outbreak of war contained more Captains and Lieutenants (though slightly fewer Commanders) than they had at the end of the previous war. The usual famine of officers was not present at the start of what was to be a war more than twice as long as ever before. In these circumstances the Navy's traditional system of promotion, run as it always had been run, was very likely to produce too many officers.

There was, moreover, a particular problem with Commanders and Captains. In the absence of any system of decorations, the only reward for gallantry or good service by junior officers was promotion. Ratings were sometimes given money; Captains might be given a medal or a knighthood, and Admirals a peerage, but for Lieutenants and Commanders promotion was normally the only available distinction. It had long been the rule of First Lords of the Admiralty to promote those who distinguished themselves in action. Anson made it,

> my constant method since I have had the honour of serving the King in the station I am in... to promote the Lieutenants to command whose ships have been successfully engaged upon equal terms with the enemy, without having any friend or recommendation, and in preference to all others, and this I would recommend to my successors if they would have a fleet to depend upon.[42]

Twenty years later Lord Sandwich took the same line:

> The Candidates for promotion in the Navy are so numerous, that it is absolutely necessary for me to hold the same language to all who address themselves to me upon that subject, and I am obliged to have the most strict attention to the seniority of those who either by themselves or friends sollicit preferment.

> The rule of seniority indeed usually gives way in cases where officers have the good fortune to distinguish themselves in battle, but I cannot agree with your Lordship that exertions on harbour duty tho' very meritorious should give the same pretension. There are many young men of fashion in the Navy who are equally sollicitous for preferment and their friends are equally pressing; your Lordship will find on enquiry that my answer to all of them is the same, whatever their connections may be.[43]

Gallantry in action was the only exception St.Vincent would admit to his ban on promoting new Commanders and Captains:

---

[41]   PRO: ADM 1/5119/3 contains working papers from this exercise.

[42]   Sir Lewis Namier, *The Structure of Politics at the Accession of George III* (London, 2nd edn. 1957), p. 34.

[43]   NMM: SAN/ V/13 pp. 244–245, to Lord Berkeley, n.d.

I shall seek merit, and reward it, to the utmost of my power, in every branch of the navy, civil, and military; but at present I am restrained from promoting, by the very great number of meritorious officers on the list of post-Captains and Commanders, now, and for a great length of time, unemployed; and it is my fixed determination not to attend to any recommendation whatsoever, except on occasion of brilliant services against the enemy, until they are provided for.[44]

The problem was that in a long war there were many examples of gallantry – and all the more of them as young officers realised that this was their only chance of promotion. The number of those it was just to reward bore no relation to the number it was possible to employ. The practice of advancing all the First Lieutenants of the ships of the line which had fought in a fleet action had a particularly devastating effect on the Commanders' List. St.Vincent, Camperdown and the Nile between them increased it by more than a third in two years. In 1801 St.Vincent found 'almost all the First Lieutenants who were made Commanders on the Battle of the Nile, several of those of St.Vincent, of Camperdown, of Lord Bridport's action, before L'Orient, upon half pay; and I feel myself bound, by every principle of justice, to bring them forward in the first instance.'[45] Presently the battle of Copenhagen added another batch of deserving candidates for whom little could be done.

One further factor may have been at work. Lord Spencer was First Lord of the Admiralty from 1794 to 1801. He was by general consent an able and conscientious minister, but he was also a great Whig grandee, with all the normal political expectations of his age and class, and no previous experience of the Navy to educate him in a different way of handling political patronage. Rightly or wrongly, some contemporaries believed that Spencer filled the Navy with the sons of his friends at the expense of merit and service. Nelson and St.Vincent, among others, complained of the destructive effect of 'the Honourables'.[46] 'Your encouragement for those Lieutenants who may conspicuously exert themselves,' Nelson told his chief, 'cannot fail to have its good effect in serving our Country, instead of their thinking that if a Vessel is taken, it would make the son of some great man a Captain, in place of the gallant fellow who captured her.'[47] When he took office, St.Vincent contrasted his own rectitude with his predecessor's laxity: 'The circumstances of the war, and the numerous

---

[44]   Edward Pelham Brenton, *Life and Correspondence of John, Earl of St.Vincent* (London, 1838, 2 vols), II, 52; to Chief Justice Pipon, 19 Feb 1801.

[45]   Jedediah Stevens Tucker, *Memoirs of Admiral the Right Hon. the Earl of St.Vincent* (London, 1844, 2 vols), II, 175; to Sir W. Dickson, 1 Mar 1801.

[46]   Sir N.H. Nicolas, *The Despatches and Letters of Vice Admiral Lord Viscount Nelson* (London, 1844–45, 7 vols), II, 398.

[47]   Nicolas, *Despatches*, II, 406–407; to Jervis, 5 Jul 1797.

XV

connexions of the Spencer Family, have contributed to swell the list of post-captains and commanders to an enormous size, insomuch I have determined not to promote to those ranks, except in cases of extraordinary merit and service, until the worthy on half-pay are provided for.'[48] To another correspondent he complained that 'the list of lieutenants abounds with improper persons who have obtained promotions by influence.'[49] When he retired, St.Vincent told the king

> that a sprinkling of nobility was very desirable in the Navy, as it gives some sort of consequence to the service; but at present the Navy is so overun by the younger branches of nobility, and the sons of Members of Parliament, and they so swallow up all the patronage, and so choke the channel to promotion, that the son of an old Officer, however meritorious *both* their services may have been, has little or no chance of getting on.[50]

Until Spencer's papers are thoroughly studied, it will not be possible to say if St.Vincent's insinuation was justified. What is rather clearer is that St.Vincent himself was not as rigorous towards his own friends and connections as he wished people to think. 'The officers of the *Ville de Paris*,' he wrote to one applicant in April 1801, 'remain as they did when I left her; and my own nephew, commander of the *Stork* sloop, who is reputed an officer of uncommon merit and acquirements, stands as he did before I came into office ; and I have refused to promote at the request of four princes of the blood.'[51] What he did not mention was that he was at the same time encouraging overseas commanders-in-chief to create false vacancies by bogus resignations.[52] The Peace of Amiens gave him the excuse for a large promotion, apparently modelled on Keppel's of 1782: 'I agree with you that the Board should be governed by former practice at the close of such a successful naval war as we have witnessed.'[53] When the war resumed, St.Vincent adopted the same austere promotion policy, in public. On 18th May 1803 he assured the Marquis of Douglas, 'I have not forgot Lord Cochrane, but I should not be justified in appointing him to the command of an 18-pounder frigate when there are so many senior Captains of great merit without ships of that class.'[54] Douglas might have been surprised to read the letter St.Vincent had written the previous day to Sir Andrew Mitchell at Halifax:

[48] Smith, *St.Vincent Letters*, I, 331, to Sir J. Carter, 17 Feb 1801.
[49] Brenton, *St.Vincent*, II, 72, to Visct. Bulkeley, 18 Jun 1801.
[50] Tucker, *St.Vincent*, II, 267.
[51] Brenton, *St.Vincent*, II, 62; to Mrs Montagu, Admiralty 6 Apr 1801.
[52] Smith, *St.Vincent Letters*, I, 270.
[53] Brenton, *St.Vincent*, II, 86; to Sir P. Stephens, 5 Oct 1801.
[54] Smith, *St.Vincent Letters*, II, 337.

This will be delivered to you by Captain Fane of the *Driver*, son of Mr Fane, Member of the County of Oxford, who is sent out to you with a view to his being promoted to the rank of Post-Captain... Captain Fane is a near relation of mine and every way worthy your good offices and protection.[55]

St. Vincent was not quite breaking the conventions he had inherited, but he was certainly stretching them for a young cousin whose career, though respectable, was not remotely as distinguished as Cochrane's.

There is at least circumstantial evidence, therefore, that political and personal influence was gaining promotions more easily during the Great Wars than they had done during the Seven Years War or the American War.[56] Collingwood had a good opinion of Lord Mulgrave as First Lord, but he also thought that political influence on promotions was inescapable: 'the truth is, that he is so pressed by persons having parliamentary influence, that he cannot find himself at liberty to select those whose nautical skill and gallantry would otherwise present them as proper men for the service. A hole or two in the skin will not weigh against a vote in Parliament...'[57] Further research is needed before we can say whether Collingwood was right, and identify who, if anybody, relaxed the strict resistance to political interference which had marked Anson's and Sandwich's handling of naval patronage. It is in the nature of historical statistics that they seldom provide complete answers in themselves, and this paper certainly does not. What these graphs and tables do is to make clearer than before exactly how the naval promotion system worked, and to demonstrate beyond any reasonable doubt that it broke down during the Great Wars against France.

---

[55]   Smith, *St. Vincent Letters*, II, 329.

[56]   For which see Rodger, *Wooden World*, pp. 331–343; and *Insatiable Earl*, pp. 172–192.

[57]   G.L. Newnham Collingwood, *A Selection from the Public and Private Correspondence of Vice-Admiral Lord Collingwood: Interspersed with Memoirs of his Life* (London, 4th edn. 1829), pp. 549–550; to Capt. J. Clavell, 20 Oct 1809.

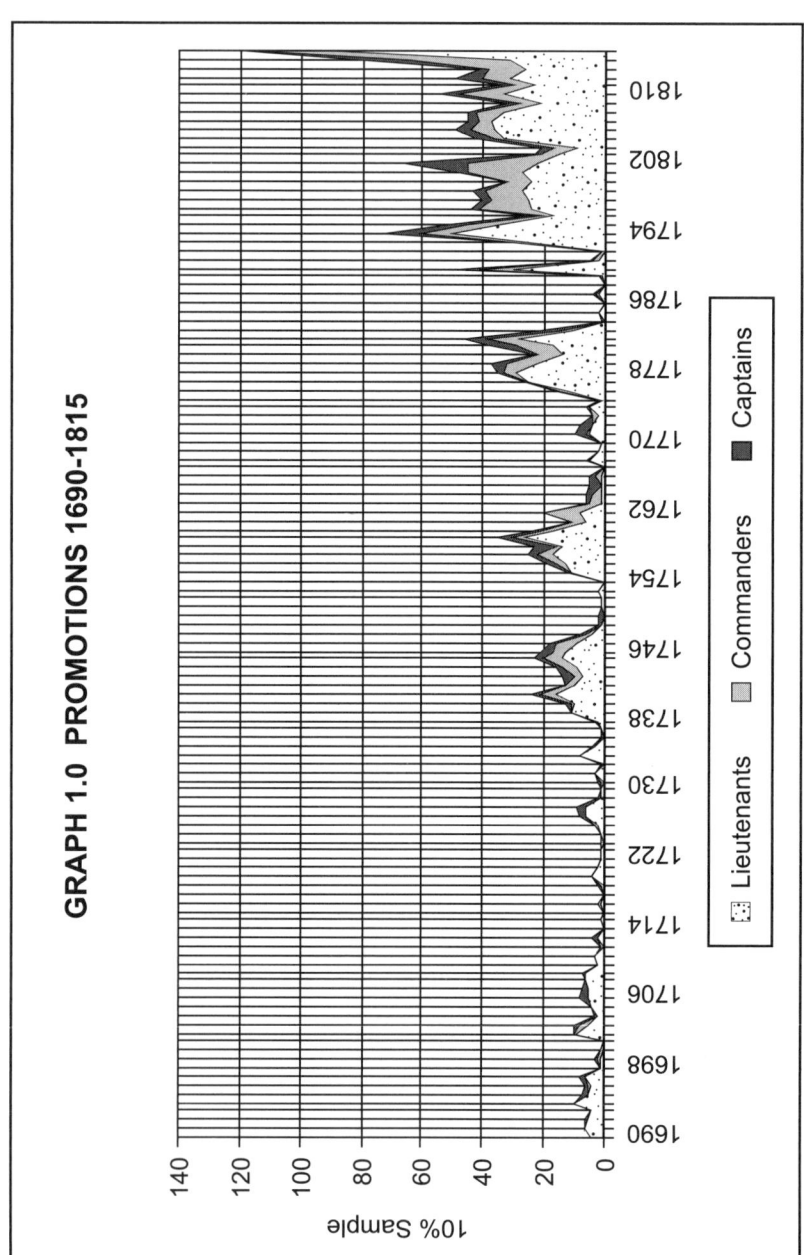

GRAPH 1.0 PROMOTIONS 1690-1815

10% Sample

Legend: Lieutenants · Commanders · Captains

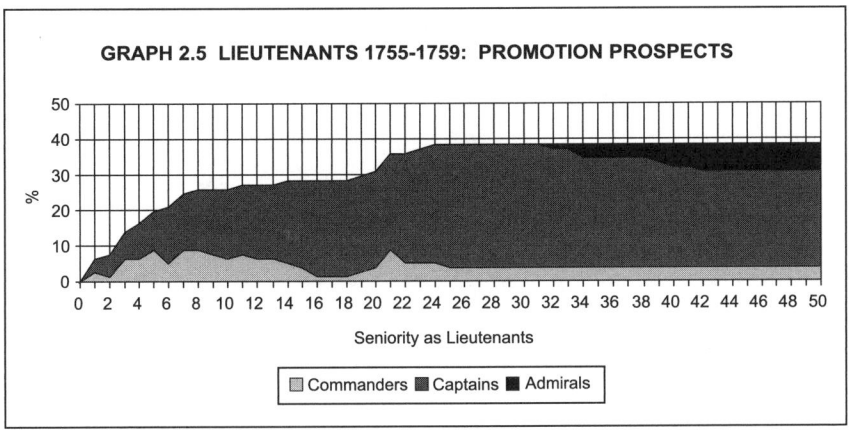

Source: *CSO*; Sample: 81.

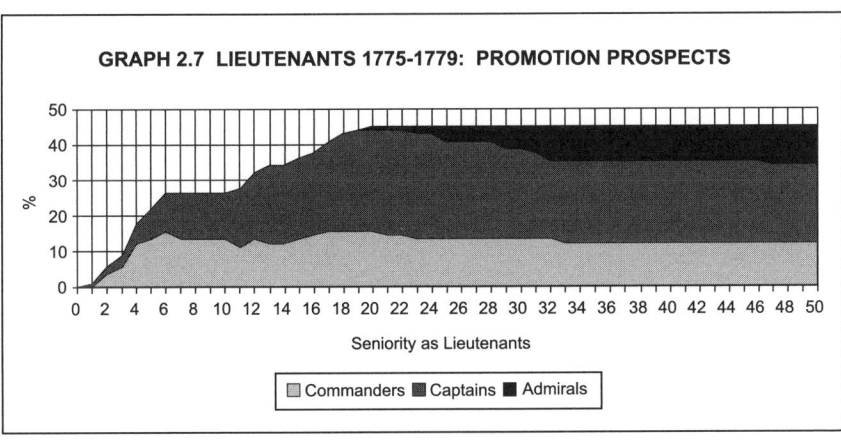

Source: *CSO*; Sample: 89.

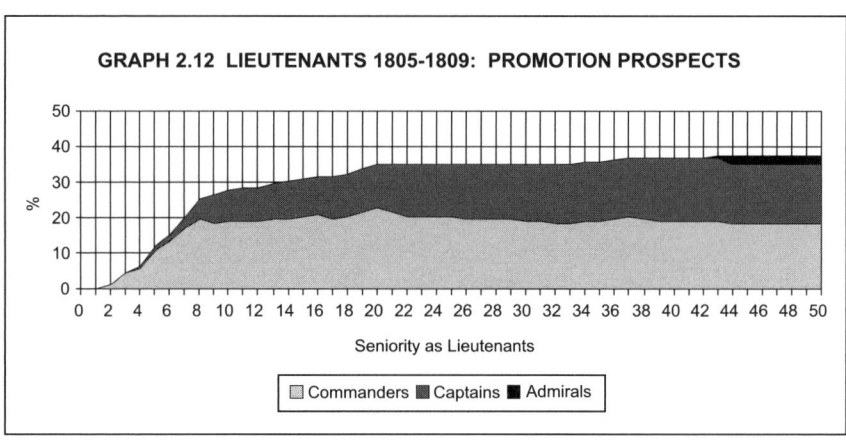

Source: *CSO*; Sample: 160.

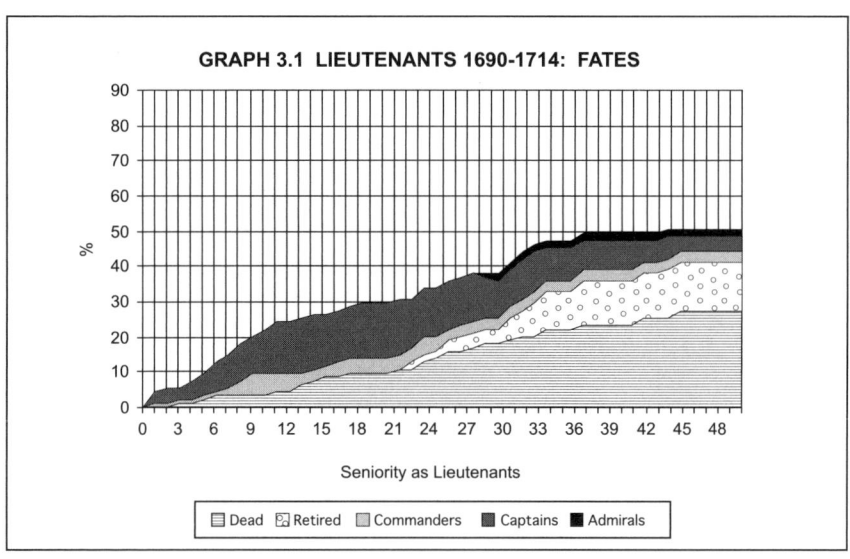

Source: *CSO*; Sample: 94.

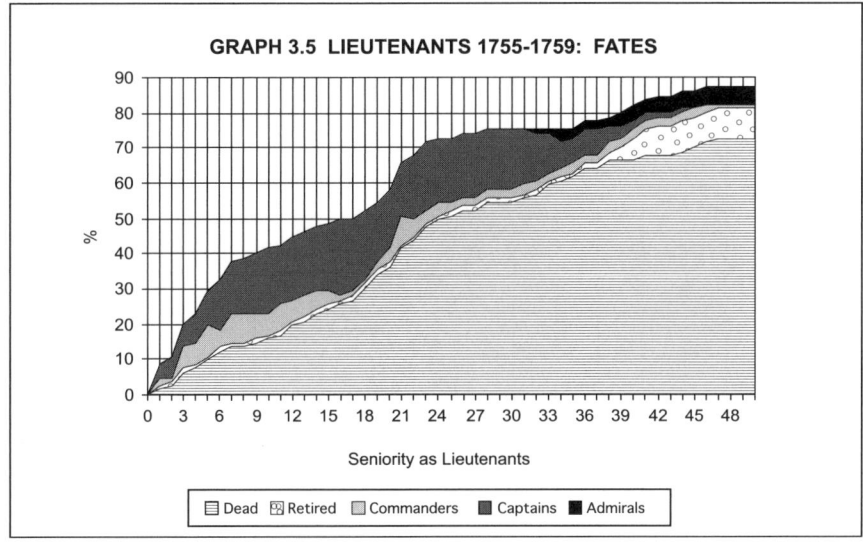

Source: *CSO*; Sample: 81.

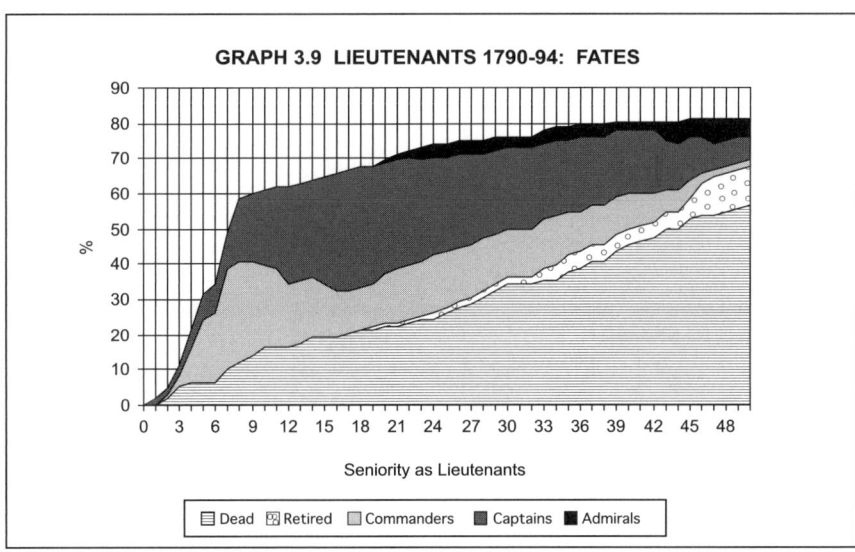

Source: *CSO*; Sample: 108.

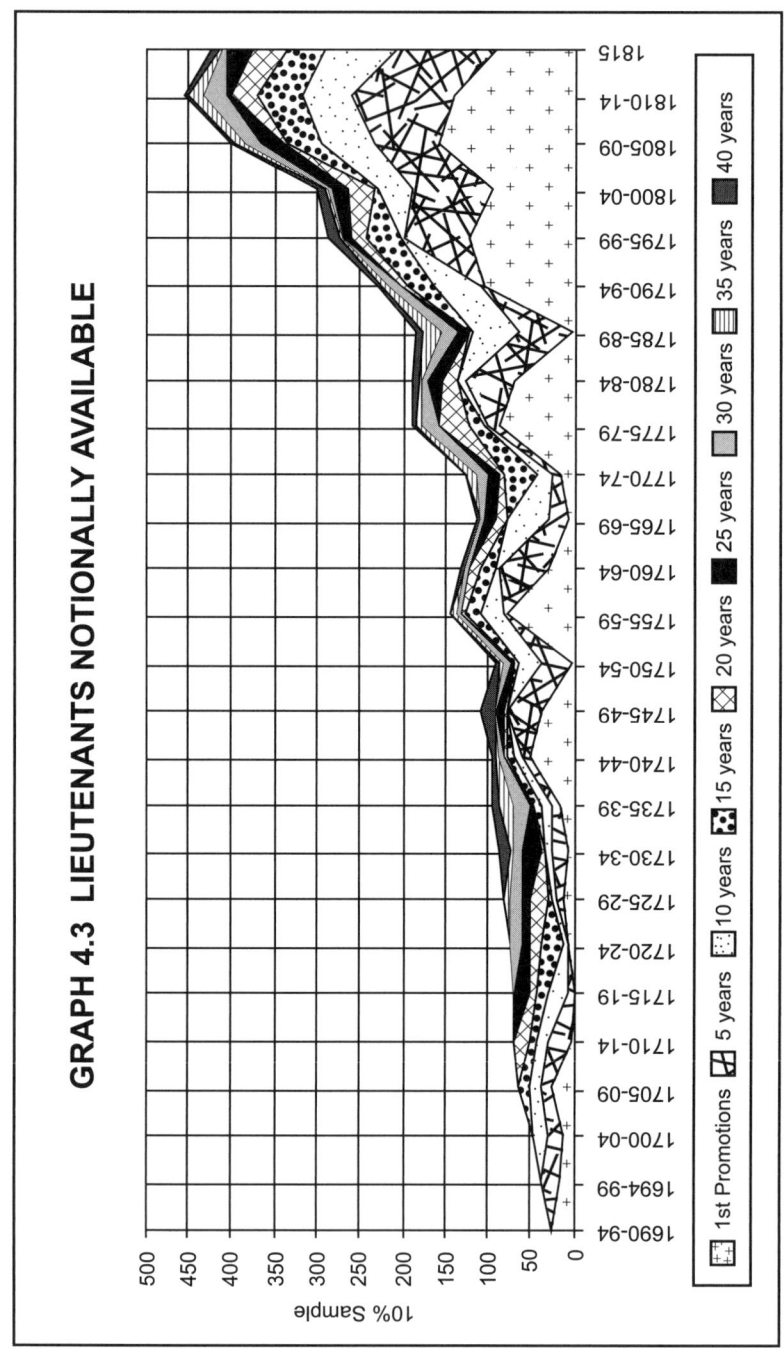

GRAPH 4.3 LIEUTENANTS NOTIONALLY AVAILABLE

Source: *CSO*.

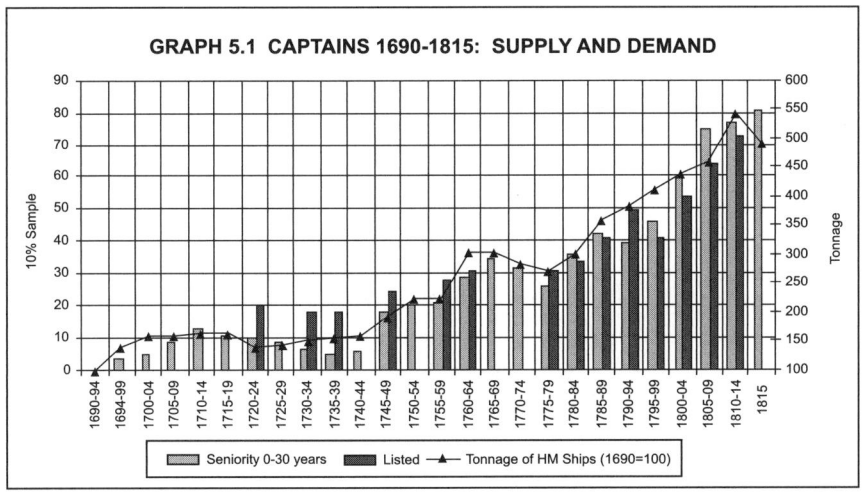

Sources: ADM 118/1–2, 5–6, 26–27, 29, 31 & 71. *Steel's Navy List* Aug 1790, Jul 1792, Jun 1794, Jul 1795, Jul 1800 & Jun 1810. Jan Glete, *Navies and Nations: Warships, Navies and State Building in Europe and America, 1500–1860* (Stockholm, 1993, 2 vols) II, 551–553.

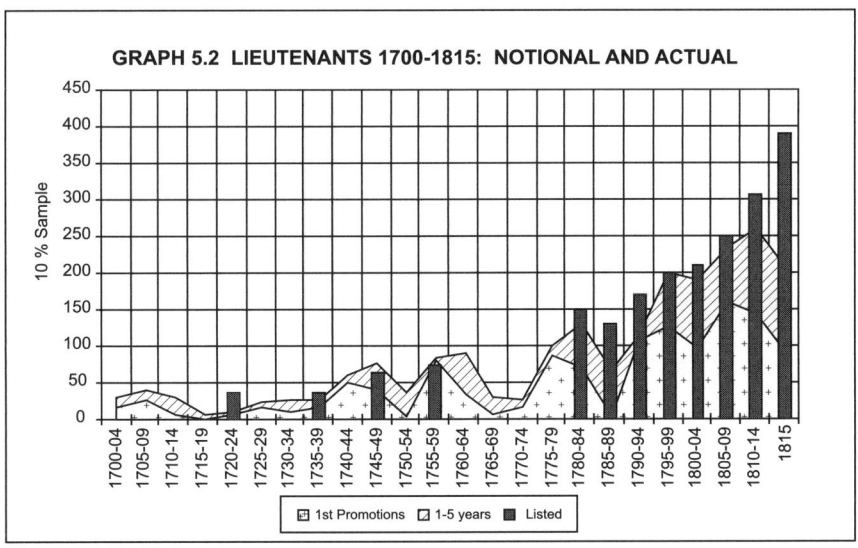

Sources: ADM 118/1–2, 5, 31–32, 71 & 84. *Steel's Navy List* Aug 1790, Jul 1792, Jun 1794, Jul 1795, Jul 1800 & Jun 1810. *Naval Promotions* (House of Commons Sessional Papers 1833 XXIV 279), p. 282.

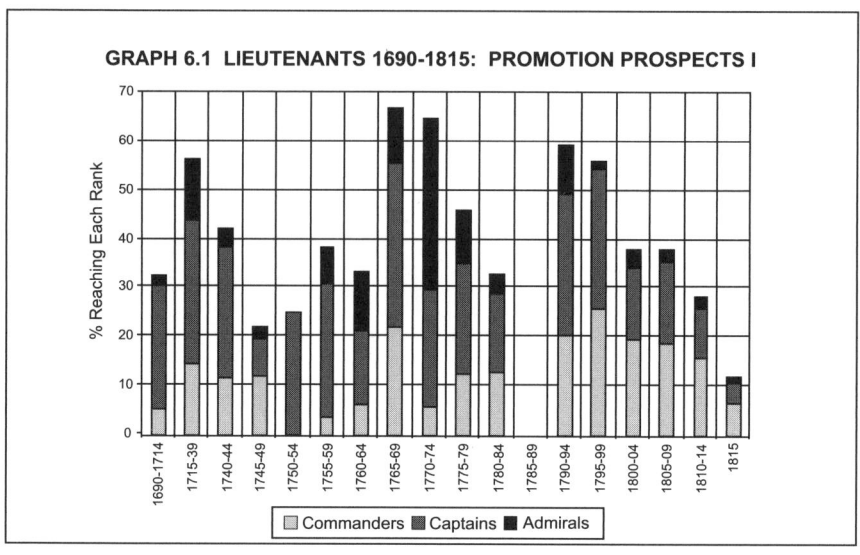

Source: *CSO.*

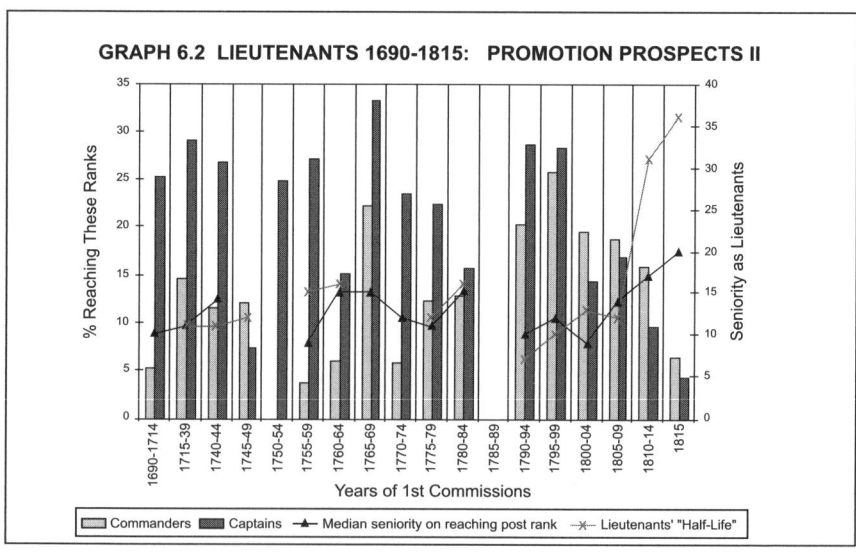

Source: *CSO.*

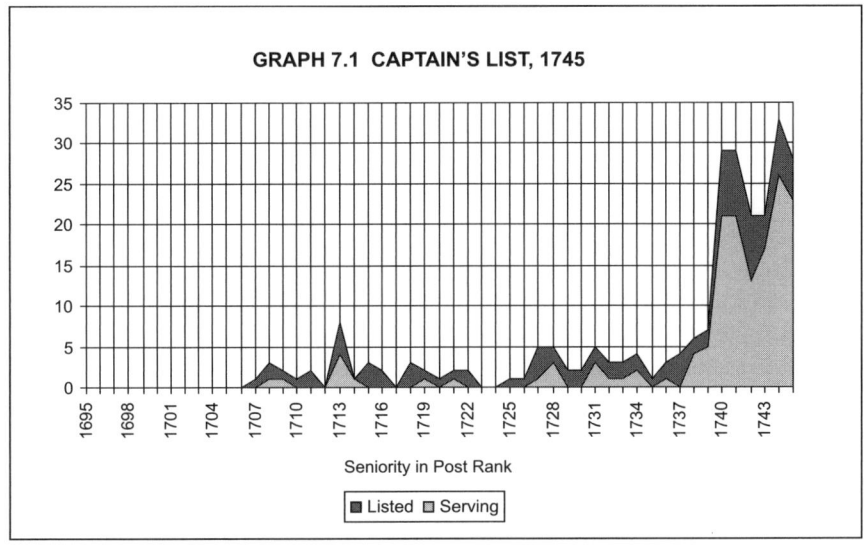

Source: ADM 118/2.

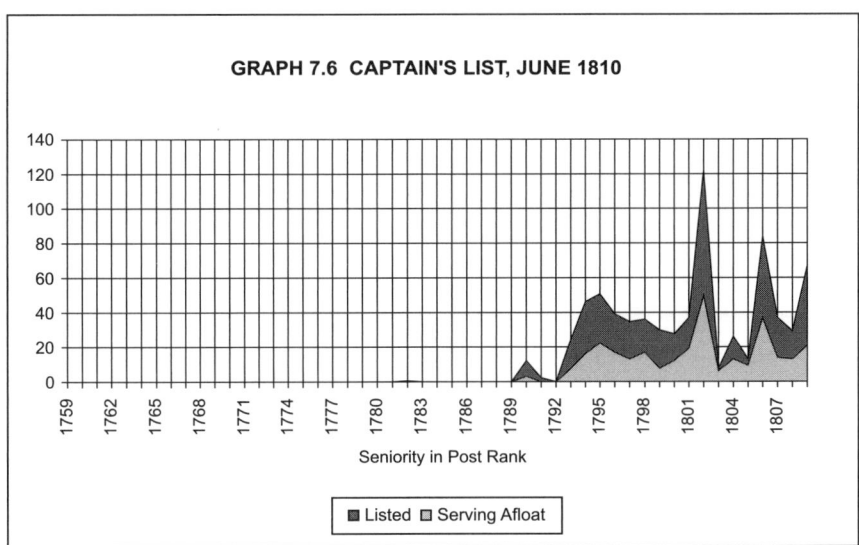

Sources: *Steel's Navy List* June 1810; ADM 118/84.

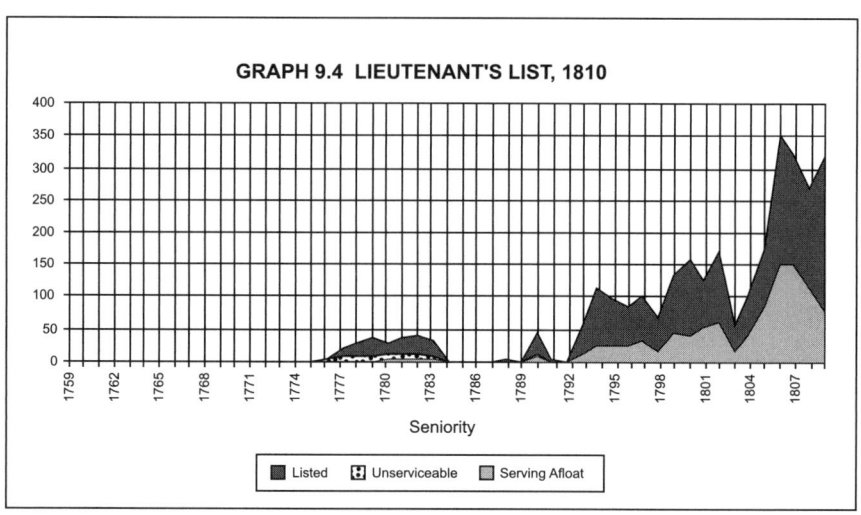

Sources: *Steel's Navy List* June 1810; ADM 118/84.

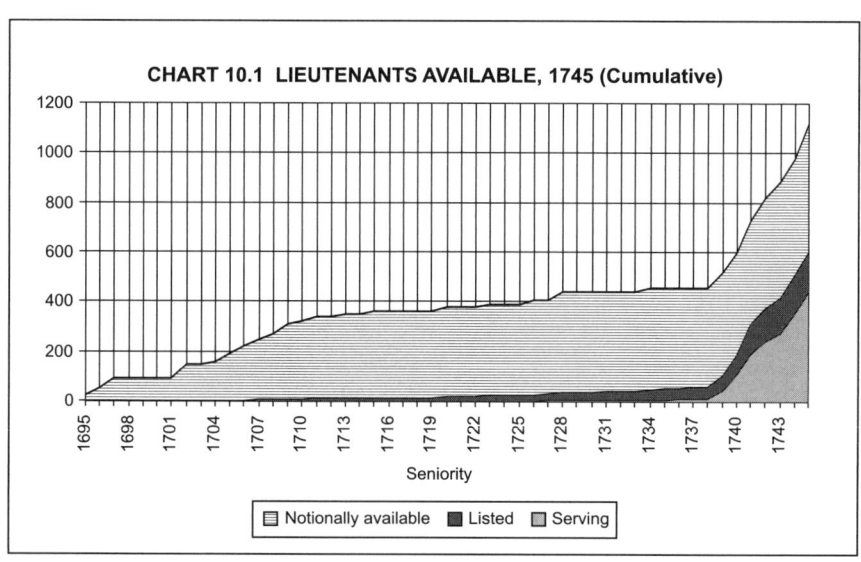

Sources: *CSO*; ADM 118/2.

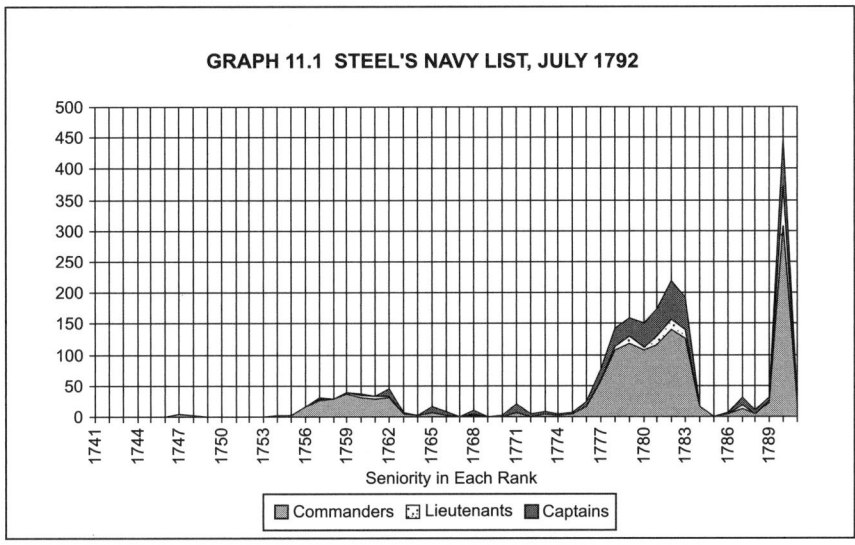

GRAPH 11.1 STEEL'S NAVY LIST, JULY 1792

Seniority in Each Rank

☐ Commanders ☐ Lieutenants ■ Captains

Source: *Steel's Navy List* July 1792.

XVI

Mutiny or subversion? Spithead and the Nore

For a number of reasons, it is – or at least, it ought to be – still difficult to write about the 1797 naval mutinies. The first problem is the lack of research. Until relatively recently naval historians tended to be uninterested in social history and somewhat embarrassed by the great mutinies themselves. Historians in general during most of the twentieth century have not been much interested in the Navy. The 1797 mutinies were spectacular events, not to be ignored, and scholars have been ready enough to cite them in support of their arguments, but rather less ready to undertake any serious research into them. The result is that the first, and nearly the last, serious study of these mutinies was published in 1913.[1] Only in recent years has scholarly interest revived, and most of the recent research is still unpublished.[2] Moreover several of the most important categories of evidence are still unexploited,[3] and the social history of the Navy in this period has still not been extensively studied.[4] The time is therefore not yet ripe to attempt any serious reconsideration of the significance of the mutinies.

1   Conrad Gill, *The naval mutinies of 1797* (Manchester, 1913). Since then two further studies have been published. G.E. Manwaring and Bonamy Dobrée, *The floating republic: An account of the mutinies at Spithead and the Nore in 1797* (London, 1935) use documents and add some material facts, but they are less than impartial, and their underlying purpose is evidently to comment on the 1931 Invergordon Mutiny; James Dugan, *The great mutiny* (London, 1966) is not without merit, but romantic, unhistorical and wildly partisan.
2   I refer in particular to the (as yet unpublished) papers given at the two '1797' conferences organised by Ann Coats and Philip MacDougall. I am extremely grateful to Miss Coats, Dr MacDougall and Dr Doorne for the chance to read these papers in advance of their publication. See also the theses of Neale, Oprey and Doorne, referred to below.
3   Notably the ships' musters (Coats' and Doorne's work excepted), and the bulk of the admiralty intelligence records.
4   Michael Lewis, *A social history of the navy, 1793–1815* (London, 1960) was a pioneer effort, but Lewis was mainly interested in officers, and scarcely used documents at all. J.D. Byrn, *Crime and punishment in the Royal Navy: Discipline on the Leeward Islands station, 1784–1812* (Aldershot, 1989) is solid and useful. Brian Lavery, *Nelson's navy: The ships, men and organization, 1793–1815* (London, 1989) deals intelligently but briefly with social history. Dudley Pope, *Life in Nelson's Navy* (London, 1981) is a good popular account based on wide reading and some documentary research. John Masefield, *Sea life in Nelson's time* (London, 1905) still has its admirers, but none among those who know anything at all of the subject.

550

This may not be a subject which inspires much research, but it certainly inspires interest, commitment, and sometimes passion. A number of those who have written about the 1797 mutinies have been more or less explicitly applying their history to support modern political or social causes;[5] and at least one is candid enough to admit that he has selected his evidence accordingly.[6] In Irish history likewise, objectivity has not always been regarded as a virtue, and the intersection of the two subjects in the 1797 mutinies makes it particularly difficulty to maintain ones balance while standing firmly on the evidence.

Fortunately this does not mean that it is impossible to say anything at all about the 1797 mutinies. Before attempting to do so, however, it may be well to sketch briefly the actual events. It is customary to speak of two great naval mutinies, at Spithead and the Nore, but it would be more accurate to distinguish four – the first and second Spithead mutinies, the Nore mutiny, and the mutiny of the North Sea Squadron off Yarmouth which subsequently joined the Nore mutiny. These mutinies differed significantly from one another, and it is not safe to assume that they all had the same origins; indeed, it has been for some time usual among naval historians to draw a clear distinction between the 'unpolitical' (benign, morally justified) Spithead mutinies, and the 'political' or 'revolutionary' (malign and dangerous) mutinies on the East Coast.[7] It is also relevant to look briefly at a number of single-ship mutinies or conspiracies later in 1797 and in 1798, because they were possibly connected with the Irish rebellion, and because several historians have deduced from them evidence of widespread underground movements.[8]

The Channel or Grand Fleet, which was the principal British squadron, had been commanded from the outbreak of war by Lord Howe, under whose command it won the battle of 1 June 1794. Howe was by this time sixty-eight and

5   Roger Wells, *Insurrection: The British experience 1795–1803* (Gloucester, 1983), with its frequent references to the 'Peace Movement', hints at such an engagement. Joseph Price Moore III, '"The greatest enormity that prevails": Direct democracy and workers' self-management in the British naval mutinies of 1797', in Colin Howell and R.J. Twomey (eds), *Jack Tar in history: Essays in the history of maritime life and labour* (Fredericton, N.B., 1991) pp 76–104, makes no secret of it: 'In the late capitalist world, the story of the meanings we have been trying to locate here is still, despite many of our battles lost, very far from having ended': p. 103.

6   Jonathan Neale, *The cutlass and the lash: Mutiny and discipline in Nelson's Navy* (London, 1985), p. 12 n.7. The author acknowledges (p. x) the encouragement of the Socialist Workers' Party; a healthy corrective to the quarter-deck view, perhaps, but not without some risk of another bias. Cf. the introduction to the same author's 'Forecastle and quarterdeck: Protest, discipline and mutiny in the Royal Navy 1793–1814' (unpublished Ph.D. thesis, University of Warwick, 1990). But in his thesis especially, Neale's handling of the evidence he has chosen to use is exemplary, and his work is highly useful even to those who do not share his politics.

7   This interpretation derives from Manwaring and Dobrée, *Floating republic*, implicitly commenting on the 1931 Invergordon Mutiny. Ann Coats in 'Spithead Introduction' argues that the contrast has been over-drawn.

8   Wells, *Insurrection*, pp 145–50; Marianne Elliott, *Partners in revolution: The United Irishmen and France* (New Haven, 1982), pp 138, 143.

XVI

Mutiny or subversion? Spithead and the Nore 551

anxious to retire, but the king was reluctant to part with him, and for three years he remained officially in command though for much of the time he was actually ill ashore, while his second-in-command Lord Bridport took the fleet to sea. This uncomfortable arrangement might have strained the warmest friendship, and the two admirals were not on good terms. Howe, unlike Bridport, had long been a believer in distant blockade, keeping the main fleet safely at anchor, especially in winter, while frigates watched the enemy ports until their observations, combined with intelligence from other sources, gave warning that the enemy was preparing to sail. In principle there was much to be said for this strategy, but it depended on good intelligence and communications.[9] Its disadvantages were well illustrated by Hoche's midwinter expedition to Ireland, which the Channel Fleet altogether failed to intercept; Bridport was generally blamed for this failure, though the fault was arguably Howe's, and Vice-Admiral Colpoys was actually commanding part of the fleet at sea at the time.[10] The strategy also involved keeping the main fleet at anchor for long periods, which saved damage and danger to the ships but gave the men much leisure to think and talk about their situation. In February and March 1797, Howe, convalescing at Bath, received a number of anonymous petitions purporting to come from various ships of his fleet (which was then at sea), requesting higher pay. On his own account he did not take them very seriously, but he made some enquiries in the fleet, apparently without informing Bridport, and unofficially passed the petitions to the admiralty. Similar petitions had already been received there, and ignored. In this case Lord Spencer, the first lord of the admiralty, sent the petitions to Bridport for his comments.[11]

By the time he received them it was too late. The fleet returned to Spithead on 30 Mar. After waiting two weeks for a reply, the seamen put their plans into motion. Only in the last few days did it become obvious to their officers that something was afoot. Bridport from the start advised negotiation and conciliation, but the admiralty's reaction to the rumour of discontent was to order the fleet to sea. This gave the signal for the outbreak of the mutiny on Easter Sunday 16 April.[12] The mutiny was essentially a collective refusal to obey the order to weigh anchor. For the next week the fleet was immobilized by the mutineers while a body of elected delegates, two from each ship, negotiated first with

9   A.N. Ryan, 'The Royal Navy and the blockade of Brest, 1689–1805: Theory and practice', in Martine Acerra, José Merino and Jean Meyer (eds), *Les marines de guerre Européennes, XVII–XVIIIe siècles* (Paris, 1985), pp 183–4; John Barrow, *The life of Richard, Earl Howe, K.G.* (London, 1838), pp 216–18.

10 Richard Saxby, 'Lord Bridport and the Spithead mutiny', in *Mariner's Mirror*, lxxix (1993), 170.

11 Gill, *Naval mutinies*, pp 7–12. One of the petitions is printed with other documents by D. Bonner Smith, 'The naval mutinies of 1797' in *Mariner's Mirror*, xxi (1935), 428–49; xxii (1936), 65–86.

12 Gill, *Naval mutinies*, pp 16–21; Saxby, 'Lord Bridport', pp 171–3.

552

Bridport, and later with the board of admiralty itself led by Lord Spencer. Although a few unpopular officers were sent ashore, no violence or disorder occurred, and the mutineers did not interfere with the ordinary routine of their ships. On 19 April, indeed, the grand duke of Württemberg, in England for his marriage to Princess Charlotte, paid a state visit to the fleet accompanied by Spencer and the lords of the admiralty, the mutineers politely manning the yards and firing the appropriate salutes.[13] The mutineer delegates insisted throughout on their readiness to sail immediately if the French fleet put out from Brest, and would not allow frigates and convoy escorts to join them, lest trade should suffer. They strongly denied any political motives and proclaimed their loyalty to the king. Their principal demands were for an increase of wages, together with various improvements in the quality and quantity of victuals and the treatment of the wounded. Most of these were eventually conceded, and with the arrival of a royal pardon on Sunday 23 April the first Spithead mutiny was officially over.[14]

The necessary legislation was now set in motion, but the motions of parliament were too slow for the seamen, who became increasingly suspicious that they had been deceived. On 7 May the mutiny broke out anew. This time there was violence, though not from the mutineers: Colpoys ordered the officers of his flagship, the *London*, to fire on the mutineers, several of whom were killed. The enraged men nearly hanged the admiral and one of his officers in retaliation, but were dissuaded by two of the leading delegates. Colpoys, Vice-Admiral Gardner, ten captains and one hundred other officers (about one-fifth of the total) were now sent ashore and the mutineers took effective command of the fleet, but the remaining captains and admirals, including Bridport, remained aboard. Two days later the necessary act of parliament finally passed the Lords and received the royal assent. Lord Howe had at last been allowed to resign his command in April, but he now came to Portsmouth on behalf of the king to persuade the mutineers that their demands really had been granted. In addition they now insisted that a list of named unpopular officers (about half of those who had been sent ashore) should be replaced, and this Howe conceded. The reconciliation was completed with ceremonies on 15 May, culminating in a banquet given by Howe for the delegates of the fleet. Two days later Bridport was able to sail to take station off Brest.[15]

Meanwhile another mutiny had broken out among the ships at the Nore. This anchorage off Sheerness dockyard, at the junction of the Thames and Medway, was a focal point where ships coming from Chatham and the river yards, or those returning from sea, often spent a few days. It was also a major distribution centre for new recruits, and an old line-of-battleship, the *Sandwich*, lay permanently off Sheerness as 'guardship', which in practice meant floating barracks. A flag offi-

---

13 Manwaring and Dobrée, *Floating republic*, p. 54.
14 Gill, *Naval mutinies*, pp 360–76, prints the main documents bearing on these negotiations.
15 Ibid., pp 55–82.

XVI

Mutiny or subversion? Spithead and the Nore 553

cer, Vice-Admiral Buckner, supervised the business of the port, and flew his flag on her. There was no fleet at the Nore, accustomed to operating together, simply a small, transient population of ships most of which stayed there only briefly. When mutiny broke out there on 12 May, it initially aroused little alarm, and virtually no official reaction. Only after twelve days, when it became clear that the concessions made at Spithead were not going to satisfy the new mutineers, did the admiralty react. The Nore mutineers demanded not only the same concessions given at Spithead (which in reality had already been granted to the whole Navy), but more regular pay, advance wages for pressed men, a right to leave in port, a more equitable distribution of prize money, a standing pardon for returning deserters, and an effective veto on the appointment of officers.[16] (Neither at Spithead nor the Nore did the mutineers mention either impressment or flogging as grievances, and the mutineer leaders themselves flogged men for drunkenness.)[17] To cement their cause the mutineers imposed rigorous discipline, stopping all communication with the shore in order that the men should not discover the concessions made at Spithead, and not hesitating to fire on ships which offered to leave the anchorage.[18]

The board of admiralty arrived on the scene on 28 May, but from the beginning they refused to make further concessions, and stopped shore supplies to the mutineers. They must have known that the new mutiny had little of the public support of the old and virtually none of the leverage. The Channel Fleet was the country's principal strength and only safeguard against invasion; the small group of ships at the Nore had limited opportunity to do mischief, and several of them were visibly reluctant to remain in the mutiny. On 30 May the frigates *Clyde* and *San Fiorenzo* escaped under fire from the mutineers. The Nore mutiny was then on the verge of collapse, but it was saved by the mutiny of Admiral Duncan's North Sea Squadron off Yarmouth on 27 May, after which most of the squadron sailed to join the Nore mutineers. This was another crisis, potentially worse than the Spithead mutinies, for Duncan's task was to blockade the Dutch fleet in the Texel, which (unlike the French in Brest) was known to be ready for sea and preparing for an expedition. For some days Duncan was reduced to keeping up a pretence of blockade with two ships only. Moreover the reinforced Nore mutineers became increasingly extreme in their attitudes as their situation grew more difficult. For three days they attempted a complete blockade of the Thames, and when that failed they discussed sailing their ships to an enemy or neutral port. But supplies were short, the navigation buoys had

16 The mutineers do not seem to have known that their demand to be paid up to six months in arrears on sailing was already law under the 1758 Navy Act. See Stephen Gradish, *The manning of the British navy during the Seven Years War* (London, 1980), pp 88–96.

17 Gill, *Naval mutinies*, pp 43, 278–81; Dugan, *Great mutiny*, p. 477.

18 Gill, *Naval mutinies*, pp 107–41; D. Bonner-Smith, 'The mutiny at the Nore, 1797', *Mariner's Mirror*, xxxiii (1947), 199–203.

been removed, more and more ships found means to desert the mutineers, and when they gave the signal to sail on 9 June no ship obeyed it. After fighting on board, all the mutinous ships had been recaptured by loyalist seamen by 13 June, and the last of the great mutinies was over.[19]

There were however a number of mutinous incidents in individual ships over the next few years. Besides those on overseas stations, they included the conspiracy that same month aboard the *Pompée* of Bridport's fleet, in which a number of men apparently planned to seize the ship and, possibly, hand her over to the French at Brest;[20] and the discontent aboard the *Mars* that summer which led to another court martial.[21] In the summer of 1798 undoubted United Irish plots were detected aboard the *Caesar* and *Defiance*, and a possible one aboard the *Glory*.[22] At the same time individuals aboard several other ships were convicted of using 'mutinous or seditious expressions'.[23]

Broadly speaking, four different explanations have been offered for the 1797 mutinies. The first might be called the traditional naval historians' explanation, except that there is no strong tradition among naval historians of studying the mutinies. According to this understanding, the Spithead mutinies were in part what they pretended to be, a strictly professional movement for purely naval ends, conducted and resolved with good sense on either side; a regrettable incident but one demonstrating the English virtues of moderation and tolerance. Behind them, however, and much more clearly in the East Coast mutinies, we can detect the evil influence of outside agitators working on the simple sailors in the interests of the country's enemies – even though here, too, good sense eventually triumphed when the loyal majority overthrew the troublemakers.[24]

It is implicit, and often explicit, in this interpretation that the seamen were essentially loyal but unsophisticated men, whose generous sympathies were easily perverted by designing landsmen without whose malign influence politics would never have corrupted the Arcadian simplicity of naval life. Certainly the Spithead mutineers had grievances and were justified in bringing them to the authorities' notice, but their mutiny was not a political action. The Navy's principal fleet remained undefiled by civilian politics. At the Nore it was different,

---

19 Gill, *Naval mutinies*, pp 151–240.

20 Dugan, *Great mutiny*, pp 340–1; Gill, *Naval mutinies*, pp 84, 117, n.2; Wells, *Insurrection*, p. 101.

21 Ibid., p. 101; Dugan, *Great mutiny*, p. 366.

22 Ibid., pp 427–8; Neale, 'Forecastle and quarterdeck', pp 332–4; Wells, *Insurrection*, pp 149–50. Doorne, who has studied these incidents in detail, regards the evidence of United Irish involvement as circumstantial, but strong.

23 Dugan, *Great mutiny*, pp 427–8.

24 Manwaring and Dobrée, *Floating republic*, pp 14–17; Lewis, *Social history*, pp 123–6. Of these three authors, Manwaring (a librarian) had written a good deal of naval history, Dobrée was a Professor of English, and Lewis was Professor of History at the R.N. College, Greenwich. Gill, *Naval mutinies*, pp 300–46, takes essentially the same line with rather more sophistication.

XVI

Mutiny or subversion? Spithead and the Nore   555

and the question was how and whence the evil influence of civilians had pene-trated the Navy.

There was an obvious answer, already proposed at the time, and subsequently adopted by most historians – the Quota Acts.[25] During 1795 and 1796 the gov-ernment passed a series of five acts which laid obligations on local authorities in England, Wales and Scotland to provide fixed numbers of recruits for the Navy or army. These recruits were implicitly to be volunteers, since no mechanism for compulsion was provided in the acts, only the means to raise money with which to pay bounties. Those authorities which failed to meet their quotas were to pay fines instead.[26] The 1795 acts, which coincided with a time of dearth and unem-ployment, appear to have been successful, but the 1796 acts proposed much smaller quotas, and produced so few men that the scheme was then abandoned. The suggestion usually made is that these acts had introduced numbers of landsmen – and what was worse, landsmen of some education – whose evil influ-ence had corrupted the simple sailors; 'the pernicious leaven working, or striving to work, in the healthy lump'.[27] One outstanding piece of evidence supports this argument; Richard Parker, the leader (or in some interpretations, figurehead) of the Nore mutiny, was a Quota man, and a former pupil of Exeter Grammar School who at one period in his life had kept a school – though he was also a professional seaman and a former inferior officer in the Navy.[28] The Quota Acts have served subsequent historians as the perfect vehicle for every theory, each proposing their own favourite candidates as the Quota men who must have inspired the mutinies.

For the naval historians it was sufficient that the Quota men were, or could be assumed to be, outsiders, landsmen, alien to the naval character. Non-naval his-torians, however, have found it needful to identify the Quota men with an appro-priate category ashore. The first of these interpretations is what we might call the romantic socialist view. It may be conveniently summed up in a quotation from E.P. Thompson:

25 Ibid., pp 315–17; Manwaring and Dobrée, *Floating republic*, p. 16; Lewis, *Social history*, pp 121–3; Wells, *Insurrection*, p. 94.
26 The Quota Acts were: 35 Geo.III c.5, which levied all English and Welsh counties for the Navy (9,420 men in total); 35 Geo.III c.9, which levied English, Welsh and Scottish seaports for the Navy (19,866 men in total, each able seaman to count as two); 35 Geo.III c.29, which levied Scottish counties, cities and burghs for the Navy (total 1,814 men); 37 Geo.III c.4, which levied English and Welsh counties, some for the army and some for the Navy (naval total 6,146 men); and 37 Geo.III c.5, which levied Scottish counties, cities and burghs for either service at the volunteers' choice (total 2,219 men). In addition there were several amending and explaining acts.
27 Lewis, *Social history*, p. 123.
28 Gill, *Naval mutinies*, pp 124–8. Parker's own account of his life is printed in *Private papers of George, second Earl Spencer*, J.S. Corbett and H.W. Richmond (eds), Navy Records Society (vols xlvi, xlvii, xlviii and lix [1913–24]), ii, 160–73.

556

> It is foolish to argue that, because the majority of the sailors had few
> political notions, this was a parochial affair of ship's biscuits and arrears
> of pay, and not a revolutionary movement. This is to mistake the nature
> of popular revolutionary crises, which arise from exactly this kind of con-
> junction between the grievances of the majority and the aspirations artic-
> ulated by the politically conscious minority.[29]

The true meaning of the mutinies was nothing so trivial as naval affairs, which
Thompson had no idea of investigating; they were to be understood as a significant moment in that most significant of all historical movements, the rise of the
English working class. As an extension of this interpretation, it has since been
argued that the mutinies were the product of a native English 'peace movement',
centred on the Corresponding Societies and learning from the French example,
whose objective was to drive Britain out of the war and Pitt out of office, if not
to engineer another English republican revolution.[30] Pitt's 'reign of terror' was
on this interpretation thoroughly justified (pragmatically if not morally) for
exactly the reason with which he and his supporters justified it; the real and
grave threat posed by English revolutionaries to the survival of the regime.[31] But
not everyone agrees that the English were capable of revolution unaided, and the
same 1797 mutinies have been adduced as prime examples of the work of the
United Irishmen. Again it is argued that outside agitators were at work; again
the Quota Acts are offered as the mechanism by which they were introduced into
the Navy. In this case the outsiders are United Irishmen, their first target was the
large numbers of Irishmen in the Navy, and the 1797 mutinies join the list of
Irish revolutions which nearly worked.[32]

It has also been argued that Thompson was insufficiently rigorous in his
Marxism, that romantic notions of working-class solidarity are no substitute for
pure dialectic, and that the only way to understand the life of the Navy is in
terms of the struggling proletarians striving to escape the shackles of the capitalist mode of production. This tends to the unusual, almost unique, conclusion
that the seamen were not an isolated profession needing outsiders to teach them
their revolutionary responsibilities, but members of a radicalized working class
quite capable of mounting their own insurrection without the instruction of the
Quota men.[33]

---

29 E.P. Thompson, *The making of the English working class* (London, 1978), p. 184.
30 Wells, *Insurrection*, pp 81–150.
31 Ibid., p. 28.
32 Elliott, *Partners in revolution*, pp 135–44.
33 Neale, 'Forecastle and quarterdeck', pp 13–30, 329–31, 494, though he deals primarily with
    mutinies other than those of 1797. Moore, 'The Greatest enormity', is not far from this posi-
    tion, but he offers an eschatological interpetation of the mutinies and their significance in
    terms of Marxist salvation history; he has no clear view of their origin.

XVI

Mutiny or subversion? Spithead and the Nore 557

This, however, remains an eccentric position. Almost all historians who have written about the mutinies are agreed that they can only be explained by outside influence, and for all but the naval historians, it is clearly this which lends the subject its attraction. A purely naval mutiny, 'a parochial affair of ship's biscuits and arrears of pay', could be of no interest unless it involved an issue of historical importance, if not a cause worthy of the historian's commitment. Little writing, and less reading, have been bestowed upon the social history of the Navy itself, and historians have been happy to believe the most unlikely facts. The Spithead mutineers, for example, demanded the abolition of what they claimed to be the 'totally new' rating of landsman. It is an interesting question what they meant by this, but there is no question whatever that the rating of landsman and its equivalents ('landman' in the older form, and before that 'grommet') had been in continuous use in the Navy since the sixteenth century,[34] as anybody would know who had any acquaintance with the subject, but nobody does know who has actually published about it.[35] Almost without exception, the historians of the 1797 mutinies have preferred a leap of faith to a painful trawl through the naval archives.[36] Even Gill, the first and most scholarly student of the mutinies, who was interested in them for their own sake, was prone to abandon his notes in favour of assumptions unsupported by evidence or argument,[37] and his example has been willingly followed by those whose real interests lay elsewhere.

Three related aspects of the question may be used to support this charge; the leadership of the mutinies, the Quota Acts, and the sources of naval recruitment. Clearly if the mutinies were really led by Quota men, it is important to identify the leaders. In the case of the Spithead mutineers, there is no difficulty in doing so, for the delegates of the fleet put their names to documents and negotiated publicly. We know not only who they were, but their ages, ratings and places of

---

34   In sixteenth-century references, it is not always easy to distinguish a formal rating from a loose description, but 'grommets' are listed in the 1626 scale of sea pay, midway between seamen and boys; cf. *The naval tracts of Sir William Monson*, M. Oppenheim (ed.), Navy Records Society, vols xxii–xxiii, xliii, xlv, xlvii [1902–14], iii, 185–6.

35   Gill, *Naval mutinies*, p. 32; Manwaring and Dobrée, *Floating republic*, p. 52; Wells, *Insurrection*, p. 86; John Ehrman, *The younger Pitt: The consuming struggle* (London, 1996), p. 21, n.5. Even Lewis, *Social history*, pp 85, 94, is adrift on this point, though he did know something about the Navy.

36   I emphasise the *naval* archives; many of these writers have done admirable research into the subjects central to their interests.

37   Gill, *Naval mutinies*, for example – 'the secret societies to which many of the seamen belonged': pp 305–6; 'a widespread and dangerous conspiracy': p. 310; 'I have treated sedition and the belief in revolutionary theories as synonymous terms', (the evidence for 'revolutionary theories' being the use of language reminiscent of Paine): p. 314, n. 1; quota men 'as a rule, either debtors or men who had been convicted of petty fraud … persons of comparatively good education … [with] a slight and mischievous knowledge of the new political theories': pp 315–16; 'it is probable that several of the ringleaders at Spithead and at the Nore had been sent into the navy by the civil authorities': pp 316–17.

birth.[38] Moreover all this information has been in print since 1935, and it could easily be amplified from the available documents.[39] It has been ignored because it does not support any of the popular theories. Without exception the delegates were able seamen or seamen petty officers, ratings which they could not have reached without long experience at sea; none of them was a Quota man, and only four out of thirty-three were Irish.[40] Though the fact was long since disproved, it is still frequently repeated that Valentine Joyce, the delegates' spokesman, was a Belfast tobacconist and a Quota man.[41] In fact he was born in Jersey, had been a professional seaman all his life, and on his own statement had served in the Navy since he was eleven. His family lived in Portsmouth where his father was serving in the garrison.[42] It is only possible to believe that the mutiny was really led by Quota men if one believes that the delegates were straw men concealing the real leaders[43] – or the real leader, that shadowy Macavity of the Channel Fleet, the mysterious genius who 'must' have organized the mutiny but who covered his tracks so perfectly that no evidence of his existence survives.[44] Here we are in the presence of the conspiracy theory in its purest form, in which the entire absence of evidence only serves to prove the fiendish cunning of the conspirators.

In fact the most plausible candidate for a straw man is Richard Parker, an undoubted Quota man but not certainly the true leader of the Nore mutiny.[45] At present, however, we have little hard evidence about his colleagues. For obvious reasons the leaders of this mutiny were not keen to be identified afterwards: some escaped, others concealed themselves, and we cannot be sure that those executed were the true leaders. Captain Bligh of the *Director*, to name one deeply-involved ship of the North Sea squadron, prevented any of his ship's company being hanged.[46] Though the names are known of at least some of the most active mutineer leaders at Yarmouth and the Nore, no systematic attempt has been made to trace their origins.[47] All that can be said at present is that Parker is the only identified Quota man among them. We now have, however, an

38 Ibid., pp 361–2.
39 Manwaring and Dobrée, *Floating republic*, pp 262–3, but they did not attempt to trace the delegates' previous careers.
40 Ann Coats, 'The Delegates: A radical tradition'.
41 Elliott, *Partners in revolution*, p. 143; Dugan, *Great mutiny*, pp 63–4; Neale, 'Forecastle and quarterdeck', p. 317.
42 Coats, 'The Delegates', pp 18–19.
43 Lewis, *Social history*, pp 124–5.
44 Manwaring and Dobrée, *Floating republic*, pp 16–17.
45 Gill, *Naval mutinies*, pp 249–50; Philip MacDougall, 'The East Coast mutinies, May–June 1797', argues that he was a moderate who tried unsuccessfully to restrain the extremists. Christopher Doorne, 'A floating republic? Conspiracy theory and the Nore Mutiny of 1797', discusses the same question.
46 Neale, 'Forecastle and quarterdeck', pp 325–6, where the name of the ship is mistaken.
47 MacDougall, 'The East Coast mutinies', and 'Mutiny and the North Sea squadron' assembles the evidence, but has not used the ships' musters.

XVI

Mutiny or subversion? Spithead and the Nore   559

analysis of all men accused at court martial of mutiny or sedition anywhere in
the Navy during the year 1797, which shows that 43 out of 462 were identifiable
as Quota men, plus another 40 or so volunteers who, from the date of their
appearance on board, might possibly have been recruited under the Quota Acts.[48]

It remains to consider how the Navy was recruited, what effects the Quota
Acts had, and in particular how many Irishmen were serving in the mutinous
squadrons of 1797. The eighteenth-century Royal Navy was largely demobilized
in peacetime, and there was no form of continuous or career service for ratings. It
followed that the Navy had to draw its seamen from the general pool of seamen
and seafaring men, so that there were relatively few pure 'men-of-warsmen', but
very many with experience of merchantmen and fishing boats. Professional seamen, above all topmen, were very scarce in wartime. Their skills took many years
to learn, normally starting in boyhood, and the existing supply could not suddenly be increased on the outbreak of war. Since wartime demand (from the Navy
and merchant service together) exceeded supply by at least two to one, both the
Navy and merchant shipping had a permanent manning crisis, and all ships had
to resort to a substantial dilution of skill by recruiting landsmen.[49]

The Navy initially mobilized during 1793, when its total strength rose from
16,600 to nearly 70,000. The total reached 87,000 in 1794, 96,000 in 1795,
114,000 in 1796, and nearly 119,000 in 1797 (12,000 more than the maximum
number attained in the last year of the American War).[50] This voracious demand
for manpower was the background to the Quota Acts, which, it has been
claimed, wrought 'something of a revolution in the social composition of the
lower deck'.[51] They certainly would have done that, were it true that 'in 1797
over 100,000 of the 120,000 to 135,000 strong naval force had been recruited in
the preceding three years, primarily products of the Quota Acts'.[52] That would
imply that the English, Scottish and Welsh local authorities had outperformed
their quotas by three fold – an astonishing patriotic excess for which there is no
precedent, and no evidence.[53] It would also oblige us to account for the disap-
pearance of most of the 100,000 or so men who were already serving before the

48 C.J. Doorne, 'Mutiny and sedition in the Home Commands of the Royal Navy, 1783–1803'
    (unpublished Ph.D. thesis, University of London, 1998), tables 6.1, 6.2 and 6.3.
49 D.J. Starkey, 'War and the market for seafarers in Britain, 1736–1792', in L.R. Fischer and
    H.W. Nordvik (eds), *Shipping and trade, 1750–1950: Essays in international maritime economic
    history* (Pontefract, 1990), pp 25–42.
50 Christopher Lloyd, *The British seaman* (London, 1968), pp 288–9. These are averages of the
    monthly totals borne; numbers mustered were somewhat lower. Note that the table in Lewis,
    Social history, p. 119, is based on the numbers voted by parliament, which were an accounting
    fiction.
51 Wells, *Insurrection*, p. 83. Wells actually writes 'lower decks', which I take to be a printer's error.
52 Elliott, *Partners in revolution*, p. 136.
53 The total naval recruitment from all the five acts together would have reached 39,465 if every
    quota had been completely filled; no able seamen had been entered under 35 Geo. III c.9, and
    no volunteer had elected for the army under 37 Geo. III c.5.

first Quota men reached the fleet. In fact the net increase in the manpower of the Navy from 1795 to 1797 was only 22,000 men,[54] though the gross recruitment was certainly much greater. We do not have accurate figures for the wastage or turnover of the Navy, but a figure between 20 per cent and 25 per cent per annum would be a plausible guess.[55]

Fortunately the evidence for the Quota Acts allows us to do considerably better than plausible guesses. Although the naval muster books have not yet been analysed to give overall figures for the Navy, records of the workings of the Quota Acts survive from at least thirteen English counties, and possibly from the seaports and from Scotland as well.[56] The best estimate is that the 1795 acts recruited about 31,000 men, the 1796 acts much fewer.[57] Possibly no more than one sixth were seamen,[58] but the remainder were overwhelmingly young working men from a cross-section of the usual trades, mostly from the counties they were recruited for or nearby. Though there were some from more distant parts, only 3 per cent were Irish. There is no evidence at all of the disqualified attorneys, cashiered excisemen, fraudsters, debtors, bankrupts, vagrants, beggars, poachers, pickpockets, Sunday-school pupils, schoolmasters and other undesirables supposed to have been recruited by these acts.[59] All the evidence is that these

54 Lloyd, *British seaman*, p. 289.

55 N.A.M. Rodger, *The wooden world: An anatomy of the Georgian navy* (London, 1986), pp 148, 203; R.G. Usher, 'Royal Navy impressment during the American Revolution', *Mississippi Valley Historical Review*, xxxvii (1950), 673–88. These estimates apply to earlier periods, but at present we have none better.

56 Clive Emsley, A.M. Hill and M.Y. Ashcroft (eds), *North Riding naval recruits: The Quota Acts and the Quota Men, 1795–1797* (Northallerton, 1978). This is essentially two publications in one: an analysis by Emsley of returns from Kent, Leicestershire, Lincolnshire, Northumberland, Nottinghamshire and Sussex; and a transcript (by Hill and Ashcroft) of returns for the North Riding of Yorkshire; Christopher Oprey, 'Schemes for the reform of naval recruitment, 1793–1815' (unpublished M.A. thesis, University of Liverpool, 1961), considers records from Lancashire, Kent, Essex, Nottinghamshire and London; for Lincolnshire, see also F.W. Brooks, 'Naval recruiting in Lindsey, 1795–7', *English Historical Review*, xliii (1928), 230–40. To my knowledge the returns for Essex, London and the Isle of Wight in the Public Record Office (ADM 7/361–362 and ADM 30/63/8) have never been studied.

57 Oprey, 'Naval recruitment' – the most extensive study of these acts – is cautious about committing himself to figures, but implies (p. 127) that the 1795 quotas (total 31,100) were more or less achieved, at least in England.

58 This, however, is based on Emsley and Oprey, who have analysed only county records. The 1795 Port Quota Act (35 Geo. III c.9) called for 19,866 men (or half that number of able seamen), to be levied by committees of shipowners. This means that half the notional product of the Quota Acts was not to be raised by local authorities, and that half was obviously meant to be seamen. Until records of this Act have been studied, therefore, it is better not to be dogmatic about the proportion of landmen to seamen, but see Oprey, 'Naval recruitment', pp 221–7, for the Port Act in Liverpool.

59 Gill, *Naval mutinies*, pp 315–16; Manwaring and Dobrée, *Floating republic*, p. 16; Lewis, *Social history*, pp 117–18; Wells, *Insurrection*, pp 81, 84–5; *The private correspondence of Admiral Lord Collingwood*, ed. Edward Hughes, Navy Records Society, vol. xcviii (1957), p. 85. Cf. Coats, 'The 1797 mutinies'.

were not educated trouble-makers, but respectable working men in need of employment.[60]

The Quota Acts did not apply to Ireland, and brought in only a few Irishmen. It is often argued, however, that the proportion of Irishmen in the Navy was very high. We are told that there was 'a huge Irish contingent, reinforced further by political prisoners',[61] meaning those sent to sea under the 1796 Insurrection Act. Another historian, referring to the same act, tells us that, 'the proportion of Defenders or United Irishmen sent to the navy in those years must consequently have been considerable', but prudently avoids explaining what proportion, of what, or how much might be 'considerable'.[62] There does not at present appear to be any evidence to prove that 'thousands' of men were sent into the Navy under this act.[63] In November 1796 Thomas Pelham incautiously offered that 15,000 men had been recruited in all for the Navy in Ireland since the outbreak of war, but he was later obliged to withdraw this as an exaggeration.[64] It has been suggested that 25 per cent of the Navy was Irish,[65] and Theobald Wolfe Tone believed the figure was two-thirds or more.[66] Though no one is so incautious as to say outright that all Irishmen were United Irishmen, it is freely insinuated that United Irish leadership, or at least participation, can be assumed wherever large numbers of Irishmen can be identified. The *Mars* of the Channel Fleet, for example, is described as 'manned principally by Irishmen', and as 'one of the most militant ships at Portsmouth'.[67] The *Defiance*, we are told, 'the most troublesome ship at Spithead, had an unusually large component of Irish sailors'.[68] It has been claimed that the ships which mutinied in 1798 were 50 per cent manned by Irishmen.[69]

It is not possible to replace these figures with satisfactory evidence until the ships' musters are systematically analysed, but some things can be said with confidence. In the ships which sent delegates to the Spithead mutiny, an average of 26 per cent of the crews were Irish-born, though as we have seen the proportion

---

60 Emsley, in *North Riding naval recruits*, pp 7 20; Oprey, 'Naval recruitment', pp 155, 159, 170, 263.

61 Wells, *Insurrection*, p. 84.

62 Elliott, *Partners in revolution*, p. 138.

63 Wells, *Insurrection*, p. 82.

64 Elliott, *Partners in revolution*, p. 138; Wells, *Insurrection*, p. 82, adopts the figure uncritically. I take it to be the unnamed source for Manwaring and Dobrée's claim that 16,515 Irishmen were recruited during this period: *Floating republic*, p. 101. Note that recruits in Ireland are not the same as Irish recruits; professional seamen in particular were very likely to have been pressed at sea.

65 Wells, *Insurrection*, p. 82.

66 Elliott, *Partners in revolution*, pp 331 2.

67 Wells, *Insurrection*, p. 101.

68 Elliott, *Partners in revolution*, p. 143.

69 Ibid., p. 138, apparently citing Lewis, *Social history*, p. 129, which contains nothing to the purpose.

among the leaders was much lower. The *Mars*, so far from being 'manned principally by Irishmen', had the lowest figure of all (15 per cent), while the highest (72 per cent) came from the *Monarch*, which did not initially participate in the mutiny.[70] Of the total of 462 men who were charged at court martial with mutiny or sedition in home waters during 1797, 106 had been born in Ireland.[71] There are also some indications of the level of Irish recruitment for the Navy as a whole. A sample of ships commissioning at Plymouth during the American War had 20 per cent Irish ship's companies; in a similar sample from 1804–5, this had risen to 29 per cent.[72] Since Plymouth was the nearest dockyard port to Ireland and the one to which recruits from Ireland usually came, the figures for the Navy as a whole would presumably have been lower, though a sample of ships which served on the Leeward Islands station between 1784 and 1812 shows 30 per cent Irish.[73] What proportion of these Irishmen may have been disaffected is a matter of too much speculation, though it is worth noting that the captains in the Channel Fleet who in 1798 were invited by the admiralty to state what proportion of the Irishmen serving in their ships were 'evilly-disposed', returned a figure of 21 per cent.[74]

Overall we can certainly assume the presence of Irishmen in most ships, and the presence of United Irishmen is likely in some ships in 1798, but we are far from establishing any clear connection between the United Irishmen and the 1797 mutinies.[75] The mutinies took the United Irish leadership as completely by surprise as they did the French.[76] The fact that the mutineer leaders enforced the swearing of oaths does not in the least establish an Irish connection, particularly as the form of the oaths was quite different from those used by the United Irishmen.[77] After the event, according to Dublin Castle's intelligence, the United Irish leadership discussed the possibility of fomenting discontent in the fleet, but this is no proof that they tried, still less succeeded in doing so.[78] The most that can be said is that there are strong suggestions of United Irish involvement in some of the 1798 incidents.[79] By that stage the first target of some United

---

70 Coats, 'The Delegates', table 1. There are no figures for the *Defiance*.

71 Doorne, 'Mutiny and sedition', tables 6.2 and 6.3.

72 N.A.M. Rodger, 'Devon men and the navy, 1688–1815', in Michael Duffy et al. (eds), *The new maritime history of Devon*, 2 vols (London, 1993–4), i, pp 213–14.

73 Byrn, *Crime and punishment*, p. 76, n.2.

74 328 seamen out of 1,517, and 83 marines out of 460: Wells, *Insurrection*, p. 150.

75 *Pace* Wells, *Insurrection*, p. 84: 'Although the sources are not very revealing ... there can be no question that the United Irish started its offensive in the navy prior to the mutinies.' Cf. Elliott, *Partners in revolution*, pp 140–2.

76 Gill, *Naval mutinies*, pp 336–8.

77 Coats, '1797 mutinies', and 'The Delegates'.

78 Gill, *Naval mutinies*, p. 334.

79 Wells, *Insurrection*, pp 145–7; Doorne, 'A floating republic'. In September 1798 William Nugent of the *Minerve* was court-martialled for 'having declared himself to be a United Irishman with many other improper expressions', and assaulting the master-at-arms: Roger Morriss, *Cockburn and the British Navy in transition: Admiral Sir George Cockburn, 1772–1853* (Exeter, 1997), p. 43.

XVI

Mutiny or subversion? Spithead and the Nore 563

Irish plotters was said to be Protestants rather than officers, and their plots were swiftly betrayed by other Irishmen.

What then, can we say about the 1797 mutinies? Much less, is the answer, than has been said; but not so much as might be said if the needful research were to be done. There is no reason to argue that seamen were political innocents incapable of collective organization without outside help. It is certainly true that the occasions on which the ratings of the Navy had directly participated in national political events were relatively few, though by no means unimportant: in the seventeenth century, the Navy had made and unmade several régimes.[80] More relevant to the great mutinies is the fact that the seamen were the heirs of a native political tradition of shipboard organization, which went back as far as our evidence allows us to see it. In the middle ages, maritime law expected a ship's company to take collective decisions in matters of commerce and navigation, and held the seamen jointly liable with the master for the consequences of decisions in which they were assumed to have participated.[81] Much had changed since then, but by no means everything. Seamen in merchant ships were still liable to bear the cost of damaged cargo, and no doubt many men serving in the Navy in 1797 had previously suffered deductions from their wages in consequence.[82] The old traditions of consensus were probably strongest in fishing boats and coasters rather than deep-sea merchantmen or the Navy, but many of the 1797 mutineers would have had experience of one or both, and even in the Navy the law still required that the ship's company give their consent in certain cases, notably to the disposing of their common property in prizes. Within recent memory it had still been customary in certain circumstances for the captains of men-of-war to consult their men on critical decisions.[83] Professional seamen like the delegates of the fleet at Spithead were the heirs of an ancient tradition which owed nothing to outside tutelage. Arguably the harsher attitude towards collective protest adopted by the admiralty since the 1780s had forced the men to tighten up their organization, but they did not have to invent or borrow a tradition of collective action.[84] The whole experience of shipboard life was an education in teamwork and initiative. Men like Valentine Joyce who had passed their boyhood afloat and aloft were steeped in the complex machinery of a sailing ship, in which everyone's safety depended on co-ordination and mutual trust, and in which the topmen in particular had to

80 Bernard Capp, *Cromwell's Navy: The fleet and the English Revolution, 1648–1660* (Oxford, 1989), pp 115–51; Hans-Christoph Junge, *Flottenpolitik und revolution: Die Entstehung der Englischen seemacht während der Herrschaft Cromwells* (Stuttgart, 1980), pp 81–107.

81 Dorothy Burwash, *English merchant shipping, 1460–1540* (Toronto, 1947), pp 61–2; Sir Travers Twiss (ed.), *The black book of the admiralty* (London, 1871–6), i, pp 89–94; Jacques Bernard, *Navires et gens de mer à Bordeaux (vers 1400–vers 1550)* (3 vols, Paris, 1968) ii, pp 638–9, 642–6.

82 Ralph Davis, *The rise of the English shipping industry in the seventeenth and eighteenth centuries* (2nd edn, Newton Abbot, 1972), pp 144–5.

83 Rodger, *Wooden world*, pp 136–7, 235–6.

84 Ibid., pp 237–44; Neale, 'Forecastle and quarterdeck', pp 49, 330–1.

think for themselves for the survival of all. As petty officers and leading hands they had been trained to carry responsibility. They knew far more about collective organization than shopkeepers or schoolmasters.

All this should make us pause before we attempt to impose interpretations on events which have to be understood in their own terms before they can be interpreted in any other. Much remains to be discovered about these mutinies, but whoever undertakes research into them will have to be prepared to understand naval life itself, and not simply treat the Navy as a blank screen onto which to project a favourite plot. When we have a complete social history of the late eighteenth-century Navy, we may be able to see more clearly in what respects the 1797 mutinies differed from naval tradition, and in what ways they may, perhaps, have been influenced from outside. Until then, modest caution best becomes us.

Additional Note [2009]

Written for a conference marking the two-hundedth anniversary of the Irish rebellion of 1798, this piece was marginal to the interests of Irish historians, and has not attracted much notice from political, naval or social historians of Britain, all of whom ought to pay much more attention than they do to the naval mutinies of 1797, arguably the nearest Britain ever came to a French revolution.

Training or Education: A Naval Dilemma over Three Centuries

My starting point is a scurrilous anecdote. The scene is a classroom in the United States Naval War College, where a class of naval and Marine officers is struggling with the novel challenge of writing an essay. The instructor is trying to persuade them that essays are a valuable means of learning clarity of thought and expression. One of the Marine officers objects: 'Lieutenant, the only thing you are trying to do is to teach me how to speak English. I am going back to the Marine Corps and I don't need to speak English.[1]

Probably not many US or British officers would dispute that an ability to speak English is a necessary skill, but how far beyond that an officer's education need advance is a serious question, and the answer is not necessarily obvious, especially not for the officer in that most complex and technical of all services, the Navy. What is the difference between training and education, how much of either does an officer require, and who should administer them? How far is it proper to distinguish between handling ships and handling people; between the science of navigation and the art of war? How much is to be learnt in the classroom and how much at sea? Should theory come before practice, or after it, or instead of it, or nowhere at all? At what age should future officers be recruited and how long should they be trained? Is the object to produce a lieutenant, a captain or an admiral? These are difficult questions, and I do not pretend to have ready-made answers to them to offer to the Navy today. What I can do is survey the ways in which the Navy has tried to answer them over the three centuries or so from the 1650s to the 1950s, and draw some general conclusions about what has, and has not, worked in the past.

In the 17th century, the concept of military rank was only slowly emerging as an alternative to 'rank' as it was normally understood in civilian society. The only natural authority, universally understood and very widely accepted, was the authority of birth. In armies, a formal structure of military rank was already more or less established, but it did not represent a serious alternative to the order of society at large because army officers were everywhere recruited mainly, and in many armies exclusively, from the nobility and gentry, and general officers were usually noblemen of high rank.[2] In navies the situation was more delicate. Not only was there no formal structure of rank, and no established tradition of recruiting officers from the nobility and gentry, but sea command required two unrelated skills. On the one hand it was indispensably necessary to master navigation and ship-handling, a difficult and complex business requiring long experience. On the other hand ships and fleets, like armies, had to be led by men who possessed understanding of the arts of war, physical and moral courage, and natural authority; none of which came necessarily from experience commanding merchantmen. Furthermore the mid-17th century was an age of political instability and civil war in most of the major European states, above all in England, where the Navy was directly involved in making and unmaking several successive regimes, and where the political loyalty of the officer corps was a matter of high sensitivity.

The English republic and Commonwealth, relatively relaxed about the social origins of its sea officers, were content to find most of them from among professional – that is, merchant – seamen. Political and religious loyalty to the military regime were the government's main concern. To ensure it, the naval officer corps was repeatedly purged, and high command was almost entirely reserved to army officers.[3] This approach was not an unqualified success. The State's Navy encountered serious problems of cowardice and indiscipline in action; the Generals-at-Sea had to learn to handle fleets while fighting a war against admirals like Maarten Harpertszoon Tromp who had been at sea all their lives; while in the end the Navy on whose political loyalty so much had depended, played a major part in restoring Charles II.

The Restoration Navy then had to develop its own solutions to the problem of choosing, and training, sea officers.[4] At one level, the decision was simply whether to choose those who already knew the sea, or train those who did not. 'Tarpaulin' officers, bred up in merchantmen, did not need to be taught to handle ships – but there were obvious political risks in depending on men who had been appointed by the Cromwellian regime, or who came from the social and religious background associated with republicanism. The First Dutch War, moreover, had clearly shown that experience of trading voyages did not necessarily fit a man for the command of fleets in wartime.[5] The natural, obvious, decision was to make men admirals, if not also captains and lieutenants, who had undoubted personal authority, whose birth and upbringing had accustomed them to taking responsibility, and who had acquired that knowledge of the world beyond the sea and the Navy which enabled them to judge of questions of strategy and policy. All navies saw the necessity of these qualities, and so 17th-century fleets were commanded by generals, princes, diplomats or archbishops most of whom relied on subordinates for the mechanical arts of handling their ships. Even in the Dutch fleets, many (though by no means all) of whose senior officers were professional seamen, more was required than mere sea experience. That great admiral Tromp, 'unversed in letters, but bred up upon the restless sea' as he put it himself, spoke French and English, while his compatriot De Ruyter, also at sea from his boyhood, was familiar with French, English, Spanish, Portuguese and Irish.[6] They knew the world as well as the sea.

For Charles II and his brother the Duke of York, Lord High Admiral and later King James II, the critical problem was not so much the choice of admirals – for they were lucky enough to dispose of a number of fleet commanders of diverse origins but real ability, starting with the Duke of York himself – but the formation of a loyal and competent officer corps, not tainted with republicanism and yet capable of facing Dutch fleets commanded by the finest seamen of the age. One obvious answer, seriously advocated in the 1660s by some of the king's ministers, was to ensure natural authority, courage and political reliability by choosing only noblemen and gentlemen.[7] Another solution, widely practised during those years, was to honour and advance men of long experience but relatively humble birth and, in many cases, politically doubtful origins. In the long run, however, Charles II and his advisers were clear that they had to make the Navy acceptable to gentlemen if it were ever to be a reliable support of the Crown. Moreover a permanent service could not long meet its requirements by recruiting ad hoc from the merchant service or anywhere else. A regular career path had to be established, and it had to be attractive to gentlemen. The key question was what, if anything, the gentlemen ought to learn about their new profession, and how they were to learn it. Fortunately there were many senior officers of the Restoration Navy of undoubted rank and loyalty who were also capable seamen keenly interested in the technicalities of their profession. The Duke of York and Prince Rupert, both princes of the blood and originally soldiers, were able naval tacticians, and Rupert was the boldest seamen of all the English admirals. Lord Sandwich, a gentleman by birth and a Cromwellian soldier and politician by origin, was one of the most accomplished navigators and mathematicians of his age.[8] Another gentleman officer, Captain Sir William Booth, told Samuel Pepys;

'…that he would undertake to teach a man enough of the sea to talk as a seaman in a year, but to do the work and know the business his whole life is little enough, he answering to me that now he finds one thing or another to learn every day and that he did believe himself a better seaman after the first three years of his service than he knows himself to be now…'[9]

It was their influence which led the English Royal Navy towards a distinctive solution to the recruitment problem. In an historic debate at the Admiralty on 8 December 1677, in the presence of the king, the Admiralty and Navy Boards and a number of senior officers, it was decided to oblige all candidates for the rank of lieutenant to prove a minimum service of three years at sea, one of them as a midshipman, and to pass an examination in seamanship. The idea of a qualifying examination was then extremely unusual, and the idea of forcing young noblemen and gentlemen to serve in a common petty officers' rating, and prove their ability in a practical, mechanical skill, was socially revolutionary, indeed subversive. It was the united opinion of the gentlemen officers present on this occasion which carried the day.[10]

In France, at roughly the same time, Colbert was establishing a system by which young gentlemen, having first proved their noble status, were admitted to colleges where they could be trained for the sea in conditions, and under teachers, proper to their social rank. They went to sea for the first time as adults, familiar only with the theory of their new profession, and a permanent social gulf divided them from their subordinates who had been bred up as seamen.[11] The Spanish Navy followed with a similar system early in the 18th century.[12] The English Navy, by contrast, obliged future officers to go to sea to learn their profession, 'to make themselves masters of it', in Pepys's words, 'by learning and doing and suffering all things.'[13] They did so alongside, and in the same ratings as petty officers and seamen. There was until 1794 no equivalent of the later naval cadet, and 'midshipman' was a working petty officer's rating. Moreover the qualifying sea time was raised to four years in 1703 and six years in 1728. Since lieutenants were supposed to be not less than 20, it was normal for young gentlemen to go to sea in their early or mid-teens, and spend their formative years learning to handle ships and men at sea. While the future French or Spanish officer passed his time in the classroom, the future British officer was working afloat, and often aloft.

This gave British officers the pre-eminent skill as practical seamen in which they took intense pride, and which they never ceased to stress was the essential foundation of a naval career;

'...In the early part of Life, the Shorter time a young Sea Officer is on Shore the better, Practice is fully as necessary, as Theory, think I, that is my old fashioned Creed, and that is absolutely for young Seamen to be bred in the Fore Top, as well as the Quarter Deck...'[14]

That is identifiably the voice of a retired admiral, but his views were not in the least out of date. At almost the same date, and in the same vein, Captain John Jervis warned his sister of what her son would have to endure if he chose the Navy for his profession;

'...He must lie in the Berth with the other midshipmen, live as they do, and have no other distinction whatsoever: for the first year, he must rise at break of day, and apply closely to his Studies, and to his Seamanship; be very subordinate and respectful to all in authority over him, and never repine at the hardships and impositions he is bound to bear, in common with others – the life is a very rigorous one, and what few Boys educated as he has been, can bear... After the first year, in which, I expect he will become Master of the Theory of Navigation, he must watch and do his duty with punctuality, and alertness; and at least with as much precision, as the best midshipman in the ship: for I shall always exact more from a very near Relation, than from those I receive, on recommendation…'[15]

— it was a tough, dangerous career, attractive to boys who preferred adventure to school.

In this there was a disadvantage, which became increasingly obvious to thinking officers as the 18th century progressed. Young gentlemen who went to sea at 13 or 14 (let alone eight or nine, as some did)[16] had little formal education before they started their naval career, and limited opportunities to better it afterwards. Only big ships carried a schoolmaster; a sober, capable schoolmaster was something of a rarity; not all captains took as much care of their young gentlemen as Jervis did; and a ship at sea made an indifferent classroom.[17] Yet serious learning of one kind at least was indispensable to the sea officer, for navigation required a good knowledge of mathematics, especially after the introduction in the 1750s of lunar distances as the first generally practicable method of determining longitude at sea. To meet this requirement it became increasingly common for young gentlemen to attend specialist mathematical schools, either before they went to sea, or in the intervals of sea service, while their ships were in port or in dock. Here again the Navy was in social terms notably progressive. The use of mathematics was well recognised in the 18th century, but they still belonged mainly to the vocational world of the workshop, the counting-house or the Excise office. Many gentlemen were;

'…so Brisk and Airy, as to think that the knowing how to cast Accompt is requisite only for such Underlings as Shop-keepers or Trades-men, but unnecessary and below Persons of plentiful Estates…'[18]

Henry Legge, as Chancellor of the Exchequer in the 1750s, was sneered at for his 'clerk-like knowledge of finances,' so demeaning to a gentleman minister.[19] The schools these young gentlemen attended were in many cases conducted by Nonconformists, and instructed boys for careers in trade, finance and merchant shipping with which gentlemen were not normally connected. Moreover they taught to a high standard. The curriculum of one such school proposed to teach boys of 13 or 14:

1. Arithmetic, Vulgar and Decimal.
2. The Extraction of the Roots, with their Application to various Purposes in the Mathematics.
3. Geometry Practical, with some necessary Theorems demonstrated.
4. Mensuration, and Cask Gauging.
5. Trigonometry Plain, with its application to the measuring of Heights, Depths, Distances and c.
6. Navigation, in all its Parts, with an exact Method of keeping a Journal.
7. Surveying and Planning of Harbours.
8. The Use of the Globes, Maps, Charts and Nautical Instruments.
9. Spheric Geometry, with the Projection of the Sphere.
10. Spheric Trigonometry, with its Application to Practical Astronomy; also Variety of Methods for determining the Latitude at Sea. Also the use of the Globes, Maps, Charts and other Mathematical Instruments.[20]

This was an education strikingly unlike what other young gentlemen received in the public schools, and marked the Navy's character as a modern, 'scientific' service in the Enlightenment mould.[21]

What it did not do was provide any sort of general education. It was perfectly possible for an officer to reach post and even flag rank without any secondary education except mathematics. Though Henry Medley (a Vice-Admiral of 1745) was probably the last flag officer unable to write a legible hand, John Elliot rose to be a full Admiral as late as 1795 without having learned to spell the simplest English words. Contemporaries complained of captains and admirals unable to compose an intelligible report, speak a word of a foreign language or make a presentable appearance in polite society.[22] Thinking officers, moreover, were concerned that an upbringing devoted exclusively to seamanship and navigation bred a very narrow understanding of an officer's duty. 'It is certainly necessary', Admiral Vernon wrote;

'that a sea officer should have some natural courage: but it is equally just that he should have a good share of sense, be perfect master of his business, and have some taste for honour; which last is usually the result of a happy education, moderate reading, and good company, rarely found in men raised on the mere credit of being seamen... The general notion about sea officers is that they should have the courage of brutes, without any regard to the fine qualities of men, which is an error themselves too often fall into. This levels the officer with the common seaman, gives us a stark wrong idea of the nature design and end of the employment, and makes no distinction between the judgement skill and address of a Blake, and a mere fighting blockhead without ten grains of common sense.'[23]

'There is one thing extremely obvious', he wrote on another occasion;

'which is that our sea officers despise theory so much, and by trusting to their genius at the instant they are to act, have neither time, nor foundation whereby to proceed on; their consultations are all in a hurry; and by want of either theory or experience, which should furnish them with a competent number of areas distinct and clear, their thoughts are puzzled, perplexed and confounded...'[24]

These are the opinions of an unusual figure in the 18th-century Navy, an Oxford man who had not gone to sea until he was nearly 17, by which time he had mastered Latin and Greek, studied mathematics, navigation, geometry, fortification and gunnery, and made some progress in Hebrew.[25] But other, less self-consciously intellectual contemporaries had similar opinions. In 1745, the First Lord of the Admiralty was sent an anonymous character of the ideal admiral;

'There should be in an Admiral, who is to Command, a great deal of Historical Learning, a thorough knowledge of Geography, and the Mathematicks; He should be of a Generous cheerfull nature, temper'd by an excellent sedate Understanding; a Cool head and, a warm heart... Free from all the infirmities of old age, or other bodily complaints; with a mind Active and Vigilant...'[26]

All this, the writer continued, would require more education than most officers possessed. Too often they were judged 'excellent sea commanders' because they made much noise about the details of rigging, which was their subordinates' business. Just the same point was made a few months later by Commodore Curtis Barnett;

'I am stupid enough to think that we are worse officers though better seamen than our neighbours [the French]; our young men get wrong notions early, and are led to think that he is the greatest officer who has the least blocks in his rigging.'[27]

This remark bears scrutiny. The blocks in question are leading blocks for the running rigging. The fewer the blocks, the better the lead, the less the friction losses and the less effort needed to work the ship. Attention to this sort of detail was important; it spared the men, and in the long run it helped British ships to be manned with smaller crews than French or Spanish ones, which in turn allowed Britain to man a bigger fleet. The matter was not unworthy of an officer's attention – but the officer concerned should have been the boatswain, not the captain. In the same vein Lord Howe told George III;

'that he thinks in our service the attention is carried so long alone to seamanship that few Officers are formed, and that a knowledge of the military is necessary to open the ideas to the directing large fleets'.[28]

Collingwood likewise urged young officers;

'Read – let me charge you to read. Study books that treat of your profession, and of history…Thus employed, you will always be good company. Nature has sown in man the seeds of knowledge; but they must be cultivated to produce fruit.'[29]

These were influential opinions, but they had no general effect in an age when the recruitment and training of future officers was entirely in the hands of captains, each of whom had their own ideas. It was not until the 19th century that the Admiralty gained control of the choice and the training of naval officers, and then it was as much concerned with officers' breeding as with their education either before or after joining the Service. Whereas the 18th-century Navy, in which almost all officers began their careers at least formally as ratings, erected no barrier to the young man of talent but humble origin, the 19th-century Admiralty established informal but watertight tests of birth and fortune. Moreover the majority of future officers were now chosen by political nomination, and drawn largely from families closely connected with the party in power at Westminster. This provided the Navy with the most aristocratic and well-connected officer corps that it had ever had.[30]

Three successive systems of officer entry and training were adopted during the 19th century. First, between 1806 and 1837, the Royal Naval College at Portsmouth trained the young gentlemen entering the Navy under Admiralty patronage, a proportion which, by the 1830s, had risen to about one third of the total. The Admiralty's educational ideas were not enlightened by the standards of the previous century. Sir John Barrow, Secretary of the Admiralty from 1804 to 1845, was prepared to admit that midshipmen required to know something more than navigation, but only gunnery, French, and the wording of the Queen's Regulations.[31] That formidable mathematician Professor James Inman, principal of the Royal Naval College, taught the following curriculum to boys in their final year (aged 14 or 15):

Fifth half-year: Fortifications, doctrine of projectiles and its application to gunnery: principles of flexions and application to the measurements of surfaces and solids: generation of various curves, resistance of moving bodies: mechanics, hydrostatics, optics, naval history and nautical discoveries.

Sixth half-year: More difficult problems in Astronomy, motions of heavenly bodies, tides, lunar irregularities: the Principia and other parts of Newton's Philosophy to those sufficiently advanced.'[32]

Sufficiently advanced indeed, but narrowly technical, this formation magnified both the best and worst features of 18th-century naval education.

In 1837, the Royal Naval College ceased to be concerned with young gentlemen, all of whom now entered the seagoing Navy directly, in the eighteenth-century fashion, with no prior training ashore. A very modest educational test was now imposed: candidates (not younger than 12) had to be 'able to write English correctly from dictation, and be acquainted with the first four rules of arithmetic, reduction and the rule of three'. In 1851, the standard was slightly raised, and for the first time the regulations contemplated the remote possibility that a boy might fail the examination. The real test of course was to obtain a nomination, most of which were now in the hands of the members of the Admiralty Board, and dispensed to the sons of their political colleagues and connections.[33] Those who succeeded were supposed to acquire all the secondary education they needed while serving afloat. From the educational point of view, this system was an almost unmixed disaster. What the naval instructors tried to teach afloat were the same advanced and highly theoretical subjects as the old Royal Naval College had taught ashore (indeed was still teaching to older officers, at a yet higher and more abstract level[34]), but not many boys were sufficiently educated and intelligent to cope with them, and the interstices of shipboard work left them little opportunity to try. Moreover, by taking its new entries directly into the Navy the Admiralty found it was difficult and expensive to get rid of incompetents, and nearly impossible to match the supply of officers to the demand, while in spite of the rise of political nomination, there was still disquiet that the social selection of future naval officers was insufficiently rigorous.[35]

To meet these objections another system of entry was established in 1858. Now the future officers, ('naval cadets' since 1843), joined the training ship Britannia for three years at what was intended to be a naval public school. The level of fees was carefully set high enough to exclude social undesirables (with a lower scale for the sons of naval officers, who could not possibly be undesirable), while three years at the parents' expense allowed time for any who had passed that filter to be identified and eliminated. Though the fact was not made clear to the boys, or even their parents, cadets were not legally in the Navy, and could be summarily dismissed without process. The educational test for entry, though not completely negligible, remained low.[36] But though the Britannia was intended to function in some respects as the Navy's public school, its curriculum and internal management were quite different. The subjects taught remained very heavily dominated by mathematics, at a level well above the real understanding of the average 13-year old. Teaching, or rather cramming, was entirely by the rote-learning of lectures delivered by civilians. A harsh and inflexible system of discipline was enforced by petty officers; the captain and lieutenants of the ship had hardly any contact with the boys, so that bullying, extortion and corruption flourished unobserved by them.[37]

Those who knew this system were almost unanimous in condemning it. A foreign observer commented that;

'the high scientific and professional attainments of many English naval officers are not in consequence, but in spite, of their early education.'[38]

A cadet's real education 'stopped, to all intents and purposes, the moment he entered the *Britannia*.'[39] Anyone who had had the misfortune of having learned to think before arriving was likely to suffer for it.[40] Those who prospered there were boys of retentive memory and conformist character, who gained 'Firsts' in their examinations and were rewarded with seniority on passing out. But three years of classroom theory had not equipped them to be useful officers. As midshipmen, they passed from theoretical classroom instruction in the *Britannia* at Dartmouth to theoretical classroom instruction afloat in battleships which spent most of their time in port. They passed from the rigid and mechanical discipline of the training ship to the rigid and mechanical discipline of the gunroom. Having been bullied and humiliated by the cadet captains (whom seem in many cases to have been badly chosen),[41] they were bullied and humiliated by the sub of the gunroom (the most senior sub-lieutenant was often the least promising officer who had waited longest for promotion). After three more years of this, they still knew very little of the practical work of an officer. Even seamanship they learnt entirely as a theoretical subject, by the memorisation of textbooks. As sub-lieutenants, they passed to more courses, again concerned entirely with theory, again taught entirely by classroom lectures, again concluded by examinations which were purely tests of memory. After seven years of unbroken instruction, the young men joined the fleet to become watchkeeping officers almost without practical experience;

'In the *Britannia*, for example, about one-third of the syllabus was devoted to the mathematics of navigation, but one never took a sight nor fixed a ship's position. The same kind of work continued in the gunroom for three and a half years under the appropriate title of 'school'. As for the Greenwich examination, an experienced navigator might be as incapable of passing it as the average Sub-Lieutenant [is] of navigating a ship. On first going to sea as a Lieutenant, my head was crammed with useless theory, but as navigating officer of the Marathon, I was seriously handicapped by lack of practical training. An analogy would be found if candidates for a driving licence were given long lectures on thermodynamics and were then courtmartialled for running into a lamp-post. The only mathematics required in working out sights is simple arithmetic and a book of logarithms. Spherical trigonometry, etc., has just as little bearing on practical navigation as the theory of gravitation on bricklaying. A youth of average intelligence can learn how to work out observations in three or four weeks and it is ridiculous devoting several years to the subject.'[42]

From an exclusive concentration on practical seamanship, the Navy had passed in less than a century to the almost complete exclusion of all practical training from the formation of its officers.[43]

The worst effect of this upbringing was, however, not on training as such. Though the British are traditionally supposed to prefer character to intellect, the late 19th-century Royal Navy took almost the opposite view. Brains by themselves were not regarded as objectionable, so long as they ran in safe and predictable courses. It was independent thinking which was dangerous;

'Though it is true that some boys came through it [the *Britannia*] with little apparent harm, and ultimately became fine officers who rose high in the service, others were undoubtedly ruined by it and either left the navy totally disgruntled at the first opportunity or served on with increasing dislike of the life which they had chosen, or had been chosen for them by parents, to become thoroughly bad officers. The system was based on forcing cadets into a pre-conceived and rigid mould by the application of harsh, even inhuman discipline. Obedience to orders was the hallowed principle of the system, and woe betide any boy who was deemed to have transgressed that tenet. Any signs of originality or independence were severely frowned on - if not actively suppressed; while intellectual accomplishments always came a bad second to athletics.'[44]

'From the very beginning our future naval officers were surrounded by a converging pressure of convention in the form of a set of senseless rules tending to suppress independence and originality.... the repressive atmosphere of the Britannia and the gunroom unconsciously checked initiative and self-confidence.'[45]

The training of midshipmen and sub-lieutenants;

'was purely technical, tempered by a pathetic faith in mathematics as an instrument of culture. The importance of a sound technical training cannot, of course, be overrated, but mere technical knowledge is not enough. The system did little to develop intelligence or character. It crammed with facts instead of equipping with faculties. The petty routine of watchkeeping without responsibility, combined with the continual study of machines always worked for the same purpose in the same way, did not encourage critical questioning minds, whilst the enormous importance attached to examinations tended to accentuate the spirit of mental inertia which such a system inevitably develops. It was also something of a paradox that although so much was sacrificed to technical subjects, the competence of the finished product left much to be desired. Few Captains trusted a Sub-Lieutenant to keep watch at sea and I know from my own experience that I only learnt my job as a Lieutenant by doing it. The reason is not far to seek. Instruction was not only divorced from responsibility but it was mainly focused on work which had no practical bearing on the duties of a Lieutenant.'[46]

As sub-lieutenants, the young officers spent a year at Greenwich 'studying mathematical physics, mensuration, kinetics, statics, kinematics, hydrostatics and chemistry. Though the average age of my class was about 24, the methods of tuition were those of the secondary school rather than the university.' The writer of this memoir then went on the Long Course in gunnery at HMS *Excellent*;

'If hard work were any criterion, Whale Island would have been an extremely efficient establishment, but unfortunately the Staff never seems to have decided whether to train the long course as gunnery officers, gun manufacturers, ordnance artificers, gunners, gunner's mates or seamen gunners. The only thing we were not taught was good shooting.'[47]

The result of this upbringing was that the late-Victorian Navy was largely devoted to 'narrow seamanship, housekeeping and show-piece talents,' to the neglect of anything connected with war.[48] 'In the British Navy of the 1890s, the work of Lieutenants was done by Commanders, the work of the Captains by the Admiral, and the work of the Admiral (formulation of war plans, tactics and preparation for war) was not done at all.'[49] An intelligent officer such as the young Commander

John Fisher found himself employed as;

'a sort of upper housemaid, devoting severe thought to the cleaning of paint-work and, by way of relief to the mind, investigating the correctness of Midshipmen's watch bills or (still more interesting) following the trail of a missing bucket.'[50]

The consequences of this on the Navy's fighting efficiency during the First World War have been vividly described by Andrew Gordon in *The Rules of the Game*,[51] and they were obvious to independent-minded officers at the time. Fisher himself was the worst of many senior officers who ruthlessly suppressed critical or simply independent thought;

'In the British Navy…capacity to think was a handicap and an independent or critical mind was a definite disability.'

'In such cases, serious thinking may be more dangerous than secret drink-ing'.[52]

H.W. Richmond served as flag-captain to Sir William May as Commander-in-Chief of the Channel Fleet, 1909-1911. May was one of the most open-minded flag officers of his generation, yet;

'He detests sitting down and arguing a thing out. When he has to deal with concrete things, he is very good, but abstract thought he is incapable of. He reads nothing and finds great difficulty in expressing himself on paper…More than ever it has been impressed [on] me how essential it is that the Commander-in-Chief of such a Fleet as this should be a man free from the small details of administration. The unfortunate thing is that May is quite unable to appreciate this. To him minor details of gunnery are matters of real importance, small things like drills, exercises and dress possess him, while the really big things never enter his head…He will spend hours over some very minor, usually easy, tactical question, because it involves no deep thinking and enables him to spend several hours on the bridge making signals to people and finding fault with their manner of handling ships, but the really big things which require concentration of thought and real brain work he never touches…With all this he is in his way a hard-working man – as long as the work is easy. He will spend hours at his desk, but that is not what is wanted in a Commander-in-Chief if the work done there is concerned with the disposal of so much ammunition, the fit of a seaman's boots, or the best method of training the Captain of a 12-pounder.'[53]

The consequences for the Navy and the country during the First World War have been very fully studied, and there is no need to go into them in detail again. Before the war, however, the education of naval officers had again been reformed by the introduction of the Selborne Scheme in which Fisher played so large a part. The objectives of this scheme were several, but it was influenced by the ideas of H.W. Richmond, Julian Corbett and other critics, and it included an important element of educational reform.[54] To oversee the scheme a contingent of progressive educationalists was recruited, notably the new Director of Education J.A. Ewing, formerly Professor of Engineering at Cambridge; and the new Headmaster, first of Osborne and then of Dartmouth, Cyril Ashford, formerly Head of Science at Harrow. They were determined to replace the narrow cramming of the *Britannia* with a broad education based on history, modern languages, mathematics and English, comparable to the 'modern side' of a contemporary public school. Though Ewing was an engineer himself, he rejected Fisher's enthusiasm for engineering as the basis for officer training.[55] The result was, on paper, one of the most progressive schools in England;

'Experimental work in the College laboratories is used as a means of imparting much of the knowledge of mechanics, electricity and heat. Mathematics are taught as a tool for useful application to problems in engineering, gunnery and navigation, and not as an end in themselves… As a whole, it is an education for the boy who is to become a man of action, not a philosopher. If it makes no claims to develop the ruminating side of his character, it fosters habits of activity and quick decision.'[56]

A Board of Education inspector in 1912 was impressed;

'As a whole the work appears to be singularly successful in teaching the cadets to express themselves in clear and vigorous English, and in inspiring them

with a taste for reading... In intelligence and in the range of their general education the more capable sets compare very favourably with most boys of similar age
who have been educated in Public Schools.'[57]

Reality was less satisfactory. Selection, essentially by interview, at the age of
13 when neither character nor intellect could be well developed, tended in practice
to be selection by appearance.[58]

'What was the Board looking for? Poise? What they saw might have been sed-
ulously laid over a shaky interior. Brains? Certainly not. Many of the boys they
passed were astonishingly stupid. Manners, breeding or smartness? Perhaps those
were sought but how difficult to detect smartness in a boy when he is palpitating
with anxiety and has just endured hours of waiting in a billiard room...'[59]

The curriculum was dominated by the engineering workshops (controlled by
the Captain and not the Headmaster), which turned out many capable handymen,
and one outstanding physicist (the future Lord Blackett) of the generation of
research scientists who had to make their own equipment, but which were not
used in the fashion Ashford intended, as an instrument of general education;

'Technical education is begun too young, and at the same time an attempt is
made to teach too much. Instead of laying a good foundation of principles upon
[which] the mechanical and practical work, in so far as they are necessary, can be
superposed, the small boys are put straight to work of that kind. They do not
understand what they are doing. Instruction at the Colleges becomes a mere cram
– it is not education in any sense. Development of the mind is sacrificed to learning
technical, or quasi-technical, facts. The boys are not sufficiently developed mentally
to absorb what is going on round them; and altho' they succeed in passing examinations, their real knowledge is very small. What there is is superficial and consequently very quickly forgotten.'[60]

The curriculum was;

'monstrously mechanical and included a great deal of practical and theoretical
engineering... The humanities were hardly recognized. One of the results of this

kind of mechanized education was to produce a brand of naval officer incapable of expressing himself either in speech or on paper and without any conception of the strategical and tactical problems of defence.'[61]

What was worse, the disciplinary regime of the *Britannia* was carried over almost unchanged;

'From the moment of their arrival they [the cadets] were disciplined as if they were delinquents, regimented as if they were both unreliable and untrustworthy and deprived of all means of exercising character or originality...'[62]

The late Professor Marder was able to quote a chorus of senior and distinguished officers who passed through Dartmouth between the wars, united in lamenting that;

'Enterprise, iniative, enthusiasm, inventiveness, departure from the official mould, and a host of valuable attributes were all discouraged if not regarded almost as objectionable; even individuality, or a too-enquiring mind were out of place'[63]

The Navy's approach to training its future officers remained, at least as late as 1939, centred on forcing young and impressionable minds into a standard mould;

'Despite ameliorative efforts made by some of the more humane and understanding civilian masters, this system... stifled any tendency to show originality.'[64]

'For the most part what emerged was a definite breed of fit, tough, highly trained but sketchily educated professionals, ready for instant duty, for parades or tea parties, for catastrophes, for peace or war; confident leaders, alert seamen, fair administrators, poor delegators; officers of wide interests and narrow vision, strong on tactics, weak on strategy; an able, active, cheerful, monosyllabic elite.'[65]

'A mixture of savage discipline, ruthless mental processing and the simultaneous development of extreme idealism produced a standard young naval officer for the Fleet... Their professional standards and their devotion to duty were of the highest order. They accepted themselves as Naval officers unthinkingly because they had never had the opportunity to consider anything else...'[66]

Moreover the same pattern persisted of theoretical studies as cadets ashore succeeded by theoretical studies as midshipmen afloat in big ships which seldom went to sea. The young men were given no experience of responsibility;

'Rather, we confine them to the naval barrack yard, give them little interesting work to do, make them responsible for nothing, but keep them under constant instruction and inspection. This is not the way to strengthen their characters; and it is one of the direct results of sending them to sea young with their education so incomplete that they must spend all their time in continuing it on board ship. The very fact that their instruction has to continue at sea makes it necessary that the ship should be a large one; and in a large ship they can have little responsibility ...Thus, early entry involves us first in herding the boys together in a college, then, continuing them in large herds still under tuition, in the great ships.'[67]

Though much is made in some officers' memoirs of the educative effect of handling a steam piquet-boat, the average 20th-century battleship had two steam-boats and over 20 midshipmen, few of whom were trusted to take charge of such valuable craft without supervision. There were pulling and sailing boats as well, and there was enough practical work to interfere with the midshipmen's studies, but not enough to teach them much that would be useful to them as lieutenants, let alone as captains or admirals.

'On coming to sea the boys' scholastic education is still incomplete and naval instructors have to be carried in all ships bearing midshipmen. This is in contradiction to the opinions of every committee that has sat upon naval education since 1870, the reports and recommendations of which have in every case drawn attention to the incompatibility of the position of an officer and a schoolboy. Notwithstanding these recommendations, theoretical instruction continues under every sort of disability; there are few holidays; the effort put out is small. And at the same time the object of sending the boys to sea young is defeated. They come to ships to acquire experience as seamen and officers in the performance of their duties; but they cannot be given the opportunity of acquiring experience, as their whole time is spent under instruction at a cabin table.'[68]

That was the opinion of the Director of Education in 1919, but it was still only intellectual malcontents who maintained that;

'The acid test of naval training is not, as some people imagine, ability to pass examinations but its influence on character and intellect, and we should ask ourselves whether initiative and intelligence are likely to be developed by herding boys into a naval college between the ages of 14 and 18. May not four years under a disciplinary regime, unaccompanied by any responsible work, be four years too long? No doubt the cadets absorb a lot of information, but do they learn to think for themselves? The nature of the syllabus and thoroughness of the instruction may stop them thinking altogether. Similar questions might be asked concerning midshipmen, for the gunroom is an intellectual desert, barren and sterile as the Sahara, and that particular type of training is unlikely to encourage either initiative or self-reliance. This protracted tutelage does not end on promotion to Sub-Lieutenant, for Greenwich and the technical schools then cut him off from responsible duties for another 12 months. But even that is not the end of the story. After only about a year as a Lieutenant, our future Admiral probably returns to school for another two years or so in order to specialise in gunnery or torpedo. If his mental faculties are not impaired by this intensive cramming he will have had a narrow escape. On completion of the long course, he spends another year on shore and subsequently employment, as a specialist, may completely isolate him from more important functions....'

By the time our future Admiral reaches the age of 28, he may have done over 11 years under formal instruction and only about two on responsible duties at sea. This long academical schooling robs him of practical experience and does nothing to develop the essential qualities of character and intellect. Dartmouth, Greenwich and Whale Island would soon have withered Nelson's genius and moulded him to the conventional pattern. Incidentally, the inordinate length of this schooling also causes periodical shortages of officers. During 1895, 1898 and 1936 we had to enter Lieutenants direct from the mercantile marine. But why should we take 10 years to train Lieutenants when the merchant service can produce them without any special training? The only difficulty in answering such questions is that our educational system teaches officers not to ask them.'[69]

Once the young officer passed his Sub-Lieutenant's examinations;

'education (except in so far as experience is education) ceases. No further mental effort is called for unless the officers become specialists; and these form a proportion only [of] the whole, and their work is of a purely technical character. At the age at which a young man in medicine, the law or the arts is putting forth his whole effort, applying his mind which his previous education has trained [to master problems][70] to the solution of those problems particular to his profession, the young naval officer ceases to apply his mind to anything more abstruse than mechanical details which can be mastered by any intelligent workman. Thus, while in the early stages the instruction fails to establish a habit of thinking – substituting for it a process of memorising – in the later stages the reasoning powers are neither exercised nor developed.'[71]

All this was the product of what was meant to be the Navy's principal if not sole source of executive officers; entry into Osborne, later Dartmouth, at the age of 13. This method, however, taking at least seven years to produce an officer, was extremely inflexible as well as extremely costly, and the Navy repeatedly found itself with either too few or too many officers as a consequence. On three occasions, as we have seen, it was obliged to enter lieutenants directly from the merchant navy. In 1913, only 10 years after the Selborne Scheme had started and just as its first products were entering active service, it had to be supplemented by the 'Special' or Public School entry, which took boys at 18, their education already completed elsewhere, and made them into officers in only two years. The 'Pubs' were widely considered to be as good officers, if not rather better, than the 'Darts'. They formed a substantial fraction of the seamen officers, and provided most of the engineers. This form of entry was increasingly popular with boys and parents. By 1936 it was not possible to fill all the places offered at 13 even by admitting candidates who had failed the interview.[72]

Moreover during both world wars the Navy recruited large numbers of additional officers into the RNR and the various branches of the RNVR. The Navy made no attempt to educate them, but sent them to sea after minimal training to learn their new trade at sea, in small ships where they had to take immediate responsibilty.

'Temporary service officers of the RNR and RNVR have been employed in destroyers and other smaller craft, where they obtained experience as fighting men and seamen under the finest conditions – the conditions of active service. Midshipmen, RN, of the same age, intended for permanent service, have been locked up on board battleships in order to be under instruction. They acquired neither sea – nor fighting experience. The reason for this was that if they went to small vessels, they would not be able to pass their examinations, this being rated of greater importance than practical war experience.'[73]

The same was true to a much greater extent during the Second World War, when RNVR officers eventually amounted to 88 per cent of all the officers of the Navy, and when the Battle of the Atlantic – surely the most crucial campaign the Navy has fought this century – was almost entirely left to them.[74] No time was wasted preparing these young officers for the Navy. In 1939, new entry Sub-Lieutenants RNV(S)R were receiving a maximum of 10 days' training before going to sea. The limiting factor was not training but tailoring; 'The standard to be reached by a Sub-Lieutenant RNVR in September 1939 was the possession of a full uniform. An additional pair of trousers would almost certainly have led to accelerated promotion.'[75] All of these new officers were already educated, many of them university graduates. All of them of course had experience of the world outside the Navy. Many of them were promoted from the lower deck. They went quickly to sea, where most of them served in small ships and bore immediate responsibility. Unwittingly, uninentionally, by force of circumstances, the Admiralty was forming these officers much as the young gentlemen of the 18th century had been, with the crucial difference that they were not boys but young men already educated. There is no doubt that this enormous influx of outsiders, many of whom stayed on in the post-war Navy, transformed the character and outlook of the Navy for the better.[76] Their example cannot but have hastened the final end of the Dartmouth 13 year-old entry in 1949, and the final adoption between 1955 and 1960 of entry at 18 or later.[77]

Until then, the RNVR or ex-RNVR officers were almost the only officers in the Navy who had been educated as well as trained. The whole naval system of entry and training was directed at producing junior officers who were neither supposed to need, nor encouraged to acquire any intellectual experience outside their own Service. The experience of the First World War, however, had cruelly demonstrated that good lieutenants did not automatically make good captains, still less good admirals. Lacking both a broad education and experience of the world beyond the Navy, many senior officers had had no opportunity to develop their powers of rational analysis or informed judgement. At the War Course, as revived at Greenwich in 1919 to form the future leaders of the Navy;

'It is curious, though it is not really surprising, to see how unable most officers are to express themselves at all. They cannot analyse a situation. They cannot define their objects in a given situation. The contrast between the naval and military officers is remarkable. Of the soldiers, of whom four – Colonels – have been in the Course, all could write a clear appreciation and make a better plan than the Captains or Admirals. Many of the Captains cannot spell even passably. They think nothing of contradicting themselves two or three times within as many sentences, and are astonished to find they have done so. Yet these are our future guides in all high matters. No wonder the average statesman can make them say anything, and make a hash of their proposals.'[78]

The problem was thrown into high relief by the new requirement for staffwork. The Naval Staff as originally formed in 1912, and as it worked throughout the First World War, was a failure partly because there were few officers available who were capable of clear thinking or clear expression.[79] (There were also few admirals available who welcomed them). Though the Navy emerged from the First World War convinced of the value of the Naval Staff, which the Admiralty fought hard in the 1920s and 1930s to preserve against its civilian critics,[80] little was done to supply it with suitable officers. Whereas in the army, promotion beyond regimental rank was into the Staff, in the Navy the best officers were chosen for sea command, which was the only route to flag rank. The middle ranks of the Naval Staff tended to get whoever was left after the Fleet had made its choice: at best, officers of ability whose health or temperament unfitted them for command afloat; at worst, the unemployed or unemployable. In the Naval Intelligence Division in 1926;

'all the officers in the ID were on their way out, that is to say that they had been passed over for promotion and had no prospects. They were soldiering on for a pension and most of them were dead from the neck up.'[81]

Even the ablest officers arrived in the Naval Staff completely unequipped for the job.[82] Though H.W. Richmond, the main architect of the post-war Naval Staff, strove to alter the formation of lieutenants in order to fit them for future staff or flag appointments, he had few supporters and limited success.[83] His greatest triumph was the 1919 scheme to send junior officers to Cambridge for a year, which lasted only to 1923.[84] In the 1930s, the Admiralty at first reduced and then abolished the Sub-Lieutenants' Greenwich course which represented the only, tentative, element of adult education remaining in the standard naval career. It was not until the Second World War that the urgent need began to be recognized for officers of real intellectual capacity to fill staff positions.[85]

Many of these officers found themselves working for the first time in joint headquarters and staffs, alongside army, RAF and foreign officers. Comparisons were inevitable, and not necessarily to the Navy's advantage. After the war, retrenchment and inter-service rivalry called for First Sea Lords able to speak for the Navy on equal terms with politicians and statesmen (to say nothing of Field Marshals and Air Marshals). They were not easy to find among flag officers still drawn almost entirely from the Dartmouth entry. The creation of the Ministry of Defence in 1968, and the consequent loss of the dedicated body of Admiralty civil servants whose abilities had done so much to complement the technical knowledge of the naval officers, further exposed how ill-equipped many senior officers were to defend the interests of the Navy in the wider world.[86]

Yet the Navy continued until recently to concern itself almost exclusively with the training of junior officers. It devoted no sustained attention to encouraging them to think about their profession, still less about the wider world. The unspoken assumption was that a good lieutenant was the best possible foundation for a good captain or admiral, and a good lieutenant was a leader not an analyst. Practical experience and technical expertise were the routes to promotion. Sea time in command, and shore time in technical (above all gunnery) establishments were the making of the admiral. The necessity of staff work was understood, but it was addressed by sending officers on staff courses in mid-career. After a sketchy education finished at 16 or 18, the future staff or flag officer passed 20 years in an active and demanding profession which left him hardly any time for study or reflection. Then the Navy expected an officer who had spent all his adult life as a man of action, to convert in six months to an intellectual; thoughtful, analytical, building logical analysis on the foundation of a broad knowledge of the world. Some outstanding officers succeeded: the men who would have succeeded in any system or none. Most officers found it very difficult – as anyone would, however intelligent, who had been brought up as they had.

What conclusions can we draw from this hasty survey of naval officers' training over three centuries? Clearly there is a great deal worth avoiding. However effective in teaching officers not to think, naval training was until recently gravely deficient as professional training. Whereas the 18th-century Navy thoroughly trained its officers in what they would have to do, at least as lieutenants, for much of the 19th and 20th centuries the Navy has devoted enormous efforts to training officers to become, not officers, but theoretical mathematicians or practical mechanics. Much of the training was far beyond the officers' abilities or requirements; much of it (especially at Dartmouth) was far beneath them. Their actual duties had to be learnt on the job, after a remarkably long and costly period of instruction in matters which they did not need to know, or could not understand. Magnificent at instilling *ésprit de corps* and devotion to duty, the *Britannia* and Dartmouth systems stunted education, and deferred real training until officers were well into their twenties.

What was worse, when future officers entered at 13, the formation of character frequently meant in practice the suppression of character, or at least of independence. No fighting service can afford weak discipline, but neither can it afford weak thinking. If junior officers are not taught and encouraged to think for themselves they cannot be trusted with responsibility, initiative is stultified and it becomes impossible to cope with the unexpected. Naval history is littered with examples of failures generated by senior officers who could not or would not trust their juniors with information or responsibility.[87] Sir Henry Oliver, Chief of the War Staff 1914-1918, personally drew up sailing orders, drafted signals, plotted ships' movements on his chart, and typed his own letters. Meanwhile the First Sea Lord, Sir Henry Jackson, diverted himself from the crisis of the naval war by studying junior officers' excessive wine bills.[88] Inability to delegate and unwillingness to trust subordinates were the characteristic weaknesses of British admirals at least as late as the 1940s;

'The fundamental problem is that the men at the top will not leave details to subordinates. Their fatal remark − "let me see the signal before you send it" − damns so many of us. The leaders ought to decide the policy, the juniors execute it.'[89]

Too often, however, junior officers lacked the experience and self-confidence to manage for themselves, while senior officers took refuge from big issues by interfering in their subordinates' work. Important though it is that future admirals should be trained to think for themselves, it is no less necessary that future lieutenants should as well. This must be true in any fighting service which expects to allow junior officers the slightest responsibility. It is moreover doubly important today that officers should be able to analyse complex issues and express themselves lucidly, for they are likely to encounter staffwork as lieutenant-commanders if not before. Incompetent staffwork, and a general failure by senior naval officers ashore and afloat to analyse new problems with logical rigour or even common sense, very nearly lost Britain the First World War. The country survived that war at sea, just, in spite of the Navy's follies, by the application of overwhelming force against an outnumbered enemy in an unfavourable strategic position.

It seems unlikely that in future we shall be able to rely on this luxury. We cannot afford today to deploy our resources with anything less than the maximum skill and intelligence, and we cannot expect to get it if our future officers have not been educated at least to graduate level. This is what society expects as well as what the Navy needs, and the Service will not be able to recruit able candidates if it aims any lower. The Navy was not mistaken in its traditional insistence on rigorous training for its junior officers, and command experience for its senior officers. These things were, and are, certainly necessary, but they never were sufficient, and they are even less so now. The challenge today is to combine action and reflection, habits of thought and powers of command. History suggests, however, that the Navy itself has no special talent in forming the mind or imparting a broad general culture. Schools and universities have their weaknesses, but they unquestionably do a better educational job than the Navy ever did. What the Navy has to do is take future officers whose minds are already formed and receptive and train them, not in the theory but the practice of what they will have to do. The real challenge is to impart that training thoroughly but quickly, so that officers entering the Navy in their twenties still have time to reach high rank before they have passed the age of physical stamina and mental vigour.[90] Then the Navy has to retain and nourish junior officers' intellectual abilities so that they will be prepared and qualified for staff work and high command. Hardest but most essential of all, modern naval formation has to impart loyalty, self-discipline and devotion to duty: undoubtedly the best qualities of the old Dartmouth system, the worst qualities of the modern school, and the most difficult qualities to acquire late in life.

Additional Note [2009]

The training of naval officers has received a good deal of study over the years, most recently in H.W. Dickinson, *Educating the Royal Navy: Eighteenth- and Nineteenth-Century Education for Officers* (London, 2007), but there is a strong tendency for scholars to discuss education and training as though they were self-contained subjects rather than different aspects of a single subject. This rapid survey, originally given as a Hudson Memorial Lecture at Oxford University, is an attempt to tie these themes together.

References

1 Ex. inf. Professor B. Hattendorf.

2 Christopher Storrs & H.M. Scott, 'The Military Revolution and the European Nobility. c.1600-1800', *War in History* Vol.iii (1996) pp.1-41.

3 Bernard Capp, *Cromwell's Navy: The Fleet and the English Revolution,* 1648-1660 (Oxford, 1989), pp.55-56 &116-170.

4 The standard work on the subject is J.D.Davies, *Gentlemen and Tarpaulins: The Officers and Men of the Restoration Navy* (Oxford, 1991).

5 Notably the career of Captain Henry Appleton in command of the Mediterranean squadron; for which see R.C. Anderson, 'The First Dutch War in the Mediterranean', *Mariner's Mirror* XLIX (1963) pp.241-265;& F.W. Brooks, 'Captain Henry Appleton', *Yorkshire Archaeological Journal* XXXVl (1946) *pp.357-365.*

6 Johanne K. Oudendijk, *Maerten Harpertszoon Tromp* (2nd ed., The Hague, 1952), p.14. *See also* C.R. Boxer, M.A. De Ruyter, 1607-1676, *Mariner's Mirror* XLIV (1958) pp.3-17, at p.5.

7 Robert Latham ed., *Samuel Pepys and the Second Dutch War: Pepys's Navy White Book and the Brooke House Papers* Navy Records Society Vol. 133, (Aldershot, 1995) pp.221-226.

8 R.C. Anderson ed., *The Journal of Edward Mountagu, First Earl of Sandwich, Admiral and General at Sea 1659-1665,* (Navy Records Society Vol.64, 1929) pp.135, 151, 153. See also, Richard Ollard, *Cromwell's Earl: A Life of Edward Mountagu, 1st Earl of Sandwich* (London, 1994) pp.3-5, 9, 15, 123-124, 157 & 243.

9 Edwin Chappell ed., *The Tangier Papers of Samuel Pepys* (Navy Records Society Vol.73, 1935) p.233.

10 J.R. Tanner., *A Descriptive Catalogue of the Naval Manuscripts in the Pepysian Library,* Navy Records Society Vols. 26, 27, 36, 57, (1903-23) iv, pp. 543-544.

11 Michel Vergé-Franceschi, *Marine et Education sous l'Ancien Regime* (Paris, 1991). Philippe Henwood, 'L'Enseignement des Gardes de la Marine d'après l'Ordonnance de 1689', *Chronique d'Histoire Maritime* No.15 (1987) pp.36-39.

12 José P. Merino Navarro, *La Armada Española en el Siglo* XVIII (Madrid, 1981), pp.34-35.

13 Chappell, p.234.

14 Public Record Office: PRO 30/20/22/3, ff.125-126, Lord Rodney, 1 May 1783.

15 British Library: Add.MSS 29914, ff.145-146, Capt.J.Jervis to Mrs Mary Ricketts, 29 Aug 1780.

16 N.A.M. Rodger, *The Wooden World; An Anatomy of the Georgian Navy* (London, 1986) p.254.

17 F.B. Sullivan, 'The Naval Schoolmaster during the Eighteenth Century and the Early Nineteenth Century', *Mariner's Mirror* LXII (1976) pp.311-326.

18 Keith Thomas, 'Numeracy in Early Modem England', *Transactions of the Royal Historical Society* 5th S.XXXVII (1987) pp.103-132, quoting (at p.111) Edward Wells, *The Young Gentleman's Course of Mathematicks,* of 1714.

19 Henry Roseveare, *The Treasury: The Evolution of a British Institution* (London, 1969), p.110.

20 J.H. Plumb, 'The New World of Children', in *The Birth of a Consumer Society: The Commercialization of Eighteenth-Century England* ed. Neil McKendrick, John Brewer & J.H. Plumb (London, 1982) pp.286-3 15, at p.315. Cf. J.R. Oldfield, 'Private Schools and Academies in Eighteenth-Century Hampshire', *Proceedings of the Hampshire Field Club & Archaeological Society* XLV (1989) pp.147-156.

21 Keith Thomas, 'Numeracy in...' p.131. *See also,* MV. Wallbank, 'Eighteenth-Century Public Schools and the Education of the Governing Elite', *History of Education* VIII (1979) pp.1-19.

22 Rodger, *Wooden World,* pp.260-262.

23 H.W. Richmond, *The Navy in the War of 1739-48* (Cambridge, 1920, 3 vols) I, xii.

24 B.McL. Ranft ed., *The Vernon Papers.* (Navy Records Society Vol.99, 1958) pp.287-288, quoting Vernon's (anonymous) pamphlet *An Enquiry into the Conduct of Captain Mostyn,* 1754.

25 Richmond, *Navy in the War of 1739-48* I, pp. 39-40.

26 Woburn Abbey: 4th Duke of Bedford's MSS, Vol.IX p.98, Anon ['M.I.'or 'M.J.'] to Bedford, 7 Feb 1744/5.

27 British Library: Add.MSS 15955 fo.113, C. Barnett to George Anson, 16 Sep 1745.

28 A.Aspinall ed., *The Later Correspondence of George III.* (Cambridge, 1962-70, 5 vols) I,xvii.

29 G.L. Newnham Collingwood, *A Selection from the Public and Private Correspondence of Vice-Admiral Lord Collingwood: Interspersed with Memoirs of his Life* (London, 4th ed. 1829), p.15.

30 N.A.M. Rodger, 'Officers Gentlemen and their Education', 1793-1860, in *Les Empires en Guerre et Paix*, 1793-1860 ed. Edward Freeman (Vincennes, Service Historique de la Marine, 1990) pp.139-151. Michael Lewis, *The Navy in Transition,* 1814-1864 (London, 1965) pp.19-26.

31 Sir John Barrow, *The Life of George Lord Anson* (London, 1839), pp.87-88.

32 Michael Lewis, *England's Sea-Officers: The Story of the Naval Profession* (London, 2nd edn 1948), pp.91-92.

33 Rodger, 'Officers, Gentlemen and their Education', pp.145-146. Lewis, *Navy in Transition,* pp.108-109.

34 P.H. Colomb, *Memoirs of Sir Astley Cooper* Key (London, 1898) pp.64-69.

35 Rodger, 'Officers, Gentlemen and their Education', pp.148-150. Philip Payton, 'Naval Education and Training in Devon', in *The New Naval History of Devon* ed. Michael Duffy et al (London, 1992-94, 2 vols) II, 191-203, at p.192. 'Report of the Committee on the Higher Education of Naval Officers' [C 203, 1870] (Parliamentary Papers: HC 1870 XXV pp.835ff) p.viii/842. B.S. Mends, *Life of Admiral Sir William Robert Mends* (London, 1899), pp.3 17-319. Lewis, *Navy in Transition,* pp.109-110. H.W. Dickinson, '*Britannia* at Portsmouth and Portland', *Mariner's Mirror* LXXXIV (1998) pp.434-443; idem, 'Britannia Rules: The Early Years of Modern Royal Naval Officer Training', in *New Interpretations in Naval History: Selected Papers from the Twelfth Naval History Symposium* ed. William B. Cogar (Annapolis, Md., 1997) pp.141-153.

36 Rodger, 'Officers, Gentlemen and their Education', pp.148-150.

37 Admiral Sir Hugh Tweedie, *The Story of a Naval Life* (London [1939]), pp.16-19. Tweedie entered the *Britannia* in 1890.

38 J.R. Soley, 'Report on Foreign Systems of Naval Education' (Washington, 1880: 46th Congress 2nd Sess.Senate Exec.Doc.No.51), p.90.

39 Lewis, *England's Sea-Officers,* p.108.

40 Vice-Admiral Humphrey Hugh Smith, *A Yellow Admiral Remembers* (London, 1932), p.11.

41 S.W.C. Pack, *Britannia at Dartmouth* (London, 1966), pp.117, 179, 184-185 & 200-201; These hints are the more telling coming from a rather uncritical admirer.

42 K.G.B. Dewar, *The Navy from Within* (London, 1939) pp.359-360.

43 Dewar, *The Navy from Within,* pp.14-17. Smith, *A Yellow Admiral Remembers,* p.19.

44 Stephen Roskill, *Admiral of the Fleet Earl Beatty: The Last Naval Hero* (London, 1980), pp.21-22.

45 Dewar, *The Navy from Within,* pp.14-15.

46 Dewar, *The Navy from Within,* p.46.

47 Dewar, *The Navy from Within,* pp.58 & 61-62.

48 Andrew Gordon, *The Rules of the Game: Jutland and British Naval Command* (London,

1996), p.176.

49 Dewar, *The Navy from Within,* p.24.

50 Ruddock F. Mackay, *Fisher of Kilverstone* (Oxford, 1973), p.93.

51 Andrew Gordon, *The Rules of the Game....*

52 Dewar, *The Navy from Within,* pp.74 & 119.

53 Arthur J. Marder, *Portrait of an Admiral: The Life and Papers of Sir Herbert Richmond* (London, 1952), pp.64 & 67-68.

54 Mackay, *Fisher of Kilverstone,* pp.274-275. D.M. Schurman, *The Education of a Navy: The Development of British Naval Strategic Thought, 1867-1914* (London, 1965), pp.117-119.

55 E.L. Davies & E.J. Grove, *The Royal Naval College Dartmouth: Seventy-five Years in Pictures* (Portsmouth, 1980), pp.12-13. Mackay, Fisher, pp.266-267. Payton, 'Naval Education and Training', p.195. Pack, *Britannia at Dartmouth,* p.145.

56 Pack, *Britannia at Dartmouth,* p.157, quoting Ashford.

57 Quoted by Payton, 'Naval Education and Training', p.195.

58 Marder, *Portrait of an Admiral,* p.321.

59 John Wells, *The Royal Navy, An Illustrated Social History* (Stroud, 1994) p.133, quoting the future Captain Hugh Gairdner who entered in 1918.

60 Marder, *Portrait of an Admiral,* p.334, quoting Richmond's 1919 paper for Lord Haldane.

61 Stephen King-Hall, *My Naval Life 1906-1929* (London, 1952), p.47.

62 Arthur J. Marder, Mark Jacobsen & John Horsfield, *Old Friends, New Enemies: The Royal Navy and the Imperial Japanese Navy* (Oxford, 2 vols, 1981-90) 1,281.

63 Marder, *Old Friends, New Enemies* 1,281-282.

64 Roskill, *Beatty,* p.22.

65 Wells, *Social History,* p.152, quoting Charles Owen of the 1929 entry.

66 C.C. A[nderson], 'Dartmouth between the Wars', *Naval Review* LXXIII (1985) pp.247-250, 346-349 & LXXIV pp.49-53, at p.250. The author was one of the Exmouth Term of 1930.

67 Sir H.W. Richmond, *Naval Training* (London, 1933), pp.59 & 61.

68 Marder, *Portrait of an Admiral,* pp.334-335, quoting Richmond's 1919 paper for Haldane.

69 Dewar, *The Navy from Within,* pp.358-359.

70 The words in brackets, printed by Marder, seem to be superfluous to the sense.

71 Marder, *Portrait of an Admiral,* p.335, quoting Richmond's 1919 paper for Lord Haldane.

72 Davies & Grove, *Dartmouth,* pp.15-16. Lewis, *England's Sea-Officers,* p.117. Dewar, *The Navy from Within,* p.18.

73 Marder, *Portrait of an Admiral,* p.335, quoting Richmond's Haldane memorandum.

74 Wells, *Social History,* pp.194 & 211.

75 J. Lennox Kerr & Wilfred Granville, The RNVR; *A Record of Achievement* (London, 1957). p.151. Wells, *Social History,* p.166.

76 Wells, *Social History,* pp.208-209. The present writer has often heard this opinion from regular RN officers of the wartime generation.

77 Davies & Grove, *Dartmouth,* pp.18-21.

78 Marder, *Portrait of an Admiral,* p.365, quoting Richmond, as Director of the course in 1920.

79 Arthur J. Marder, *From the Dreadnought to Scapa Flow: The Royal Navy in the Fisher Era, 1904-1919* (London, 1961-70, 5 vols) V,315. Dewar, *The Navy from Within,* pp.215, 228-229 & 248-249. Marder, *Portrait of an Admiral,* pp.22-23, 104-142 & 165. Alfred C. Dewar, *On Certain Aspects of Organisation* (Kirkwall, 1917), p.5. Schurman, *The Education of a Navy,* p.125.

80 Stephen Roskill, *Naval Policy between the Wars* (London, 1968-76, 2 vols) I, pp. 128-129.

81 King-Hall, *My Naval Life,* p.215.

82 *British Naval Documents, 1204-1960* ed, John B. Hattendorf et al. (Navy Records Society Vol.131, Aldershot, 1993) p.892.

83 Roskill, *Naval Policy between the Wars* II, p. 341.

84 S.W. Roskill, 'The Navy at Cambridge', 1919-23, *Mariner's Mirror* XLIX (1963) pp.178-193. Marder, *Portrait of an Admiral,* p.26.

85 Roskill, *Naval Policy between the Wars* II, pp. 343-344.

86 Eric J.Grove, *Vanguard to Trident: British Naval Policy since World War II* (Annapolis, Md., 1987) p.261.

87 H.W. Richmond, *On Informing Subordinates, in National Policy and Naval Strength and other Essays* (London, 1928) pp.204-216.

88 Marder, *Dreadnought to Scapa Flow* II,92 & 300; III,153, IV,60. Marder, *Portrait of an Admiral* p.256. Sir William James, *A Great Seaman: The Life of Admiral of the Fleet Sir Henry Oliver* (London, 1956) pp.141-143. SW. Roskill, *Hankey, Man of Secrets* (London, 1970-74, 3 vols) I, 253.

89 *The Somerville Papers* ed. Michael Simpson (Navy Records Society Vol.134, Aldershot, 1995) p.28. Admiral Somerville is here commenting on his experience when attached to the Signals Division in 1940.

90 Perhaps not as hard as it seems, when one considers that those who entered at around fifteen under the *Britannia* scheme did not begin their practical training until at least seven years later.

INDEX